Social Work in Mental Health

Social Work in Mental Health

Areas of Practice, Challenges and Way Forward

Edited by
Abraham P. Francis

⊛SAGE www.sagepublications.com
Los Angeles • London • New Delhi • Singapore • Washington DC

First published in 2014 by

SAGE Publications India Pvt Ltd
B1/I-1 Mohan Cooperative Industrial Area
Mathura Road, New Delhi 110 044, India
www.sagepub.in

SAGE Publications Inc
2455 Teller Road
Thousand Oaks, California 91320, USA

SAGE Publications Ltd
1 Oliver's Yard, 55 City Road
London EC1Y 1SP, United Kingdom

SAGE Publications Asia-Pacific Pte Ltd
3 Church Street
#10-04 Samsung Hub
Singapore 049483

Published by Vivek Mehra for SAGE Publications India Pvt Ltd, Phototypeset in 10/12 Adobe Garamond Pro by RECTO Graphics, Delhi and printed at Sai Print-O-Pack Pvt Ltd, New Delhi.

Library of Congress Cataloging-in-Publication Data

Social work in mental health : areas of practice, challenges and way forward / edited by Abraham P. Francis.
      pages cm
   Includes bibliographical references and index.
   1. Psychiatric social work—India. I. Francis, Abraham P., editor of compilation.
   HV690.I4S63   362.2'0425—dc23   2014   2014018213

ISBN: 978-81-321-1740-7 (PB)

The SAGE Team: Supriya Das, Saima Ghaffar, Nand Kumar Jha and Dally Verghese

To
my fellow authors
and
my family

Thank you for choosing a SAGE product! If you have any comment, observation or feedback, I would like to personally hear from you. Please write to me at <u>contactceo@sagepub.in</u>

—Vivek Mehra, Managing Director and CEO,
SAGE Publications India Pvt Ltd, New Delhi

Bulk Sales

SAGE India offers special discounts for purchase of books in bulk. We also make available special imprints and excerpts from our books on demand.

For orders and enquiries, write to us at

Marketing Department
SAGE Publications India Pvt Ltd
B1/I-1, Mohan Cooperative Industrial Area
Mathura Road, Post Bag 7
New Delhi 110044, India
E-mail us at <u>marketing@sagepub.in</u>

Get to know more about SAGE, be invited to SAGE events, get on our mailing list. Write today to <u>marketing@sagepub.in</u>

This book is also available as an e-book.

Contents

Part 1: Areas of Social Work Practice in Mental Health

List of Illustrations

Tables

Figures

Boxes

Foreword

I am pleased to introduce this book titled *Social Work in Mental Health: Areas of Practice, Challenges and Way Forward* edited by Abraham P. Francis, Senior Lecturer at the James Cook University in Australia. It has been quite a challenge for him to bring together a range of professionals, mostly social work educators and practitioners from Australia and India on social work practice in mental health. This book will be useful in teaching, skill development of social work practitioners and for future researches and collaborations. The chapters cover current practices, theoretical debates, social work interventions and challenges faced by the social workers in the field of mental health.

Mental, neurological and substance use disorders are common in all regions of the world, affecting every community and age group across all income countries. While 14 per cent of the global burden of disease is attributed to these disorders, most of the people affected—75 per cent in many low-income countries—do not have access to the treatment they need (WHO 2013). Only between 76 per cent and 85 per cent of people with severe mental disorders in low- and middle-income countries receive no treatment for their mental health conditions compared to the corresponding figures for high-income countries, which were also unenviable, that is between 35 per cent and 50 per cent (WHO 2011 and 2013).

There is a growing recognition of the global community that countries, especially low- and middle-income countries need to pay greater attention to mental disorders and prevention of mental health problems as a large number of those can be prevented and treated. As people living with mental disorders have to suffer the dual burden of the disease and the stigma arising out of gross misconceptions, there is great need to develop appropriate interventions to change attitudes and to protect the human rights of this highly vulnerable population. Among those caretakers and health care providers, professional social workers play a major role in working with the affected individuals, their families and the community at large. Professional social work also has a very significant contribution to make in the prevention of these disorders and for the promotion of mental health.

I am sure that this book will find a place in many of our social work educational institutions, especially in the Asia and Pacific region, and will be a good reference book for our social work students and faculty.

Vimla V. Nadkarni, PhD
President, International Association of Schools of Social Work (IASSW)
Vice-President, Bombay Association of Trained Social Workers (BATSW)
Founder Dean and Professor (Retd), School of Social Work
Tata Institute of Social Sciences
Mumbai, India

References

World Health Organization. 2011. *Global Burden of Mental Disorders and the Need for a Comprehensive, Coordinated Response from Health and Social Sectors at the Country Level.* Report by the Secretariat. Retrieved on 14th April 2014 from http://apps.who.int/gb/ebwha/pdf_files/EB130/B130_9-en.pdf
———. 2013. WHO Mental Health Gap Action Programme (mhGAP). Retrieved 14th April 2014 from http://www.who.int/mental_health/mhgap/en

Acknowledgements

It is with a great sense of hope, excitement and accomplishment that I would like to present this book to the readers, especially social work students. There have been a number of people who have been instrumental in bringing this book project to fruition. I would like to first of all acknowledge the loving providence of God, who protected me, and blessed me with some fantastic colleagues and friends to work on this project. Likewise, support and assistance have come from many corners for which I am indebted and grateful.

Mental Health as a subject has always been a fascination for me. During the course of my own studies and practice I developed a passion for this subject. The greatest of all learning in this field occurred when I started working with my clients. They taught me a lot—many of which were matters that I had not learned through my formal studies. Therefore, I would like to thank all my clients and colleagues who supported me, guided me, and challenged me in my clinical practice. In particular, I would like to thank all my team members at Clare Mental Health, South Australia, and very specially John Banister, our then team leader who allowed and supported me to venture into community mental health practice, and Pat Glenister for mentoring me in mental health social work. Their support has been a key inspiring aspect of my journey in editing this book.

I would like to thank Vimla V. Nadkarni, Professor and Founder Dean, School of Social Work, Tata Institute of Social Sciences, and the President of the International Association of Schools of Social Work for writing a foreword for this book. I would like to also express my gratitude to all chapter authors for offering the readers excellent insight into social work practice within a mental health setting. I am aware that many of them were extremely busy with their teaching, research and other academic commitments, but nevertheless found time to be a part of this wonderful project. You honour me with your participation in this project, and for that I am truly grateful.

This book would not have been possible without the help and assistance of my students and colleagues at James Cook University. Very special thanks to S. Sharma who provided with some anecdotal evidence for this project and for being part of this work. At each step of this journey, my colleagues provided me with overwhelming support and encouragement, particularly

Mark David Chong, Debra Miles, Wendi Li, Peter Jones, Ines Zuchowski, Nonie Harris and Beth Tinning.

I am equally indebted to Professor Robert Bland, from the University of Queensland, who constantly encouraged me, provided feedback and mentored me in this project. I am likewise thankful to John Ashfield, from the Australian Institute for Male Health Studies, for his tireless support and inspiration. I also thank Professor Sanjai Bhatt from Delhi University for his support to this project.

During the course of this project, I have been blessed to have come into contact with so many scholars hailing from different walks of life. Some have been able to contribute to this book, while others offered me words of appreciation, direction and further references. I thank them all. I would like to especially thank Professor R. Srinivasa Murthy, who graciously allowed me to reproduce his outstanding paper as a chapter in the book.

I am also deeply touched and honoured by the support of my friends. To that end, I would like to thank my friend Kalpana Goel from the University of South Australia, for her support and excellent suggestions. Special thanks are also due to my friend and colleague Professor Ilango Ponnuswami from Mangalore University for his encouraging words, reviewing some of the chapters and for his insightful comments. My gratitude likewise goes out to my friend and colleague Venkat Pulla, University of the Sunshine Coast, for sharing his knowledge and understanding of strengths-based social work practice and mental health issues with me. He has been a keen supporter of this project and I really thank him for all he has been to me through the various roles that he has played over this period as an author, colleague, supporter and critic. I thank Shoba Ramachandran, for critically reviewing some of the chapters that came to us for this book, and doing such a good job at it.

On the production side, I wish to thank Rekha Natarajan, the executive editor of SAGE Publications, Sutapa Ghosh, the commissioning editor, and Supriya Das, Anupam Choudhary, Saima Ghaffar for their professional support, comments, suggestions and commitment to seeing this work published.

As you can imagine, this has been a long but passionate journey for me and for my family. I thank my wife, Mini, for her critical questions, deep and meaningful reflections and her invaluable suggestions for the book. I also thank my children, Abhijith and Alka, for their understanding, and for patiently waiting for me to help them with their academic work and sports activities.

Abraham P. Francis

Prologue: The Making of the Book

The inspiration to lead a book on social work practice in mental health did not just happen overnight. There were a couple of incidents and events that influenced my thinking and practice in the field which motivated me to take this work. Social work practice in mental health is an important area of practice. This collection deals with a variety of gaps in the literature and also provides a fresh outlook for an international audience. This book finds a niche for itself as it brings academia that are involved in interdisciplinary practice. A series of incidents has prompted me to shape this book. As a faculty member in social work some 15 years ago, I was responsible for a field placement for one of my students in a mental health hospital in India. At that time, it was not a course unit taught at the college, but a mere placement option in a psychiatric hospital setting that was made available to interested students, although subject to discussion and negotiation with the said medical facility. A number of my peers were a bit concerned about sending students to a place that represented great misery and disappointment for social workers at that time. The question then arose as to whether it would be a prudent action to place a young and naive social work student in a mental health setting that offered a difficult practice context and a grim future. I still remember that a student came bravely to express her keenness. While some of my colleagues were apprehensive about sending her into such a potentially harsh environment, the student not only received a start but finished her placement and went on to do a masters in social work. While I deeply appreciated the practical issues that many of my colleagues in the 1990s warned me about, clearly there was an ideological difference that permeated our discussions in those years. The primary issue was: Is this place suitable for an undergraduate placement? Or was there an undercurrent of resistance due to stigma attached to mental illness even in the social work field 15 years ago? I did not have a clear answer then; but this made me reflect about the role of social workers in the field of social work practice and was a key motivating factor behind the making of this book.

Meanwhile, I was very keen to provide a safe, supportive environment for my student and an opportunity to see, grasp and fathom for herself and to experience what a gigantic task it would be to be involved with mental health issues. The student was well supported and received much appreciation from many, which not only motivated her but also later motivated other students to undertake placement in a psychiatric setting.

I felt that mental health is everybody's business and social workers have a special role to play in this field. Thus began an impulse to write a book for new students about the role of social work in rehabilitation and/or treatment. For a long time, nearly 15 years, this remained a dream. In the meantime, another student of mine took up the cudgel and wanted to do his placement in a mental health facility, and upon successfully completing it, both these students gave me the confidence, courage and anecdotal evidence to engage in developing culturally appropriate literature and trainings for students in mental health. On reflection, these early challenges really spurred me on to develop meaningful materials that would attempt to de-stigmatise and demystify issues in mental health for my students.

After a long hiatus, I came into contact with my first mental health placement student again in 2011. She was by then actively engaged in social work and was settled in the United States. While we were catching up, she said something to me which rekindled this idea to lead this book. This is what she had to say:

> Being a Social Work student in India was always a choice everyone questioned. It was hard for even my own family to sometimes understand what good a degree in social work could be as a career? After all these years of its presence, social work still struggles for its place in the working world as a profession. Starting a career in social work was a decision that I made not just because it was different but also because it offered learning through working. So far, pursuing a career in this field has meant a great experience for me. It has moulded me into the person that I am today and how I perceive the world around me.
>
> During the course of my study (Bachelor's in Social Work), there were several challenges I was faced with, but the major one arose in the final year. I was to be placed for my concurrent fieldwork at a mental health hospital. There were doubts raised by the hospital social workers that Bachelor's students lacked the experience required to make the best of the training in a mental health set up and to make any contribution as a part of their team. Similar doubts were raised by some of my college faculty members as well, stating that Psychiatric Social Work was much too complicated for Bachelor's students, and had not been attempted before. There also was an unfounded fear within me, making me doubt my own ability to work in that place, since it was so overwhelming to see as much sadness and people dealing with all the problems they had that it almost depressed me. I felt at a personal level that I might not be able to deal with it.

So the first hurdle in my way I had to leap over was my own mindset, and I did overcome my fear. After my first couple of visits to the hospital, I had an epiphany and realised this is what I wanted to do. I saw that all the people coming in to the clinics everyday were dealing with so much and still doing what they must despite their problems. The people I observed and I was going to work with, themselves, became my inspiration to work there. I believed that this is what I was meant to do, no matter how hard it may seem.

Fortunately for me, our college supervisor had faith enough in my willingness to work there and my readiness to take on what everyone else thought was an oddball of a task. He discussed these issues with the college as well as the hospital's social work department and thus my training started. It was decided that for the first quarter I would only be making observations in the OPD clinics and if the hospital supervisor felt I had learnt enough by then, I could be an active participant in the team's work.

And so it happened, the training began, I made the most of my hours of observation in various outpatient clinics, reading at the library and discussions with the doctors and gaining from the perspective of teams of all professionals and understood the role of social workers in the whole scenario. Upon completion of the first quarter I was gauged by the supervisors and was then allowed to practise at the hospital. With guidance from my supervisors and the hospital doctors I gained knowledge about various psychiatric, psychological and other mental health disorders. But most of all I learnt of the social issues surrounding mental health problems. I came to realise that, till date in our country (India) mental health problems were considered a 'taboo'. The families most of the times failed to recognise the actual problems of the patients. Even when they do find out about the problem, they do not wish to seek help for it, for the fear of being ostracised by the society. There were several patients in the rehab centre who had been brought over by their families for treatment, but never taken back by that family member, thinking of them as a liability. This display of sheer apathy on the part of family members was the most difficult to comprehend and saddening. But the reason for such behaviour was clearly the fact that our society still does not understand mental health; even something as depression is looked down upon and people refuse to see doctors for it, fearing what others might think of them. So one can safely say that the role of a social worker in the field of mental health is quite crucial especially in a country like India, where awareness needs to be brought about amongst the masses about these issues and people need to be rid of their biases and prejudices against those ailing.

At the end of the year, my determination and my teachers' belief in me paid off, and I completed the training successfully. Thanks to this experience and all that I learnt from it, I want to be a social worker in the field of mental health. (Personal communication with S. Sharma, 2012)

My professional experience of working in the mental health sector has definitely influenced my thinking and I was very keen on including the consumer's voice in the subjects that I was responsible for teaching. All of these experiences, reflections and ambitions have in a way directly or indirectly affected my ethos and created a thirst in me for wanting to contribute to the social work fraternity. Unfortunately, it has taken almost 15 years for me to crystallise this dream into reality.

The need for such a book was also another factor which spurred me on. This book, therefore, represents an effort to bring together various academics in this field from Australia and India to share their knowledge. There are a number of Indian-born social workers employed as mental health social workers in Australia, and there are many others who aspire to provide their therapeutic expertise in this country as well. I hope that this text will intellectually scaffold these groups by facilitating greater awareness of the areas of convergence as well as the points of departure between social work theory and practice in Australia and India.

> One in four people develop some kind of mental illness at some point in their lives. But although mental illness is one of the most common health conditions worldwide, it can be one of the hardest to come to terms with. Both for those who are ill, and for those who are close to them. People suffer twice over—from the illness itself, and because they are shunned by their families, exiled from their communities and isolated by society. (*Mental Health Atlas 2011*)

From this account, it is apparent that mental health problems are very common in contemporary society. The key message from the *Mental Health Atlas 2011* is that the gap between what is needed for mental health care and what is available, remains very large. This gap is also replicated in social work education, especially in developing countries. It is likewise hoped that this book will be useful in teaching, enhancing practitioners' skills and facilitating future research and collaborative endeavours among social workers in these nations. As explained by Professor Robert Bland, 'All social workers, whether in specialist or generalist settings, need specific knowledge, skills and values to work effectively with people with mental health problems' (Bland et al. 2009). The book is therefore aimed at: (*a*) students pursuing Bachelor of Social Work, Master of Social Work and MPhil in Medical and Psychiatric Social Work; (*b*) social work practitioners; (*c*) field educators; (*d*) researchers; and (*e*) social work educators. This book will orient the reader through the various local and international concepts used in mental health, the intellectual base for such practice, current practices, models, debates in the field and challenges for social work practice. The contributors to this book have come from various backgrounds and they are from social work, psychology, psychiatry, law, criminology and education, which presents a multidisciplinary view of the current practice models. The book is also enriched by the voice of the consumers, which is also a new direction of practice. Principles of 'social justice and human rights' are the core values that underpin the philosophical framework of this book as social workers are called to advocate on behalf of the marginalised, under-represented and vulnerable sections of society.

The book is divided into two parts, with each part containing a number of related chapters. The first part explores the various practice models, and the second part outlines the challenges that confront social work practice in the area of mental health. At the end of the book, you will find two appendices. Appendix 1 explains the key terms that are used in this book and Appendix 2 provides you with a set of reflective questions that will help the reader to engage in critical reflections and help you formulate an action plan for practice.

I present this book to you in the hope that it will be useful for your critical thinking, education and practice.

Abraham P. Francis

References

Bland, R., N. Renouf and A. Tullgren. 2009. *Social Work Practice in Mental Health.* Crows Nest, New South Wales: Allen and Unwin.

WHO. *Mental Health Atlas.* 2011. 'Transcript of the Podcast', retrieved from http://www.who.int/mediacentre/multimedia/podcasts/2011/mental_health_17102011/en/(accessed: 20 January 2012).

Introduction

Abraham P. Francis*

Welcome to *Social Work in Mental Health: Areas of Practice, Challenges and Way Forward*. This book has two parts: the areas of social work practice in mental health, and the challenges and ways forward. The Australian Association of Social Workers (AASW) identifies social justice as a key value integral to ethical practice. Social justice considers issues of stigma, disadvantage, discrimination and marginality, and values the lived experience of mental illness and the importance of partnerships, mutuality, participation and choice (AASW 2010). Human rights are based upon the recognition of the inherent dignity and worth and inalienable rights of every person; it is the foundation of freedom, justice and peace in the world and is endowed to all humans regardless of mental health status or culture (Hunter 2007). 'Human rights refer to the basic rights and freedoms to which all humans are entitled. They are socially sanctioned entitlements to the goods and services that are necessary to develop human potential and well-being' (Ife 2010: 148).

---

* This book is conceived and edited by Abraham P. Francis. He has had extensive discussions with the contributors of this book at every stage of the production. It is a work that has involved many authors from various backgrounds, professional disciplines, professional backgrounds and countries. The focus of the book is about social work practice and mental health. The ideas, concepts and practice frameworks discussed in this book are useful in any social context, but with a caution that it needs to be adapted with cultural sensitivity and appropriate level of consultation/guidance with supervisors while engaging in clinical/community practice. The effort of the editor of this book has been to orient the students or practitioners to the current areas of practice in mental health and provide a common platform for further reflection and action in their respective field of practice. The editor is responsible for the ideological framework, identifying the authors for this book and providing an overall structure and presentation of this book, while the individual author/authors are responsible for the key ideas presented in their respective chapters. Some of the chapters are based on research studies and others are views, experiences and reflections of the authors engaged in this field of research and professional practice.

The second philosophical ideal underpinning the social work profession is social justice, which can be described as an act of working towards combating human rights violations (Taylor et al. 2008). According to Ife,

> Social justice refers to the concept of a society in which justice is achieved in every aspect of society, rather than merely through the administration of law. It is generally considered as a social world which affords individuals and groups fair treatment, equality and an impartial share of the benefits of membership of society. (Ife 2010: 148)

Individuals who experience poor mental health are more likely to be discriminated against and to have their rights violated than people with optimum mental health. Due to individuals with mental illness being more likely to be discriminated and have their human rights violated, it is essential to provide a supportive and understanding service that seeks to promote mental health well-being. The Australian social work *Code of Ethics* (AASW 2010: 12) states there are three key values that are fundamental to all social work practice: 'respect for persons, social justice and professional integrity'. Social workers are required to value and seek to preserve each individual's unique worth, and all individuals are entitled to dignity, respect, self-fulfilment and self-determination. The social work profession values honesty, transparency, reliability, empathy, reflective self-awareness, discernment, competence and commitment (AASW 2010). This requires social workers to have open and honest communication with the people they work with. It is also important for social workers to provide mental health consumers with information on their rights and responsibilities. Throughout this book, we will explore as to how these important issues are identified and addressed in a practice context.

In the first part of the book, we will look at the various areas of social work practice. With one in five Australians experiencing mental illness at some stage in their lives, social workers will engage with individuals who experience mental health concerns in almost every specialist area (Australian Government Department of Health and Ageing 2009). The interventions, interactions and expectations of social workers differ depending on at what point the contact is and the context of their work. As Bland et al. (2009) remind us that social workers will have to be equipped to handle any such issues that may come before them in their practice. We also need to understand the social contexts in which social workers practice. Social workers are employed in a wide variety of settings and contexts, from individual case management to community development, from clinical work to non-clinical work, from a solo practitioner to a member of a multidisciplinary team or working in a rural/remote background to urban settings. Wherever the social worker is employed, one will definitely come across the issue of mental health. The content of this book is aimed to throw some light on the current areas of social work practice. You will find some chapters that deal with children, youth, women migrants and older people, and the authors discuss the implications for practice. These chapters not only give you a good understanding about the context and relevance of practice, but it also challenges you and gives you the opportunity to engage in further readings and research. You can devote more time to the specific areas of interest by immersing in the literature which is given at the end of the chapters.

In the second part of the book, we will focus on the challenges faced by social workers in the mental health field, gain an understanding about the emerging knowledge base and will discuss some of the strategies that will strengthen the profession itself, and also will equip the necessary skills needed for individual workers to be effective in their practice. Mental health is a complex area with many social, environmental and psychological influences as well as physical illness and other stressors impacting on an individual's mental wellness. Individuals who experience poor mental health are more likely to be discriminated against and have their rights abused than individuals who do not experience poor mental health. It is for this reason that social workers must treat mental health consumers with the utmost respect and advocate social justice. Social workers need to work with 'head, heart and hand' (Kelly and Sewell 1991: 120).

Reviewing the direction that current mental health policy is taking in Australia, it is important to be able to continue promoting an emphasis on concepts such as participation, recovery and social inclusion in a way that will improve the access to and relevance of services, whilst accommodating the standardised measures of practice (Bland et al. 2009). The social work profession's strength is its ability to understand the social context and consequences of mental illness and the need for culturally appropriate practices to be utilised (AASW 2004). Therefore, social work practice has a role in building understanding that people, who may be experiencing mental illness, are impacted by direct and indirect discrimination, a general lack of understanding of their specific needs and current policy reforms that are not always culturally sensitive adding to barriers of access to support services, and that this affects them in many domains including employment, housing, education and welfare. This is both a challenge and opportunity for the social worker. Bland et al. (2009: 65) state that 'Care is effective when multidimensional solutions are provided which build on existing community strengths and capacity and include counselling and social support, and when necessary, support during family re-unification'.

In order to provide effective and reliable service to individuals who experience mental illness, it is important for social workers to continue professional development through research, supervision and critically reflecting on current practices within mental health (AASW 2010). Working in this manner ensures that the social worker provides a service that is of high quality, promotes the principles of social work and is impartial. It is vital that our own personal values, views and preferences do not impact on the people we work with. It is also important that as a social worker, service to humanity is the foundation of our practice. This involves ensuring the interest of the human well-being and social justice takes precedence before a worker's individual aims, views or objectives (AASW 2010).

So, with this purpose in mind let us now look at the sections in the book. Towards the end of this book, you will find two appendices. Appendix 1 explains the key terms used in the book and Appendix 2 provides you with a list of reflective questions. I hope you will find them useful and will be able to engage with these questions and resources to critically reflect your practice in the best interest of providing a great service to your clients and community.

References

Australian Association of Social Workers (AASW). 2004. *The Development of Competency Standards for Mental Health Social Workers*. Barton.

———. 2010. *The AASW Code of Ethics*. Canberra.

Australian Government Department of Health and Ageing. 2009. *Response Ability: Overview of Mental Health in Australia*. Retrieved from http://www.responseability.org, 7 January 2014.

Bland, R., N. Renouf and A. Tullgren. 2009. *Social Work Practice in Mental Health*. Crows Nest, New South Wales: Allen and Unwin.

Hunter, E. 2007. *Disadvantage and Discontent: A Review of Issues Relevant to the Mental Health of Rural and Remote Indigenous Australians*. Cairns, Queensland: National Rural Health Alliance.

Ife, J. 2010. 'Human Rights and Social Justice', in M. Gray and S. Webb (eds), *Ethics and Value Perspectives in Social Work*, pp. 148–159. Basingstoke, UK: Palgrave Macmillan.

Kelly, A. and S. Sewell. 1991. *With Head, Heart and Hand: Dimensions of Community Building* (4th edn). Brisbane, Queensland: Booralong Press.

Taylor, J., D. Wilkinson and B. Cheers. 2008. *Working with Communities in Health and Human Services*. Melbourne: Oxford University Press.

PART 1

Areas of Social Work Practice in Mental Health

Introduction to Areas of Social Work Practice in Mental Health

Rosamund Thorpe

After a lifelong career in social work practice and education—first in the United Kingdom (UK) and then Australia—I have come to the firm conclusion that mental health is every social worker's concern, since, irrespective of their place of practice, country, nature of employment, most (if not all) social workers will come in contact with people with mental health issues and often may feel that their skills and practice confidence are challenged. Thus, an understanding of the context and areas of practice is important, along with an understanding of the needs and rights of people whose lives are touched by mental ill health.

Accordingly, in this part of the book, the chapters provide us with examples of social workers in a range of different agency contexts, working in ways to support and reinforce strengths in people who live with mental health issues or may be vulnerable to their development. The chapters focus on work with children, adolescents, women escaping family violence, migrants, people caught up in problematic substance use, older people and those contemplating suicide. They contain detailed discussion of the authors' respective areas of practice and pose a number of questions for us to consider in our professional practice. Together, the chapters highlight the social work commitment to practice in ways which promote the well-being of each and every person we encounter, including not only those who are living with diagnosed mental ill health but also those whose lives are affected by the debilitating impacts of loss and trauma.

Plainly, this commitment to value and respect the dignity and worth of all persons is a fundamental expectation in codes of professional social work ethics around the world. A second expectation in both the Australian and the international social work codes of ethics is to work towards enhancing and increasing social justice for all persons, and especially for the most vulnerable or disadvantaged. This is a crucial commitment in relation to mental health, since there is much progress still to be made in reducing discrimination, disadvantage and stigma associated with mental ill health.

Even in Australia, an advantaged society in global terms, I know from my experience as carer for a family member who lives with disabling effects of mental health issues, that barriers to acceptance and difficulty accessing our preferred kinds of support continue to be challenges in my own and my loved-one's struggle to live satisfying lives. And I know from those I meet in a women carers' support group, Together Women Thrive, that this situation is exacerbated for those whose income is low or who live in poverty, whether in the First World or in developing countries.

Social workers can make positive differences in people's lives at both personal and social system levels. Indeed action at one level without complementary action at the other is insufficient, even though individual social workers may concentrate their efforts at either level, as caseworkers and case-managers or as community activists. Nonetheless, regardless of the area in which a social worker may operate, it is imperative that all social workers recognise and address both the essential humanity of people living with mental ill health and the extent of social injustice which may darken their lives.

Wherever social workers work, we can have significant influence, given our dual focii on the individual and wider social systems, and given our social science background, which enables social workers to take a holistic view of an individual and their social situation. For social workers employed as part of multidisciplinary mental health teams, the perspective which we bring to our work can be significant alongside other professionals who typically are more steeped in a biomedical model of diagnosis and intervention, focusing more on treatment of personal pathology than on reinforcing strengths and protecting human rights. Power dynamics within such teams, especially with the dominance of medical and psychiatric trained personnel, sometimes lead social workers to feel that our perspective is not respected and, in consequence, we feel our ability to work in ways compatible with promoting social justice is constrained. Such feelings, however, should not lead us to lose confidence in the essence of a social work approach, since there is evidence to suggest that we are achieving far more than we realise.

In one Australian study, consumers and carers living with schizophrenia readily identified how they could differentiate social workers from other mental health professionals, clearly appreciating the more holistic understanding of themselves which social workers have and the more empowering ways of practising which social workers use. These experiences of those on the receiving end contrasted starkly with the self-effacing doubts expressed by their social workers themselves. Thus the findings provide a vital vote of confidence in the distinctive contribution which social work can make to the work of multidisciplinary teams in mental health (Flanagan 2007). As social workers, we need to be assertive about what we can offer and, indeed, we can consider taking initiatives in facilitating participation of service users and carers, and thereby bridging gaps between the progressive rhetoric of mental health policy in many jurisdictions and the more traditional realities of practice.

Across the world in recent years, consumer advocates and some professionals in the mental health field (social workers, especially) have been challenging both the ethos and the power dynamics in relationships between service providers and service users. With the emerging shift in emphasis from treatment to recovery, there has been growing recognition that professionals do not have a monopoly on mental health expertise. Rather, there are two sets of experts—professional experts and experts by lived experience—and there is a need to move from user and carer 'involvement' (in practice often tokenistic) to a genuine mutual respect in processes of shared decision making in service design and delivery, and a focus on self-management rather than 'fixing' people—in short, a move from an exclusively 'therapeutic' model to an educational approach, and a process of co-creation between service providers and service users as equals (Perkins 2013).

The aim of this movement is not only to recognise and respect the expertise of mental health consumers in knowing what works for them in reclaiming a worthwhile life, but equally to recognise that consumer (and carer) involvement in decision making about their own recovery is in itself a powerful force for facilitating healing and recovery.

This said, it is sometimes challenging for professionals, including social workers, to change from seeing ourselves as 'experts' with a monopoly of knowledge to sharing power with people we tend to see as 'different' and sometimes, subconsciously perhaps, as 'lesser' on account of this difference.

At a recent workshop in Western Australia on 'Changing Mental Health Practice', Perkins (2013) argued that in order to facilitate recovery, professionals need to be 'on tap' not 'on top', incorporating the following strategies into our work:

- respect each person's right to define their own experience and reality;
- promote shared decision making at an individual level;

- support self-management rather than 'fixing' people;
- develop an educational approach;
- move from 'user and carer involvement' to a genuine process of shared decision making in service operation, design and delivery;
- include the expertise of lived experience in the workforce; and
- change relationships between services and local communities, creating communities that can acknowledge people with mental health problems as equal citizens

While these strategies are proposed for use in mental health services, they can be adapted well for use by social workers in any area of practice. Essentially they signify rethinking the power dynamics in 'professionalism' and recognising that power sharing is a rather more effective way of working with and alongside people, whether in government or non-government services. Moreover, this rethinking can include working with involuntary service users, for example in child protection or community corrections, even when there may be constraints on the exercise of power by service users. The challenge in such areas of practice is to restrict constraints to a minimum and to facilitate empowerment and self-determination wherever possible, including when working with people who have mental health issues. Far too often, involuntary service users who grapple with mental ill health, or the effects of loss and trauma, are judged negatively and dealt with by control or punishment, even by social workers—often to the extent that I am left wondering whatever happened to care and compassion, and the commitment in social work to respect the dignity and worth of all persons.

Thirty years ago, my mentor Bob Holman—a social work professor in the UK who left academia to resume work as a practitioner—conceptualised the role of a community social worker as a 'resourceful friend' (Holman 1983). In doing so, Holman affirmed the knowledge, skills, experience and access to resources which a professional social worker is able to share in a relationship of mutual respect with service users who, themselves, have not only the expertise of 'lived experience' but also, more often than not, a multitude of other skills and abilities, or 'strengths' as modern-day social workers name them. For me, being a 'resourceful friend' encapsulates the essence of the social work role not only in facilitating recovery but also in preventing the development of mental health issues.

Many of the chapters in this part of the book provide examples of social work not only at the micro level but also at meso and macro levels, recognising the need to address both the social environment of vulnerable individuals and structural issues of social injustice, in order to fully enhance mental health recovery and promotion.

Clearly, in addition to social work with individuals, working with people in groups or through community development and community action can be powerful ways to promote and strengthen recovery. For example, in my own current work in The Family Inclusion Network (FIN) with parents who have lost their children into public care, we draw explicitly and very usefully on the work of Judith Herman (1997). Accordingly, FIN operating principles include the statement that

> FIN provides safe space for the 'voice' of parents who, as stakeholders, are invariably devalued, to be expressed and heard. This safe space is an essential part of the healing process from trauma and loss, leading to hope, growth, personal change and, in time, collective action. (FIN 2013)

The statement continues to endorse Herman's assertion that 'activism is both a means for achieving social change and also, in itself, an additional powerful therapeutic tool, which can strengthen healing through the experience of dignity and a positive identity' (Herman 1997: 1).

While social workers may rail against the constraints of practice—shortage of resources, facilities or trained professionals, bureaucratic requirements, medical dominance, to name but a few—it is empowering for ourselves and for our service users to recognise that, nonetheless, much can be accomplished through practice which endorses and enacts a commitment to both respecting the humanity, dignity and worth of all persons, and to advancing the cause of achieving greater social justice.

What we need is vision and passion. Our service users hope that you will embrace this challenge!

References

Family Inclusion Network Queensland (Townsville) Inc. 2011. *About FIN: Information Booklet.* Retrieved from http://www.fin-qldtsv.org.au/FIN%20 information%20booklet%20A4%20size4.pdf, 24 February 2014.

Flanagan, C. 2007. 'Participation and Partnership: The Development of a Social Work Model of Service Delivery for Consumers and Carers Living with Schizophrenia'. PhD thesis, James Cook University.

Herman, J. 1997. *Trauma and Recovery: The Aftermath of Violence from Domestic Abuse to Political Terror.* New York: Basic Books.

Holman, B. 1983. *Resourceful Friends: Skills in Community Social Work.* London: The Children's Society.

Perkins, R. 2013. 'Changing Mental Health Practice: Professionals "On Tap" Not "On Top"', One-day Workshop, Richmond Fellowship of Western Australia, 3 May.

1

Engaging Children with Mental Health Issues: Review of Approaches to Practice

Abul Khan

Introduction

Children, below the age of 18, who attend child and adolescent mental health services (CAMHS) generally experience abuse, neglect, trauma and insecure attachment. Eventually they develop confusion, a sense of emotional isolation and distrust (Mullan et al. 2007). The idea of psychosocial approach draws on psychological therapies in the domain of the profession of social work, for a more comprehensive response to the complexity of child and adolescent mental health. The multidisciplinary principles in CAMHS are inspired by Erikson's person-in-environment approach, which proposed that human development is a bio-psychosocial process that takes place throughout one's lifespan (Greene 2008). The psychosocial approach combined person-centred, psychodynamic and systemic perspectives to support and empower children. The person-in-environment approach focuses on the living experiences of the children while recognising the impact of past developmental experiences. Payne's (1997) reflexive therapeutic approach delineates social work's contribution in terms of seeking the best possible well-being for individuals, groups and communities in society, by promoting and facilitating growth and self-fulfilment. A constant process of interaction with others modifies the ideas of the social workers and allows them to influence others. This process of mutual influence is what makes social work reflexive. In these ways, people gain power over their own feelings and ways of life. Through this personal power, they are enabled to overcome or rise above sufferings and disadvantages.

Adopting appropriate strategies of engagement in psychosocial therapy is recognised as effective for many child and adolescent mental health disorders such as attention-deficit/hyperactivity disorder (ADHD), oppositional-defiant disorder, bipolar and other mood disorders, depression, anxiety, social phobia and so on (Beynon et al. 2008; Probst 2006; Tetley et al. 2011). However, there are enduring concerns regarding low engagement in case of work intervention leading to premature case closure. The actual status of disengagement is still not clear but some research indicates that the number of premature case closures due to non-engagement of clients could be as high as 82 per cent (Ben-Porath 2004; McMurran et al. 2010; Wierzbicki and Pekarik 1993). Low engagement or premature case closure in psycho-social therapy can have adverse consequences in terms of clinical outcomes (Ben-Porath 2004; O'Brien et al. 2009; Tetley et al. 2011), cost-effectiveness of the service and morale of the staff as well as the clients (McMurran et al. 2010; O'Brien et al. 2009; Tetley et al. 2011). In this critical situation, an empowerment-based child- and environment-centred intervention can play a pivotal role in supporting and building resilience in the child.

The purpose of this chapter is to discuss some creative ideas for engaging children and adolescents under psychosocial perspectives. The selection of the therapeutic approaches has been guided by person-centred, systemic and psychodynamic approaches. The goals of the therapeutic approaches include empowering the children and adolescents by becoming aware of their mental illness and behavioural consequences, freely expressing their wishes and feelings, gaining insight into their social environment and realistic expectations, developing skills to manage emotions (anger, fear and anxiety), understanding their own mind and rationally judging others' minds and improving and strengthening support networks. The therapeutic approaches discussed in this chapter may also be modified to accommodate more creative ideas based on the living experiences of the client.

First Step in Therapy: Overcoming the Testing Period

Therapeutic alliance is the key to a successful therapeutic intervention. It is always a challenging process to overcome the testing period of the children who are carrying negative experiences out of trusting adults around them. The children like to see whether the therapist is genuine and committed to help them and in this regard they humbly attempt to examine the credibility of the therapist on their own terms, which is often exhibited through disengaging and sometimes by even displaying manipulative behaviour (Hughes 1997) by providing some disclosures to control the therapy session.

Figure 1.1 depicts a representation of the powerful impact of childhood abuse, neglect and trauma that could potentially halt the natural human developmental motion and even drive it in the opposite direction leading to living in confusion, distrust and negative coping strategies (e.g., substance abuse, self-harm). The challenges of the psychosocial therapy are to first halt the anticlockwise motion and then to face the consequent jolt (this particular part may be referred to as the *testing period*) and continue to empower the gear (i.e., overcoming the testing period) to bring back its premorbid natural motions (normal developmental progress) through consistent therapeutic intervention.

Figure 1.1
Challenges of Therapy: The Clockwise Motion of Human Developmental Gear is Challenged and Halted by the Effect of Anticlockwise Motion of Abuse, Neglect and Trauma

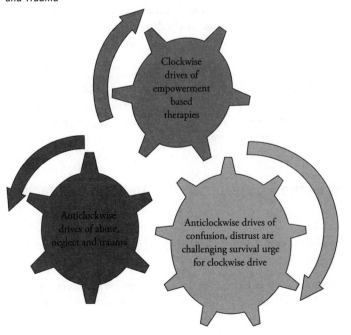

Facilitating active participation of a child in the therapy not only requires professional skills and competence but also a comprehensive approach with a strong commitment to engage and empower the child to develop self-reliance for future management of his/her needs (Khan and Miles 2011). Axline (1989) developed eight basic principles that contribute to an atmosphere which enables the participation of a child in psychosocial treatment. These principles are as follows:

- *Develop* a warm and friendly relationship with the child.
- Accept the child as he/she is.
- Establish a sense of permission in the relationship so that the child feels free to express his/her feelings completely.
- Recognise the feelings of the child and reflect back these feelings in such a manner that the child gains an insight into his/her behaviour.
- Maintain a deep respect for the child's ability to solve his/her problems and give the child the opportunity to do so. The responsibility to make choices and to institute change is the child's.
- Be nondirective towards the child's actions or conversations. The child leads the way, the therapist follows.
- Engage in a gradual therapeutic process.
- Establish only those limitations necessary to anchor therapy in the world of reality and to make the child aware of his/her responsibility in the relationship.

In the process of creating a conducive therapeutic atmosphere, the therapist should be passionate about the job, believe in it and be committed to it. A therapist's own emotional well-being is critical for managing any potential risks of transference and countertransference in the process of case work (Backer-Weidman and Hughes 2008).

Review of the Psychosocial Therapeutic Approaches

Person-centred Approach (PCA)

PCA is a dynamic force of human development that Carl Rogers conceptualized in the 1970s. The idea of PCA is based on the hypothesis regarding three different selves of a human being: self-concept, real self and ideal self and it aims to bring greater congruence among the selves of the client through unconditional positive regard and empathetic understanding (Holosko et al. 2008). The role of the therapist is that of just a partner, not a problem solver, who will establish a genuine and empathetic relationship with the client and aim to facilitate self-actualizations (positive self-esteem, self-worth and self-image) and freedom of choice. PCA creates an empowering atmosphere that allows children and young people to heal themselves through the experiences of positive social interaction (Axline 1989).

Hughes (1997: 61) referred to a person-centred therapy as a relationship-centred approach paying equal importance to the child's relationship with the therapist as well as the primary caregiver; it facilitates a playful and emotional interaction and a 'here and now therapeutic relationship'. Hughes also strongly emphasised on appropriate touch to help the child understand the reality of human connectedness:

> In the course of the therapy, she (therapist) often touches the child's hand, arm, shoulder, hair, back, puts her arm around him (the child), briefly tickles, gently pokes, wrestles, places her hands on the chin, on either sides of his eyes. The therapist holds the child as he screams in anger, shakes with fear or cries with profound sadness.

Shore (in Hughes 1997) emphasised on preverbal attachment development through appropriate eye contact, facial gestures and communications, physical movement of body and posture.

Now there is a question of safe practice with regard to touch-based intense therapeutic interaction, which may be taken into consideration in context of the child's gender, age, statutory and organisational policy and cultural circumstances while keeping everybody safe.

PCA (Holosko et al. 2008) is the foundation of any psychosocial therapeutic intervention, which is preceded by a therapeutic rapport with the child. It offers a respectful environment for human interaction that necessitates a child to attend therapy. The advantage of this approach is in engaging the abused, neglected and traumatised children who are struggling to trust people. However, PCA demands a strong commitment to go to the extra mile in creating an enabling pace through a warm welcome, unconditional acceptance and respectful treatment under the values of social justice and lasting recovery and well-being.

Psychodynamic Approach

Psychodynamic model is one of the bio-psychosocial perspectives in understanding mental illness. Although the model is derived through psychological concept, it has been presented here in psychosocial perspective with appropriate focus on the children's living experiences, environmental circumstances and its potential impact on behaviour and relationships. Psychodynamic model refers to the origin of human mental illness as a conflict of different developing components of psychology, the resistance we show against the conflicts, the maladaptive behaviour and its impact on human relationships (Shooter 2008: 9). The psychodynamic perspective helps us understand and interpret the impact of the past and the ongoing experiences of abuse, neglect and trauma of parents and children on their cognitive, perceptual and affective experiences and related behaviour (Hughes 1997). Psychodynamic theory is an insight-oriented therapy that focuses on the unconscious components which determine the person's current social behaviour against the background of past developmental experiences (Haggerty 2006). For example, a child with an experience of abuse represents in sand tray–based therapy situation by hurting and burying a doll who he identifies as the perpetrator. The focus of the therapy, in this case, will be to help the child to connect the perpetrator doll with the actual perpetrator who abused him and then enable him to gain insight and emotional skills to manage his behaviour. Therefore, the purpose of psychodynamic approach is to help the person with developmental trauma and to understand its impact on his/her social and emotional well-being and to develop strategies to manage his/her behaviour (see Figure 1.2).

Haggerty (2006) has outlined the history of different schools of psychodynamic ideas. The psychodynamic psychotherapy also needs to be understood in the background of four different schools of psychology. These are: (a) Freudian psychology, (b) Ego psychology, (c) Object relation psychology, and (d) Self-psychology.

Freudian psychology refers to the human defense mechanism as a construction of the ego to minimize the feelings of pain and suffering and to exercise and maintain psychic equilibrium. It is the super ego formed during the period of latency (age 5 to puberty) as a natural process to manage id-related behavioural implications.

Ego psychology has evolved from Freud's ego psychology of managing the demand of reality through the capacity to defend and reality testing.

Figure 1.2
Progress of Psychodynamic Interventions

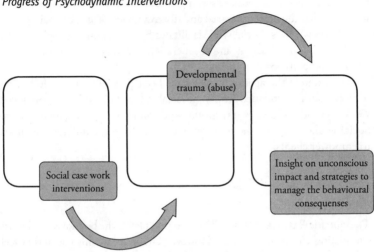

This also clarifies the rationale of children and young people's challenging behaviour in therapy.

Object relation psychotherapy is advocated by Melanie Klein, W. R. D. Fairbairn, D. W. Winnicott and Harry Guntrip (Haggerty 2006). Accordingly, human behaviour is shaped in relation to the significant others surrounding them. Our constant struggles and goals in life revolve around maintaining relations with others and at the same time in differentiating ourselves from others.

The construct of human behaviour in terms of experiences and demands of its social environment can be appropriately assessed and addressed through the social work principles of social study, social diagnosis and social treatment. For example, a child with experiences of abuse or trauma and negative care will be likely to develop a negative self-image, sense of insecurity and distrust and will construct a consequent defensive behaviour that may not be socially appropriate. The psychodynamic approach attempts to offer some thoughts regarding diverse complexities of human experiences and related behavioural consequences. The approach also clarifies the challenges of engaging with children and young people with empowerment-based psychosocial therapies that are organised in a conducive environment with empathy, curiosity and interest, playfulness (Hughes 1997) under the social work values of non-judgemental listening and social justice. Socialist–collectivist theory sees social work as seeking co-operation and mutual support in society so that the most oppressed and disadvantaged people can gain power over their own lives. Social work facilitates by empowering people to take part in a process of learning and co-operation, creating institutions that can all own and participate in (Payne 1997).

Some simple therapeutic games have been presented in the following section that are grounded in psychosocial values but essentially on social work methods of case work, group work and community organisation. Social workers can use the tools by freely exploring the different methods to empower clients.

Snakes and Ladders Game

Therapeutic Rationale: It is well known that play is the best loved and most stimulating activity for children. However, children can only play if they feel safe in the environment. Snakes and Ladders is generally a familiar, joyful, competitive but non-threatening game that may reflect children's ability to maintain rules and boundaries, accept loss and defeat, manage emotions, talk about experiences affecting his/her life and reflect social presentation skills. The game also offers opportunity to manage social and emotional well-being through individual interaction with the therapist.

Descriptions: Materials needed: A 'Snakes and Ladders' game set
The therapist introduces the game to the child, discusses the rules and boundaries with him/her, selects the counters (lets the child pick his/her counter first) and starts playing turn by turn. The therapist should be particular in expressing positive social gestures (*thank you, I am sorry, you got the snake or well done you got the ladder*) and also giving honest reflections if the child breaks the rules or attempts to change rules in his/her favour. The therapist should not give any undue favour or show leniency, he/she should rather maintain a competitive atmosphere that will help the child to continue to engage in the game. However, in between, the therapist can use some quality time to explore the discomfort zone by directly asking the child about his/her difficult experiences and wishes and feelings.

Applications: The game is appropriate for young children (6–11 years) who have difficulty to regulate emotions, have poor social skills and have difficulty to verbalise feelings.

CARD ACTING GAME

Therapeutic Rationale: This is a nondirective engagement tool that allows a child to create his/her own imaginary character before acting it out alongside the therapist. It allows the child to build-up a rapport with the therapist, to express creativity and imagination, recognise feelings, social and emotional presentation skills and also to facilitate dyadic developmental attachment with the caregiver (Baker-Weidman and Hughes 2008). There will be a marking system for right or wrong guessing of characters to maintain a competitive temperament and to maintain the child's consistent interest in the activity.

Descriptions: Materials needed: Ten 3 inch square-shaped white cards (this number could be evenly increased as appropriate) and two pens.

The therapist will explain the rules of the game to the child and demonstrate about its progress very clearly. Accordingly, the therapist and the child will have an equal number of cards and each of them will write imaginary characters secretively, one on each card; turn by turn the child and the therapist will enact the characters while the other person will guess and awards scores. For example, if the other person (the therapist or the child or the carer if he/she joins) is able to guess the character correctly then he/she will get 1 mark but if he/she guesses wrongly, the score will be a 0. At the end, the scores will be calculated to declare the winner with the full involvement of the child.

Application: The game will be beneficial for children, of any age group, who struggle to express their feelings, have insecure attachment experience and have difficulty understanding their own mind and other people's minds due to personality constellation (Cohler and Weiner 2011).

MY IMAGINARY WORLD

Therapeutic Rationale: Children can explore their wishes and feelings regarding circumstances better through nondirective and visual media. This nondirective therapeutic tool helps a child to explore his/her feelings, positive as well as negative, acknowledge the quality of relationships in his/her social environment and also give the therapist an opportunity to work through his/her imaginary world with diversities of relationships and its impact on perceptual, cognitive and affective development. The therapist can also use the interpretations to help the child gain congruence of the developmental experiences in terms of self-concept, real self and ideal self (Figure 1.3).

Figure 1.3
My Imaginary World

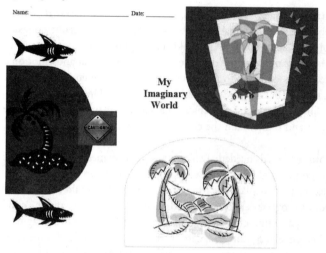

Descriptions: Materials needed: A4-sized white paper.

The therapist can draw a scene of three islands surrounded by water in front of the child or bring a computer-generated image. The therapist then describes the three islands: the first is the best island, where there is everything available as per the interest of the child; the second is a good island that is just good (but not like the best island); and the third is the worst island, which is deadly in terms of living arrangements, being fully isolated and if anybody from the island tries to flee, the deadly sea creatures will seriously harm the person. Meanwhile, the descriptions of deadliness should be developmentally appropriate to the child. Then the therapist very passionately asks the child to imagine that he/she is the owner of the three islands and can bring people or anything from his/her social circle to any of the three islands. He/she can make an imaginary bridge between the two nice islands or allow the child to draw anything that he/she wants to own on it without tampering the fundamental concept of the game. Meanwhile, the therapist will ensure that the child is reassured regarding the confidentiality and spontaneous participation. Then the therapist will hand over the pen and the paper to the child to bring people or animals from his/her social environment into the three islands. The therapist, by being very passionate, will help the child to engage in the game without being judgmental. At the end, with the child's permission, the therapist will help the child to revisit the people in the identified island and their impact on the child's social and emotional well-being by developing a realistic insight about his/her developmental experiences, to gain confidence and to develop resilience.

Application: The game will be beneficial for children, five years and above, with social phobia, generalised anxiety, who tend to internalise feelings, self-harm and have anger issues and are not able to connect with the feelings in terms of social relationships in their significant environment.

MY FEELINGS BAROMETER

Therapeutic Rationale: My Feelings Barometer is a systemic tool that may be developed with full participation of the child, carer and the therapist to recognise signs and symptoms of feelings and emotions, to understand the degree of behavioural consequences of feelings and emotions and to develop strategies to manage feelings and behavioural consequences as a part of early intervention.

Figure 1.4
My Feelings Barometer

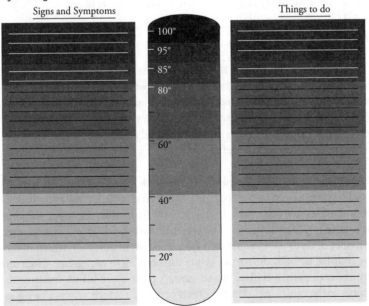

Signs and Symptoms   Things to do

100°
95°
85°
80°

60°

40°

20°

Name:

Descriptions: Materials needed: The tool consists of degrees of stages of feelings and emotions and corresponding behavioural consequences that are identified through a symbolic barometer.

The therapist will support the child to understand that the purpose of this activity is to support him/her to manage feelings and emotions in the right time before it escalates. Then the therapist will support the child to gain ownership of the document by inviting him/her to name the stages of the barometer by giving different names to each stage and identifying the emotional and behavioural symptoms in the 'Signs and Symptoms' sections followed by developing strategies to manage the symptoms in the 'Things to Do' sections. Initially, the child will engage and then, with the child's permission, the parents/carers can join in on the development of the strategies. The intervention may take more than one session depending on the quality of the engagement. At the end, with permission of the child, the completed document can be laminated and a copy given to the child and his/her carer to put up in a convenient location of the house so that the child can be supported to identify and arrest a difficult feeling and emotion before it escalates.

Application: This systemic tool for managing emotions can be applicable for children with anger issues between 12 and 17 years of age.

BLUFF MASTER GAME

Therapeutic Rationale: The Bluff Master game aims to create a comfortable and relaxing environment, to enhance social communications and presentation, relationships building and also helps in mind reading. The game focuses on creating a joyous situation with an opportunity of playfully fooling each other by appropriately managing the cards and acting out own facial expressions as well as carefully judging other people's facial expressions.

Descriptions: Materials Needed: Playing cards.

The game can be introduced once the child is settled in the therapy environment. Initially, the therapist will play the game with the child, and later, the carer can join the game. The therapist and the child will take an even number of cards (7–15 cards each for a game of 30 minutes), which should be shuffled by both the parties before distributing to each other. Then one by one each party will place his/her card/s upside down before declaring the status of the card/s (e.g., king or queen or 3, etc.), which may not be necessarily true. Now the second contestant will judge the status of the card by checking it (if the card/s match the declared status then the second contestant will have to take the card/s back but if the status does not match, then the first contestant will have to take the card/s back) or decides to continue further and places his/her card by declaring the same status, which again may not be of the matching status. It is upto the opponent party to judge carefully before picking the card to check its status or placing his/her card. In this process, the contestant, who will have only one card left, will place the card after declaring himself/herself Bluff Master and wins the competition.

Application: The game can be played with children between the age group of nine years and above with Autism Spectrum Disorder, insecure attachment experience and anxiety issues and dissociative symptoms.

BEHAVIOUR MANAGEMENT REWARD CHART

Therapeutic Rationale: This is a systemic reward chart to manage a child's behaviour at home. It allows the child to be fully involved, alongside the carer/s, in managing his/her feelings and emotions and respond to rules and boundaries at home under the motivation of rewards. As the plan is set out jointly, the child feels the ownership and control of the programme and attempts to participate actively. The progress of the plan also depends on the carer/s to enforce it passionately under a firm and calm approach.

Descriptions: Materials Needed: A generic chart has been designed as an example that could be reworked as per the needs of the child and family circumstances by the carer/s and the child (see Table 1.5).

The therapist will discuss the plan with the child in consideration of parental concerns of behaviour issues at home and then with his/her consent, involve carers to draw up a plan appropriate to the situations of the family and the child. To enforce the plan, carers will ensure a firm and calm approach as well as be deeply encouraging towards the child's positive progress and keep their word irrespective of the child's performance. The progress could be reviewed in therapy in the joint session in a very positive and supportive atmosphere.

Application: Children in the age group of 5 to 12 years.

DRAWING GAME

Therapeutic Rationale: Drawing has been recognised undeniably as a significant medium of expression by children (Hamama and Ronen 2009). In the absence of adult-like developmental maturity, children use drawing

Figure 1.5
Behaviour Management Programme

Week	Breakfast	Lunch	Study	Help	Dinner	Clean	Go to Bed	TOTAL
Monday	/1	/1	/2	/2	/1	/1	/2	/10
Tuesday	/1	/1	/2	/2	/1	/1	/2	/10
Wednesday	/1	/1	/2	/2	/1	/1	/2	/10
Thursday	/1	/1	/2	/2	/1	/1	/2	/10
Friday	/1	/1	/2	/2	/1	/1	/2	/10
Saturday	/1	/1	/2	/2	/1	/1	/2	/10
Sunday	/1	/1	/2	/2	/1	/1	/2	/10

Full 10 marks in a day = can have longer TV time
Less than 6 marks in a day = go to bed early
Less than 4 marks in a day = no TV time
Less than 25 marks in a week = no pocket money for next week

Signature......................(child). Signature.................... (carer)

Signature................. (therapist)

as an alternative language to express their inner world, feelings and thoughts (Leibowitz 1999). There are different thoughts on whether children's drawing should be used as a diagnostic tool or not. Thomas and Jolley (1998) outlined drawing as an unreliable option for assessing children's personalities; however, it can reflect on the children's emotional attitudes towards the topic. Also, they suggested that drawings should be used alongside other information from the home and the school, the two key settings in a child's life.

Descriptions: Materials needed: White paper, crayon and so on.

The child should be provided with drawing materials without any instructions. The therapist may choose to draw something, while carefully leaving drawing materials on the table, as an indirect encouragement for the child to draw. If the child chooses to draw, the therapist may carefully show interest regarding the drawing while allowing the child to continue to remain focused on the drawing. The therapy environment should be safe and the child should be ready.

Application: This medium is applicable for children of 12 months or above.

THE FEELING WORD GAME

Therapeutic Rationale: The Feeling Word Game (by Hall et al. 2002) is about helping children identify and connect with their feelings. This rationale is based on the understanding that children find it difficult to verbalise their feelings due to lack of developmental maturity or they have not been able to connect with their feelings. The game will be beneficial for children to express feelings in a non-threatening manner.

Descriptions: Materials needed: Eight sheets of A4-sized paper, a marker and a tin filled with poker chips.

The therapist will explain the game to the child in a developmentally appropriate way. Accordingly, the therapist will invite the child to name some feelings and when the child starts talking about the feelings, the therapist will add the feelings the child missed. The therapist will write the feelings on the top of the A4 sheets (one feeling on each sheet). The therapist will help the child to understand the meaning of the feelings and if necessary, the therapist will draw the feelings. Then, with the permission of the child, the therapist will tell a story that involves different feelings and in the end he/she will place poker chips of different amounts (as per degree of feelings) on the 'feelings' sheets. Next, the therapist will tell a non-threatening story about the child with both positive and negative feelings and then the child is encouraged to place the poker chips on different feelings. Next, the child will be encouraged to tell a story to put down his/her feelings. The whole intervention will progress at the child's pace. The story sessions will continue until significant presenting issues are explored and addressed.

Applications: The game will be beneficial for children with anxiety issues and ADHD.

LIFE RIVER MAP GAME

Therapeutic Rationale: Children with a background of multiple changes due to a difficult family situation, experience significant separation and loss and are often confused with regard to the meaning and impact of the changes. The Life River Map Game will allow a non-threatening environment for children to recreate their story in their own terms and gain realistic insight regarding the changes that affected them.

Descriptions: Materials needed: Two A3-sized sheets of white paper, two markers, two crayon boxes and so on.

The therapist will first draw a wide and appropriately long river, so that it is divided into a number of parts (one part for each year of age) as per the child's total chronological age on the chart paper. Next, start writing or drawing in the part, significant incidences, both positive or negatives of the child's life. Invite the child to draw/write his/her own life map, which can be done simultaneously also after explaining the process to the child. However, the therapist should consider the developmental functioning of the child. The child may find it hard to remember or be guarded about writing incidences. The therapist needs to be careful to acknowledge the difficulty and reassure him/her by skipping over a topic or just drawing something instead of writing. When the maps are completed, the therapist and the child will talk about each other map and this will generate more conversations and reflections which the therapist will manage appropriately.

Application: The children with multiple placement changes will benefit particularly.

MAGIC KEY

Therapeutic Rationale: Magic Key (developed by Crenshaw 2008) is a form of projective drawing that aims to reconnect the children with the feelings and wishes associated with the background of separation and loss experienced in their lives. In general, children find it difficult to verbalise or connect with feelings and wishes; however, projective drawing and storytelling along with play therapy and symbols can offer them the language and the means to explore the loss, longing and missing aspects of their lives.

Descriptions: Materials needed: Chart paper, crayons, pencils, marker and so on.

The following instructions should be given to the child in a developmentally appropriate way:

> Imagine that you have been given a magic key that only can open one door in a huge castle. There are four floors in the castle and since the castle is huge there are many, many rooms in the castle. Pretend that you go from room to room, and from floor to floor, trying your magic key in each door until you finally come to the door that your key opens. You turn the key and the lock open. Because you have been given a magic key that only opens this door, what you see is the one thing that money cannot buy which you always thought would make you happy. Pretend that you are looking into the room. What is it that you see? What is that thing that has been missing that you think would

make you happy? When you have a clear picture, please draw it as best you can. (Crenshaw 2008: 16)

Application: Children with a history of trauma, anxiety and depressive symptoms will benefit from this intervention that will facilitate a therapeutic dialogue to express their wishes and feelings regarding past and current experiences. However, this intervention demands positive therapeutic alliance. Crenshaw (2008) suggested that the tool could be used in group situations as well.

ABOUT-ME GAME

Therapeutic Rationale: Children can explore their wishes and feelings about significant life experiences in a distracting situation that facilitates nondirective and playful experiences. The game creates a sensory atmosphere to generate thoughts with short incomplete statements that are relevant to their day–to-day social affairs.

Descriptions: Materials needed: Figure 1.6 or an adopted version, according to the circumstances of the child, in full A4-sized paper. Pen or pencil and marker (if needed).

In the individual psychosocial therapy session, the therapist should provide a brief introduction of the tool in colour form including reassurance about confidentiality and voluntary participation (i.e., he/she may choose to leave any part/s if the child is not comfortable with). Then offer the child the *About-me* copy and a pen. The child may choose to write with pen or pencil and even draw a picture in certain section/s. Once this is completed, with permission of the child, the therapist should have a look at it and ask if he/she wants to add anything further. This will give the therapist a reasonable background regarding the child's understanding of his/her environment for future appropriate intervention.

Applications: The tool may be applicable for children of the age group of five years or above with any mental health symptoms in the background of difficult developmental experiences.

PSYCHODRAMA OR ROLE-PLAY GAME

Therapeutic Rationale: The role-play activity is about reframing an experience of the past in the light of new perceptual, cognitive and affective feelings and experiences (Hughes 1997). Psychodrama uses re-enactment

Figure 1.6
About Me

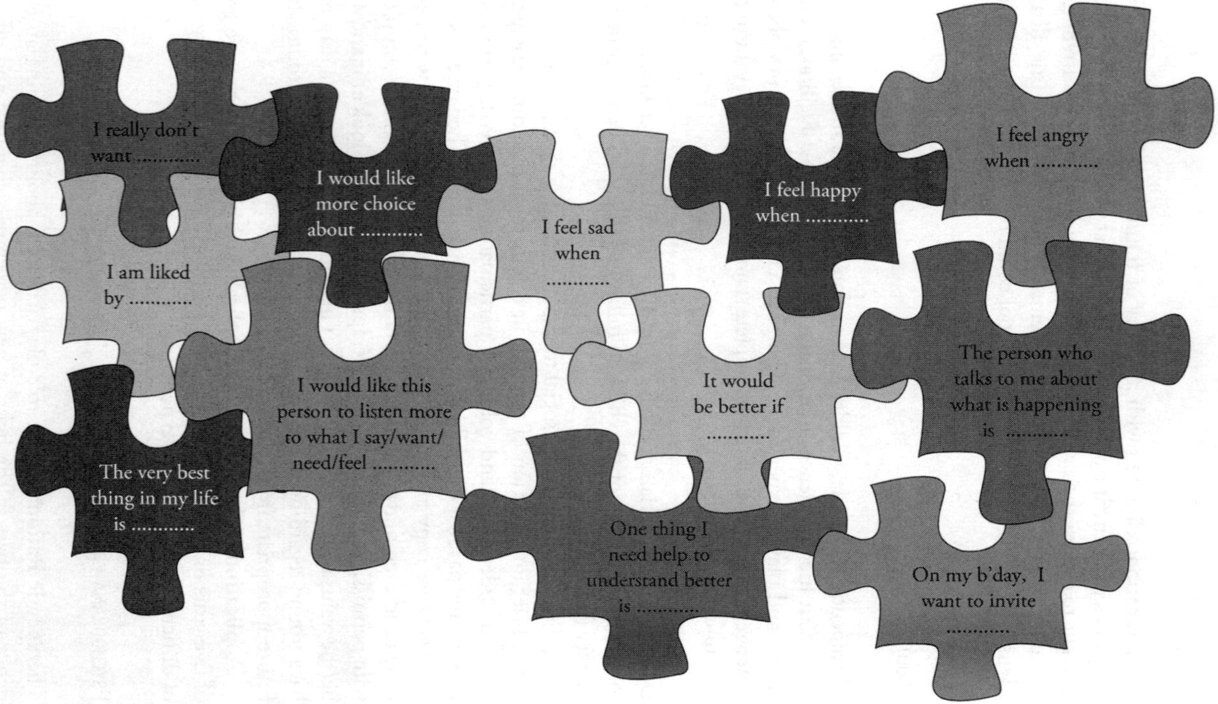

of past trauma and abusive relationships with the child's primary caregiver to explore wishes and feelings as well as replacing it with positive and pro-social experiences. The new experience, in a safe and supportive therapeutic environment, helps the child to reconnect with the past or ongoing difficult developmental experiences and simultaneously internalise the feelings in a positive and developmentally-appropriate ways.

Descriptions: Actors needed: Apart from the child and the therapist, the child's supportive family members may also participate in the drama. This is a simple exercise.

Role-play needs very careful planning as it requires considerable sensitivity to the child's current psychosocial functioning. If the child becomes regressed, rigid or frantic, the therapist should immediately change the focus or reframe the drama or reduce the intensity (Hughes 1997). Accordingly, the therapist will first discuss and plan out the role-play exercise with full permission and to the comfort of the child. Initially, the therapist and the child will start by playing different roles (the therapist should not take the role of an abusive parent/caregiver, rather the role of the child and vice versa) and then gradually expand by involving supportive family members (Hughes 1997). For example, the author, had an experience of working with a 10-year-old boy who was very upset due to his father's consistent missing contact. During the role-play exercise, the author became the child and the child was playing the role of his father. Although the author attempted to highlight his strong sense of understanding of the child's experiences, feelings, empathy and compassion in the role, still the child (from the other side) did not find the author's expression adequate and this forced him to return to his actual self and natural response. In another, similar situation, the child became very upset when the author had to reframe the topic and the focus.

Application: Children with the experience of abuse, trauma and neglect or other difficult developmental experiences will benefit from the psycho-drama activities.

Systemic Approach

The systemic component of psychosocial therapy stems from Erickson's person-in-environment perspective, recognising the impact of wider physical and social environment (Mattaini and Lowery 2007) in the child's functioning under the values of social justice. Mattaini (2008) has expressed concerns that the person-in-environment concept has been defined and redefined since the last century but the social work practitioners have switched sides in keeping with their own preferences and have ignored either the person or the environment. This isolated practice approach has led them to often attempt to intervene with clients by amputating them from their environment and interactional realities. In child and adolescent mental health, the environment consists of significant key players such as parents and family, school, health and social care systems and cultural development opportunities (Figure 1.7a).

These factors are deeply integrated and interdependent. For example, if the child does not feel safe at home, he/she will struggle to engage in either school or in therapy. If the child has any medical, mental or developmental conditions, he/she will be particularly vulnerable in the absence of appropriate health and social care resources. The cultural perspective recognises the importance of cultural connectedness and also culturally-appropriate practice. Tseng's (1999) work identifies that practitioners, if not appropriately matured, can face cultural transference and countertransference in cross-cultural practice. Tseng (1999: 161) outlines:

> Cultural transference refers to a patient developing a certain relationship, feeling or attitude towards the therapist because of the therapist's ethno-cultural background; cultural countertransference implies the reverse phenomenon, namely, a therapist developing a certain relationship with the patient mainly because of the patient's ethno-cultural background.

Figure 1.7a
Systematic Factors of Child Development and Well-being (Outer Factors)

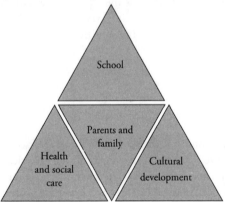

School

Parents and family

Health and social care

Cultural development

FAMILY DEVELOPMENT FACTORS

The Department of Health (2000: 17) practice guidance has offered a comprehensive tool for the process of psychosocial assessment and intervention. However, the therapists need to have skills and competence to clarify the impact of family and environmental factors in the mental health needs of the children apart from maintaining appropriate partnerships with parents/carers (see Figure 1.7b).

CO-ORDINATION WITH SCHOOL

Besides family, school is the other significant setting in a child's life. School plays a central role in not only teaching children literacy, numeracy and wide range of creative physical activities, but also about the world beyond their childhood home (Wilson 2008). It is also a crucial place that may capture the mental health needs of children as part of early intervention. Australian government's recent policy decision to introduce a mental health screening programme in the primary school (*Sydney Morning Herald* 2012) recognises the importance of school-based intervention. United Nations International

Figure 1.7b
Systematic Factors of Child Development and Well-being (Inner Factors)

Developmental needs
- Basic needs, health, education, social and emotional identity
- Social presentation, self care and family and social relationships

Parenting capacity
- Basic care, ensuring safety, emotional warmth and stimulation
- Guidance, boundaries and stability in parent's lifestyle

Family and environmental factors
- Family history and functioning, support networks, support from extended family
- Housing, employment and income

Children's Emergency Fund's (UNICEF) *State of the World's Children Report 2011* (UNICEF 2011) suggests that one in every five adolescents suffers from mental health or behavioural problem. These reports set the rationale for appropriate clinical initiative in the school setting like co-ordination with schools on specific case management levels as well as advocating for a whole school approach to facilitate an 'emotionally-literate school' where students, teachers, parents and other members of the school community feel integrated, valued, listened to and respected (Weare 2008: 143). The focus should be on creating a positive learning environment and an absolutely no-tolerance policy for not just bullying and violence but also sarcasm and belittling (Weare 2008). The idea of whole school approach is in tune with Erickson's person-in-environment approach that children need to have a safe, secure and welcoming place that will facilitate their social and emotional well-being. Ferguson (2011) emphasised for social workers to go the extra mile to better understand the child in his/her intimate space, that is, home, school and so on, to get a pragmatic feel regarding the child's circumstances for appropriate action in partnership with the people in the system.

CULTURALLY APPROPRIATE INTERVENTION

Culture is embedded in a person's way of life. Cultural experiences create social values and norms in a person's mind that frequently exist at an unconscious level and influence social functioning. Malinowski (in Jenks 1993: 12) states that 'culture is inherited artifacts, goods, technical process, ideas, habits and values'. He included within his definition a notion of social structure, which, he felt, could not be understood apart from culture.

Culturally appropriate clinical practice is about being aware of the socio-cultural values and norms of the child and thereby structures an intervention strategy that is most appropriate to protect the best interests of the child. Culturally appropriate intervention strategy is not just empowering but also adherence to children's human rights. Article 4 of the United Nations Conventions on the Rights of the Child (UNCRC) states, 'With regard to economic, social and cultural rights, States Parties shall undertake such measures to the maximum extent of their available resources and, where needed, within the framework of international co-operation' (OHCHR 1989). The literature clearly outlines the necessity of evidence-based culturally appropriate intervention. This is not an uphill task but rather needs an open mind, respectful attitude and reasonable knowledge about a culture and its values and norms. However, at times, professionals' stereotypical perceptions about indigenous, black and minority-ethnic populations due to cultural ignorance, racism, stigma and anxiety lead to inappropriate practice (Street 2008: 38). Appropriate culture-specific training, regular supervision and a commitment to social justice in terms of cultural diversity may lead to culturally appropriate practice.

Conclusion

This chapter reviews the scope of a comprehensive psychosocial practice framework in the domain of social work to support and empower the vulnerable children in mental health services. It offers the social workers with different therapeutic tools under social work values and principles. The intervention framework demands high-standard professional skills and competence to use the tools in the background of person-centred, psychodynamic and systemic approaches. The therapeutic games discussed are just few ideas but can be redeveloped to meet the new demands of diverse individual therapeutic situations.

Children and young people attending mental health services often find it difficult to engage due to various needs and create potential risks of disengagement. The complex needs of the children sets the rationale for a broad-based child–friendly treatment approach by taking into consideration their diverse social and emotional needs while upholding their rights of dignity and fairness. This chapter outlines a psychosocial approach that advocates multi-dimensional treatment perspectives in coordination with psychological theories and social work values to empower and build resilience. The discussion draws on integration of person-centred, psychodynamic and systemic perspectives in attempting to contribute to a more comprehensive response to the challenges in child and adolescent mental health social work and services in general.

The discussion also reflects on how the social work profession has undergone significant changes in the last hundred years in terms of its scope and horizon while maintaining its essential values of social justice and human welfare (Showers and Dulmus 2008). While this chapter offers different therapeutic models and practice ideas, it also compliments the strengths of social work and behavioural sciences in integration.

References

Axline, V. 1989. *Play Therapy*. London: Ballantine Books.

Backer-Weidman, A. and D. Hughes. 2008. 'Dyadic Developmental Psychotherapy: An Evidence-based Treatment for Children with Complex Trauma and Disorders of Attachment', *Child and Family Social Work*, 13 (3): 329–337.

Ben-Porath, D. D. 2004. 'Strategies for Securing Commitment to Treatment from Individuals Diagnosed with Borderline Personality Disorder', *Journal of Contemporary Psychotherapy*, 34 (3): 247–263.

Beynon, S., K. Sares-Weiser, N. Woolacott, S. Duffy and J. Goddes. 2008. 'Psychosocial Interventions for the Prevention of Relapse in Bipolar Disorder: Systemic Review of Controlled Tricks', *The British Journal of Psychiatry*, 192: 5–11. Doi: 10.1192/bjp.bp.107.037887

Cohler, B. and T. Weiner. 2011. 'The Inner Fortress: Symptom and Meaning in Asperger's Syndrome', *Psychoanalytic Inquiry*, 31(3): 208–221.

Crenshaw, D. A. 2008. 'Magic Key', in L. Lowenstein (ed), *Assessment and Treatment Activities for Children, Adolescents and Families*. Canada: Champion Press.

Department of Health. 2000. *Assessing Children in Need and Their Families: Practice Guidance*. London: HMSO.

Ferguson, H. 2011. *Child Protection Practice*. Great Britain: McMillan.

Greene, R. 2008. 'Psychosocial Theory', in B. A. Thyer, K. M. Showers, and C. N. Dulmus (eds), *Comprehensive Hand Book of Social Work and Social Welfare: Human Behaviour in the Social Environment*. New Jersey: J Wiley.

Haggerty, J. 2006. 'Psychodynamic Therapy', *Psych Central*. Available from: http://psychcentral.com/lib/2006/psychodynamic-therapy/. (accessed in June, 2011)

Hall, T. M., C. E. Schaefer and H. G. Kaduson. 2002. 'Fifteen Effective Play Therapy Techniques', *Professional Psychology: Research and Practice*, 33 (6):515–522.

Hamama, L. and T. Ronen. 2009. 'Children's Drawing as a Self-Report Measurement', *Child and Family Social Work*, 14 (1): 90–102.

Holosko, M., J. Skinner and R. Robinston. 2008. 'Person Centered Theory', in B. Thyer, K. Sowers and C. Dulmus (eds), *Comprehensive Hand Book of Social Work and Social Welfare: Human Behaviour in the Social Enviornment*. New Jersey: J Wiley and Sons.

Hughes, D. 1997. *Facilitating Developmental Attachment: The Road to Emotional Recovery and Behaviour Change in Foster and Adopted Children*. New Jersey: Jason Aronson.

Jenks, C. 1993. *Cultural Reproduction*. London and New York: Routledge.

Khan, A. and D. Miles. 2011. 'Talk to Me, Not my Illness: Relevance of Human Rights and Social Justice in Child and Adolescent Mental Health Intervention', in P. Jones, D. Miles, A. Francis and S. P. Rajeev (eds), *Eco-social Justice: Issues, Challenges and Ways Forwards*. Bangalore: Book For Change.

Leibowitz, M. 1999. *Interpreting Projective Drawings: A Self Psychological Approach*. Philadelphia: Brunner/Mazel.

Malinowski, B. 1993. 'Review of Six Essays on Culture by Albert Blumenthal', in C. Jenks (ed), *Cultural Reproduction*. London and New York: Routledge.

Mattaini, M. A. and C. T. Lowery (eds). 2007. *Foundations of Social Work Practice* (4th edition). Washington, DC: National Association of Social Workers Press.

Mattaini, M. A. 2008. 'Ecosystem Theory', in B. A. Thyer, K. M. Showers and C. N. Dulmus (eds), *Comprehensive Hand Book of Social Work and Social Welfare: Human Behaviour in the Social Environment*. New Jersey: J Wiley and Sons.

McMurran, M., N. Huband and E. Overton. 2010. 'Non-completion of Personality Disorder Treatments: A Systematic Review of Correlates, Consequences and Interventions', *Clinical Psychology Review*, 30 (3): 277–287.

Mullan, C., S. McAllister, F. Rollock and L. Fitzsimons. 2007. 'Care Just Changes Your Life: Factors Impacting upon the Mental Health of Children and Young People with Experiences of Care in Northern Ireland', *Child Care in Practice*, 13 (4): 417–434.

O'Brien, A., R. Fahmy and S. P. Singh. 2009. 'Disengagement from Mental Health Services', *Social Psychiatry and Psychiatric Epidemiology*, 44 (7): 558–568.

OHCHR. 1989. 'Convention on the Rights of the Child', High Commission for Human Rights, Geneva.

Payne, M. 1997. *Modern Social Work Theory*. London: Macmillan.

Probst, B. 2006, 'Re-Framing and De-Pathologizing Behavior in Therapy for Children Diagnosed with Psychosocial Disorders', *Child and Adolescent Social Work Journal*, 23 (4): 487–500.

Shooter, M. 2008. 'What is Mental Health?' in C. Jackson, K. Hill and P. Lavis (eds), *Child and Adolescent Mental Health Today: A Handbook*. Brighton, UK: Pavilion.

Showers, K. M. and C. N. Dulmus. 2008. 'Hand Book Preface', in B. A. Thyer, K. M. Showers and C. N. Dulmus (eds), *Comprehensive Hand Book of Social Work and Social Welfare: Human Behaviour in the Social Environment*. New Jersey: J Wiley.

Street, C. 2008. 'Delivering Accessible and Culturally Competent Services', in C. Jackson, K. Hill and P. Lavis (eds), *Child and Adolescent Mental Health Today: A Handbook*. Brighton, UK: Pavilion.

Sydney Morning Herald. 2012. 'Government Stands by Child Mental Health Tests'. Available from: http://news.smh.com.au/breaking-news-national/govt-stands-by-child-mental-health-tests-20120610-204bf.html. (accessed in December, 2012)

Tetley, A., M. Jinks, N. Huband and K. Howells. 2011. 'A Systemic Review of Measures of Therapeutic Engagement in Psychosocial and Psychological Treatment', *Journal of Clinical Psychology*, 67 (9): 843–980.

Thomas, G. V. and R. P. Jolley. 1998. 'Drawing Conclusions: A Re-examination of Empirical and Conceptual Bases for Psychological Evaluation of Children from Their Drawings', *British Journal of Clinical Psychology*, 37 (2): 127–246.

Tseng, W.-S. 1999. 'Culture and Psychotherapy: Review and Practical Guidelines', *Transcultural Psychiatry*, 36 (2): 131–179.

UNICEF. 2011. 'UNICEF: Investing in Adolescents Can Break Cycles of Poverty and Inequity'. UNICEF Press Centre. Available from: http://www.unicef.org/media/media_57728.html (accessed in May, 2012)

Weare, K, 2008, 'Taking a Whole School Approach to Promote Mental Health', in C. Jackson, K. Hill and P. Lavis (eds), *Child and Adolescent Mental Health Today: A Handbook*. Brighton, UK: Pavilion.

Wierzbicki, M., and G. Pekarik. 1993. 'A Meta-Analysis of Psychotherapy Dropout', *Professional Psychology: Research and Practice*, 24 (2): 190–195.

Wilson, P. 2008. 'Mental Health Promotion in Primary Schools', in C. Jackson, K. Hill and P. Lavis (eds), *Child and Adolescent Mental Health Today: A Handbook*. Brighton, UK: Pavilion.

Web Resources

http://www.marketingisland.com/mi/tmm/en/cataloguemanager/CMHA/CMHA_mh_pamphlet_04_EN.pdf (accessed on 11 March 2014)

http://www.gway.org/websites/gway/images/creative%20interventions.pdf (accessed on 1 May 2014.

http://www.scie.org.uk/publications/practiceguides/practiceguide06/index.asp (accessed on 11 March 2014)

http://www.health.qld.gov.au/mentalhealth/abt_us/qpfmh/vision.asp (accessed on 11 March 2014)

2

School Mental Health Practice: Challenges for School Social Work in India

V. Sayee Kumar

Introduction

School mental health often evokes a feeling of stigma among school community members comprising students, teachers, school administrators and parents. The problems assume significance due to their occurrence in schoolchildren as a captive population, the public health dimension and our moral duty to address them suitably. The chapter discusses the significance of the problems and brings out the extent of mental health problems among schoolchildren. The human resource dimension with reference to mental health professionals in this regard, especially with reference to social work profession, is deliberated. Various studies have shown that childhood problems, such as anxiety, emotional disorders, dyslexia, scholastic backwardness, mental retardation and suicide, are fairly common among schoolchildren. And it is a big challenge to address them with very limited resources in India. The author makes an attempt to trace the past as well as identify the present trend. A mention is made on development in this regard. This is especially true with the available infrastructure and human resources for mental health services. An effort is made to understand the relationship between school social work and psychiatric social work. The chapter indicates emerging trends of practice and scope for future interventions.

'School mental health' is a term that often evokes a sense of social stigma within school circles. However, mental health professionals cannot avoid using this term to cover a wide range of child and adolescent psychiatric problems prevailing among school-going children and adolescents. Of course, they can also occur in non school-going children, but professionals prefer to use the term 'school mental health' due to its captive and specific coverage. The non school-going children's mental health problems, it appears, have been left to non-governmental organisations (NGOs) and governments to study or deal with. Alas, there are a significant number of children in India outside the umbrella of school. But this chapter has restricted its scope of discourse on the topic to the school system only.

Why the Problem

A wide variety of diagnostic categories of childhood psychiatric problems is present in the school population. In India, studies have been more pointedly done with the child guidance clinic population in Bombay, Delhi, Vellore, Chandigarh and Amritsar, and sometimes in schools. The community surveys have been very limited. Researchers have used terms such as 'behavioural problems', 'neurotic disorders', 'emotional problems', 'emotional disturbance' and 'behavioural disorder'.

Why School Mental Health is Important

According to the *Report of the Surgeon General's Conference on Children's Mental Health, 2000*, in the United States, both the promotion of mental health in children and the treatment of mental disorders should be the major public health goals. When we look into India's new National Mental Health Policy, it commits for inclusive services for children too.

The extent, severity, and far-reaching consequences of mental health problems in children and adolescents are far more severe than what can happen to adults. School mental health affects the future and our vibrant economy. So it deserves its priority and place in national policies related to health, mental health and education.

In this context, offering school mental health services will be realistic and hence important for the following reasons:

- Adjustment and learning outcomes are related to mental health of children.

- Children learn and imbibe many of their healthy behaviours from the schools due to their presence in school for most hours of the day, constant interaction, exposure and interface with the school environment.
- School is an ideal centre to combine the mental health care efforts of teachers, families, mental health service providers and school managers.
- It is easy to identify the problems very early and make interventions.
- The services can be made affordable and accessible easily in school.
- We can integrate mental health inputs into general education, student counselling/guidance programmes and school health services.

While we struggle to address the need to offer basic mental health services to the vast majority of our population, in spite of our proclaimed National Mental Health Programme (NMHP), 1982, child mental health does not figure as a priority.

Extent of Mental Health Problems among Schoolchildren

The incidence of mental health problems among school and non school-going children reported by different authors is interesting to note. Basu (1962) noted 36 per cent, Chacko (1964) 9 per cent, Raju et al. (1969) 10.6 per cent, Singh and Gupta (1970, in Ilango 1986) 4.6 per cent and Teja et al. (1970, in Ilango 1986) 36.8 per cent, out which 10.5 per cent had conduct disorders.

Murthy R. S. et al. (1974, in Ilango 1986) felt that there were only a few studies from India relating to the epidemiological, clinical and follow-up aspects of behaviour disorders of childhood. Nagaraj (1978, in Ilango 1986) published an analysis of over 12 years and showed that primary schoolchildren showed more adjustment problems while adolescents had more neurotic complaints. While reviewing the studies, Ilango (1986) remarks that the prevalence of psychiatric morbidity in children is 15–20 per cent. Parvathavardhini (1983) in her survey among rural schoolchildren, found 30 per cent conduct disorders, 15 per cent neurotic disorders and 37 per cent mixed and conduct disorders. Suresh and Sebastian (2003) report that dyslexia, a common form of learning disability, is observed in 10 per cent of the school-going population. However, the magnitude of the problem and prevalence in India have not been fully understood.

Most of the studies pertaining to child psychiatry in India are confined to analysis of clinical data and a few relate to monosymptomatic disorders like enuresis, speech problems, abdominal pain and mental retardation. With the explosion of information technology, news and information, the expanding economic growth story of India since liberalisation has had an impact on the educational sphere, especially on stress experienced by students as well as teachers. The topic of mental health gets episodic attention every now and then, especially when school, schoolchildren or school teachers are held responsible for some bad news. It then occupies prime news space and social discourse. This is true when media flashes an incident, especially if it involves a student committing suicide in a tragic manner, a teacher is disciplined for meting out corporal punishment in a lethal or brutal manner, and stress experienced by students during annual board examinations. As per a recent health ministry report, over 16,000 school and college students in India committed suicide in the last three years, shedding light once again on the sorry state of mental health care in the country ('16,000 students lost to suicide in 3 years', *sify news*, 3 May 2008). As per the ministry, 5,857 students committed suicide in 2006 and the figure for 2005 was 5,138. Similarly, in 2004, 5,610 students committed suicide. The suicide rate in the city of Chennai (Madras) was 17.2 per 100,000 (Vijayakumar and Rajkumar 1999, as cited in Young et al. 2003). But these figures tactfully cover the whole gamut of childhood and adolescent psychiatric problems that can be cited, observed, elicited and dealt well in school settings. All it needs is a very concerted and coherent strategy.

Malhotra (1995) studied schoolchildren by using the sophisticated three-stage assessment of the epidemiology of disorders in school population in the age group of 4–12 years. This study compared children's groups based on clinical assessment, and responses of teachers (by using Rutter's B scale) and parents. It revealed the prevalence rate of psychiatric disorders between 7 and 20 per cent. Overall, the most conservative estimate of severe psychiatric disorder in India is 10 per cent of the population under age 14, representing 35 million children (Malhotra 1998: 321–34).

Mental retardation and epilepsy are the most common mental disorders in India (Lal and Sethi 1977; Malhotra and Chaturvedi 1984). Rozario (1991, in Kapur 1995), in a study of 110 children of nine years of age in a school serving middle, socio-economic children had found that 32 children were labelled as scholastically backward and having learning disabilities. Shenoy 1992 (cited in Kapur 1995) conducted an epidemiological study of 1,535 five-to-eight year-old school-going children. In this study, 11 per cent of the boys and 9.38 per cent of the girls were rated as scholastically backward by the teachers, yielding the prevalence rate of 10.2 per cent. Twenty-six per cent of the scholastically backward were also rated as psychologically disturbed as against 7 per cent in the non-disturbed population.

Sarkar 1990 (cited in Kapur 1995), in an epidemiological study of 408 children in the age of 8–12 years from the middle, socio-economic background, found 33 per cent of children to be scholastically backward as per the reports of teachers. Of the children who were rated as psychologically disturbed, 42 per cent were also reported to be scholastically backward, while only 32 per cent of the non-disturbed were reported to be so (Kapur 1995).

In a primary school with 1,522 students in Bangalore, Rao, Moorthy and Parthasarathy (1983) studied children's classroom behaviour which was perceived by teachers as 'problems' other than scholastic backwardness. They had found 72 children as problem children. In a randomly selected representative sample of 963 schoolchildren in the 4–12 years age range in Chandigarh, the prevalence of overall psychiatric disorders was 9.34 per cent, with the following psychiatric diagnoses: enuresis 2.28 per cent, conduct disorder 1.66 per cent, attention deficit hyperactivity disorder 1.35 per cent, specific developmental disorder 0.93 per cent, disorder of emotions 0.62 per cent, mild mental retardation 0.41 per cent, somatoform and conversion disorder 0.2 per cent and adjustment disorder 0.2 per cent. Thirteen children had dual diagnosis and two had three diagnoses. Dual diagnosis was more in males, and the commonest condition was enuresis. While the study documents the rates of psychiatric disorder in India, it is interesting to note that the prevalence rates are much lower than what are reported from Western countries. The reasons for this could be related to sociocultural and family factors (Indian Council of Medical Research 2005). The magnitude is fairly clear from the editorial analysis made by Sharan and Rajesh (2008) about child and adolescent psychiatric problems. It says that 10–20 per cent of children and adolescents develop mental health problems with 5–12 per cent suffering from functionally impairing conditions.

Human Resources for Child and Adolescent Mental Health Services

Children and adolescents with mental health complaints are generally attended to by general practitioners, family physicians, paediatricians, and sometimes mental health professionals.

Although mental health care for our schoolchildren cannot be completely given by trained clinical psychologists or psychiatric social workers, there certainly is a need for school psychologists, school social workers trained at masters level, and teachers and special educators trained at bachelors level.

We see a recent trend of appointing school counsellors, across the country, but we do not have clear statistics since they belong to a set of heterogeneous disciplines of social and behavioural sciences, education, guidance, human resource development trainers and self-claimed professionals in counselling. However an ideal school mental health programme needs the input of a mental health team, with members such as psychiatrists, clinical psychologists, psychiatric social workers, psychiatric nurses, occupational therapists and special teachers.

The *Mental Health Atlas* (World Health Organization 2005) highlights the low numbers of mental health professionals in India. The figures are not at all encouraging, particularly given the magnitude of mental health needs. The average national deficit of psychiatrists is estimated to be 77 per cent; more than one-third of the population has more than 90 per cent deficit of psychiatrists. Only the populations of Chandigarh, Delhi, Goa and Pondicherry have a surfeit of psychiatrists. Kerala and Maharashtra have less than 50 per cent deficit, while all the other states have more than 50 per cent deficit of psychiatrists. There is a vast and striking variation in the distribution of psychiatrists across the country. The figures for psychologists, psychiatric social workers and psychiatric nurses working in mental health care are equally inadequate.

According to Murthy (2011), there is an acute shortage of manpower in the field of mental health, namely, psychiatrists, clinical psychologists, psychiatric social workers and psychiatric nurses. This is a major constraint in meeting mental health needs and providing optimal mental health services to people.

The other major development is the growth in human resources. At the time of the formulation of the NMHP, the number of psychiatrists was under 1,000 and in the past 27 years, it has more than tripled, to about 3,500. However, the number of trained clinical psychologists, psychiatric social workers and psychiatric nurses is inadequate, and this is unfortunate because they form a vital part of the team. The existing training infrastructure in India produces about 320 psychiatrists, 50 clinical psychologists, 25 psychiatric social workers and 185 psychiatric nurses per year.

The present author presented some findings of a study on child and adolescent mental health content available in the websites of state and central educational bodies in India. He went through the websites of

42 educational boards apart from the National Council of Educational Research and Training (NCERT), Regional Institutes of Education, and the University Grants Commission, and presented some findings. Of all the sites, the website of the Central Board of Secondary Education (CBSE) (http://cbse.nic.in) was good in terms of clarity, updates, friendly navigation, content, resources available for students, teachers and parents, and online and hotline telephone services. The sites of Kendriya Vidyalayas were good and included a note on guidance and counselling programmes. Child and adolescent mental health were mentioned in the sites of Haryana (deaf, dumb and dyslexia; exemptions), West Bengal (mentions and commits community mental health, but does not elaborate), Kerala (adolescent health education), Uttaranchal, National Institute of Open Learning (adolescent health education), Rajasthan (personality development programme), Meghalaya, Mizoram (ragging, self-esteem, coping with stress, dealing with anger, coping with emotions),and Orissa (menu on student welfare, future plan on grievance cell).

In this study it was found that except for the CBSE, no other board had put anything significant on school mental health on their website. The CBSE has started telephonic counselling, especially during examination times. This is due to student suicides—both attempted and completed—which are reported in the media between March and June, and triggered by acute examination stress or disappointment arising out of published results of public examinations. The CBSE offers good guidelines to students, teachers and parents through their website (Kumar 2009). It is also evident that there is a lack of co-ordination between central and state boards to have or develop a unitary vision on various issues of policymaking in this regard (unpublished paper).

Some Thoughts for the Future

The new economy of India demands a vast number of skilled employees in every sphere of economic activity. So the emphasis is laid on human resource building through professional and technical education. Newly emerged middle-class parents are caught up in this competitive environment to push their ward for higher performance for a decisive professional career. The present world of work and higher education has thrown up huge varieties of new lucrative careers for the youngsters to choose from, but students are ill prepared to choose a career befitting their aptitude and interest. This kind of situation has changed the priorities of schools and parents to focus on school mental health. Since the competition can be beaten only by excellent performance in board exams, the school system follows that order of rote learning. The teachers are targeted if the students fail to reach the targets fixed by schools. This has thrown up new emotional challenges to the students.

The student and teacher communities need to know that India faced the daunting task of providing mental health for all by 2000, as envisaged in the NMHP, but missed an opportunity. And we still struggle to provide reasonable care even to major mental disorders like schizophrenia in the community. India is yet to utilise the allotted fund of INR 1.39 billion during the 10th Five-Year Plan for mental health. In fact, mental health professionals were criticised in the Parliament for failure of the flagship NMHP of 1982. Now the hope is to do justice by renewed efforts to follow the National Mental Health Policy, 2001. This policy hopes to address the district mental health programme, modernisation of mental hospitals, upgrading of undergraduate and postgraduate psychiatry curricula, strengthening of state/central mental health authorities, and research/training in community mental health, substance abuse and child/adolescent psychiatric clinics. About 70 per cent of health care contacts in India occur within the private sector (Nizamie and Goyal 2010). This may pose challenges while considering public–private partnerships, like in other sectors.

However, during the 11th Five-Year Plan, there has been a substantial increase in the funding support for the NMHP. The total amount of funding allotted is INR 4.73 billion (a three-fold increase from the previous Plan). The areas identified for support include manpower development, completion of spillover activities of the 10th Plan, modernisation of state-run mental hospitals, implementation of the existing district mental health programme and integration of the NMHP with the National Rural Health Mission (Murthy 2011).

But the government or public sector has almost withdrawn itself from welfare services, leaving it to private players under the policy of liberalisation, privatisation and globalisation. The private sector has little interest in the welfare of state, or to offer free or even subsidised services. But hopefully this may change hereafter due to the new statutory requirement for companies to spend a mandatory amount of their profit under the corporate social responsibility programs. Earlier it was left to their discretion. The situation is not very different in the education sector which is dominated by private unaided schools and universities. Any effort to regulate them is met with stiff resistance due to strong political and commercial interests and connections.

So the mental health issues have to be understood and services availed of in this context. The state needs to have a clear policy on mental health in schools and link it with the National Mental Health Policy and the Ministry of Human Resource Development (MHRD).

Possible Solutions

It is worthwhile to recollect what was mentioned in the Indian Psychiatric Society (IPS 1964, in Murthy and Burns 1992), which was repeated in the Indo–US Symposium on Community Mental Health in 1992. In the words of Murthy and Burns (1992),

> Even if almost all five year plan efforts in the field of health were only geared to increasing the number of psychiatric doctors, it would be impossible to provide an adequate number of hospital beds and mental specialists even in the next 50–100 years; even if the training facilities in the country are doubled and trebled, which is not easy, it could still require nearly 100 years to provide an adequate number of psychiatrists for working in the curative field.

So, it is better that we gear our school mental health programme from a non-clinical perspective and involve stakeholders, such as school teachers, parents and the society at large. It is important to make the educational bodies more responsive to the contributions of other professionals like school social workers and school psychologists. But unfortunately these are not very well established professions in the eyes of society and the school community. They suffer from many inadequacies in terms of their status, statutory authority, professional standing and acceptance in the school system. Compared to social work, psychology is better in terms of references and role clarity. We also face the problem of too many professionals, para-professionals, self-claimed counsellors and psychotherapists crowding the schools and offering services.

The schools are also helpless and encourage them knowingly or unknowingly. They are likely to look up to the CBSE, the NCERT, and state and national boards of school education for guidance and regulation. We need mental health professionals to actively work with the MHRD.

The challenge of school mental health lies in ensuring primary and secondary prevention of childhood disorders which seriously affect emotional and school adjustment. It has to be done without any stigma creeping into it.

So a good guidance programme which blends well with the general education programme for all the students is needed. The next challenge is to change the attitude of teachers in the school. It involves sensitising, motivating and facilitating them for early identification and supportive but simple interventions, such as active listening, referral for professional help and maintaining confidentiality. This means that a good amount of continuous teachers' training has to take place.

Training is required especially in recognition and sensitisation of mental health issues. Here we need to mention the findings of Ilango (1986) who undertook a study covering 130 teachers working in three schools of Bangalore city, out of whom 60 were selected based on a questionnaire with regard to 127 items of problem behaviours. It was found that a sizeable number of them considered only self-destructive, inattentive, nervous, over-active and aggressive behaviours as problems. They did not consider anxiety, social withdrawal and unpopular behaviour as problems. They did not have any idea of professional help for the management of problem behaviours.

The management needs to commit itself to a belief in counselling and professionalised personal services to children. In the absence of good, suitable legislation governing strong professional bodies in school social work, it becomes a losing battle to offer any meaningful school mental health services by social workers. There is little work done in the area. Schools of social work across the country offer traditional and popular specialisations, but not school social work, although they keep talking about it in and out of classrooms. Without any assured job market for the young trainees in social work and psychology, the professional opportunities of working in child mental health gets depleted. Moreover, there are no proven models and documented work in school mental health programmes and services. However, we cannot deny the possible availability of clusters of experiences across the country which need to be brought to light, for sharing, learning and replicating if found to be good.

Psychiatric Social Work and School Social Work

The number of psychiatric social workers, with advanced MPhil-level training in psychiatric social work from mental health or medical institutions, available in the country will not be adequate to handle school mental health programmes in the entire country. So social workers at Master of Social Work (MSW)–level and having any specialisation can be encouraged to work and contribute. Ideally, we need one school social worker for every 1,000 students, but it may not be achievable in the short term; so, the realistic approach will be to train the existing teachers in a ratio which can be worked out by planning along with the educational boards and the MHRD. The existing mental health policymakers need to form a separate task force for school mental health and promote school mental health programmes, and it needs to seek the patronage of good student ambassadors, such as Dr A. P. J. Abdul Kalam, former President of India, who has been a great visionary and is able to reach out to the entire student community of India. There is an urgent need for social work institutions to start a specialisation of School Social Work and popularise it as a career for MSW students. Schools also have realised that emotional issues of present-day students are beyond their behavioural knowledge, time, capacity, competency and skills. However, they are still groping in the dark as to how to proceed and organise school mental health services. They are used to organising good general health or, of late, even dental health services. For mental health they face a challenge of stigma to serve as well as save children. There are many other allied professionals in the field operating for a common cause but with different orientation.

There is no statutory recommendation to appoint a full-time student counsellor in schools for student guidance and career counselling. Perhaps an amendment to the Right to Education Act recommending the appointment of social workers for psychosocial help in schools, on the lines of appointing social workers as welfare officers in industries according to the Factories Act, 1948.

It is pertinent to look into the seminal work done by Gandhi (1990) on school social work. It is the only major study done in India exclusively on school social work. Perhaps we need to take such documented work seriously before we plan and formulate anything on school social work.

Present Trends in School Mental Health

The 2008 National Consultative Meeting of the District Mental Health Programme suggested a pragmatic approach for school mental health care in India. In the background of scarce resources and huge demands for mental health care, it recommended that the teachers, in life skills education approach, address issues related to health, family relationships, developmental crisis, substance abuse, violence, bullying, sexuality and career choice. It also advocated a predominantly preventive and promotional interventional component in it. The school mental health programme in India needs to have the aims of training class teachers in identification and referral services. It also suggested involving stakeholders such as parents and community leaders in the efforts. The district mental health programme was to be primarily responsible for facilitating the training of teachers and responding to the referral in a meaningful manner. There have been some voluntary efforts in the NGO sector, like the one from the School Health Annual Report Programme (SHARP). It primarily works for schoolchildren, with a professionally managed team of medical experts, sociologists, educationists, psychologists, nutritional specialists and others who have vision of promoting the health care of children. SHARP started in July 1998 with participation from some schools in Delhi. The programme is, at present, operational all over the country, with its various projects running in schools of Mumbai, Pune, Bangalore, Chennai, Hyderabad, Kolkata and Lucknow, and various towns of Haryana, Punjab, Himachal Pradesh and Uttaranchal. It has computerised health records of hundreds of thousands of children and made them accessible via the internet. But the author was not able to locate the relevant contents on its website; moreover there is no mention of child mental health (www.schoolindia.org).

Here, we may mention the work of the Promise Foundation from Bangalore (www.thepromisefoundation.org), which takes care of counselling services for underprivileged school students. It focuses on career counselling, training teachers in career guidance and developing indigenous career guidance materials. Many telephonic helplines are available like the one from SNEHA, a centre for prevention of suicide (www.snehaindia.org). Popular among them is 1098–Child Help Line. There are also hotlines which become operational during board exams, like the one from the CBSE.

There are numerous private players in major Indian cities and towns offering a wide range of services like counselling, psychological assessment, speech therapy, special education, personality development and soft skills training. But they mainly cater to the middle- and upper-income groups. There are many NGOs working in the area of counselling, but are all community based. Some, like the Madras Dyslexia Association on Learning Disabilities at Chennai, work in special areas (www.mdachennai.com).

There are also a few individual initiatives in school social work in the country. A small publication titled *Journal for School Social Work*, from Chennai, has made some presence in the region by motivating professional social workers to write on various topics in school social work (Naidu 2012).

Significance of Social Workers' Services in Schools

Prasad (1993) mentions three channels for providing mental health services to children in India: (a) child guidance clinic, (b) school mental health (both of which include school social work and educational and vocational counsellors) and, (c) government schemes for physically challenged children (offered by various ministries of welfare and education). The Tata Institute of Social Sciences became a pioneer in starting child guidance clinics as part of its extension services in 1960. This was later followed with some reasonable success in other schools of social work in Delhi, Bombay and Ahmedabad. Gandhi (1990) observed that the growth achieved so far is attributed to the efforts made by colleges of social work, child guidance clinics, associations of social workers, a few progressive educationists and local parent–teacher associations.

Moreover, our schools suffer from chronic problems like very poor infrastructure, severe shortage of teachers, remote locations of schools in rural and hilly regions and underfunded education schemes. Under these circumstances, pursuing an interest in school mental health by committed professionals is a real challenge. It is very important that the school system, along with the government education departments, gets aligned with mental health professionals for prevention, early detection and active treatment of all major childhood mental disorders.

Professional social workers are better placed and equipped to deal with the challenges provided they are employed in adequate numbers with reasonable career benefits. They can bridge the systems, co-ordinate with the district mental health programme, liaise with government/non-government agencies, create awareness, offer crisis interventions, organise or even offer parent coun-selling services, educate parents, train teachers and work with managements to shape school policies favourable to school mental health. Significantly, they can offer student/parent counselling services which can fill the mental health needs in prevention and promotion areas. All stakeholders—schools, families and communities—need to come together for a collaborative and co-ordinated effort to ensure that all children and adolescents achieve good mental health adjustment.

Postgraduates with MSW degree are far more in number than those with MPhil in Psychiatric Social Work. So, with renewed interest in school social work, and if social work institutions introduce school social work as a specialisation, it will make the service more focused. Significantly, school social work can deal not only with stigma effectively but in fact remove it while offering quality mental health care in Indian schools. What we have to keep in mind is the existence of multiple service professionals who are qualified with MSc in Applied Psychology, Counseling Psychology, Counseling and Psychotherapy, Postgraduate Diploma in Guidance and Counseling, Masters in Education with Guidance and Counseling, and other related disciplines. School managements are not aware of the differences between these disciplines vis-à-vis social work. It is then our professional responsibility to sensitise and educate them through social work professional bodies at the national and local levels.

The author's personal experience, as a student counsellor in two large major Indian Schools with more than 6,000 students studying under the CBSE in Bahrain and Muscat, reveals that it is possible to create a sea change in the minds of parents, teachers and students to accept mental health services under the umbrella of student counseling. It also helps to take away the stigma, especially when it is integrated with personal, educational, social and career guidance. It is possible if schools of social work and professional bodies in social work engage educational boards fruitfully at both national and state levels on matters of school social work. Social work institutions with proven capabilities in undertaking and executing major projects can be given this task to lead for change. It will be successful only if the process is linked with fieldwork training and job placements of social work students.

Conclusion

The new millennium has exposed children to multifaceted challenges that are stressful for parents, educators, social workers and society in general. Today's children face daunting challenges in academics, emotions, peer relationships and relationships with parents. The biggest challenge that the parents face is helping the child manage peer pressure, maintain harmonious relations and discipline, develop time management skills, choose the right career and cope with psychological problems. Social work interventions like teaching coping skills and maintaining good relationships with teachers, parents and peers can help the turbulently troubled child achieve a smooth transition to be a successful adult (Angeline 2012). In this context, it is relevant to recollect the concept of life skills education of the World Health Organization to improve the immediate functioning of children as well as the potential to prevent problems of drug abuse, suicide, delinquency and risk-taking behaviour. School mental health is achieved by aligning the psychosocial forces in and out of the school through school social work interventions. Hence school mental health is not complete without the contribution of school social work.

References

Angeline, M. 2012. 'Life Challenges in the New Millennium' (Editorial Note), *Journal of School Social Work*, VIII (2): 2.

Basu, D. M. 1962. 'An Analysis of Cases Attending Child Psychotherapy Centres', *Indian Journal of Psychiatry*, 4 (3): 139–144.

Chacko, R. 1964. 'Psychiatric Problems in Children', *Indian Journal of Psychiatry*, 6 (3): 147–152.

Gandhi, A. 1990. *School Social Work: The Emerging Models of Practice in India*. New Delhi: Commonwealth Publishers.

Ilango, P. 1986. 'School Teachers' Opinions about Mental Health Problems of Children', MPhil thesis, National Institute of Mental Health and Neurosciences and Bangalore University, Bangalore.

Indian Council of Medical Research. 2005. *Mental Health Research in India* (Technical Monograph on ICMR Mental Health Studies). New Delhi: Division of Non-Communicable Diseases, Indian Council of Medical Research.

Kapur, M. 1995. *Mental Health of Indian Children*. New Delhi: SAGE Publications.

Kumar, S. V. 2009. 'A Study on Child and Adolescent Mental Health Content Available in Websites of State and Central Educational Bodies in India', paper presented at the World Congress of Psychosocial Rehabilitation, Bangalore.

Lal, N. and B. B. Sethi. 1977. 'Estimate of Mental Ill Health in Children in An Urban Community', *Indian Journal of Paediatrics*, 44 (3): 55–64.

Malhotra, S. and S. K. Chaturvedi. 1984. 'Pattern of Childhood Psychiatric Disorders in India', *Indian Journal of Paediatrics*, 51 (409): 235–240.

Malhotra, S. 1995. 'Study of Psychosocial Correlates of Developmental Psychopathology in School Children', Report to Indian Council of Medical Research. New Delhi, India.

Malhotra, S. 1998. 'Challenges in Providing Mental Health Services for Children and Adolescents in India', in J. G. Young and P. Ferrari (eds), *Designing Mental health Services for Children and Adolescents: A Shrewd Investment.* Philadelphia: Brunner/Mazel.

Murthy, R. S. 2011. 'Mental Health Initiatives in India (1947–2010)', *National Medical Journal of India*, 24 (2): 98–107.

Murthy, R. S. and B. J. Burns. 1992. *Community Mental Health: Proceedings of the Indo-US Symposium held at NIMHANS*, 5–9 March 1987. Bangalore: National Institute of Mental Health and Neurosciences.

Naidu, P. J. 2012. 'Focus: Life Challenges', *Journal of School Social Work*, VIII (2): 12.

Nizamie, S. H. and N. Goyal. 2010. 'National Mental Health Programme of India: A Reappraisal', *Indian Journal of Social Psychiatry*, 26 (3–4): 79–83.

Parvathavardhini. 1983. 'Psychosocial Problems among Rural Children: An Epidemiological Study', MPhil dissertation submitted to the Bangalore University, Bangalore.

Prasad, B. 1993. 'Child Mental Health: A Neglected Area', in P. Mane and K. Gandevia (eds), *Mental Health in India: Issues and Concerns.* Mumbai: Tata Institute of Social Sciences.

Raju, V. B., N. Sundarvalli, O. Somasundaram and G. V. Raghavan. 1969. 'Neurotic Disorders in Children', *Indian Journal of Paediatrics*, 6 (5): 296–301.

Rao, V. N., M. V. Moorthy and R. Parthasarathy. 1983. 'Teacher's perception of Behaviour Problems: Primary School Children—An Exploratory Study', *Child Psychiatry Quarterly*, 16 (4): 192–197.

Rozario, J. 1991. Intervention Strategies for Scholastic Backwardness. Unpublished Doctoral Thesis, Bangalore University, NIMHANS, Bangalore in Kapur, Malavika. 1995. *Mental Health of Indian Children*. New Delhi: SAGE Publications India Pvt Ltd.

Sharan, Pratap and Sagar, Rajesh. 2008. 'The Need for National Data on Epidemiology of Child and Adolescent Mental Disorders', *Journal of Indian Association for Child Adolescent Mental Health*, 4 (2): 22–27.

Shenoy, J. 1992. A Study of Psychological Disturbance in 5 to 8 Year Old School Going Children, Unpublished Doctoral Thesis, Bangalore University, NIMHANS, Bangalore, in Kapur, Malavika. 1995. *Mental Health of Indian Children*. New Delhi: SAGE Publications India Pvt Ltd.

Suresh, P. A. and S. Sebastian. 2003. 'Epidemiological and Neurological Aspects of Learning Disabilities', in P. Karanth and J. Rosario (eds), *Learning Disabilities in India.* New Delhi: SAGE Publications.

Vijayakumar, L. and S. Rajkumar. 1999. 'Are Risk Factors for Suicide Universal? A Cross Control Study in India', *Acta Psychiatrica Scandinavica*, 99: 401–11. (in G. J. Young et al. 2003).

World Health Organization. 2005. *Mental Health Atlas.* Geneva: World Health Organization.

Young, Gerald J., Pierre Ferrari, Savita Malhotra, Samuel Tyano and Caffo Earnesto. 2003. *Brain, Culture and Development—Tradition and Innovation in Child and Adolescent Mental Health.* Delhi: Macmillan India Ltd. (Published as part of the ICCAPAP—book series of the Child and Adolescent Psychiatry and Allied Professions.)

Web Resource

www.schoolindia.org (School Health Annual Report Programme [SHARP])

3

Child and Adolescent Mental Health in India

Archana Dassi

Introduction

Child and adolescent mental health (CAMH) is defined as 'the ability to achieve and maintain optimal psychological and social functioning and well-being' (World Health Organization 2005: 2). This definition views CAMH as a positive dimension considering it as 'a resource that is essential to subjective well-being and to our ability to perceive, comprehend and interpret our surroundings, to adapt to them or change them if necessary, and to communicate with each other and have successful social interactions' (Lehtinen et al. 2005: 46).

CAMH is about an ability to be productive and to learn, and a capacity to tackle developmental challenges and use cultural resources to maximise growth. The children and adolescents with good mental health have a sense of identity and self-worth, enjoy sound family and peer relationships, and actively participate in social and economic life. On the other hand, child and adolescent mental ill-health is about the inability of a child to reach the optimum level of competence and functioning reflected in disorders, such as depression and learning disabilities. While CAMH is a broad concept which goes well beyond the simple absence of a mental disorder, the burden of child and adolescent mental disorders (CAMD) is the primary indicator of mental health status. The present chapter attempts to understand the mental health concerns of adolescents in India. It analyses their situation with reference to their sociocultural environment, the favourable and the unfavourable circumstances they live in, and its impact on their mental health. Finally, it looks into the initiatives taken by the government and non-governmental organisations (NGOs), emphasising the role of social work profession, for addressing the mental health concerns of adolescents.

In all the cultures around the globe, the characteristic attributes of adolescence are considered to be physical changes and raging hormones. In studying adolescent development, adolescence can be defined as: biologically, the physical transition marked by the onset of puberty and the termination of physical growth; cognitively, as the change in the ability to think abstractly and multi-dimensionally; and socially, as a period of preparation for adult roles. Major pubertal and biological changes include changes to the sex organs, height, weight and muscle mass, as well as major changes in brain structure and organisation. Cognitive advances encompass both increase in knowledge and ability to think abstractly and reason more effectively.

India has a population of over one billion, of which children under the age of five years constitute 11 per cent, and children and adolescents under the age of 18 years constitute about 38 per cent of the total population (Census of India 2011). Though steadily decreasing over the last two decades (1990–2007), the infant mortality rate (50/1,000 live births) and under-5 mortality rate (64/1,000 live births, with average annual rate of reduction for under-5 mortality rate being 2.7 per cent) are still alarming (Census of India 2011). A large proportion of the children still suffer from low birth weight and its complications, under-nutrition, wasting, stunting and lack of nutrition, and lack of immunisation.

Over the last two decades, government policies and health programmes have claimed to address child health in a holistic manner and have consistently focused on efforts to achieve these goals. But a closer look at the health programmes reflects that these commendable efforts have been in the area of only physical health of children, for example, immunisation, prenatal care and nutrition; CAMH is still a highly neglected area.

In the field of mental health, adult psychiatry has received much attention, especially in the areas of clinical care, research and training. Mental health, especially CAMH, still receives scanty attention from the policymakers. The policies and health programmes in the field of mental health have been directed solely towards the treatment, care and rehabilitation of mental disorders in adults.

Children under 16 years of age constitute over 40 per cent of India's population, and information about their mental health needs is a national imperative. From the early 1960s, there have been efforts at conducting epidemiological studies in community, clinic and school settings. Community surveys have the advantage of being more representative; they include children and adolescents who do not attend schools and those who do not access mental health services. Based on a number of studies carried out in clinics and communities, the total prevalence rate of mental health problems ranged from 0.48 per cent to 29.40 per cent. Most Indian studies report lower psychiatric morbidity than large-scale studies from other countries. This difference may not necessarily imply truly lower rates of psychiatric disorders in Indian children and adolescents. There are other reasons, such as poor awareness and lack of psychological sophistication, leading to lower sensitivity to certain disorders, higher threshold of tolerance for certain symptoms, sociocultural factors leading to stigmatisation and discrimination of persons with mental disorders, insufficient skilled human resources, low priority by policymakers, high service load and greater concern for child mortality than morbidity. Similar findings have been revealed in a study conducted by the Indian Council of Medical Research (2005), where it was found that abnormal psychosocial situations in family and other social environment of children—such as familial over-involvement, mental disturbance in other family members, discordant intrafamilial relationship, inadequate/inconsistent parental control, and stress in school environment—were associated with childhood mental health problems. A study by Srinath et al. (2005) in Bangalore suggests that in urban slums low awareness of the importance of psychiatric disorders, increased tolerance for deviance, poor living conditions and the presence of multiple stressors could have combined to decrease the focus on children's mental health problems. The number of affected children and adolescents is still staggering, given India's total population figures.

Historically, the landmark World Health Organization (WHO) studies on the burden of CAMD in Low- and Middle-Income Countries (LAMIC) represent the first systematic attempt to measure and describe these conditions (Giel 1982; Giel et al. 1981). Since then, a series of population- and school-based studies have built the evidence based on the prevalence and risk factors for CAMD. There is also, now, a small evidence base arising from longitudinal studies of CAMD. These studies represent research from only a few countries and may not be representative of all countries or settings within countries. CAMD may pose a significant burden on public health of LAMIC due to the larger populations and the higher proportion constituted by children and adolescents (up to 50 per cent in some LAMIC), lack of resources and human power, and lower recognition and priority allocation. There are even greater variations in the pattern of disorders seen in communities compared to clinics. For example, rates of severe intellectual disability are much higher in some developing countries than in the western countries (Stein, Durkin and Belmont 1986), and enuresis is one of the most common disorders found in a good number of community-based studies (Giel et al. 1981;

Lal and Sethi 1977; Malhotra and Chaturvedi 1984; Malhotra, Kohli and Arun 2002; Patel et al. 2007; Srinath et al. 2005). Like most mental disorders, symptoms of CAMD are distributed continuously in a population. However, many children and adolescents who experience symptoms of poor mental health, but do not meet the diagnostic criteria for disorder, are affected by their mental ill health. Furthermore, the scope of CAMH incorporates community development issues, which are the key to sustaining social and economic progress in the countries and go well beyond CAMD as defined by the major sociological systems. The Millennium Development Goals (MDGs) represent a development agenda which has been adopted by the global community and commits to an expanded vision of development that vigorously promotes human development as the key to sustaining social and economic progress in all countries (Sachs and McArthur 2005). While the attainment of all these goals is likely to have profound implications for health in general, and CAMH in particular, our concern here is whether addressing CAMH in itself may be a factor in attaining some of the MDGs. In this regard, we consider evidence which indicates that promoting mental health of children, adolescents and mothers may be associated with the attainment of Goals 2 (to achieve universal primary education), 4 and 5 (to reduce child mortality and improve maternal health respectively), and 6 (combat HIV/AIDS and other diseases). A key target for MDG 2 is to ensure that by 2015 children everywhere, boys and girls alike, will be able to complete a full course of primary schooling. This goal will never be attained unless educational systems address the needs of children and adolescents with developmental and mental disorders. While much attention has been paid to pedagogical and socio-economic determinants of child educational attainment, there has been little acknowledgement of the role of developmental and mental disorders and other CAMD in this regard. As mentioned, brain damage and consequent neuro-psychiatric morbidity, intellectual disability and epilepsy are more common in LAMIC than in high-income countries, and this has a direct bearing on the educational attainment of children and its lifelong impact including secondary morbidity (Grantham-McGregor et al. 2007). Thus, in educational systems already challenged by inadequate resources, crowded classrooms and inconsistent quality, it is plausible to hypothesise that learning and emotional problems are important risk factors for dropout (Patel and De Souza 2000). Studies specifically examining the causes of school failure have found that emotional and learning disorders are amongst the most important risk factors. A survey of 1,535 primary school children drawn from schools in Bangalore city found that 18 per cent and 15 per cent suffered from psychological disturbance and learning disability, respectively (Shenoy, Kapur and Kaliaperumal 1998). Learning problems were associated with low quality of academic work, poor concentration, not carrying out tasks, low motivation and under-achievement (ibid.). In rural primary school children in India, 13 per cent of those having an IQ of greater than 90 were found to have poor achievement in an arithmetic test and a teacher's assessment (Agarwal et al. 1991). This study suggested a high prevalence of specific learning disabilities in these children, none of which were identified by the educators or health service providers. Another study conducted in rural India found that more than 80 per cent of the 172 children in a group of dropouts suffered from learning disability as diagnosed by a psychological screening test (Pratinidhi et al. 1992).

The improvement of maternal mental health has a potential to play an important role in the attainment of MDGs 1, 4 and 5, which address child mortality, child under-nutrition and maternal health. Nearly one-fifth of all pregnancies occur in women under the age of 19 years in LAMIC, and such pregnancies are associated with adverse health outcomes for mother and child (Mehra and Agrawal 2004). Maternal depression during pregnancy and following childbirth is associated with an increased risk of low birthweight, cessation of breastfeeding, infant diarrhoeal episodes, infant under-nutrition and stunting over the first year of life (Patel and Rodrigues 2003; Rahman et al. 2004). Depression during motherhood in adolescence may contribute to both maternal mortality and morbidity. Thus, promoting the mental health of adolescent girls is likely to be an important public health intervention to improve maternal and child health in LAMIC. Finally, MDG 6, which is explicitly concerned with controlling HIV/AIDS, has a number of indicators which are concerned with children and adolescents, for example improving the percentage of 15–24-year-olds with comprehensive correct knowledge of HIV/AIDS. There is not much research evidence on the associations between CAMD and HIV/AIDS, but in a Brazilian study with adolescents seeking HIV testing, those who were seropositive had significantly higher scores in all dimensions of psychiatric symptomatology (Bassols et al. 2007). Another study of schoolgoing adolescents in Goa (in India) reported that sexual risk behaviours were more common among adolescents with emotional disorders than their counterparts who did not suffer from such disorders (Patel and Andrew 2001). This study also showed that adolescents themselves perceived psychosocial factors, including poor educational achievement and relationships with parents, to be a more important priority than sexual health. This suggests that integrating these concerns in sexual health promotion programmes would make them more acceptable (Andrew et al. 2003). It has been seen that adolescents are in search of their identity, both physical and sexual. In case they are not able to establish their identities as per the societal expectations, they develop low self-esteem and frustration reactions, and might go into depression, which is again a mental health concern.

All young people in India today face significant stresses in their lives. This is because of the fact that the Indian family is going through structural and functional modifications that have a bearing on adolescent's socialisation and parent–child relations. Weakening of social support from kinship, movement for women's empowerment, exposure to media, increasing competitive demands of the market economy and higher standards of achievement are a few aspects that have changed the family dynamics in the recent past. The need for differential values, competencies and coping styles between parents and adolescents is a source of anxiety and stress, both for adolescents and parents (Verma and Saraswathi 2002).

The ambiguity of values that adolescents observe in the adult world, the absence of powerful role models, and increasing gaps between aspirations and possible achievements, not surprisingly, lead to alienation and identity diffusion (Singh and Singh 1996).

Stress also results due to problems of growing up. Some changes are part of normal growing up, for example, growth and hormonal changes as well as changes in the relationships that young people experience with parents and society. Other stresses are more individual involving pressures to achieve in academics, to earn a living, family relationships, parental quarrels and parental separation and divorce, peer pressures, pressures to engage in substance abuse and pressures of establishing one's identity leading to identity disorder, alienation and low self-esteem. Sexual and physical mistreatment, AIDS, natural catastrophes, armed conflicts, and severe or chronic physical illnesses like juvenile diabetes may also cause significant stress. Young people negotiate these stresses with varying degrees of resilience and maturity.

In India, family and school are the most important social institutions in a child's life. Rapid population growth, geographical mobility and urban migration, increased number of single-parent families, technological change, and easy access to potentially life threatening mechanisms, substances and activities have weakened family and cultural structures that formerly protected and supported young people. Nearly one in every five children and adolescents develops emotional/behavioural disorders regardless of where they live and how well to do they are. Their emotional disturbances are manifested in many ways—scholastic backwardness, feeling of socially rejected and development of a poor self-image. They may have difficulties in relating to peers and adults, and may have little respect for the laws of the society. Their mental health problems are aggravated if they live within financially and emotionally impoverished environments. As a consequence, such children drift away from mainstream society and become targets of socially dysfunctional elements. Since all the children develop ability to cope up with their life situation in varied ways, it is not possible to determine which children will develop mental health problems before they occur.

Generally, schools assume a central position in the potential development of the lives of many children, especially when families are unable to assume a leading role. Therefore, for a large number of children, school is the most important point of intervention for mental health promotion programme. However, all children do not attend schools. A large proportion of such children are on the streets, as working children, child labourers, children living in hazardous neighbourhoods, and a large number of them living in urban slums without any guidance and supervision. This is a group of 'at risk' children. Therefore, it is important to have a multi-pronged approach to reach out to all the children who are in school and out-of-school.

Theoretical Framework

Theoretically, it has been determined that CAMD is a result of maladjustment between children and their environment. When the maladjustment is not addressed or remains untreated for a long time, it results in a disorder. The dysfunctional relationship with the environment has an effect on the mental health of the child. Social ecology theory goes beyond assessing the relations and interactions between the parent and the youth. It looks at the effects of all the systems in the youth's social ecology. According to the theory, a developing individual is affected by the environments in which he/she resides as well as by settings in which he or she is not (Bronfenbrenner 1979).

The relationship between people and the environments in which they are embedded is dynamic. Each affects the other. These components of ecological systems are the micro-, meso-, exo- and macro-systems (Bronfenbrenner 1979). It is within the micro-system that an individual resides, and it is the micro-system which has the most influence on the individual. An example of a micro-system is the family unit of a child. The child's school would be an example of a meso-system. The meso-system includes settings outside the micro-system in which an individual participates (Bronfenbrenner 1979). Individuals are members of multiple social groups, or meso-systems, at the same time (Earls and Carlson 2001). A setting such as the workplace of a child's parent is an exo-system to a child. A child may not come in direct contact with the workplace of a parent; yet, the workplace has an effect on the child, and the child has an effect on the workplace. For instance, a parent over-stressed due to pressures of employment may lack energy to provide a child adequate attention and care. On the other hand, a parent may perform poorly at work due to stress resulting from difficult issues of the child. The political government would be an example of a macro-system. Policies and laws developed through the local, state and/or national governments affect the support and services that a child and family receive (Painter 2010).

According to this theory, it is understood that children and adolescents develop stress during their growing-up years, which if not dealt with properly by the parents (at micro level) and school (at meso level) can result in maladjusted personalities. Similarly, the role of the state and policymakers, who need to develop mental health services for children and adolescents, is equally significant. At the same time, parents and teachers who are vigilant towards the mental health needs of children and adolescents can address them at the nascent stage itself.

Risk and Protective Factors

The aim of mental health promotion is to enhance positive mental health. Promoting resilience provides the dominant approach for mental health promotion, while reducing the impact of factors that may be considered to increase vulnerability is focused in prevention. Factors which promote mental health or prevent mental ill health are present in the environment and have a direct impact on the person who is exposed to them. Thus the factors that make you vulnerable to mental illness are risk factors and the ones which promote resilience are protective factors. Keeping this in view, it is essential to consider all the factors together while dealing with CAMH.

Much of child psychiatric epidemiology has focused on describing risk factors for CAMD. Much less research has focused on protective factors which decrease the probability of suffering mental health problems and the promotive factors which actively enhance positive psychological well-being (Patel and Goodman 2007). An understanding of these risks, protective and promotive factors is crucial in a discussion on promotion of CAMH. Risk and protective/promotive factors may be grouped in different ways—factors arising from individual determinants, family determinants, and social or community-level determinants.

Socio-economic deprivation, family disruption and psychopathology, early childhood insults (physical and psychosocial), childhood temperamental difficulties, violence and intellectual impairment are all widely recognised risk factors in child development. Other individual determinants influencing the risk of CAMD include temperament and cognitive impairment. Similarly, seizure disorders in childhood are strongly associated with behaviour and emotional disorders. Disruption in family functioning constitutes a significant risk factor for CAMH.

However, there are cultural differences in parenting styles. In India, traditionally there is a strong family system, abiding faith in religion and belief in destiny. There are prescriptions for child-rearing which are generally authoritative and hierarchical; children are encouraged to be obedient, less expressive and follow decisions made by parents. Adults are expected to provide a loving, secure and protective environment and window to the world. All conflicts are expected to be resolved within the family setting. These factors may contribute to resilience, although there is no research that addresses this issue.

There is evidence that abuse and corporal punishment are risk factors for mental disorders. In a study of school-based adolescents in India, 6 per cent reported a lifetime experience of coercive sexual intercourse; other types of sexual harassment and abuse were commonly experienced, and sexual abuse was strongly associated with educational failure, poor physical health and mental health (Patel and Andrew 2001).

Conversely, sensitive and democratic parenting, decent educational opportunities, psychological autonomy and good physical health are widely recognised protective factors. Secure attachment, developmentally appropriate and sensitive parenting, and firm and consistent handling are related to better adjustment in children.

Life skills are living skills/abilities for positive adaptive and positive behaviour that enable an individual to deal with demands and challenges of everyday life effectively (WHO 1997). Considering this definition, the current situation warrants urgent inputs to young people and adolescents in view of a rapidly changing society, technological developments facilitating information dissemination at an unimaginable speed, rapid urbanisation and nuclearisation of families. All of these factors have an impact on the value system of the community. These factors often confuse the adolescents and raise a storm in their mind about their competence. They often learn to survive in the race by doing things at their disposition. It is important to recognise that life on earth should be lived by design, rather than by chance, to ensure a sense of well-being. The art of living by design cannot be learnt by merely reading the syllabus, and from the guidance and support of family and community. With each preoccupied with their own agenda to compete and achieve, nurturing adolescents to make them competent to face opportunities and challenges in their life needs systematic and ongoing inputs at a time when it is most needed. Nurturing is most important in adolescence since it represents a transition from childhood to adulthood, that is, from being dependent on parents and carers to being independent and autonomous. This change in attitude can pose several problems in nurturing. While it is important to accept that transition is a development phase in one's life, it is crucial to keep in place a process which helps the adolescent learn abilities to do the best he/she can with opportunities and challenges that come in his/her way. It is well recognised that mere education about the values and morals to be imbibed in oneself, and to behave in a manner that is appropriate, are not relevant to the development phase of adolescents. Changing values in the family and larger society will pose a major barrier for such an input at home. Therefore, an alternative method which involves experiential learning has been in practice for the last two decades to enable the development of competencies.

Governmental Interventions

During the past six decades, there has been a wide range of governmental initiatives in mental health care in India. These range from humanising mental hospitals, moving the place of care from mental hospitals to general hospital psychiatry units, the formulation of the National Mental Health Programme (NMHP), the adoption of the District Mental Health Programme (DMHP) approach to integrate mental health with general health care, the setting up of community treatment facilities, the provision of support to families, the use of traditional systems of care, legislative revision, and public education and research to support these initiatives. Although considerable efforts have been done by the state to improve the facilities for mental health, sadly all of them are adult-centred, ignoring the specific needs of children and adolescents.

It has been observed that only the DMHP includes early detection and treatment of mental ailments, life skills training and counselling in schools and colleges, and active collaboration with NGOs in all the activities. There have been no significant efforts of the government in establishing or promoting child guidance clinics (through NGOs), which are specialised to provide mental health services to children and adolescents at a stage when the behavioural problem has not turned into a mental ailment.

Legislation

The Mental Health Act, 1987 changed the penal approach to mental health care to an approach which centres around promotion, prevention and rights. The Persons with Disability Act, 1995 is important because for the first time, mental illness was included as one of the disabilities. The UN Convention on Rights of Persons with Disabilities, 2006 adds a new dimension to the rights of the mentally ill. It is expected that some of the other existing laws will be changed to bring them in harmony with the current thinking and approach towards the mentally ill in India. Since there were a number of gaps in the existing Mental Health Act, 1987, a new Mental Health Care Bill 2013 has been introduced. The legislation will provide access to mental health care and services for persons with mental illness, and protect, promote and fulfil the rights of persons with mental illness during delivery of mental health care and services. It also recognises the rights of a mentally ill person and recognises mental illness as a disability. It promotes 'institutionalisation' of mental health care facilities and gives patients the right to choose in advance the kind of treatment for the mental illness he/she suffers from. As far as children and adolescents are concerned, certain specific treatment guidelines have been included for those who are suffering from mental illnesses such as schizophrenia. To sum up, the legislation gives more recognition to mental illness only when it precipitates and becomes a problem for the family and society to be managed by them. Again, children and adolescents are just provided lip service.

Initiatives by NGOs

Historically, NGOs have played a critical role in promoting and facilitating health and educational activities in India. Despite the considerable challenges faced in developing mental health programmes, it is gratifying to note the achievements made by many NGOs throughout the country. However, these interventions are in urban areas and in states where there are relatively less pressing problems posed by poverty and communicable diseases (for example, the south Indian states). The concept of CAMH has broadened from its earlier focus on mental retardation to include the far commoner mental health problems seen in children, such as autism, hyperactivity and conduct disorders. NGOs such as Sangath Society (Goa) and Umeed and the Research Society (Mumbai) provide out-patient and school-based services for such problems. Adolescent health interventions based on the life skills model have become very popular in secondary schools around the country; many such programmes are run in collaboration with local NGOs focusing on reproductive and sexual health issues. Better Life for Adolescent Girls is a life skill programme by Centre for Development and Population Activities (CEDPA), which has been implemented by a number of NGOs in slum and rural communities with the non school-going adolescents. Sneha (Chennai), Medico Pastoral Assocation (Bangalore), Snehi and Sanjivini (Delhi) work on suicide prevention activities and Saarthak (Delhi) runs helplines for distressed persons, especially children and adolescents during examinations. Similarly, the Richmond Fellowship Society is the oldest NGO in India working in the field of child mental health, and in particular, mental retardation.

Social Work Interventions

Social workers are especially aware that illnesses and mental disorders afflicting individuals, their families and their communities are signs of social inequalities and the current imbalance between human beings and their environment. The fight to alleviate human suffering, and the causes and consequences of illnesses and mental disorders, thus enriches humanity as a whole. A significant proportion of students in schools and colleges have recognisable mental disorders in the form of depression, anxiety, severe examination fear, somatoform disorders, adjustment disorders, personality disorders and alcohol and drug abuse. Many more children and adolescents, whether in school or out of school may be suffering from subclinical symptoms and emotional disturbances. These contribute to the observable behavioural abnormalities such as aggression, being hostile to others, hopelessness and helplessness, fears and apprehensions. Children and adolescents who are especially out of the school system also reflect conduct disorders like lying, stealing, running away from home, criminal activity, sexual promiscuity and immoral sexual activities. Since there is a growing evidence of increased rates of adolescent behaviour problems and suicides, Life Skills Approach is the only strategy to promote the mental health of children and adolescents as it equips them with the skills and the abilities to live an effective and healthy life. An empowered adolescent has the competence to cope with the challenges of life using the available resources even amidst adversities.

Life skills which need to be taught to adolescents, both at the school and the community levels are: critical thinking and creative thinking, decision making and problem-solving, communication skills and interpersonal relations, coping with emotions and stress, self awareness and empathy. Life skills training can be imparted through trained social workers by conducting interactive sessions with adolescents in the schools and through NGOs in the communities.

Keeping this in view, mental health with specific focus on CAMH should be recognised as a public health concern. There is a need to start dedicated and specialised mental health service for children and adolescents at all departments of psychiatry and paediatrics that have postgraduate courses in India. There is a need to advocate a national policy on child mental health that has a holistic and integrated perspective. Child mental health issues should figure in all development-related policy and planning in India. All academic and research institutions should promote research in the field of CAMH in India to create the necessary database, need and programmes, developing models of care and intervention that are relevant, appropriate and cost-effective.

Conclusion

In India, there is no separate, comprehensive policy dealing with the child and also with child mental health. The needs of children are covered in other policies, namely, the National Health Policy (1983), the National Policy on Education (1986) and the National Mental Health Programme (1982) or National Trust for the Welfare of Persons with Autism, Cerebral Palsy, Mental Retardation and Multiple Disabilities Act (1999) but only in a piecemeal fashion. These policies provide for guidelines focusing on nutrition, immunisation, mother and child health services, school health programmes, physical and social rehabilitation and so on. The Persons with Disabilities Act (1995) includes mental retardation and mental illnesses in its proviso and aims to meet the needs of disabled people as far as access to opportunities and prevention is concerned.

In summary, CAMH is as important as adult mental health, if not more. There is urgent need for a multi-pronged approach, which means working at various levels such as sensitising the state to create the necessary service infrastructure, organising capacity building programmes for trained human power to work with children and adolescents, and mobilising support from the families and the communities to meet the challenge which is not only mandated by the constitutional framework but is also a moral necessity.

References

Agarwal, K. N., D. K. Agarwal, S. K. Upadhyay and M. Singh. 1991. 'Learning Disability in Rural Primary School Children', *Indian Journal of Medical Research*, 94 (1): 89–95.

Andrew, G., V. Patel and J. Ramakrishna. 2003. 'Sex, Studies or Strife? What to Integrate in Adolescent Health Services', *Reproductive Health Matters*, 11 (21): 120–129.

Bassols, A. M., R. A. Santos, L. A. Rohde and F. Pechansky. 2007. 'Exposure to HIV in Brazilian Adolescents: The Impact of Psychiatric Symptomatology', *European Child and Adolescent Psychiatry*, 16 (4): 236–242.

Bronfenbrenner, U. 1979. *The Ecology of Human Development: Experiments in Nature and Design*. Cambridge, MA: Harvard University Press.

Census of India. 2011. Retrieved from http://censusindia.gov.in/vital_statistics/ SRS_Bulletins.

Earls, F. and M. Carlson. 2001. 'The Social Ecology of Child Health and Well-being', *Annual Review of Public Health*, 22 (1): 143–166.

Giel, R. 1982. 'An Epidemiological Approach to the Improvement of Mental Health Services in Developing Countries', *Acta Psychiatrica Scandinavica*, 65 (Suppl 296): 56–63.

Giel, R., M. V. De Arango, C. E. Climent, T. W. Harding, H. H. A. Ibrahim, L. Ladrigo-Ignacio, R. S. Murthy, M. C. Salazar, N. N. Wig and Y. O. A. Younie. 1981. 'Childhood Mental Disorders in Primary Health Care: Results of Observations in Four Developing Countries', *Pediatrics*, 68 (5): 677–683.

Grantham-McGregor, S., Y. B. Cheung, S. Cueto, P. Glewwe, L. Richter and B. Strupp. 2007. 'Developmental Potential in the First 5 Years for Children in Developing Countries', *Lancet*, 369 (9555), 60–70.

Indian Council of Medical Research. 2005. *Mental Health Research in India*. New Delhi: Division of Non-communicable Diseases, Indian Council of Medical Research.

Lal, N. and B. B. Sethi. 1977. 'Estimate of Mental Ill-Health in Children in an Urban Community', *Indian Journal of Pediatrics*, 44 (350): 55–64.

Lehtinen, L., H. Ozamiz, L. Underwood, M. Weiss, H. Herrman, S. Saxena and R. Moodie. 2005. 'The Intrinsic Value of Mental Health', in H. Heeman,

66   *Archana Dassi*

S. Saxena and R. Moodia (eds), *Promoting Mental Health: Concepts, Emerging Evidence, Practice*, pp. 46–58. Geneva: World Health Organization.

Malhotra, S. and S. K. Chaturvedi. 1984. 'Patterns of Childhood Psychiatric Disorders in India', *Indian Journal of Pediatrics*, 51 (409): 235–240.

Malhotra, S., A. Kohli and P. Arun. 2002. 'Prevalence of Psychiatric Disorders in School Children in India', *Indian Journal of Medical Research*, 116 (1): 21–28.

Mehra, S. and D. Agrawal. 2004. 'Adolescent Health Determinants for Pregnancy and Child Health Outcomes among the Urban Poor', *Indian Pediatrics*, 41 (2): 137–145.

Painter, K. 2010. 'Multisystemic Therapy as an Alternative Community-Based Treatment for Youth with Severe Emotional Disturbance: Empirical Literature Review', *Social Work in Mental Health*, 8 (2): 190–208.

Patel, V. and G. Andrew. 2001. 'Gender, Sexual Abuse and Risk Behaviours: A Cross-Sectional Survey in Schools in Goa', *National Medical Journal of India*, 14 (5): 263–267.

Patel, V., N. De Souza and M. Rodrigues. 2003. 'Postnatal Depression and Infant Growth and Development in Low-income Countries: a Cohort Study from Goa, India', *Archives of Disease in Childhood*, 88: 34–37.

Patel, V. and N. De Souza. 2000. 'School Drop-out: A Public Health Approach for India', *National Medical Journal of India*, 13 (6): 316–318.

Patel, V. and A. Goodman. 2007. 'Researching Protective and Promotive Factors in Mental Health', *International Journal of Epidemiology*, 36 (4): 703–707.

Patel, V., A. Simbine, I. Soares, H. Weiss and E. Wheeler. 2007. 'Prevalence of Severe Mental and Neurological Disorders in Mozambique: A Household Key Informant Survey in Rural and Urban Settings', *Lancet*, 370 (9592): 1055–1060.

Pratinidhi, A. K., P. V. Kurulkar, S. G. Garad and M. Dalal. 1992. 'Epidemiological Aspects of School Dropouts in Children between 7-15 Years in Rural Maharashtra', *Indian J. Pediatrics*, 59 (4): 423–427.

Rahman, A., Z. Iqbal, J. Bunn, H. Lovel and R. Harrington. 2004. 'Impact of Maternal Depression on Infant Nutritional Status and Illness: A Cohort Study', *Archives of General Psychiatry*, 61 (9): 946–952.

Sachs, J. D. and J. W. McArthur. 2005. 'The Millennium Project: A Plan for Meeting the Millennium Development Goals', *Lancet*, 365 (9456): 347–353.

Shenoy, J., M. Kapur and V. Kaliaperumal. 1998. 'Psychological Disturbance among 5- to 8-year old School Children: A Study from India', *Social Psychiatry and Psychiatric Epidemiology*, 33 (2): 66–73.

Singh, L. B. and A. K. Singh. 1996. 'Alienation: A Symptomatic Reaction of Educated Employed Youth in India', *International Journal of Psychology*, 31 (2): 101–110.

Srinath, S., S. C. Girimaji, G. Gururaj, S. Seshadri, D. K. Subbakrishna, P. Bhola and N. Kumar. 2005. 'Epidemiological Study of Child and Adolescent Psychiatric Disorders in Urban and Rural Areas of Bangalore, India', *Indian Journal of Medical Research*, 122 (1): 67–79.

Stein, Z., M. Durkin and L. Belmont. 1986. '"Serious" Mental Retardation in Developing Countries: An Epidemiological Approach', *Annals of the New York Academy of Sciences*, 477: 8–21. doi: 10.1111/j.1749-6632.1986.tb40316.

Verma, S. and T. S. Saraswathi. 2002. 'Adolescence in India: Street Urchins or Silicon Valley Millionaires?', in B. B. Brown, R. Larson and T. S. Saraswathi (eds), *The World's Youth: Adolescence in Eight Regions of the Globe*, pp. 105–140. New York: Cambridge University Press.

World Health Organization. 1997. *Life Skills Education in Schools*. Geneva: Programme on Mental Health, World Health Organization.

———. 2005. 'Mental Health Policy and Service Guidance Package: Child and Adolescent Mental Health Policies and Plans'. Geneva: WHO.

4

Psychosocial Intervention Model for the Well-being of Institutionalised and Non-institutionalised Adolescent Girls in the Institutions for Care

Sheeja Remani B. Karalam

Introduction

The *Adolescent Girls' Fact Sheets* of 2009 by the United Nations Interagency Task Force, United Nations Children's Fund (UNICEF) reports that more than 600 million of adolescent girls live in developing countries. Many of them lack access to education and health services, and are exposed to unsafe practices in society (UNICEF 2009). Unlike the young generation just decades ago in India, the adolescents of this millennium are growing up in a dynamic, changing country, with a range of opportunities before them in career, leisure and everyday life. However, surplus of preferences seems to have produced a generation of young people who end up confused and conflicted. At the extreme, most of them are prone to taking their own lives ('Teen Suicides', *India Today*, 28 April 2008). The most unfortunate and astonishing thing is that the number of adolescents' suicides in the state of Kerala is increasing. The magnitude of mental health problems in children in India and adolescents has not been recognised sufficiently by many governments and decision makers (Remschmidt and Belfer 2005). Adolescent girls are the world's second largest population with very little available research to guide mental health practice and policy (Raval et al. 2010). Kumar (2001) emphasises that there is a need for social work intervention to test its efficacy in improving child and adolescent mental health. This necessitates establishing linkages with psychiatric social workers, clinical psychologists, psychiatrists and nurses to facilitate professional and paraprofessional social workers through training and guidance.

At the individual level, the physiological and psychological changes in this age cause a dilemma in the adolescent. Literature reviews also stress the condition of adolescent girls as vulnerable and disadvantaged. This chapter attempts to bring out the success of implementation and evaluation on a model psychosocial intervention programme aimed at improving the well-being of adolescent girls in institutions and in communities, instead of only conducting exclusive sex education for them.

Adolescence

Adolescence is the period of transition in a distinct and dynamic phase of development in the life of an individual. During this period, an individual is neither a child nor an adult. Foundations of adequate growth and development are laid during childhood and adolescent years. Children reach puberty at this age. Girls attain puberty earlier than boys. This maturation marks the transition of a girl to a woman capable of begetting children. In boys, its beginning is marked by the onset of voice change followed by rapid physical growth and psychological changes. The changes happen due to the development of secondary sex characteristics in the body and its effect on the mind because of hormonal changes. The child may not be aware about the changes happening in her/his body and mind (Karalam 2011). It is common in adolescence that psychosomatic problems and stress frequently play a role in their development maintenance.

Adolescent mental health is associated with psychological changes like high intensity and volatility in feelings, the need for immediate gratification, awareness of probable consequences and misunderstanding others' feelings, lack of self-esteem, awareness of the world around them, which is quite different from that of an adult. From an adolescent's perspective, adolescence is the time when intelligence is at its peak, permanent personality traits begin taking root, and decisions regarding future profession have to be taken during a period of extreme emotional instability and identity crisis (Bodhakar 2002). During this period, they should be aware about their body and mind. When adolescents arrive at the wrong conclusion, they need support and supervision of parents and adults to guide them and to learn from their experiences. It is very important that parents play a significant role in determining the personality of their child during adolescence. A positive standard of psychological well-being in adolescence includes both the development of an independent sense of identity and the maintenance of close relationships with parents

(Bulanda and Majumdar 2009). Home is considered to be the ideal place for every child, since the home and family provide a protective and stimulating medium for the child's physical, mental and spiritual growth. But not all children are blessed with such continued care and protection at home from infancy to adulthood. Vulnerable circumstances like absence of one or both parents due to either death, separation or divorce, marital discord, being born out of wedlock, chronic or contagious illness, single-parent families, displacement, disaster, communal riots, extreme poverty, unemployment, employment of the mother, migration, breaking up of joint families, and abuse and misuse by the family, create situations where children cannot live with their parents. Under these situations, alternative forms of care such as children's homes and treatment for the child become inevitable.

The manner in which the children's homes are organised and run, the kind of socialisation facilities, and the care provided as per their objectives largely affect, mould and reflect the personalities of the inmates. Lack of proper environmental support will affect negatively the quality of well-being of any individual. Physical facilities are not enough to accomplish a well developed personality in which psychological support could make the mission complete. While these children attain the age of adolescence, they lack a lot of necessary inputs for proper growth and development, such as nutritious food, psychological support, positive environment, freedom and love. All are supposed to be received by a normal child with supporting parents (Siddiqui 1997). While psychological changes happen, someone should be there to understand the adolescents, support and strengthen their ego, and divert their negative attitudes to a positive attitude. A study on psychosocial aspects such as insecurity, self-esteem and adjustment problems among 252 institutionalised adolescents and 252 adolescents from socially and economically poor families but in parental care found that those who were institutionalised significantly differed from those in parental care. The study showed that institutionalised adolescents had higher insecurity, lower self-esteem and emotional adjustment problems (Jose 2008).

The impact of the non-conducive, familial and institutional environment manifests in the form of behavioural and other problems among children and adolescents. There is a need for improving the mental health of children who are forced into the set up. The neglect of mental health results in serious consequences and makes the adolescents unable to cope with the demands of life and future concerns. Paying importance to mental health and developing skills among children and adolescents are widely accepted as contributing to psychosocial well-being.

Well-being of Adolescents

The period during which a child grows and develops into an adult is called adolescence. Well-being can be defined as the realisation of children's rights and the fulfilment of the opportunity for every child, taking into consideration her/his abilities, potential and skills (Bradshaw et al. 2007). A well-adjusted person has the courage to face failures in her/his life and is self-confident and optimistic. She/he leads a well-balanced life of work, rest and recreation. Adolescents are a very diverse population segment. They have different needs and they have diverse problems.

It is evident that during adolescence, mental growth does not keep pace at par with physical growth. Sexual maturation is marked by menarche in girls and nocturnal emission in boys. Adolescent girls are especially suscep-tible to the biological and social changes taking place during this phase, and these effects leads to the existing inequity between the sexes. Owing to outward physical appearance, people start treating adolescent girls as adults (Chandrasekhar 2000). Throughout the adolescent period, when they are in a dilemma they need support and guidance. However, parents also find it dif-ficult to deal with the situation and hence, there is need for professional help in the early hours. It is tough to deal with adolescents because they confide only in a professional who is trustworthy and human (Mridula 2002). The well-being among adolescents aged 11 to 17 years with a deployed parent showed that older adolescents and adolescent girls were more likely than were their counterparts to face school, family and peer-related challenges (Chandra et al. 2010). The denial of information to a child or young person that is critical to her/him and which affects her/his sexual and reproductive health, is a violation of her/his right to life and health (Panda 2007). Exploring the situations of these girls will convey enormous facts to the girls, their families and communities.

Situation of Non-institutionalised and Institutionalised Adolescent Girls

An overview of research conducted among adolescent girls in the last two decades indicates that most of the studies on adolescents in general are either explorative or descriptive and covered the components of bio-socio-psycho aspects of adolescence separately. These studies were carried out among non-institutionalised adolescent girls (in schools, rural, tribal and urban communities of India), as evaluation of programmes for adolescents and projects on adolescent girls. All study findings reveal scary figures and facts about their situation in Indian society and all over the world. A majority of the studies emphasised the importance of family life education for girls and social work intervention for mental health of children and adolescents.

Non-institutionalised Adolescent Girls

The various research studies conducted among adolescent girls from schools, rural, tribal, and urban communities of India reveal that the focus is more on physical aspects than psychological aspects. Western literature is more focused on psychological rather than physical aspects. The brief contents of the conceptual and empirical work done among adolescent girls will give a picture of their situation in India.

- Importance of family support in the growth of adolescent girls (Mullick 1995)
- Ignorance of reproductive health and ill effects, lack of awareness about HIV/AIDS and importance of sex education among adolescent girls (Awasthi et al.1980; Drakshayani and Ramaiah 1994; Narayan et al. 2001; National Council of Educational Research and Training [NCERT] et al. 2000; Singh et al. 1999; UNESCO 2001)
- Need for improving well-being and self-esteem of adolescent girls (Nair and Mini 2003)
- Problems in general health, especially anaemia among adolescent girls (Bodhakar 2002; Deo and Ghattargi 2005; Joseph et al. 1997; World Health Organization 1998)
- Incidences of teenage pregnancy, abortion, trafficking and suicide attempts among adolescent girls (Bhola and Kapur 1999; Joshi 2004; Trikha 2001)
- Adolescent girl's susceptibility to biological and social changes (Chandrasekhar 2000; Pipher 1994)
- Focus on interventions with adolescents has to shift from giving information to building life skills. Family life education must be based on the needs of young people to prepare for their adult lives (Chacko et al. 2005; Mohanty and Mohanty 1997; Nair 2004, 2005; Raj 1993).

- Psychological dimensions of adolescence is emphasising that the concept of positive mental health is all the more important when we refer to adolescence (Muuss 1975; Shengchao et al. 2004; Woodhead 2004).
- It is important to identify adolescents with psychosocial problems early, and target them for intervention (De Friese et al. 1990).
- By supporting mental well-being and behavioural preparedness, life skills education can equip individuals to behave in pro-social ways, and it is additionally health giving (Birell and Orley 1996; Orley 1997; Smoker 1975; WHO 2000a).
- Skill-based health education can significantly improve the self-esteem of adolescents (Block and Robins 1993; Brennan 1985; Chauhan 1991; Chiew 1990; Rice 1990; Young et al. 1997).
- Adjustment is essential to lead a wholesome mentally healthy life (Nair and Mini 2002; Padmam 2003; Schaffer 1996; WHO 1999). Proper guidance and support to the adolescent can help to become well adjusted. There is need for social work interventions and to test their efficacy in improving child and adolescent mental health (Kumar 2001; MacCstack 1996; Raji and Nair 2006)

The reviews highlight that adolescents, especially girls, are poorly informed about their body growth and development, and matters related to sexuality and health. During adolescence, a great number of developmental changes take place to make the transition from childhood to adulthood physically, emotionally, socially and psychologically. Adolescence is a time of enormous functional development and ambivalence waiting to be an adult. Reviews also emphasise that adolescent girls are more vulnerable and disadvantaged.

Institutionalised Adolescent Girls

According to the Indian Juvenile Justice (Care and Protection of Children) Act, 2000 'children's home' means an institution established by a state government or voluntary organisation and certified by that government under section 34. Although social workers, students of social work and educationists have been visiting these institutions for care and protection in India for several decades, very few significant researches have been conducted among adolescent girls in institutions. The following findings provide glimpses of the real situation of these adolescent girls.

- The major factors leading to institutionalisation of children and adolescents in India are economic problems, broken homes and orphanhood (John 2008; Reddy 1989).
- Children's homes in India's southernmost state (Kerala) are dominated by female children (J. Fordham, 'Meeting India's Unwanted Girls', *Guardian Weekly*, 19 June 2008).
- The situation is much worse among institutionalised adolescent girls (Nayak 2000).
- Many adolescent girls are sexually active but lack information and skill for self-protection. There are instances of sexual exploitation and abuse in society towards girls, early maturity in girls, lack of proper guidance and care during adolescence from functionaries of the children's homes, lack of awareness about the developmental changes in adolescence and management among these girls, lack of sufficient functionaries with individual attention for the girls, lack of training for the functionaries to guide the inmates, lack of seriousness towards education and the future of these girls, lack of nutritious food and hygiene in the children's homes, and lack of exposure to the realities of life and society among these girls (Karalam 2011)
- There are various behavioural problems, poor peer relations, disciplinary problems and disruptive attention-seeking behaviour, problems of adjustment and intellectual deficit among the inmates (Jose 2008; Khandelkar 1977; Nagar 1992)
- There is a need for planning and organising mental health services for adolescents in general and institutionalised adolescents in particular (Sikka 1983; Viswanath 1985)
- Intervention study on the family life education programme played a successful role in bringing about significant changes in their knowledge regarding family life (Gnanasaraswathi 1994)
- Life skill education programme could bring significant levels of improvement in the mental health of juveniles in the juvenile homes (John 2008).
- The quality of post-institutional life can be improved by early intervention services (Mathew and Parthasarathy 1988).

Reviews highlight the negative impact of institutional care on infants and young children. Less is known about the fate of adolescent girls living in institutional settings in India. There is a need for improving the mental health of children who are forced into the set up. Thus it becomes imperative to look at the problems and needs of adolescents in institutions and to initiate activities for betterment accordingly.

Intervention Studies Conducted among Non-institutional Adolescent Girls

Most of the intervention studies were conducted among adolescent girls on AIDS prevention, intervention integrated into a low-income community by local non-governmental organisations (NGOs), family life education based on the needs of its members and educational needs of young people for adult life. The International Center for Research on Women co-ordinated multi-site intervention studies on youth reproductive health and sexuality in India. Findings show that with adequate information and education, reproductive health awareness may increase and may produce desirable effects on reproductive health status. The government has implemented the Kishori Shakti Yojana programme which seeks to empower adolescent girls, to enable them to take charge of their lives (Chacko et al. 2005; Crosby 1971; De Friese et al. 1990; Hassan, Jayaswal and Hassan 2003; Mensch et al. 2004; Mohanty and Mohanty 1997).

Review of MSW Dissertation Research on Adolescent Girls in India

- Master of Social Work (MSW) students study research methodology and undertake research because of the compulsory requirement for a degree.
- Very few significant research studies have been conducted on adolescent girls in institutions.
- Students prefer only descriptive designs.
- The findings are not useful for practical purpose.
- The research findings do not enhance social work knowledge base or social work practice, or aid policymakers, administrators or legislators.

- Experience sharing of those social work researchers who worked with adolescent girls in the institutions, communities and adolescents in general, the methodology applied, review of literature and study results will enrich the practice of social work research
- Students can be encouraged to undertake social work research.
- Intervention research studies can focus more on specific problems of adolescents like, health, education, behavioural problems, skill development programmes, career and vocational guidance and income generation programmes.
- Students can publish articles in journals, magazines and newspapers on their research with adolescents, along with the faculty guide. This will enrich social work knowledge.

Significance of Developing a Model Programme for the Well-being of Adolescent Girls

It is evident from the reviews that adolescent girls from the communities and institutions, their biological, social and psychological dimensions, and the importance of intervention to this group have not been investigated together by any of the researchers so far. These findings and the timeline data on management of adolescent issues reflect that not even a single programme or policy has included adolescent girls in institutions. How do these adolescent girls live? What is the kind of education they receive? What are the problems they face and what are the adjustments they make? What is the kind of food they eat? What is the kind of physical environment they have, and the kinds of fears and worries that they have? What is the kind of personality they have? How is their general health? How do they manage their changes in the body and mind during the adolescent years? Who takes care of them? How do they interact with their friends? What are their values? What are the negative feelings they have, what are the positive feelings they have, and how do they see their future?

In India every day, the number of suicide cases, abuses, missing, trafficking and teenage pregnancies is increasing among adolescent girls ('Teen Suicides', *India Today*, 28 April 2008). Now it is high time to be more protective of the girl child along with appropriate awareness. These gaps point to the need for formulating a model intervention programme to reorient expectations, and provide fair treatment and allocation of resources for the adolescent girl to protect her from social evils. Hence, a model social work intervention programme was conducted among adolescent girls in institutions and communities to identify and modify their psychosocial well-being in this crucial stage of development. Moreover, the situations faced by the adolescent girls in institutions are not exposed to society. A majority of the government programmes are designed for adolescents in general who are in community settings. The gap should be filled by the policymakers and social workers through planning and implementing programmes for adolescent girls in children's homes.

Classical Theory Framework of the Model Programme for the Well-being of Adolescent Girls

Social work approach is unique among the helping professions because it focuses on people's problems in the context of their social environment. Adolescence is the last stage before adulthood. Therefore it offers to parents, teachers and professionals the last opportunity to educate a child for his adult responsibilities. It is therefore a logical approach to provide interventions in the pre-adolescent and adolescent periods when the children have the final opportunity for catching up with growth and development (UNICEF 2005).

In order to evolve a suitable programme for adolescent girls, it was necessary to know the conceptual contributions of psychologists. The critical analysis of the following theories helped to gain substantial base material, and to get a more complete picture of the varied aspects of adolescence: Erikson's psychosocial theory of development, Freud's psychoanalytic theory of adolescence, evolutionary theory by Hall and Piaget's cognitive theory.

Erikson's psychosocial theory talks about identity formation and its roots in infancy, and establishments by the end of adolescence. Inability to establish a sense of personal identity could lead to dangers of role diffusion and identity diffusion. The result of such experiences could lead to personality confusion, personality maladjustments and various psychological disturbances (Muuss 1975). Freud believed that adolescence was a universal phenomenon and included behavioural, social and emotional changes. He stated that the physiological changes were related to emotional changes, especially an increase in negative emotions, such as moodiness, anxiety, loathing, tension and other forms of adolescent behaviour (Muuss 1975). Hall was the first psychologist to advance psychology of adolescence in its own right and to use scientific methods to study adolescents. He defined this period as beginning at puberty at about 12 or 13 years, and ending late, between 22 years to 25 years of age. Hall also described adolescence as a period of 'storm and stress' when there is simultaneous occurrence of sexual maturation, physical growth, emotional intensity, hypothetical–deductive reasoning, and moral, social and political awareness. Piaget believed that by adolescence, a person is able to conceptualise many variables, allowing for the creation of a system of laws or rules for problem solving. While Piaget focused clearly on an individual's interaction with the environment, social constructivists believe that knowledge is the result of social interaction and language, and thus is a shared experience (Newman and Newman 1979).

To comprehend the adolescent phenomenon in a total perspective, one has to study her/him from all points of view. Each of these theories provides a piece of the foundation for justifying development and differing perspectives. These theories prove to be helpful to social workers, teachers, parents and adults who are responsible in guiding the adolescents on the road to maturity.

Model Programme for the Psychosocial Well-being of Institutional and Non-institutional Adolescent Girls

The contents of the classical theories and research studies of the model programme were consolidated based on the pre- and post-intervention assessment findings of the research conducted among institutional and non-institutional adolescent girls (Box 4.1), the review of published literature on adolescent girls, discussion with experts in the communities, discussion with institutional authorities, mental health professionals and the materials already standardised and implemented by national and international organisations like the UNESCO, the NCERT, the State Council of Educational Research and Training, the Child Development Centre (CDC) and the WHO. The contents of the model programme were then put forth to some of those individuals and sections of society who were directly or indirectly concerned with the welfare of the adolescent girls, for their suggestions on the modules proposed for the model programme. The steps in the model programme are displayed in the flow chart in Figure 4.1.

Box 4.1
Excerpts from the Evaluation of the Model Intervention Programme for the Well-being of Institutionalised and Non-institutionalised Adolescent Girls in Thrissur District, Kerala

Objective: The major objective of the study was to assess the effectiveness of social work intervention programme for the psychosocial well-being of adolescent girls.

Design: The design of the two separate study samples in communities and institutions was the pre-experimental research design with pre-test–post-test without the control group.

Sample: Thirty adolescent girls from two children's homes in Thrissur District in Kerala and 30 randomly selected adolescent girls from two communities of Panachery Panchayat in Thrissur District were selected as the study group.

Tools for data collection: Questionnaire pertaining to socio-demographic profile of the respondents; questionnaire on awareness about developmental changes in adolescence (Department of Psychiatry, Government Medical College, Thrissur 2003); subjective well-being inventory (Nagpal and Sell 1992); self-esteem inventory (Battle 1981); and adolescent adjustment inventory (Reddy 1964).

Process of data collection: Was completed through five phases. First phase: pre-intervention assessment (pre-test); second phase: preparation of the intervention package; third phase: intervention; fourth phase: post-intervention assessment (post-test); and fifth phase: follow up.

Results: The ANOVA test reveals a significant difference among the three phases of intervention (F ratio $P < 0.01$) group results among two study samples. The effect size values depicting the effectiveness of the intervention programme assessed on tools such as awareness of developmental changes in adolescence, subjective well-being, self-esteem and adolescent adjustment. The results of t-test were also found significant at $P < 0.01$ level in experimental group. All effect sizes obtained for total and different variables were found to have large effect sizes, indicating that the social work intervention programme given for psychosocial well-being was highly effective both in institutional and non-institutional adolescent girls.

The major objective of the model programme is to strengthen the personality of adolescent girls to deal effectively with the demands and challenges of everyday life. Details of each step are as follows.

Step 1: Identification of the Issues Related to Adolescent Girls

This step includes the pre-assessment sessions on identification of the level of well-being and issues related to adolescent girls, by collecting data through relevant questionnaires. The micro steps are as follows.

Figure 4.1
Model Programme for the Psychosocial Well-being of Adolescent Girls

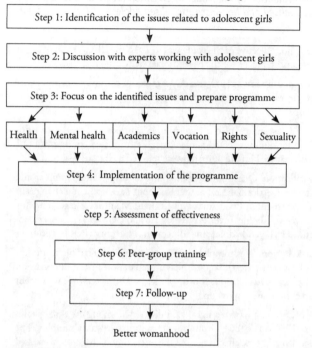

IN INSTITUTIONS/SCHOOLS

Identify the institutions to be visited, collect the contact address and get permission from the authority to visit. While visiting, discuss with functionaries the status of adolescent girls and the need for the programme. If possible, take permission to interact with the girls and understand their situation, relate to the theories and studies so far conducted, and assess the needs of adolescent girls. Convince the authorities of the need for adolescent well-being in this challenging world. Fix a time and date along with the consent of the authorities and adolescent girls for the pre-assessment of psychosocial well-being. On the day, distribute well-being assessment tools, such as the Well-being Manifestation Measure Scale (WBMMS-Masse et al. 1998), the Rosenberg Self-esteem Scale (1989), the Mental Health Inventory (Jagdish and Srivastava 1983), socio-economic status scales, body mass index, general health awareness schedule (health, hygiene, nutrition, sexuality, and reproductive and child health). Assess academic records for three years, awareness of career and vocational prospects, awareness of child rights and awareness of adolescent issues prevailing in society. Later, statistically analyse the data, highlight the areas to be stressed, identify the issues, relate to research studies and prepare pre-assessment report with issues to be dealt with, and inform the authorities about the need for the programme.

IN COMMUNITIES

Identify key resource persons in the communities, such as *anganwadi* teachers, ward members, panchayat-level health workers, ASHA (Accredited Social Health Activists) workers, primary health centre workers, schools teachers, self-help group members, and NGO field workers. Discuss the adolescent girls population in the particular community, the need for their well-being, observations of effectiveness and impacts of existing measurements. Collect all relevant data from the key resource persons in the community, and visit the adolescent girls' homes and talk to their mother. Take their consent and apply the mentioned tools for the adolescent girl. We can request the resource persons to arrange all the girl children who are in the age group of 12–19 years or those who have attained menarche to assemble in one place/community centre or anganwadi. Once they come together, inform them of the objective of the gathering, and with their consent, administer the tools for pre-assessment of psychosocial well-being. After that, statistically analyse the data, highlight the areas to be stressed, identify the issues, relate to research studies, prepare a pre-assessment report with issues to be dealt with, and inform the key resource persons and parents in the community about the importance of conducting a programme.

Step 2: Discussion with Experts Working with Adolescent Girls

Next comes the identification of local resources or experts. Get permission to meet them, prepare a note of queries based on the assessment report, or communicate (through e-mail) with those who are already in the same field. The experts in the field of adolescents should be child psychiatrists, psychiatric social workers, school teachers, counsellors, life skill educators, specialists in adolescent psychiatry, or researchers in the area of adolescent girls. While discussing with them, clarify the issues and understand the scientific way of dealing with adolescents, and finalise the methodology of the programme to be conducted based on the assessment data.

Step 3: Focus on the Identified Issues and Prepare the Programme

Literature on adolescent girls and theoretical implications have already identified general issues related to adolescent girls under major headings like health, mental health, academics, vocational, rights and sexuality. Identify the experts' opinions on assessment data and prepare the programme. The methodology should focus at the causal level, and not at the symptomatic level, to bring about deep change; hence it will be universal and scientific in approach. To retain adolescent girls' interest, attention and participation, the best use of lecturing in combination with the following methods can be used in the programme.

- Group discussion: This is a commonly used method because group discussion uses the participants' own past experiences in a very deliberate manner.
- Brainstorming: It is a process for developing creative solutions to problems. It is most effective with groups of 8–12 people and should be performed in a relaxed environment.
- Audio-visual methods: These include videos, flash cards, flannel graphs and picture scrolls, and are very important media when dealing with adolescents.
- Group games: Icebreakers or icebreaker games can be a wonderful way to ease a group from monotony, raise energy levels, and let people enjoy themselves.
- Question Box: It is an activity in which questions asked by participants are answered by the facilitator. Adolescents can ask questions freely without inhibition as the identity of the questioner is not disclosed.
- Role play: It is a simulation in which each participant is given a role to play. Participants are given some information related to the role, concerns, objectives, responsibilities and emotions.

SESSION TIME FRAME

In regard to the effectiveness and completeness of the intervention programme, the stipulated time for each session can be two-and-half hours. Before the beginning of every session, all adolescent girls have to do meditation, then review the previous session and directly come to the content of the session. The commonly followed time frame of all sessions is as follows.

10 minutes	Meditation by concentrating on the breathing
5 minutes	Attendance
10 minutes	Review of the previous session
45 minutes	Lecture-cum-activities on session concept
10 minutes	Break
45 minutes	Lecture-cum-activities on session concept
30 minutes	Reflections and experience sharing of the participants
10 minutes	Conclusion of the session
5 minutes	Information on the next session

READING MATERIALS AND OTHER RESOURCE MATERIALS

A programme kit containing a note book, pen and reading material on the contents of each session, printed in a 20-page booklet in the language of the adolescent girls should be prepared and distributed to each of them on the first day. Every day, they are expected to read and attend the session to make it more effective.

There are standardised materials prepared by the SCERT, WHO, UNESCO, and other national and international organisations that can be referred to before preparing a programme (Table 4.1).

Step 4: Implementation of the Programme

After preparation, the programme can be organised for the adolescent girls after fixing comfortable timings. Prepare the venue with sufficient physical/visual aids to impart the programme. There should be a minimum of 12 sessions exclusive of pre- and post-measurements, within two to three hours. The programme can be delivered by a team consisting of mental health professionals, medical professionals, counsellors, advocates and professional

Table 4.1
Sample Format for Preparing the Programme

Session 2	Adolescence: Growth, Development and Changes
Objectives	To make the participants understand the adolescent years' growth, development and changes. Growth and development, stages, growth pattern, physical and psychological changes happening to the body, puberty, and menstruation and importance of reproductive organs.
Methodology	Interactive lecture, with visual aids on the topics, group discussion and individual doubt clarification.
Materials needed	Paper, pen, reading material, charts showing adolescent years' growth and development, charts showing pictures of reproductive organs.
Total session time	150 minutes (2 hours, 30 minutes).
Activities	1. Adolescent growth and development, stages, growth pattern, physical and psychological changes happening to the body. 2. Introduction to puberty, menstruation, anatomy, functions and importance of reproductive organs (introduction of the concepts through stories, question box and explanation of the doubts in general through flip charts/videos, photographs and identification by the participants). 3. Group discussion on puberty, menstruation, anatomy and functions of reproductive organs.
Contents of the session	Adolescent years, characteristics of adolescence, puberty, growth in girls and boys, the female and male reproductive organs, menstrual hygiene, abnormal and normal menstruation, marriage, sexual reproduction, fertilisation, pregnancy and family planning.

social workers. The major part of the methodology can be employed informally with an interactive participatory approach, and the activities with audio and visual aids. A brief sample of each session is given in Box 4.2.

Box 4.2
Sample Sessions

Session 1 / Introduction to the Programme and Meditation: This session aims to introduce the intervention programme, give information about forthcoming sessions, establish rapport with participants, and introduce and train them in meditation.

Session 2 / Adolescence—Growth, Development and Changes: The objective of the session is to make the participants understand adolescence growth, development and changes. The following are the topics covered in the session:

(Box 4.2 Contd)

(Box 4.2 Contd)

growth and development, stages, growth pattern, physical and psychological changes happening to the body, puberty, and menstruation and importance of reproductive organs.

Session 3 / Adolescence—Sexuality, Sexually Transmitted Diseases (STDs) and HIV/AIDS: The objective of this session is to make them understand human sexuality, STDs, and HIV/AIDS. It helps to clarify misconceptions and teach preventive measures.

Session 4 / Adolescence—Developmental Issues and Management: The objectives of the session are to make them understand how adolescent girls are at risk (of abuse/exploitation, violence, sex rackets), to prepare them to respond in the right way (assert, say 'No'), to make them understand common factors related to school adjustment, scholastic backwardness and its management, and to make them aware of the problems around them and their management.

Session 5 / Life Skills Session 1—Communication and Interpersonal Skills: The objectives of the session are to introduce the participants to communication and train them in communication and interpersonal skills to improve day-to-day interactions.

Session 6 / Life Skills Session 2—Decision Making, Critical Thinking and Creative Thinking Skills: The aim of this session is to introduce and train the participants to learn decision making, critical thinking and creative thinking skills to prepare the participants to deal satisfactorily with the daily events of life.

Session 7 / Life Skill Session 3—Coping and Self-management Skills: This session aims to introduce and train the participants to learn coping and self-management skills, train the participants to develop their realistic self, improve self-esteem, make them understand the importance of positive self-regard, prepare the participants to deal satisfactorily with the daily events of life and also identify those participants who are not easy to get along with and discuss and solve their issues.

Session 8 / Legal Awareness and Gender Issues: The objective of the session is to impart information about the legal system, how it supports women and children, and existing gender issues in the country.

Session 9 / Career and Vocational Guidance: The objective of the session is to guide the respondent to choose a career and perform in fields/vocations that most suit them.

Session 10 / General Health Check up and Awareness Class on Health: The objectives of the session are to assess participants' general health conditions by consultation with a professionally qualified doctor, to give a heath awareness class, and to clarify participants' doubts regarding their health.

(Box 4.2 Contd)

(Box 4.2 Contd)

Session 11 / Personal Counselling and Plan for the Future (better womanhood): The objectives of the session are to sum up all the sessions conducted in the previous days and clarify their doubts regarding topics/concepts, introduce the importance of planning for the future, and help each participant in the preparation of future plans in life based on the inputs of the intervention programme.

Session 12 / Peer Group Training: The objectives of the session are to conduct one-day training in the skills necessary for peer educators, select possible peer educators, impart the skills needed for the peer educator for informational and educational purposes (that is, technical, teaching and teamwork skills for the adolescent girls in the communities and institutions).

Step 5: Assessment of Effectiveness

It is important to evaluate any programme after its implementation. Therefore, immediately after the programme, the same tools previously used have to be administered, for post/after measurement, to the participants to know the effectiveness. Along with this, collect participants' individual evaluation on the total programme in a separate paper. After this, analyse the data statistically and prepare the report. We can identify from the report the areas to be considered more and that had gone astray. If any topic is to be added, do so with expert validation, and prepare a final modified programme for the next group.

Step 6: Peer Group Training

Peer groups are an important influence throughout one's life, but they are more critical during the developmental years of childhood and adolescence. In the beginning, introduce the terms 'peer group' and 'peer group training' once intervention programme is over. Plan for continuous two-day training of the skills necessary for peer educators, and select the possible peer educators or ask the participants to volunteer as peer group educators. Next, impart the skills needed for the peer educator for informational and educational purposes, that is technical, teaching and teamwork skills (Box 4.3). The peer educator has to disseminate new information and knowledge to the group members and can become a role model to others by practising what she preaches. Since peer educators are from the same group, she can empathise and understand the emotions, thoughts, feelings and language of the participants, and therefore, relate better. As part of peer education, ask the group members to gather every week on a particular day and time and conduct discussions, review the sessions covered during the programme and day-to-day life situations, and maintain the sustainability of the positive impacts of the programme.

Step 7: Follow-up

Follow-up is to be done regularly thrice a year to know the maintenance of sustainability of the programme through peer group educators. Insights imparted during the intervention sessions can be checked during follow-up, especially on planning, putting effort themselves according to the challenges, and demands of the new generation in the modern competitive world.

Follow-up can be done through regular visits and interactive sessions with adolescent girls, meetings with authorities, schools teachers, parents (especially mothers) and anganwadi workers, special case studies among success stories of the participants, personal counselling to those who are backward, and assessment with tools applied earlier.

Box 4.3
Skills Needed for the Peer Educator

Technical skills: All peer educators will need to have a basic understanding of adolescence—growth, development, changes, issues, management, life skills, career and vocational guidance, laws, gender issues and plan for future.

Teaching skills: This second set of skills places special emphasis on education, communication and presentation techniques. For example, peer educators need to know how to teach the concepts which are necessary for their group.

Teamwork skills: The activities conducted by peer educators are often done in pairs or by the entire team. Therefore, it is important that the co-ordinator encourage the cultivation of skills for working as a team.

BETTER WOMANHOOD

Continuous follow-ups are required for the effective implementation of any programme. It can be regularly done till the adolescent girls attain a level of understanding about the society and their socially accepted roles. Post-intervention programme assessment and individual follow-up sessions will reflect each one's ambitions and will give clarifications on the accepted and expected behaviour patterns and roles of women in society. The effectiveness assessment result could enable the social workers to understand the needs of children's homes and facilitate the planning and implementation of appropriate programmes. The total programme is designed for one to two years and will support them to design their future focused on better womanhood. In addition to meeting basic needs, social workers need to help the youth address issues related to grief, anger, rejection, acceptance and moving forward with hope. Social workers can do programmes to improve health and nutrition, education, psychosocial support, economic strengthening, living environments and children's rights. The model programme will prove the suitable application of social group work and social work research in issues related to adolescent girls in institutions and communities.

Feasibility and Possible Merits of Practice of Social Group Work in the Model Programme

At the heart of the social work value system there is a concern for the well-being of all people. Social group work develops the ability of establishing constructive relationship in individuals through group activities. A group in this model programme consists of a number of adolescent girls interacting with each other based on interdependence, acceptance of roles and status, similarity of goals and motives, and shared norms and values. A group of 20 is ideal to conduct this programme.

Role of the Group Worker: The role of a group worker in this model programme involves facilitating interaction among the adolescent girls, helping them learn from one another, assisting them in establishing personal goals and providing continues empathy. It also involves evaluating and following up on their leanings from involvement in the group activities and its practice in this challenging society.

Ethical Issues: Informed consent from the adolescent girls who are participating in the model programme is a significant component. The purpose of the programme, rules, and issues related to confidentiality, rights and responsibilities of group members have to be dealt with in the programme.

Instructions to MSW Students/Practitioners Who Are the Group Workers or Facilitators: Some personal traits are indispensable for the group worker to improve the well-being of adolescent girls in this model programme.

- Improve your understanding of adolescents in this millennium through reading books and research reports on adolescents, and participating in seminars and workshops on adolescents.
- Be open to all developmental happenings in this field, and keep track of innovative measures to deal with the issues of adolescent girls.
- Prepare yourself as a facilitator to interact with adolescents by planning the schedule for the day.
- Motivate and guide the adolescents by showing enthusiasm for the topics covered in the sessions and for the work that the participants have done, and by being receptive to each participant's questions and needs.
- You need to promote a friendly co-operative environment and should respond positively to the question put up by the adolescent girls. Empathise and be a companion to them.
- Facial expressions like eye movements or making comments that ridicule adolescents should be avoided.
- Your non-verbal communication, standing position, movement, gestures and hand movement should be cautiously monitored.
- You should take enough time with participants to fully answer their questions so that both the trainer and the participating adolescents are satisfied.
- Develop patience, love and affection, desire to communicate, positive attitude and sense of humour while working with adolescents.
- Group dynamics of the adolescent groups should be observed and discussed in person.
- Courage, consoling quality, willingness to confront oneself, sincerity, sense of identity and creativity are very essential.

Stages in the Development of the Group of Adolescent Girls in the Programme

Formation of the Group: This stage can be seen in steps 1 and 2 of the model and involves making the adolescent girls aware about the programme, the importance of screening and selection of adolescent girls as group members, and briefing the plan, goal and group ethics.

Initial Stage: It includes orientation and expectations of the group, understanding the expectations of the adolescent girls through the first two steps and finalisation of the model programme in step 3.

Transition Stage: This stage is included in the beginning of step 4 of the model programme. This is quite a difficult phase where adolescent girls deal with their anxiety, resistance and conflict. The group worker can help them deal with their limitations.

Working Stage: During this stage in the middle and final phases of step 4 of the model programme, the adolescent girls develop greater cohesiveness and feel a sense of belonging to the group. It also involves wide exploration of issues. Also, they strongly focus on bringing desirable changes in behaviour through involvement in psychosocial well-being exercises related to the broad areas of adolescent girls.

Final Stage: In this stage, summarising and integrating the group experience is seen in step 5 of the model programme. During the assessment phase of step 5, adolescent girls would also provide information about their insights and learning in the group, and how they are going to put it into action in their life situations.

Follow-up Sessions: This stage, in steps 6 and 7, are while discussing peer group training and follow-ups. Involvement with peer group educators contributes more to maintain the positive outcome of psychosocial well-being of the adolescent girls. The follow-up results would communicate adolescent girls' aspirations and their determination to achieve psychosocial well-being for better womanhood in this society.

The social workers need to play a vital role in imparting the concept of well-being to the adolescent girls in the institutions as well as communities of these changing societal situations. The social group work should provide the adolescent girls a comfortable environment for sharing experiences and learning. The methodology of the programme can also be used, with slight modifications, for adolescent boys. Trained social workers with concerted action can help alleviate the suffering that many of the institutionalised adolescent girls face and can provide brighter prospects for their future. The social workers' special attention should be given to their health, vocational education and future employment possibilities, and educating them where they fit in vocationally. The social worker working with adolescents should address the developmental needs of this age group and pay particular attention in providing reproductive health and HIV information, and prevention services, for adolescents in institutions and communities.

Conclusion

The components of the model psychosocial well-being intervention programme are designed in such a way that they are flexible and personally helpful to cater to adolescent girls' psychosocial needs and problems. Group participation brings out openness which helps them realise their common drawback and how effectively they can overcome them. The protection of the girl child who belongs to economically and socially deprived groups would be ensured. Even though the child may get shelter, food and clothing in institutions, that is, their basic physical needs may be met, their psychological and social needs may not be met. Positive changes in social interactions, behaviour and emotional well-being are the indicators of improved well-being. Through this intervention, psychosocial well-being of adolescent girls in institutions will improve, and they will develop a capacity to form harmonious relationship with others and respond constructively to changes in the environment. Similar results can be expected among adolescent girls in communities too. They will start to think more rationally about themselves to develop awareness and understand life situations.

References

Awasthi, N. N., B. D. Mathur, R. Mitra and R. N. Srivastava. 1980. 'A Study on the Sex Knowledge of School Going Teenagers of Jhansi, Uttar Pradesh', *Journal of Family Welfare*, 27 (1): 35–45.

Battle, J. 1981. *Culture-Free SEI. Self-esteem Inventories for Children and Adults.* Seattle: Special Child Publications.

Bhola, Poornima and Malavika Kapur. 1999. 'Brief Supportive Psychotherapy with Emotionally Disturbed Adolescent Girls', *Nimhans Journal,* 17 (2): 131–147.

Birell Weisen, R. and J. Orley. 1996. *Life Skills Education: Planning for Research as an Integral Part of Life Skills Education Development, Implementation and Maintenance.* Geneva: Program on Mental Health, World Health Organization.

Block, J. and W. R. Robins. 1993. 'A Longitudinal Study of Consistency and Change in Self-esteem from Early Adolescence to Early Adulthood', *Child Development,* 64 (3): 909–923.

Bodhakar, U. 2002. 'Adolescent Health', *Teen's Journal of Teenage Care and Premarital Counseling,* 10 and 11 (2): 1–8.

Bradshaw, J., P. Hoelscher and D. Richardson. 2007. 'An Index of Child Well-being in the European Union', *Social Indicators Research,* 80 (1): 133–177.

Brennan, A. 1985. 'Participation in the Students' Activities upon Students' Self Esteem', *Journal of Adolescence,* 20 (78): 445–466.

Bulanda R. E. and D. Majumdar. 2009. 'Perceived Parent–child Relations and Adolescent Self- esteem', *Journal of Child and Family Studies,* 18 (2): 203–212.

Chacko, T. V., S. Banu and A. C. Mathew. 2005. 'Impact of a "Modified Curriculum on Life Skills Education": On Knowledge, Attitudes and Skills of Adolescent School Girls', paper presented at the *2nd Indian Association of Social Sciences in Health National Conference on Globalization and Health Equity,* 4–5 February, Bhabha Atomic Research Centre, Mumbai.

Chandra A., S. Lara-Cinisomo, L. H. Jaycox, T. Tanielian, R. M. Burns, T. Ruder and B. Han. 2010. 'Children on the Home Front: The Experience of Children from Military Families', *Pediatrics,* 125 (1): 16–25.

Chandrasekhar, K. 2000. 'Adolescent Girls and Health Issues', in A. K. M. Nurun Nabi, F. Bourdier, G. A. O. Ersheng, K. Mahadevan, P. J. Reddy, R. Jayasree, R. Rajaram, V. K. R. Kumar, V. M. Sandeep and Y. J. Yuan (eds), *Reproductive Health of Humankind in Asia and Africa: A Global Perspective* (Volume 2). New Delhi: BR Publishing Corporation.

Chauhan, S. S. 1991. *Options for a Better Life for Young Women: The Prerana–CEDPA Partnership.* Washington, DC: Centre for Development and Population Activities (CEDPA).

Chiew, H. L. 1990. 'Relationship of Career Goals and Self-esteem among Adolescents', *Journal of Youth and Society,* 20 (1): 46–47.

Crosby, F. J. 1971. 'The Effects of Family Life Education on Values and Attitudes of Adolescents', *Dissertation Abstract International,* 31: 5839.

De Friese, G. H., C. L. Crossland, C. E. Pearson and C. J. Sullivan (eds). 1990. 'Comprehensive Schools Health Programs: Current Status and Future Prospects', *Journal of School Health,* 60 (4): 127–190.

Deo, D. S. and C. H. Ghattargi. 2005. 'Perceptions and Practices Regarding Menstruation: A Comparative Study in Urban and Rural Adolescent Girls', *Indian Journal of Community Medicine,* 30 (1): 33–34.

Drakshayani, D. K. and P. V. Ramaiah. 1994. A Study on Menstrual Hygiene among Rural Adolescent Girls', *Indian Journal of Medical Sciences*, 48 (6): 139–143.

Gnanasaraswathi, P. 1994. 'A Study on Family Life Education for Adolescents of an Institution', MPhil thesis in the Faculty of Mental Health and Neurosciences, Bangalore University, Bangalore.

Hassan, M. K., M. Jayaswal and P. Hassan. 2003. 'Reproductive Health Awareness in Rural Tribal Female Adolescents' (Research Study), Ranchi University.

Jagdish and Srivastava, A. K. 1983. *Mental Health Inventory.* Varanasi: Manovaigyanik Parikchan Sansthan Publications.

John, J. 2008. 'Life Skills Development Programme for the Mental Health of Juveniles in Kerala, India', *Loyola Journal of Social Sciences*, 22 (2): 30–37.

Jose, S. 2008. 'Psychosocial Problems of Institutionalized Adolescents'. Available at http://www.newsociety.com.inc/article/dn8736-orphaneboys. Accessed on 16 April 2014.

Joseph, G. A., S. Bhattacharji, A. Joseph and P. S. S. Rao. 1997. 'General and Reproductive Health of Adolescent Girls in Rural South India', *Indian Pediatrics*, 34 (3): 242–245.

Joshi, Kavita. 2004. *Sexuality in India: Teenager and Teacher.* New Delhi: Kalpaz Publications.

Karalam, S. R. B. 2011. 'Effectiveness of Intervention Programme on Self-esteem of Adolescent Girls in the Children's Homes, Thrissur District, Kerala, India', *BSSS Journal of Social Work*, 3 (1): 66–76.

Khandelkar, M. 1977. 'Bringing up Deprived Children at Maharashtra', *Abstract of Research Studies in Childhood Youth Welfare in India*, pp. 238–242. Mumbai: Tata Institute of Social Sciences, Mumbai.

Kumar, D. S. 2001. 'Intervention for Adolescent Mental Health' *Social Welfare*, 48 (3):18.

MacComack C. 1996. 'Promoting Psychosocial Well-being among Children Affected by Armed Conflict and Displacement: Principles and Approaches', *Working Paper*, No. 1, Save the Children Fund, London.

Masse, R., C. Poulin, C. Dasa, J. Lambert, S. Belair, and A. Battaglini. 1998a. 'Elaboration et validation d'un outil de mesure du bien-etre psychologique : L'emmbep', *Canadian Journal of Public Health*, 89: 352–357.

———. 1998b. 'The Structure of Mental Health Higher-Order Confirmatory Factor Analyses of Psychological Distress and Well-being Measures', *Social Indicators Research*, 45: 475–504.

Mathew, S. and R. Parthasarathy. 1988. 'Levels of Re-integration into the Community and Adjustment of the Ex-inmates of a Destitute Home', *Indian Journal of Social Work*, 49 (1): 75–80.

Mensch, B. S., M. J. Grant, M. P. Sebastian, P. C. Hewett and D. Huntington. 2004. 'The Effect of a Livelihoods Intervention in an Urban Slum in India: Do Vocational Counseling and Training Alter the Attitudes and Behavior of Adolescent Girls?', *Policy Research Division Working Papers*, No. 194, Population Council, New York.

Mohanty, J. and S. Mohanty. 1997. *Family Life Education (Adolescence Education)*. New Delhi: Deep and Deep Publications.

Mridula, B. N. 2002. 'Analysis of Mental Health in Terms of Adjustment of Adolescent Girls in Kerala', *Sayakta,* 2 (1): 11–14.

Mullick, P. 1995. *Text Book of Home Science*. New Delhi: Kalyani Publishers.

Muuss, R. E. 1975. *Theories of Adolescence* (Third Edition). New York: Random House.

Nagar, D. 1992. *Deprived Children*. New Delhi: Printwell.

Nagpal, R. and H. Sell. 1992. 'Assessment of Subjective Well-Being—The Subjective Well-Being Inventory (SUBI).' Regional Health Paper, SEARO, No. 24.

Nair, M. K. C. 2004. 'Family Life Education Module for Young Adults', *Teen's Journal of Teenage Care and Pre-marital Counseling,* 4 (17): 34. Child Development Centre: Medical College, Tiruvananthapuram.

———. 2005. *Handbook for Plus I and II Teachers and Students: Life Skill Education for Adolescents*. Child Development Centre: Medical College, Tiruvananthapuram.

Nair, M. K. C. and Mini K. Paul. 2002. 'Psychosomatic Problems of Adolescent, Family Life Education for Plus-one Students', *Teen's Journal of Teenage Care and Pre-marital Counseling,* 10 and 11 (2): 7–9.

———. 2003. 'Depression Prevalence', *Teen's Journal of Teenage Care and Pre-marital Counseling,* 3 (13 and 14): 9–11.

Narayan, K. A., D. K. Srinivasa, P. J. Pelto and S. Veerammal. 2001. 'Puberty Rituals, Reproductive Knowledge and Health of Adolescent Schoolgirls in South India', *Asia–Pacific Population Journal,* 16 (2): 225–238.

National Council of Educational Research and Training (NCERT), National Aids Control Organization (NACO), United Nations Children's Fund and UNESCO (2000). *Learn for Life: A Guide to Family Health and Life Skill Education for Teachers and Students*. New Delhi: NCERT.

Nayak, N. P. 2000. *Need for De-institutionalization of Children and Alternatives*. Karnataka State Council for Child Welfare's De-institutionalizing Project. Bangalore: Karnataka State Council for Child Welfare.

Newman, M. B. and P. R. Newman. 1979. *An Introduction to the Psychology of Adolescence*. Homewood, IL: Dorsey Press.

Orley, J. 1997. 'Promoting Mental Health and Teaching Skills for Life: The WHO Approach.' Available at www.healthchildrennetwork.lu/pdf/conference/1997/orleyenpdf.2003. Accessed on 16 April 2014.

Padmam, M. S. R. 2003. 'Destitute Women in Kerala: Psychological Resources and Psychosocial Needs', *Discussion Paper*, No. 51, Centre for Development Studies, Thiruvananthapuram.

Panda, A. 2007. *Adolescent Girls in India: A Report*. Advocating for the Rights of Children. New Delhi: Worldwide Trust.

Pipher, M. 1994. *Reviving Ophelia: Saving the Selves of Adolescent Girls*. New York: Ballantine Books.

Raj, H. I. 1993. *Impact of Sex Education to Higher Secondary School Students*, Master's thesis, Bangalore University.

Raji V. R. and M. K. C. Nair. 2006. 'General Adjustment in Adolescents', *Teen's Journal of Teenage Care and Pre-marital Counseling*, 1 (19): 3–5.

Raval, V. V., H. P. Raval and P. R. Stacey. 2010. 'Damned If They Flee, Doomed If They Don't: Narratives of Runaway Adolescent Females from Rural India', *Journal of Family Violence*, 25 (8): 755–764.

Reddy, N.Y. 1964. 'Development of an Adjustment Inventory for Use with Adolescents', *Journal of Psychological Researches*, 8 (1): 68–76.

Reddy, S. N. 1989. Institutionalized Children. Allahabad: Chugh Publications.

Remschmidt, H. and M. Belfer. 2005. 'Mental Health Care for Children and Adolescents Worldwide: A Review', *World Psychiatry*, 4 (3): 147–153.

Rice, F. P. 1990. *The Adolescent* (Sixth Edition). Boston, MA: Allyn–Bacon.

Rosenberg, M. 1989. *Society and the Adolescent Self-image* (rev.ed.). Wesleyan University Press: Middeltown, CT.

Schaffer, R. H. 1996. *Social Development*. Oxford, UK: Wiley-Blackwell.

Shengchao Y., H. Emily and L. Xiaodong. 2004. *Poverty, Psychosocial Well-being, and School Performance in Rural China*. San Francisco: International Health Economics Association.

Siddiqui, N. J. 1997. *Adolescent Orphan Girls in Delhi: A Sociological Profile*. New Delhi: Regency Publications.

Sikka, M. D. 1983. 'After Care Programme for Juveniles: Where Does It Stand Today?', *Indian Journal of Social Work*, 44 (2), 157–163.

Singh, M. M., R. Devi and S. S. Gupta. 1999. 'Awareness and Health-seeking Behaviour of Rural Adolescent School Girls on Menstrual and Reproductive Health Problems', *Indian Journal of Medical Sciences*, 53 (9): 439–443.

Smoker, C. B. S. 1975. 'The Development of Self-esteem and Femininity in Early Adolescence', *Journal of Early Adolescence*, 35 (7B): 3599–3600.

State Council of Educational Research and Training (SCERT). 2006. *Adolescent Education Programme: School Level Training Module*. Kerala.

Trikha, S. 2001. 'Abortion Scenario of Adolescents in a North India City–Evidence from a Recent Study', *Indian Journal of Community Medicine*, 26 (1): 48–55.

UNESCO. 2001. 'Knowledge, Attitude, Behaviour on ARSH', *Adolescent Reproduction and Sexual Health, Regional Demographic Profile*. UNESCO: Bangkok.

United Nations Children's Fund (UNICEF). 2005. *State of the World's Children 2006: Excluded and Invisible*. New York: UNICEF. Retrieved from http://www.unicef.org on 29 May 2011.

Viswanath, S. 1985. 'Concept and Extent of Destitution: Meaning, Causes and Preventive Measures', National Institute of Public Cooperation and Child Development, Bangalore.

World Health Organization (WHO). 1999. 'Creating an Environment for Emotional and Social Well Being', *Information Series on School Health*, Document 10.

Geneva: Department of Mental Health and Substance Dependence, Evidence and Research, WHO.

World Health Organization (WHO). 2000a. *Module 7: Life Skills*. Retrieved from www.unodc.org/pdf/youthnet/action/message/escap_peers_07.pdf, 11 March 2014.

———. 2000b. *Should Adolescents be Specifically Targeted for Nutrition in Developing Countries? To Address Which Problems, and How?*. Retrieved from http://www. who.org.

WHO, UNAIDS, UNESCO, UNFPA, and UNICEF. 1998. *Strategies for Adolescent Health and Development—South-East Asia Region: Report of an Inter Country Consultation*, New Delhi, May.

Woodhead, M. 2004. 'Psychosocial Impacts of Child Work: A Framework for Research, Monitoring and Intervention', *International Journal of Children's Rights*, 12 (4): 321–377.

Young, M., R. Kelley and G. Denny. 1997. 'Evaluation of Selected Life Skills Modules from the Contemporary Health Series with Students in Grade 6', *Perceptual and Motor Skills*, 84 (3): 811–818.

Web Resource

www.unicef.org/adolescence/files/fact_sheet_final.pdf2009

5

Gender-based Violence and Mental Health

Ines Zuchowski

Introduction

Violence against women is a serious violation of human rights, yet women across the globe experience violence in private and public domains. Women are disproportionally affected by '…gender-based violence, socioeconomic disadvantage, low income and income inequality, low or subordinate social status and rank and unremitting responsibility for the care of others' (World Health Organization [WHO] 2012). Violence has been identified as the leading cause of injury and harm against women and as the most common and exemplary cause for depression in women.

In this chapter, the connection of women's experience of violence and mental health is explored. Consideration is given to the extent and type of violence that women experience and the impact of it on their lives, with a particular focus on women's mental health. Social workers worldwide are responding to women who might have experienced violence and whose mental health is affected by this experience. Social workers are also engaged in community development aiming to improve the well-being of the community as a whole. As such it is important for social workers to have a sound practice framework that enables them to address gender-based violence. Social workers need to be equipped to deliver appropriate practice intervention at micro, meso and macro levels. Social work practice strategies and practice reflections for working with women, violence and mental health issues will be outlined and questions for consideration will be raised.

The aim of this chapter is to raise awareness of the connection between violence against women and mental health outcomes, and provide social work practitioners with tools to respond to violence in social welfare practice.

To set the scene, the overall context of women, violence and mental health will be explored. Gender is a factor impacting women's vulnerability to the experience of both violence and mental health. Gender is also a factor in the diagnosis of mental health. Focus of the chapter will be the exploration of how social work practitioners can work with women who present to them in practice, whether in individual case work, group work or community work. To facilitate the audience's thinking on practice implications for working with women, three examples of social welfare services who work in this field are presented and practice questions posed.

Throughout the chapter, the need to consider the impact and context of women's experience of violence in mental health social work practice is highlighted. The conclusion that violence against women is a community concern is drawn. Social work practitioners need to ensure that their practice leads to increased safety and well-being for women.

Women's Mental Health Issues

> Violence represents a crucial violation of women's rights as human beings. The experience of violence necessarily violates women's rights to liberty and security of person and to freedom from fear. The presence of violence is incompatible with the enjoyment of the highest attainable standard of physical and mental health. (WHO 2000: 66)

In this chapter, the World Health Organization's (WHO) definition for mental health is taken as a guiding principle—

> Mental health is the capacity of the individual, the group and the environment to interact with one another in ways that promote subjective well-being, the optimal development and use of mental abilities (cognitive, affective and relational), the achievement of individual and collective goals consistent with justice and the attainment and preservation of conditions of fundamental equality. (WHO 2000: 12)

While this definition does not mention gender, it is a factor in every aspect of mental health, and 'is critically implicated in the differential delivery of justice and equality' (WHO 2000). Mental health will be examined in the light of violence against women.

Violence against women is a worldwide occurrence and is permitted to continue through implicit societal support (Irwin and Thorpe 1996).

Examples of violence include the use of physical force, sexually unwanted behaviour, verbal attacks of put downs, restrictions on religious expressions or limiting the social contact with others (Ashfield 2003). The use of violence in relationships is about one person or persons controlling the other (Oberoi 2012). Violence against women and mental health outcomes are connected to gender, which is not a biological predetermining factor, but a social construct. Bottorff et al. (2012) highlight evidence that gender and gender relations impact on health outcomes. They outline that 'gender is a social construct, a multidimensional determinant of health that intersects with culturally prescribed and experienced dimensions of femininity and masculinity, and emerges in diverse individual health practices' (Bottorff et al. 2012: 435). The WHO recognises gender as a determinant of health, and suggests that it helps explain the variations in health outcomes for women and men (WHO 2000). Addressing gender-based violence is relevant to social work, whose global agenda seeks to promote social and economic equalities, to ensure the dignity and worth of the person, and to promote sustainable communities and well-being through sustainable human relationships (International Federation of Social Workers, International Association of Schools of Social Work, and International Council on Social Work 2012: 1–7).

Gender Impacts Mental Health Outcomes

When looking at the impact of gender on mental health, two main aspects will be highlighted here. First, gender impacts the lived experience of people and their mental health. Structural analysis and feminist thought highlight that women live within patriarchal structures that are oppressive, and place stress on women (Martin 2003). Second, gender impacts the way mental illness is diagnosed (Martin 2003).

It is important to recognise that gender impacts women's lived experience and consequently their mental health. The WHO (2012) highlights the role of gender determinants in mental well-being and mental ill health. Women's position in society across the globe impacts their physical and mental well-being. 'Gender determines the differential power and control men and women have over the socioeconomic determinants of their mental health and lives, their social position, status and treatment in society and their susceptibility and exposure to specific mental health risks' (WHO 2012). The reality is that many women across the world are 'caught up in struggles to survive, raise children, cope with poverty, natural disasters, corrupt regimes or varieties of social exclusion' and the 'interrelations of gender with other power relations leave the inequalities and injustices of everyday life barely changed for the most disadvantaged' (Ramazanoglu and Holland 2002: 169). Women are disproportionally affected by 'gender-based violence, socioeconomic disadvantage, low income and income inequality, low or subordinate social status and rank and unremitting responsibility for the care of others' (WHO 2012). This context alone—the struggles of daily life that mean that they are more likely to experience hardship and persecution, and have limited access to resources and status—would have an impact on a person's sense of self and their experience of the world around them. Women's overall disadvantage and vulnerabilities influence their subjective well-being, the optimal development and use of mental abilities and their ability to achieve outcomes, elements that are pivotal in the definition of mental health. It needs to be recognised that 'women continue to be placed in subservient roles that necessarily impact upon levels of health and wellbeing' (Martin 2003: 157). Gender impacts women's overall mental health. Gender also impacts on women's safety and the incidence of violence they suffer.

Violence against Women

For women there are gender-specific risk factors of mental disorders. Women's social position in the world has an impact on their life not only in terms of access to resources, but also in terms of their experience of safety and violence. Worldwide, violence is perpetrated against women. In western countries, for example, research shows that one in four women have suffered rape, and up to one in three girls sexually assaulted by a male member of their family; women experience harassment in the workplace and in public spaces (Irwin and Thorpe 1996). Across the world, women are exposed to a range of violations that takes many forms—'forced abortions, female infanticide, female genital mutilations, acid throwing, child sexual abuse, rape, forced prostitution, dowry and honour violence, domestic violence, elder abuse and more' (Redfern and Aune 2010: 77–78). Oxfam (2004: 4) reports that violence against women in South Asia is widespread—'It begins at the stage of conception; sex-selective abortions are frequent....Culture-specific forms of violence include domestic violence, rape, sexual harassment, incest, trafficking, honour killings, acid attacks, public mutilation, stove-burnings, and forced temple prostitution'. Oberoi (2012) points to the prevalence of acid throwing in India, which is committed on women 'for spurning suitors, for rejecting proposals of marriage, for denying dowry or dissatisfaction with dowry, arguing with partner etc.' (Oberoi 2012: 30). Violence against women is committed on an interpersonal level, yet, facilitated with societal support. 'Violence is embedded into many of the structures and institutions that are part of society and is, therefore, endemic in many aspects of women's lives' (Irwin and Thorpe 1996: 7).

There are serious negative consequences for women experiencing violence. For example, the WHO (2012) stresses that 'the high prevalence of sexual violence to which women are exposed and the correspondingly high rate of Post Traumatic Stress Disorder (PTSD) following such violence, renders women the largest single group of people affected by this disorder'. Moreover, 'suicide is among the leading causes of death for women between the ages of 20 and 59 years globally and the second leading cause of death in the low- and middle-income countries of the WHO Western Pacific Region' (WHO 2009: 3). Research worldwide identifies that intimate partner violence 'can cause long-term psychological effects and that domestic violence is a predictor of psychological problems' (Avdibegović and Sinanović 2006: 739–740), poor health, limiting ability to care for themselves or others, suicide, and maternal and children morbidity and mortality (Johnston and Naved 2008; Koski, Stephenson and Koenig 2011). Research shows that women who are accessing mental health services have often experienced violence. Martin, for instance, highlights that 'as many as 50 per cent of women using mental health services are survivors of sexual assault' (Cox 1994 in Martin 2003: 158). Furthermore, women who are diagnosed with a serious mental illness are in turn much more prone to experience violence from intimate partners (Laing, Irwin and Toivonen 2012).

The WHO (2009) surmises women's low status in society, their burden of work and the experience of violence as contributing factors to mental ill health. Consequently, women and men are affected differently by mental health. Women and men have different rates of mental disorders; women are more likely to be diagnosed with depression, anxiety and somatic health problem and are more likely to access health services. Men, on the other hand, are more likely to present with alcohol-related disorders (WHO 2012). Violence against women has been identified as the most common and exemplary cause for depression in women. 'This is because violence against women encapsulates all three features identified in social theories of depression—humiliation, inferior social ranking and subordination, and blocked escape or entrapment' (WHO 2000: 66). Women who are violated by their intimate partner or strangers are impacted in terms of their physical and mental health.

Diagnosing Mental Health in the Context of Women's Experience of Violence

While it is important to recognise that experiencing violence compromises women's health, a caution needs to be issued in terms of pathologising women's distress into a mental illness. Here the discussion now considers the second major impact of gender on mental health. Rummery, in her work with women survivors of child sexual assault, has found a significant correlation of incest survivors being diagnosed with a psychiatric illness. She reflects that the symptoms that had been used to diagnose mental illness in the women she had worked with, 'seemed to me to be normal reactions to abusive situations' (Rummery 1996: 151). Rummery argues that while 'some women may be genuinely suffering from psychiatric illnesses, there are also many whose emotions, responses and "symptoms" are unnecessarily deemed "sick" within a psychiatric framework' (1996: 152). Similarly, Martin (2003: 158) suggests that many people end 'up in psychotherapy or counselling and believing that there is something wrong with them, when in fact their distress is often due to disempowerment and discrimination'. She highlights that there is a 'gender bias within the formulation and application of psychiatric diagnoses' (Martin 2003: 156 citing Chesler 1972, Coppock and Hopton 2000 and Sheppard 1991) and that the main diagnostic tool used by health professionals, the *Diagnostic and Statistical Manual*, is biased in determining what seems normal and abnormal. The point to stress is that it is important to acknowledge the impact of violence on women's health, and when women experience violence, the symptoms of mental ill health cannot be explored in isolation of violence in women's lives. Experiences of violence impact women's well-being. Thus the work of a social worker is influenced by the practitioner's understanding of violence and mental health.

Working to Improve the Mental Health of Women

As part of addressing gender-based violence, it is important to work with people in various ways. Martin, for example, suggests that social workers could engage with individuals and groups to achieve empowerment and engage in community development activities and campaigns 'to address structural inequalities that necessarily impact on women's mental health and well-being' (Martin 2003: 168). Addressing structural inequalities necessitates making sure that women have equal access to resources, protection and opportunities, for example. Change needs to be implemented across communities, social systems, politics and organisations, and social workers can be part of initiating and facilitating system change. Social workers engage in various fields of practice and apply a number of methods of intervention. Within their field of practice, social workers could apply various methods simultaneously. The organisational context of their work, their own orientation towards change, and their individual skills and knowledge impact their practice (Harms and Connolly 2009). Thus, social workers have to be knowledgeable about issues that might impact their practice context. Social workers need to reflect on the context of their organisation, the specifics of their client group, and the outcomes they want to achieve and how these can be achieved. This is a complex process and is ideally facilitated through praxis, 'the process of ideologically strengthening our practice through critical reflection and reflexivity, challenging our values, ideology and beliefs and creative rethinking of issues with a view of facilitating macro change' (Harms and Connolly 2009: 7). In working to improve the mental health of women a question to be pondered would be 'Am I, as a social work practitioner, aware of women's lived experience and how this impacts their mental health?'.

Working at the Micro Level

Social workers will often work with women who experience mental health issues. Part of their work will be working individually with women to improve their well-being and at times this work will include a case-management role. The ability to engage and communicate with women are critical social work skills in these settings (Mattes 2010). Martin (2003: 162) highlights that 'The planning and delivery of mental health services for women must be developed in ways that are non-threatening, responsive, sensitive to age, cultural background, physical, emotional and social circumstances'. Social workers need to continue to talk and listen to women and recognise 'the uniqueness of individual women as well as their shared experiences as women' (Martin 200).

Often a social worker's role may be within a health setting and multi-disciplinary team. Social workers can engage in case management from a strengths-based perspective. In mental health this means moving 'away from pathologising discourses towards a focus on "resilience, rebound, possibility, and transformation"' (Saleeby 1996: 297 cited in Bland, Renouf and Tullgren 2009: 336). Strength-based practice recognises that 'All people have strengths and abilities, including the ability to build their competence, so service systems needs to be designed to give people the opportunity to display, use and build such strengths' (Bland, Renouf and Tullgren 2009: 336). Social workers can bring a clear focus on social justice to these cases; they can focus on 'listening to the wisdom of consumers and carers who have valued highly the traditional role of social workers as potentially powerful mediators of power and resources as well as providers of counselling and advocacy' (Harries 2009: 245). Social workers in this context need to build effective relationships with clients, have an awareness of available resources and services, be able to liaise with other service providers and be 'able to work with clients to identify appropriate treatment goals, clarify problems and implement interventions with those clients and their families' (Briggs and Crowe 2009: 226).

However, the focus of a social worker's role needs to move beyond treatment options to identification of life choices and exploring the impact of mental health issues (Briggs and Crowe 2009). What this means specifically for working with women who are experiencing or have experienced violence in their life, is that social workers need to have an understanding of violence and power, as well as tools available to assess women's well-being and detect the presence of violence in their lives. Part of this understanding needs to be that women are often blamed for the violence they experience, thus, for example, in the instance of rape, women's conduct is questioned and the responsibility for the rape they have suffered is placed at their feet (Redfern and Aune 2010). Social work practitioners need to be knowledgeable of this and challenge those societal constructs (Fraser 1996). Moreover, it is important to realise that 'women typically do not disclose [violence] unless asked about it and health care providers frequently do not ask' (Plitcha 2007, citing Washaw and Alpett 1999 in Laing, Irwin and Toivonen 2012: 120).

TOOLS FOR IDENTIFYING VIOLENCE

Often women do not realise that they are in a relationship that is violent. They may experience violence without realising that this behaviour is not acceptable. At the same time, social workers may not have an understanding of violence and the impact of violence. Thus, the WHO (2009: 89) highlights that, first, an 'improved detection of the depression and anxiety occurring within the context of a history of violent victimisation must occur.' Second, they identify the need to train health practitioners to better understand the links between violence and presenting somatic symptoms and disorders (WHO 2000). Laing, Irwin and Toivonen (2012) concur with both points and highlight the importance of cross-sector collaboration between health services and services that specifically respond to women experiencing violence.

It is essential to comprehend that violence does affect the mental and physical well-being of people. Violence impacts on people's sense of self and their ability to function well. Women who experience violence may assume that the behaviour that they experience is normal, and that as a woman this is what can be expected from a relationship. As a result, women could consider the effects of the violence, such as feeling depressed, feeling worried and unable to cope with life's circumstances as a sign of mental illness, a sign that there is something wrong with them and the way they feel rather than identifying these as effects of experiencing violence. There are numerous studies cited by the WHO as evidence that 'Women who have experienced violence, whether in childhood or adult life, have increased rates of depression and anxiety, stress-related syndromes, pain syndromes, phobias, chemical dependency, substance use, suicidality, somatic and medical symptoms, negative health behaviours, poor subjective health and changes to health service utilization' (WHO 2000: 75).

Many women experience violence in their own homes. 'Violence against women is perpetrated in "peace" time in their own countries and their own homes, typically by those whom they know well and to a much lesser extent by strangers' (WHO 2000: 67). Importantly, violence in relationships needs to be recognised when it happens. This can help acknowledge the woman's experience of being unwell and put this in a context of external factors that are impacting on her well-being. Moreover, unless violence is identified and named as such, it will not stop. 'Relationship violence is often a sign that a relationship is heading into serious trouble and that problems exist that will very likely not resolve without appropriate professional support and assistance. Once it is occurring, relationship violence usually worsens and becomes habitual' (Ashfield 2003: 221). Stopping violence from occurring is important to the community as a whole. Pease (2003) maintains that while most violence is perpetrated by men, not all men are violent. He argues, though, that 'men's primary model for relationships tends to be hierarchical' and that this needs to be addressed as when there is an imbalance of power between women and men there is 'a greater likelihood of male coercion and domination' (Pease 2003: 131).

Social work practitioners can help people identify when they experience violence in a relationship and do not feel safe. The WHO recognises that 'violence-related mental health problems are also poorly identified', pointing out that 'women are reluctant to disclose a history of violent victimization unless' they are asked directly about it (WHO 2012). If it is not recognised that the women experience violence, their symptoms of distress and pain may be misdiagnosed and they could be further impacted. Labelling women who display 'intense emotional distress as "disordered" or "sick," effectively silences their disclosure of abuse' (Rummery 1996: 161). A social work practitioner can gently probe in discussions with the woman what are her life circumstances are like, whether she feels safe in her relationships and also check for the occurrence of violence (with a checklist for violence). Sometimes women are not able to identify that they are experiencing violence until they actually see or hear what they are experiencing as a form of violence. One such tool is provided by Ashfield (2003), who maintains that both women and men can experience violence in relationships (Box 5.1).

Box 5.1
A Checklist for Relationship Violence

Tick the signs that are familiar

Physical violence
☐ Pushing, shoving
☐ Punching, biting, scratching, kicking, slapping
☐ Holding roughly, biting, scratching, kicking, slapping
☐ Torturing, burning
☐ Destroying belongings
☐ Hurting or killing pets
☐ Throwing objects as weapons
☐ Threatening the use of weapons or violence

Emotional and verbal violence
☐ Hurtful put downs or name calling

☐ Humiliating or shaming
☐ Playing mind games
☐ Making partner frightened
☐ Being controlling or manipulative

Social violence
☐ Not allowing partner to choose their own friends
☐ Speaking bad about friends and family
☐ Humiliating, shaming or belittling partner in public

☐ Controlling partner's every move

Financial violence
☐ Not allowing partner to have money

(Box 5.1 Contd.)

(Box 5.1 Contd.)

☐ Exploiting, manipulating, or taking advantage of partner financially
☐ Making partner beg for money
☐ Controlling or using partner's finances again their will

Religious violence
☐ Making partner feel inferior because they don't share same beliefs
☐ Making a partner feel unsafe, frightened, inferior or humiliated

by coercing them to participate in certain religious gatherings, rituals or ceremonies
☐ Using religious beliefs to control partner

Sexual violence
☐ Forcing partner to have sex against their will
☐ Humiliating partner sexually
☐ Using object to violate partner sexually

Source: Adapted from Ashfield 2003: 217–219.

Once the social work practitioner and the woman have identified that the woman is living in a relationship that is violent, it is important to work out strategies that assist the woman to be safe. Unless violence is addressed, the health of a woman is seriously compromised. 'Many women using mental health services are experiencing domestic violence or its ongoing effects on their health, but this is often not recognised, resulting in appropriate health intervention that can compound women's suffering and compromise their safety' (Humphreyes and Thiara, 2003 citing Laing et al. 2010 in Laing, Irwin and Toivonen 2012: 122). The WHO (2012) stresses that the 'complexity of violence-related health outcomes increases when victimization is undetected and results in high and costly rates of utilization of the health and mental health care system'. Mental health practitioners need to recognise and respond to domestic violence and develop treatment plans that include safety planning and referrals to domestic violence services (Laing, Irwin and Toivonen 2012).

Responses to women who have experienced violence need to be centred around the women's experiences. Rummery (1996), for example, outlines that in her work with women who have been sexually assaulted, she focuses on validating their feelings and memories, believing the women, and giving the women control over the counselling relationship. Moreover, she stresses that in her practice she clearly takes a non-neutral position in order to 'challenge dominant constructions of power and knowledge' (Rummery 1996: 159). In working with women it is important to allow for space, opportunity and information to consider their individual experience of violence in the light of broader cultural and social contexts (Rummery 1996). This helps women to commence a process of healing and regain a sense of self and self-worth.

Box 5.2 carries a social worker's reflections on working in a Women's Centre with women in socially just ways.

Box 5.2
A Practitioner's Reflections by Di Plum (Senior Counsellor, The North Queensland Combined Women's Services, Inc.)

North Queensland Combined Women's Services, Inc. (The Women's Centre) promotes and enhances the holistic health, well-being and safety of women through providing free and accessible counselling, advocacy, groups and activities, drop-in support and emergency relief. We actively encourage the development of a socially just, inclusive and respectful society in which women are valued and supported through challenging barriers and advocate for an end to violence against women.

Our framework for practice is informed by feminist principles, incorporating an analysis of the devastating impact of violence and trauma on women's mental health. Trauma-informed care provides a safe therapeutic space in which the worker and woman collaborate to understand and grapple with the enduring disruption to the establishment of a healthy sense of self, as reflected through the development of mental health issues often resulting from violence and the associated traumatic response. Experiences of violence, violation and degradation are common place across the lifespan of thousands of women and children; such experiences can profoundly affect personal agency and autonomy as well as women's quality of life and participation in society.

When supporting women at The Women's Centre, an integrated response to women's needs enables an acknowledgement of how mental health issues have robbed women of their personal power. Women who display or disclose their experiences of depression, anxiety, bipolar disorder, suicidal ideation, obsessive compulsive disorder, personality disorder, post-traumatic stress disorder or psychotic tendencies are accepted with unconditional positive regard, with an acknowledgement of how these conditions may have emerged when the intrinsic self was overwhelmed with violence and fear. Women are not judged or stigmatised for these manifestations of loss; instead, women are treated with respect and are actively included as part of the ever evolving Women's Centre 'community'. Workers who observe concerning behaviours which may place the woman herself and others at risk, either in the centre or in the community, respond to the woman within the context of duty of care, an intervention based on safety, respect and dignity. In this manner, women are provided with trauma-informed care and support which values the woman's strengths and resilience, and facilitates a conversation in which clarity and honesty about the impact of the mental health issues can be addressed.

Recognising the trauma that impacts women's mental health is important. Laing, Irwin and Toivonen (2012: 122–123) suggest that the 'development of integrated, trauma informed-therapy for women with histories of sexual and physical abuse and co-occurring mental health and substance issues (McHugo et al. 2005; Noether et al. 2005)' is a promising advancement, but also highlight the importance of safety planning so that women can escape violence.

MENTAL HEALTH CONCERNS THAT NEED TO BE REFERRED

Trauma such as experiencing violence can lead to mental ill health that needs collaboration with clinical mental health practitioners, and thus, at times, a referral to a general practitioner, the mental health unit of a hospital or psychiatrist might be necessary. As social work practitioners we need to consider what these professionals need to know, how work with them can be done in collaboration and whether there is an advocacy role for the social worker.

Working at the Meso Level

Individual or meso-level work is often the focus of intervention in western countries. However, western notions of health and illness impose a medical biological framework on emotional and social concerns, yet from 'a non-Western view, an illness model of mental health can be both alien and alienating' (Martin 2003: 160). Using collective approaches might be more relevant to women of various cultures across the globe. In Australia, for example, research highlights the importance of mental health practice with Aboriginal and Torres Strait Islander people that adopt culturally competent community development approaches and primary care models (Walker and Sonn 2010). Walker and Sonn (2010: 165) stress that to work effectively with Indigenous Australians a true partnership is needed, which is different to the 'conventional individualistic Western way of working'. Collective notions of mental health would stress 'a holistic and collective approach, integration of the individual, the family and community' (Martin 2003: 160).

Meso-level work considers the opportunities of social workers to work with other services, families and groups. Working with other services and building strong linkages are important for providing services to women, and social workers need to have a good understanding of what services are available and what services might have already been accessed by the women they are working with (Martin 2003). It is essential to conduct interdisciplinary work, as 'social work is only one contributing profession in the multidisciplinary mental health field that increasingly hinges on effective interprofessional working' (Bailey 2002: 169). Social workers in multidisciplinary teams may often be the advocates who highlight the lived experience of mental illness, the voices of clients and the importance of critical perspectives that go beyond bio-medical models. They have unique contributions to offer multidisciplinary mental health teams, but need to be familiar with the social work–informed skills, knowledge and frameworks they are bringing to the team to be effective contributors (Bailey 2002). This work 'can be an isolating experience for practitioners within a multidisciplinary team, where the power struggles associated with competing mental health discourse have the potential to thwart emancipatory relationships with users' (Bailey 2002: 171). Thus, social workers need to link with not only other social workers, their professional association, but also work to create linkages and understanding with other disciplines.

Other meso-level work includes group and family work. Group work with women who have experienced domestic violence, for instance, has been found effective to improve the well-being of women and limit violence, and similarly effective in challenging violence behaviour by perpetrators of violence (Mullender 2002). Group work allows women to realise the endemic nature of violence and to access mutual support, and may lead to consciousness raising and activism. Here group work skills and a comprehensive understanding of violence are important.

Working with women and their families might be useful; families can be sources of support, but also may need strengthening themselves. 'Social workers need to be sensitive to the needs of family members and other significant people in the woman's life and seek their involvement where appropriate' (Martin 2003: 164). It is always important, however, not to make assumptions that families are always safe places for women. As the practice example from the Townsville Multicultural Support Group (Box 5.3) shows, social workers can work sensitively with women, allowing them to explore their experience individually and in groups.

Box 5.3
A Practitioner's Reflections by Meg Davis (The Townsville Multicultural Support Group, Inc. [TMSG])

TMSG was started by a group of migrant and refugee women in the early 1990s. TMSG is committed to 'addressing needs through greater participation in and contribution to a better quality of life for our multicultural society'. Although there has been an increase in male clients in recent years, TMSG has a focus of ensuring that women's needs are met. In 2011, TMSG participated in the National Australian Women's Dialogues, contributing to a report *Hear Our Calls for Action*.

TMSG is particularly aware of the vulnerabilities of the refugee and migrant women and their lived experience of the intersection of violence and mental health. Violence is not always recognised immediately, neither by workers nor the women themselves, yet it is often an issue. If there are any concerns raised about the mental health of women, the issue of having experienced violence pre-arrival in Australia and/or currently must be explored. When TMSG first welcomes refugee people, we have a welcoming/orientation meeting during which time, it is stressed that in Australia, women and men have equal rights. This information is always greeted with great enthusiasm from the women. However, the reality is that despite their expectations and hopes, violence often continues to be experienced. Information about the law and rights in Australia serves to 'open the door' to further discussion.

Additionally, it is part of our practice that case managers meet with women separately from the men and children in the early phase of the settlement services provision. Failure to do this may result in minimising the women's role in settlement and her specific needs. The perceived level of English proficiency of refugee and migrant women by a worker can influence a perception of mental health issues...acting as another form of isolation, imprisonment or violence.

Group work is important as a means of discussing the different forms of violence. It is important to raise awareness that violence is much broader than physical violence. This work needs to done with women and men separately and often generates women seeking workers out for individual support. A successful group work tool is the use of story boards, learned through partnership with the Centre for Refugee Research, University of New South Wales. We have used this with women who have come under the visa category 'Women at Risk'. It is a way of acknowledging previous traumatic experiences of male violence, including systematic rape. Storyboards provide an opportunity for women to share previous experiences, their strengths of survival and to explore strategies in their current situation, to move through to a life free of violence. Doing this in a group setting is very empowering for women. They get support from each other and acknowledgement of their stories, and they encourage each other. Discovering that non-refugee and non-migrant women experience violence provides stimulus to a discussion about male violence as a structure of society in general, rather than being attributed solely to a background of war experiences.

Working at the Macro Level

Strategies to improve the well-being of women have to be also targeted at the community as a whole. 'Many of the main causes of women's morbidity and mortality—in both rich and poor countries—have their origins in societies' attitudes to women, which are reflected in the structures and systems that set policies, determine services and create opportunities' (WHO 2009: 5). As such, domestic violence and other forms of violence are not so much about an individual's anger problems, but rooted in the cultural and historical context of societies; 'Just as domestic abusers justify their actions by evoking patriarchal notions of male ownership, perpetrators of honour violence rationalize it through concepts of honour' (Redfern and Aune 2010: 87). Much of the violence against women is systemic or structural violence that is more implicit and indirect, yet directly affecting their lives and well-being. Irwin and Thorpe strongly argue that 'this insidious violence has to be challenged if the overall violence against women is to stop' (Irwin and Thorpe 1996: 8). Thus, macro-level work is essential for social work practice.

Importantly, public policies need fundamental change across the world to identify the risk and provide care for women (WHO 2009). This includes recognising that symptoms of mental illness can be due to the experience of violence, and intervention needs to be about recognising, acknowledging and responding to the violence and the experience of violence, rather than just labelling women as mentally ill (Rummery 1996). Social action and community work can lead to societal change, but also to communities themselves taking on issues and finding solutions. For social work practitioners, community work provides 'significant opportunities to engage with whole communities in planning to address health and well-being issues in a way that includes marginalised groups and considers the contextual issues that will impact on the program or services' (Taylor, Wilkinson and Cheers 2008: 5). Moreover, working with the whole community accesses a community's capacity and strength (Taylor, Wilkinson and Cheers 2008). Social work practice to address violence against women on a macro level includes public awareness campaigns, working to achieve legislative change and international cooperation, and organising prevention and education programmes (Redfern and Aune 2010). Change needs to occur not only in terms of gender-based inequalities, but also in terms of available resources to women in general and women with mental illness; 'what many of these women want is access to appropriate, affordable housing, a sustainable income, education and employment, friendship and social supports, information and choice, and trust and respect' (Martin 1999; Coppock and Hopton 2000 cited in Martin 2003: 163–164).

Important in community work are cross-sectoral partnerships to 'enable the community field to come together to solve problems, discuss issues, and work on new programs and initiatives' (Taylor, Wilkinson and Cheers 2008: 180). This will benefit the community as a whole, women and children as well as men. For, 'men's relationships with women will be impoverished as long as they continue to control and subordinate women (Sattel 1989)' (Pease 2003: 128). Pease suggests that a consciousness of the cost of violence and the ways violence is reinforced needs to be built and 'collective political actions to challenge institutional violence' needs to be developed (Pease 2003: 138).

The North Queensland Domestic Violence Service undertakes macro-level social welfare practice to end violence in the community (Box 5.4).

Box 5.4
A Practitioner's Reflections by Pauline Woodbridge (Co-ordinator, The North Queensland Domestic Violence Resource Service)

The North Queensland Domestic Violence Resource Service (NQDVRS) was established in 1994. The underpinning philosophy of the service is feminist and our practice is informed by an understanding that domestic violence is about power and control. It is a gender-based manifestation of the social and systemic inequalities between women and men. NQDVRS values empowerment and strengths-based responses to the victims of domestic violence, responding to each woman with the knowledge that she is the expert in her life.

This aspect can be a difficult concept for other parts of our society. Individually, she will be held accountable for the violence by questioners who ask 'Why does she stay?' The effects of the violence can be misdiagnosed as mental illness or as behavioural issues. She may be characterised as a mother who fails to protect her children as she endures frequent violent attacks from the children's father. It may be considered that she provoked the violence, and she too may well believe that and constantly modify her behaviour in attempts to avoid further abuse.

It is because of these misdirected and misguided myths and attitudes that it is important that NQDVRS also acts at the community and policy levels. Raising awareness and educating the local community is an important pathway to meeting our goal of stopping the violence against women and their children. Our public awareness campaigns such as the 'Help is Available' messages on the sides of buses and use of media to get anti-violence and healthy relationships messages out into the community, help with the understanding of the extent and seriousness of domestic violence. We are active in Domestic and Family Violence Prevention

(Box 5.4 Contd.)

(Box 5.4 Contd.)

Month, and the traditional Candlelight Ceremony reminds us all of the deaths of women, children and men as a result of domestic violence.

Using what we have learnt from the women who use our service, we tackle the systemic issues. Dovetail, Townsville's Integrated Approach to Domestic Violence, is a monthly meeting of key organisations, such as the police, the courts and a range of service providers who can monitor the systems, ensure transparency of our actions and solve problem issues. State-based networks are an important way to bring the voices and experiences of the victims and perpetrators to the broader policy development arena.

At the national level, the prime minister convened a National Council to Reduce Violence against Women and their Children, resulting in a National Plan. It is important that the recommendations of the Plan are supported not only by funding but also by people who share the aim of reducing both domestic violence and sexual assault against women. These days, there is a backlash against the feminist analysis of gender-based violence.

Domestic violence can get confused with a plethora of other issues that can serve to obscure or excuse the use of violence. Alcohol, drugs or mental illness are not the cause of domestic violence; the societal and cultural attitudes that support violence against women are where our efforts must be focused if we want to achieve a world where non-violence is the social and accepted norm.

Conclusion

Addressing violence against women needs to be a community concern and community responsibility as highlighted in the practice reflection of Ms Woodbridge. This needs to be a concerted effort and poses four critical challenges:

> 1. to challenge and change existing social and individual attitudes that accept violence against women as 'normal'; 2. to mobilise all sections of the family, community, and society to act to prevent violence against women; 3. to build popular pressure on the State to formulate and implement gender-equitable policies; 4. to bring together diverse local, national, regional, and international efforts working towards ending violence against women' (Oxfam 2004: 2)

Social workers need to raise to meet these challenges.

Across the world, violence against women has been identified as a policy concern and many countries have developed national action plans to address these concerns (Oxfam 2004). However, in practice, violence against women is still often viewed as a private concern, and work to address the roots of violence is challenging. Importantly, this work needs to be undertaken. Work at the community level is essential in order to achieve meaningful cultural and political change (Oxfam 2004).

Clearly, violence against women is a major human rights concern and is impacting women's mental health and as such negatively affecting the well-being of the community as a whole. Addressing women's mental health concerns needs to include an investigation of the potential experience of violence and women's disadvantaged position in society. Working to end violence against women and respond to women who are experiencing mental health issues because of violence needs to involve social workers at the individual, community and societal levels. Violence against women concerns all of us. As social workers we can work to end violence against women.

References

Ashfield, J. 2003. *Taking Care of Yourself and Your Family: A Resource Book for Good Mental Health*. Booleroo Centre, South Australia: Booleroo Centre District Hospital & Health Service, Inc., Jamestown Hospital & Health Service Inc., Orroroo & District Health Service, Inc., Petersborough Solderier's Memorial Hospital & Health Service, Inc.

Avdibegović, E. and O. Sinanović. 2006. 'Consequences of Domestic Violence on Women's Mental Health in Bosnia and Herzegovina', *Croatian Medical Journal*, 47 (5): 730–741.

Bailey, D. 2002. 'Mental Health', in R. Adams, L. Dominelli and M. Payne (eds), *Critical Practice in Social Work*, pp. 169–180. Basingstoke, UK: Palgrave.

Bland, R., N. Renouf and A. Tullgren. 2009. 'Case Management and Community Mental Health', in E. Moore (ed.), *Case Management for Community Practice*, pp. 323–345. South Melbourne, Victoria: Oxford University Press.

Bottorff, J. L., J. L. Oliffe and M. Kelly. 2012. 'The Gender(s) in the Room', *Qualitative Health Research*, 22 (4): 435–440.

Briggs, L. and B. Crowe. 2009. 'Mental Health Social Work in New Zealand', in M. Connolly and L. Harms (eds), *Social Work: Contexts and Practice (Second Edition)*, pp. 222–233. South Melbourne, Victoria: Oxford University Press.

Fraser, S. 1996. 'Reclaiming Our Power, Using Our Anger: Working in the Field of Sexual Violence', in R. Thorpe and J. Irwin (eds), *Women and Violence: Working for Change*, pp. 162–172. Merrickville, New South Wales: Hale and Iremonger.

Harms, L. and M. Connolly. 2009. 'The Art and Science of Social Work', in M. Connolly and L. Harms (eds), *Social Work: Contexts and Practice (Second Edition)*. South Melbourne, Victoria: Oxford University Press.

Harries, M. 2009. 'Mental Health Social Work in Australia', in M. Connolly and L. Harms (eds), *Social Work: Contexts and Practice (Second Edition)*, pp. 234–247. South Melbourne, Victoria: Oxford University Press.

International Federation of Social Workers, International Association of Schools of Social Work and International Council on Social Work. 2012. *The Global Agenda for Social Work and Social Development: Commitments to Actions.*

Irwin, J. and R. Thorpe. 1996. 'Women, Violence and Societal Change', in R. Thorpe and J. Irwin (eds), *Women and Violence: Working for Change*, pp. 1–15. Sydney, New South Wales: Hale and Iremonger.

Johnston, H. B. and T. R. Naved. 2008. 'Spousal Violence in Bangladesh: A Call for a Public-health Response', *Journal of Health, Population and Nutrition*, 26 (3): 366–377

Koski, A. D., R. Stephenson and M. R. Koenig. 2011. 'Physical Violence by Partner during Pregnancy and Use of Prenatal Care in Rural India', *Journal of Health, Population and Nutrition*, 29 (3): 245–254.

Laing, L., J. Irwin and C. Toivonen. 2012. 'Across the Divide: Using Research to Enhance Collaboration between Mental Health and Domestic Violence Services', *Australian Social Work*, 65 (1): 120–135.

Martin, J. 2003. 'Mental Health: Rethinking Practices with Women', in J. Allen, B. Pease and L. Briskman (eds), *Critical Social Work: An Introduction to Theories and Practices*, pp. 155–169. Crows Nest, New South Wales: Allen and Unwin.

Mattes, K. 2010. 'Practice Learning in Community Mental Health', in R. Giles, J. Irwin, D. Lynch and F. Waugh (eds), *In the Field: From Learning to Practice*, pp. 179–194. Melbourne, Victoria: Oxford University Press.

Mullender, A. 2002. 'Persistent Oppressions: The Example of Domestic Violence', in R. Adams, L. Dominelli and M. Payne (eds), *Critical Practice in Social Work*, pp. 63–71. Basingstoke, UK: Palgrave.

Oberoi, A. 2012. 'Domestic Violence and Acid Attacks: A Voice for the Victims', *Utthan: Thoughts towards Development*, 4 (March): 30–32.

Oxfam. 2004. 'Towards Ending Violence against Women in South Asia', *Oxfam Briefing Paper*. Oxfam International.

Pease, B. 2003. 'Men and Masculinities: Profeminist Approaches', in J. Allen, B. Pease and L. Briskman (eds), *Critical Social Work: An Introduction to Theories and Practices*, pp. 124–138. Crows Nest, New South Wales: Allen and Unwin.

Ramazanoglu, C. and J. Holland. 2002. *Feminist Methodology: Challenges and Choices*. London: Sage Publications.

Redfern, C. and K. Aune. 2010. *Reclaiming the F Word: The New Feminist Movement*. Bangalore, India: Books for Change.

Rummery, F. 1996. 'Mad Women or Mad Society: Towards a Feminist Practice with Women Survivors of Child Sexual Assult', in R. Thorpe and J. Irwin (eds), *Women and Violence: Working for Change*, pp. 150–161. Sydney, New South Wales: Hale and Iremonger.

Taylor, J., D. Wilkinson and B. Cheers. 2008. *Working with Communities in Health and Human Services*. South Melbourne, Victoria: Oxford University Press.

Walker, R. and C. Sonn. 2010. 'Working as a Culturally Competent Mental Health Practitioner', in N. Purdie, P. Dudgeon and R. Walker (eds), *Working Together: Aboriginal and Torres Strait Islander Mental Health and Wellbeing Principles and Practice*, pp. 157–180. Canberra: Commonwealth of Australia.

World Health Organization (WHO). 2000. *Women's Mental Health: An Evidence-based Review*. Geneva: WHO.

———. 2009. 'Executive Summary', in WHO, *Women and Health: Today's Evidence, Tomorrow's Agenda*, pp. 1–10. Geneva: WHO.

———. 2012. *Gender and Women's Mental Health: Gender Disparities and Mental Health—The Facts*. Retrieved from http://www.who.int/mental_health/prevention/genderwomen/en/, 8 February 2012.

Web Resources

Australian Domestic Violence & Family Violence Clearinghouse— http://www.adfvc.unsw.edu.au/home.html.

North Queensland Combined Women's Services, Inc.—http://www.thewomenscentre.org.au/

North Queensland Domestic Violence Resource Service—http://www.nqdvrs.org.au/

Oxfam International— Towards Ending Violence against Women in South Asia, http://www.oxfam.org/en/policy/bp66-violence-against-women-sasia

Queensland Centre for Domestic and Family Violence—http://www.noviolence.com.au/

Townsville Multicultural Support Group—http://www.tmsg.org.au/

Victorian Centres Against Sexual Assault—http://www.casa.org.au/index.php?page_id=1

We Can End Violence Against Women—South Asia Regional Campaign, http://www.wecanendvaw.org/

World Health Organization—Gender and Mental Health, http://www.who.int/mental_health/prevention/genderwomen/en/

6

Domestic Work and Migration: A Dual Burden to Women's Mental Health

Kalpana Goel

Introduction

Migration or human movement is a universal phenomenon. Human beings migrate for a number of reasons, such as employment, marriage, associating with family members, displacement and natural calamities. It may be a single migration where an individual makes a move alone or a family migration where the whole family migrates together. It could be for a short duration of a few months or for a longer period where the stay is prolonged from several months to years, or sometimes permanent settlement in the place of destination. This process is temporary, circulatory or permanent in nature. The distance covered through migration is also important as individuals/ family may migrate within the state, interstate in a country, or internationally. Migration also differs by nature of place whether it is rural to rural, rural to urban, urban to urban or urban to rural. Besides this, socio-demographic characteristics of migrants, such as age, sex, marital status, education, occupational status and family status may also differ.

The process of migration can be described as taking in different phases: (*a*) the pre-migration phase that focuses on factors that occur within the country of origin that influence the propensities of women and men to migrate; (*b*) the act of migrating, or national and international laws that encourage/discourage or enable/prevent an individual from migrating; and (*c*) post-migration, or the social, cultural and economic factors of the country of destination that encourage/discourage or enable/prevent an individual from integrating into the host society and settling permanently (Grieco and Boyd 1998).

The report prepared by the International Labour Organization (ILO) in 2010 provides a conservative estimate of 52.6 million women and men employed as domestic workers worldwide. Out of these 52.6 million, 21.5 million (41 per cent) domestic workers work in the Asia–Pacific region alone. This sector is also characterised as highly feminised represented by more than 80 per cent females (ILO 2010).

In India, migration is predominantly regarded as a male phenomenon, with men migrating for economic pursuits. However, there is now recognition of women's migration for reasons of employment (Shanthi 2006). Over the last four decades, there has been a continuous rise in the migration of single women from the regions of Jharkhand, Orissa, Chhattisgarh and Madhya Pradesh to the metropolitan cities in search of a livelihood. A noticeable feature is that the majority of these women are tribal and employed as domestic workers in the metropolitan cities. Migration from the regions of Bihar, Orissa, Chhattisgarh, Jharkhand, Assam and Mizoram, of women who work as domestic servants, has been roughly estimated as 20 million (Social Alert quoted in SCF 2005, cited in Deshingkar and Akter 2009: 24). These women work long hours for poor pay and with limited support and benefits. The reports and research studies undertaken by the government, non-governmental organisations and academics have highlighted the pathetic conditions of these workers (Goel 2005; Shanti 2006). The study described in this chapter relates to impacts on the mental health and well-being of women migrants in India.

The social work profession is concerned with the 'social context' or social environment of the individual as it influences their experiences of health and ill-health. Its purpose is to promote mental health and well-being of individuals, families and communities, and to enhance people's capacity to increase control over their lives (Bland, Renouf and Tullgren 2009: 10). The purpose of this chapter is to identify stressors or risk factors related to migration and domestic work that could lead to mental distress and affect mental health and well-being of migrant women doing domestic work in private households.

A framework proposed by Bhugra and Jones (2001: 219–220) based on 'phases of migration, interlinked with significant life events and chronic ongoing difficulties, as well as personal factors (e.g., self-concept, self-esteem) and relational factors (e.g., social support, cultural identity)' for analysing stressors attached to each stage of migration and its link to psychological disorder has been adopted to examine the psychosocial factors related to mental health and well-being (Table 6.1).

The conditions that may lead to mental health issues and make migrant women vulnerable to psychological disorders have been explored. The aim is to illuminate a range of potential stressors to the mental health of women who are migrants and work as domestic servants. This can help prepare social work professionals to formulate intervention strategies to work with the women migrants who are vulnerable to face mental health issues due to the nature of work and their status as migrants.

Migration and Mental Health

Migration has been defined as 'the process of social change whereby an individual moves from one cultural setting to another for the purposes of settling down either permanently or for a prolonged period' (Bhugra and Jones 2001: 216). To understand the connection between migration and mental health and well-being, it is essential to define what mental health is and what could be termed as mental health issues or mental distress. As per the World Health Organization (WHO) definition,

Table 6.1
Migration Phases and Associate Factors Linked to Psychosocial Distress

Personal Factors	Phases of Migration	Relational Factors
Age	Pre-migration	Economic
Gender		Social
Race		Educational
Personality		
Reasons of migration		
Socio-economic status		
Process	Migration	Educational
Support		Expectations
Single/group migration		Language
Social support	Post-migration	Achievement
Network		Racism
Self-esteem		Ethnic identity
Self-concept		Social isolation
		Unemployment

Source: Adapted from 'Figure 2: Factors in Migration and Psychological Distress' (Bhugra and Jones 2001: 220)

Mental health is not just the absence of mental disorder. It is defined as a state of well-being in which every individual realizes his or her own potential, can cope with the normal stresses of life, can work productively and fruitfully, and is able to make a contribution to her or his community. (WHO 2007)

Any person who is not being able to keep up to mental health is supposedly faced with mental distress or psychosocial problems.

Migration is a complex process where the emigrating person is likely to face changes in life events 'ranging from diet, family and social relations to climate, language, culture' (Carta et al. 2005: 2). These changes are compounded with post-migratory experiences, such as difficulty in finding employment, shelter, learning the norms and culture of the host society, and developing social relationships, all of which may cause considerable stress for the migrant (Bhugra and Gupta 2011).

The migrant experiences changes and needs to adapt to those changes at different levels which may vary in space and time. While it is true that mental illness is caused by multiple factors and cannot be narrowed down to a single factor, it is also important that psychosocial factors play an important role in precipitating the onset of mental illness (Bland, Renouf and Tullgren 2009). For example, inadequate employment, which is described as poorly paid, insecure and unsatisfying, is found to have the poorest mental health outcomes (Burchell 1992; Graetz 1993; Dooley et al. 2000, cited in Rogers and Pilgrim 2010: 59). A longitudinal study by Kasl et al. (1998, cited in Rogers and Pilgrim 2010: 59) rated employment with bad working conditions as the worst compared to unemployment. Migration involves a process of psychosocial loss and change that is regarded as a 'grief process' in the psychiatry of migration. People are affected through loss and change, and experience varying intensity of grief in the migratory process. Inability to express grief may lead to psychological disorders (Carta et al. 2005: 3). Kantor (cited in Kuo 1976: 297) states that 'migration in itself, does not precipitate the development of mental illness. Migration, however, does involve changes in environment which imply adjustments on the part of the migrant. These adjustments may be reflected in improved or worsened mental health'.

A study conducted by Anbesse et al. (2009: 557) with returned Ethiopian migrant domestic workers revealed that 'participants self-identified exploitative treatment, enforced cultural isolation, undermining of cultural identity and disappointment in not achieving expectations as potential threats to their mental well-being'.

There is evidence in the literature that both pre-migratory stressors such as age, low level of education, language, pre-existing physical and mental ill-health (Zahid et al. 2003) and post-migration stressors, such as little contact with family back home, working conditions and sexual abuse are associated with mental health issues.

The Phases of Migration and Migrants' Experiences

The data examined here are obtained from a large study conducted by the author with 150 tribal migrant women who migrated interstate and worked as domestic workers in the Indian metropolitan city Delhi (Goel 2005). The study was based on both quantitative and qualitative data. One hundred and ten migrant women were interviewed, and 40 women migrants participated in the six focus group discussions (FGDs). The findings from the study included the socio-demographic profile of women employed as domestic workers, reasons for their migration, working conditions, implications for marital and sexual life, and remittance. For the purpose of this chapter, I have examined their socio-demographic profile and lived experiences of women who worked as domestic workers, and identified risk factors associated with different phases of migration that could lead to mental distress and affect mental health and well-being. The percentages presented relate to the 110 interviews and excerpts are used from both interviews and FGDs.

Pre-migration Stage

The women were of tribal origin (indigenous women) from three states in India— Jharkhand, Madhya Pradesh and Orissa. The majority (78 per cent) were in the age group of 15–25 years. A large majority (72 per cent) were educated up to primary/middle level, 19 per cent of them were illiterate (with no reading and writing skills), and fewer than 10 per cent had completed secondary level school/college. The majority (86 per cent) were unmarried and all of them had migrated as individual migrants unaccompanied by their family members. These women considered their family income as insufficient to meet basic requirements of food, clothing, education and health (66 per cent). A few of them occasionally got casual work on farms prior to migration, although they worked on farms or in their own households to support the family. The FGDs revealed that despite their owning land and undertaking wage work (by quite a few families of migrant women), their general economic condition was poor. Some of the responses in FGDs were:

It is only sufficient to eat. We don't have money to buy books, clothes and medicine.
If we get work on daily wages, we do. It is not always that we get work.
If we have extra vegetables and rice, sometimes we sell those to get money.
Sometimes we just have one crop, then it becomes difficult.
This year rains were not good, crop was not sufficient.
Though it is sufficient to eat, there is no money to buy seeds and ox.

Migration Stage

The nature of migration influences the overall experience of migrants and exposes them to risk factors that can increase their vulnerability to psychological disorders.

Factors impacting on their vulnerable position include their weak financial condition (62 per cent) and lure to work in cities (52.7 per cent) that led them to take a route hidden from parents to migrate either with friends and village girls or through contractors. However, the majority of them claimed to know the person with whom they migrated as the person was distantly related or known to them in the village. A few facts became known in focus groups; some of the girls mentioned that the clothes and gifts brought by girls working in cities fascinated them.

'Their families were better off than ours were. We also wanted to earn like them. Hence, we approached them to take us.'

One of the FGD respondents said that when she went home she found out families who were in difficulty and motivated their daughters to work in the city. There were mixed feelings about the decision to migrate as the majority (72 per cent) of them felt that it was necessary for them to migrate, whereas others (28 per cent) were regretting their decision as they did not like the people in the city, the nature of work was not good, they felt lonely and were sad because they had discontinued their studies. These women felt depressed and had guilt feelings associated with their decision to migrate.

An article published in Delhi at that time ('Glare on Maid Placement Agencies', *The Hindustan Times,* 7 February 2005) supports this: 'agencies [placement] are encouraging bonded labour in the city and their operation is nothing short of human trafficking. Some maids from poorer areas of the country are exploited both sexually and monetarily.'

Post-migration

SOCIAL AND CULTURAL ISOLATION

Although women reported to be adjusting to city culture, the most problematic aspect was separation from family members and having limited opportunity to visit them either due to financial constraints or dependence on friends and the placement organisation to arrange travel. The majority of the women (82 per cent) went home once in three years. They felt socially and culturally isolated as they were often denied the opportunity to visit friends and go for religious observances. Those who were placed through church organisations were lucky to have weekly time off from work and visited the church and met friends in the placement organisation. A sense of loneliness, isolation and anonymity was visible from the excerpts gathered in the FGDs and interviews.

> She does not allow me to talk to my friends.
> They curse me in bad language.
> Employers usually do not have trust in us. In case I am late in returning they pose many questions.
> In the previous house they locked me inside for three days and went out of station. I felt miserable and did not eat properly.

The women who were brought by agents/contractors who paid their travel cost felt much more isolated and unprepared for work. They were sent for work on the day of arrival without any preparation for a new culture. Many such women who were unable to cope with a new work environment and people ran away from houses and ended up on the streets to be caught by police, who would place them in shelter homes. These women also faced physical and sexual exploitation. Life on the street made these minor girls very vulnerable—physically, psychologically, sexually and financially.

While these women faced discrimination and isolation in the place of destination, they also faced problems in getting married; city girls were not considered worthy enough in the marriage market, as their character was always questionable. According to tribal tradition, the groom's family visits the woman's family for marriage finalisation; however, in this case it became problematic due to distance and inability of women to visit their home frequently to finalise marriage. Many women reported being late for marriage and remained single all their lives, supporting their families back home. This made them psychologically and sexually vulnerable as many (38.7 per cent) expressed a desire to be married and a need for companionship. It is also associated with feelings of alienation/isolation felt by them when they were unable to visit their native village every year.

PRECARIOUS WORKING CONDITION

The nature of work that these women migrants carried out in urban households included menial and arduous kinds of work. They were faced with a plethora of problems at work, such as long working hours (42 per cent), adjustment problem (37 per cent), verbal and physical abuse (27 per cent), no place to sleep and change their clothes (18 per cent), delay in payment (17 per cent), sexual abuse (9.5 per cent) and no weekly day off (14 per cent).

Once employed as domestic workers they were overburdened with work and had limited time to sleep and rest. These conditions were precarious and women felt overwhelmed and exhausted with the workload and linked this to feeling tense, fearful and depressed. Some facts that came out in the focus groups and interviews reveal their distress, fear, sense of worthlessness, denigration and low self-esteem.

> I have to please everyone. If I don't do as per the wish of each member then I am accused. She closely supervises me and interrupts my work, irritating me; it spoils my mood and takes away my mental peace.
> Whatever I do she finds fault in that; calls me again and again and never allows me to finish one task.
> She tries to hit me in anger.
> Keeps an eye on me when I eat.
> I suffer from severe backache since I started working in the house. It is because of too much of cleaning work.
> It is a very boring job. Still I do it because I have no option.
> Though I work up to 12 o'clock, I have to get up at 5 a.m. to prepare food.
> I have to complete a year in this house; otherwise they may not give my salary.

INITIAL EXPERIENCE AT THE WORKPLACE

Almost all of the women (96.7 per cent) felt tense, scared and insecure initially at the workplace and in the different cultural environment. These feelings were triggered because of culturally different ways of doing things, different language, food habits, expectations, and values and norms of the host society. Of these 96.7 per cent, the starting work experience gave rise to tension for almost 81.3 per cent of women, while 72.7 per cent reported being scared with new people, new house and bus routes, and 60 per cent felt insecure at the workplace and in the city. A very small percent (3.3 per cent) said that they did not feel any of these. This showed that the majority were under stress initially. The arduous nature of work, long working hours and difficulties faced in day-to-day existence gave rise to feelings of abandonment (88.7 per cent), feelings of guilt (65.3 per cent), insecurity (63.3 per cent) and depression (57.3 per cent). The women spoke up of being physically and sexually abused in workplaces and traumatic experiences they or their friends had because of this. The following excerpts reveal their feelings and experiences.

> One of my friends became friendly with the neighbour's driver. Once he called her for some work and raped her. She told me about this later on.
>
> When I was seven years I had started working in a house at Mathura. After three years in the house, I was approached by one of their relatives. With great difficulty, I saved myself and informed the employers. After that incident, I did not stay there and came to Delhi with my uncle.
>
> I was in love with a boy who lives in the city and works in a factory. After a few months, I became close to him and spent a night with him. I became pregnant. The boy ditched me. Thereafter I was upset. My employers came to know about it. They were nice, and instead of throwing me out, they provided me shelter and medical care. I had to spend 10,000 [rupees] because I fell ill. My employers gave me loan.
>
> I know one of the girls who became pregnant, she left the organisation thereafter.
>
> One of the girls was molested in the house. She went and complained to the Madam. Instead of believing her, she locked her, called the agency people and told them that she was a characterless girl. She was thrown out of the job for no fault of hers.
>
> A girl was shown male organs in the house; he tried to make sexual advances.
>
> The old man in the house always approaches me when I am in the kitchen and touches me where he should not.

LACK OF SOCIAL SUPPORT

The women left their home town in small groups with their village acquaintances who were all placed in different households to work, with limited opportunity to meet each other. They were new in the city, not aware of bus routes and were not allowed to speak with their friends. They were totally dependent on the employer's family for any support they needed. An exploitative environment at the workplace evidenced that a few were literally not supported even in times of ill-health and abuse.

UNDERMINING SELF-IDENTITY, RACISM AND SENSE OF ACHIEVEMENT

The position of these women in their families was one of subjugation. Their family structure was patriarchal in nature, wherein either the father or the elder brother was the head of the family (70.7 per cent). This kind of family structure promotes gender discrimination and contributes to low self-worth/ esteem for women. Moreover, they belong to a scheduled tribe (a group of people designated as 'Scheduled', on account of their social backwardness, in the Constitution of India). The women also spoke up of facing derogatory remarks; employers changing their names for their own convenience as their names were unfamiliar for them to pronounce and some employers (nearly 20 per cent of them) keeping separate utensils for their eating. Those girls, who were not allowed to use the same utensils, felt cheated or humiliated. They did not like it. One or two girls mentioned that they broke their utensils in anger or ate using the employer's utensils whenever they were not around. In focus groups women reported that their employer:

- 'puts wrong allegations';
- 'gives secondary treatment'; and
- 'does not allow me to speak'.

FINANCIAL EXPLOITATION

The women also claimed that they were the losers and entrapped by placement agencies which exploited them.

> I had to even give a month's salary. And when it did not work out, he wanted another month's salary before he placed me again.

Another excerpt explains the extent of their financial exploitation by their employers.

> Salary is not paid regularly to girls. The employers always keep a few months' salary with them so that they can put pressure on the worker. They don't give the salary when it is required by them to go home; they cut salary on any pretext. At times, girls deposit their salaries with the employers. In a few

instances, girls were paid a lesser amount when they asked for their deposits, as they could not count and maintain proper records of the deposited money.

Financial constraints added to their misery, and lack of money could mean no access to health services and parental support in time of need.

Discussion

The exploration of the lived experiences of these women who migrated from tribal regions of India to work as domestics in the city reveals a disturbing picture of their exploitation, hardships and state of mind in the process of migration. These stressors were likely to have influenced their mental and physical well-being.

International studies on domestic workers in Kuwait highlight low levels of education, being single, and having physical and mental illness as pre-migration vulnerabilities impacting upon early onset of mental disorders in domestic workers (Zahid et al. 2003). Studies have also found a strong relationship between the lowest socio-economic status and mental health as compared to the highest socio-economic status (Bauer et al. 2005, cited in Bland, Renouf and Tullgren 2009: 176). Bland, Renouf and Tullgren (2009: 176) explain this relationship by using three hypotheses: 'social causation' where poverty-related stress factors lead to mental health problems; the 'drift hypothesis' where poverty is a result of mental illness; and a hypothesis of 'other factors' with both poverty and mental illness that could be associated with mental health problems, such as presence of physical illness and domestic violence. In this case, women did reveal economic hardships faced by them and their family members prior to migration, and that was one of the reasons for their migration and doing domestic service. The women also took hidden routes to migrate without informing parents and became entrapped in the hands of agents and mediators who had self-interest in their migration. Considering that factors such as extreme poverty, lower levels of education and being single are some of the stressors that could lead to mental health problems, it is evident that these stressors constituted severe threats for their mental well-being.

There are multiple psychosocial factors associated with post-migration conditions that may play a significant role in posing threat to the mental well-being of migrant women. The post-migration experiences revealed in the discussions clearly pointed to feelings of social isolation, loneliness and boredom in work. Such experiences have been shown to be precipitating mental illness (Weinberg 1967). Women also showed an undermining of their status due to gender, class and ethnicity. Anbesse et al.'s (2009: 566) study with Ethiopian domestic workers who returned to their country for treatment revealed that 'role frustrations and undermining of cultural identity were prominent experiences associated with emotional disturbance in the women'.

In the initial phases of the post-migration period, the majority of the women reported adjustment problems due to different cultural practice, role expectation of employers and fear of new living arrangements in city life. They associated it clearly with feeling stressed, depressed, tense and fearful. These mental problems of adjustment can be described as 'cultural shock'. According to Kuo (1976: 298), 'the cultural shock' theory posits that those immigrants entering a society extremely different from their native community will find it more difficult to adjust than will immigrants with similar 'cultural background'. As these women belonged to a tribal community, spoke a different language and had neither lived in a city nor seen city life, such cultural shock was not unexpected. The adjustment problems can be accentuated because of other 'vulnerability factors and lack of social support and may keep the migrant feeling anxious, confused and angry which may lead to apathy' (Bhugra 2004: 252). Bock (1970, cited in Bhugra 2004: 252) has shown that availability of social support was helpful in preventing depressive symptoms amongst migrants.

In considering the psychosocial stressors, risks attached to the work environment are also crucial. These women did menial jobs and worked in precarious working conditions. Experiences of long working hours without sufficient rest hours, insufficient food, abuse (verbal, physical and sexual), restrictions on meeting friends and financial problems were significant stressors to trigger anxiety and depression amongst those who faced such problems. Wong et al. (2008: 484) have cited several studies revealing 'financial and job-related difficulties' (Thompson et al. 2002), language barrier (Vedar and Virtra 2005), poor living conditions (Papadopoulos et al. 2004; Wong et al. 2003) and discrimination (Yeh et al. 2003) as stressors to mental health problems with different groups of migrants. The studies carried out by Brown and Harris (1989) and Brown et al. 1995 (cited in Anbesse et al. 2009: 564) showed that 'severe life events and chronic difficulties, particularly those characterized by humiliation, entrapment and defeat, have a well-established role in bringing about episodes of mental disorder'. This is further supported by Gilbert and Allan (1998) who postulated a model to understand depression highlighting entrapment and defeat as key factors.

In this case, it can be explained by women feeling entrapped in the vicious circle of working for the same employer in spite of being humiliated and exploited financially, unable to visit family in their place of origin to fix their marriage and being humiliated by their own community as being a city girl whose character is in doubt. All these can be seen as entrapment and social defeat which could lead to depression.

The Direction for Social Work Practice

Social workers are in a unique position to provide early intervention services to clients faced with issues of mental health as they work in a variety of practice settings and come across clients who are faced with different life issues such as homelessness, domestic violence, physical illness and mental illness. Social workers work with grass roots–level community organisations and it is likely that they become aware of social justice and human rights issues faced by migrant women. Recognising that migrant women, especially those who come from a different cultural background, have issues that are specific to their context is the first step in any helping relationship. Having a culturally sensitive approach (Schlesinger and Devore 1995) will help reduce biases, misunderstanding and miscommunication in helping relationships and that will help in making right assessments and planning early intervention strategies.

While women migrate to make their lives better and seek employment wherever it is easily available to them, it is likely that they will get entrapped with some employers or placement organisations that conceal their money and exploit them financially. Social workers need to mobilise funding from government and non-government sources to establish residential homes or shelter homes for emergency accommodation so that these women feel secure to step out from exploitative situations and can rebuild their lives. Social workers working in residential institutions should be aware of the specific needs of this young population group.

Social workers employed in service agencies need to implement programmes and services to promote mental well-being for those women who are vulnerable to different life stressors as a result of the migration process and settlement in a new place. Some of the programmes that might be useful in building capacities and resilience for migrant women may include life skill training to develop coping skills to deal with day-to-day challenges of work and being single young women in a new socio-cultural milieu. These life skills include negotiation skills, assertiveness training, communication skills, relationship building, functional literacy and numeracy, and familiarisation with services and civic infrastructure.

The other set of programmes could include self-enrichment through building self-image and self-worth. Social workers are in a unique position to assist in rebuilding their loss of identity and worth by looking at their strengths and capacities, and valuing their identity. They can skilfully apply narrative therapies, a strengths-based approach and appreciative techniques to enhance and boost their self-image, and build confidence. Yoga and spiritual education could also benefit them in building coping abilities.

The importance of support groups and social networks in mitigating effects of 'culture shock' and reducing the impact of depression has been recognised in the literature (Bhugra 2004: 252). This could go a long way towards taking care of the emotional/psychological problems faced by these domestic workers. It will also help them to become confident, less vulnerable and rely on peer support that is non-exploitative and protective of them.

Social workers need to work with migrant women to assist them realise their strengths and their rights to have a decent life and demand their dues. Social workers also need to work with the larger community to make them aware of workers' rights and advocate for humane conditions for domestic workers. The issue of trafficking by placement agents/mediators needs to be tackled at a broader policy level where legislation needs to be framed to stop human traffickers from fulfilling their own selfish motives.

Conclusion

It is evident that migration in itself is a complex process that entails a series of efforts on the part of migrants who need to make adjustments and adapt to different conditions to successfully settle in a new place. In the process of migration and at different stages of migration, they come across life-changing events that pose a threat to their physical and mental well-being. In this chapter, I have argued that migrant women, particularly those who come from disadvantaged and marginalised sections of society, are vulnerable and their mental well-being is threatened in an environment that poses risks to their physical, social, cultural and mental statuses. While undeniably women might be benefiting from migration and paid work, women migrants' mental well-being is being influenced by pre-migration stressors such as poverty, low social status and low level of education, combined with post- migration stressors like social isolation, loneliness, arduous working condition, abuse (physical, psychological and sexual), lack of social support and loss of identity. Assuming that the pull and push factors associated with migration cannot be ignored, it being a larger development issue, it needs to be addressed at the macro level; however, social work professionals are in a unique position to respond to the needs of women migrant populations who work in precarious working conditions. Social workers can use innovative techniques such as capacity building, life skill training, strengths-based approaches, and advocacy within a human rights and social justice framework to challenge the status quo and help those who are marginalised and disadvantaged.

References

Anbesse, B., C. Hanlon, A. Alem, S. Packer, and R. Whitley. 2009. 'Migration and Mental Health: A Study of Low-Income Ethiopian Women Working in Middle Eastern Countries', *International Journal of Social Psychiatry*, 55 (6): 557–568.

Bhugra, D. 2004. 'Migration and Mental Health', *Acta Psychiatrica Scandinavica*, 109 (4): 243–258.

Bhugra, D. and S. Gupta. 2011. *Migration and Mental Health*. Cambridge, UK: Cambridge University Press.

Bhugra, D. and P. Jones. 2001. 'Migration and Mental Illness', *Advances in Psychiatric Treatment*, 7 (3): 216–222.

Bland, R., A. Tullgren, and N. Renouf. 2009. *Social Work Practice in Mental Health: An Introduction*. Crows Nest, New South Wales: Allen and Unwin.

Burchell, B. 1992. 'Towards a Social Psychology of the Labour Market: Or Why We Need to Understand the Labour Market Before We Can Understand Unemployment', *Journal of Occupational and Organizational Psychology*, 65 (4): 345–354.

Carta, M. G., M. Bernal, M. C. Hardoy and J. M. Haro-Abad. 2005. 'Migration and Mental Health in Europe (The State of the Mental Health in Europe Working Group: Appendix 1)', *Clinical Practice and Epidemiology in Mental Health*, 1 (1): 13.

Deshingkar, P. and S. Akter. 2009. 'Migration and Human Development in India', *Human Development Research Papers*, HDRP-2009-13. New York: Human Development Report Office, United Nations Development Programme.

Gilbert, P. and S. Allan. 1998. 'The Role of Defeat and Entrapment (Arrested Flight) in Depression: An Exploration of an Evolutionary View', *Psychological Medicine*, 28 (3): 585–598.

Goel, K. 2005. 'Women Domestic Workers in Delhi: A Study on Tribal Migrants', Unpublished PhD thesis, University of Delhi, India.

Graetz, B. 1993. 'Health Consequences of Employment and Unemployment: Longitudinal Evidence for Young Men and Women', *Social Science and Medicine*, 36 (6): 715–724.

Grieco, E. M. and M. Boyd. 1998. 'Women and Migration: Incorporating Gender into International Migration Theory', *Working Paper Series*, WPS 98–139, Centre for the Study of Population, Florida State University.

International Labour Organization. 2010. 'More Than 52 Million Domestic Workers Worldwide', 9 January. Retrieved from http://www.ilo.org/global/about-the-ilo/newsroom/news/WCMS_200937/lang--en/index.htm, 9 March 2014.

Keung, Wong; D. F. Yan P., Lo, E. and Hung, M. 2003. 'Mental Health and Social Competence of Mainland Chinese Immigrant and Local Youth in Hong Kong: A Comparison', *Journal of Ethnic and Cultural Diversity in Social Work*, 12 (1): 85–110.

Kuo, W. 1976. 'Theories of Migration and Mental Health: An Empirical Testing on Chinese–Americans', *Social Science & Medicine* (1967), 10 (6): 297–306.

Papadopoulos, I., Lees, S., Lay, M. and Gebrehiwot, A. 2004. 'Ethiopian Refugees in the UK: Migration, Adaptation and Settlement Experiences and Their Relevance to Health', *Ethnicity and Health*, 9 (1): 55–73.

Rogers, A. and D. Pilgrim. 2010. *A Sociology of Mental Health and Illness*. Buckingham, UK: Open University Press.

Schlesinger, E. G. and W. Devore. 1995. 'Ethnic Sensitive Social Work Practice: The State of the Art', *Journal of Sociology and Social Welfare*, 22 (1): 29–58.

Shanthi, K. 2006. 'Female Labour Migration in India: Insights from NSSO Data', *Working Paper*, 4/2006, Madras School of Economics, Madras.

Thompson, S., L. Manderson, N. Woelz-Stirling, A. Cahill and M. Kelaher. 2002. 'The Social and Cultural Context of the Mental Health of Filipinas in Queensland', *Australian and New Zealand Journal of Psychiatry*, 36 (5): 681–687. Doi: 10.1046/j.1440-1614.2002.01071.x

Veder, P., and E. Virtra. 2005. 'Language, Ethnic Identity, and the Adaptation of Turkish Immigrant Youth in the Netherlands and Sweden', *International Journal of Intercultural Relations*, 29(3): 317-337.

Weinberg, S. K. 1967. 'The Relevance of the Forms of Isolation to Schizophrenia', *International Journal of Social Psychiatry*, 13 (1): 33–41.

Wong, D., X. He, G. Leung, Y. Lau, and Y. Chang. 2008. 'Mental Health of Migrant Workers in China: Prevalence and Correlates', *Social Psychiatry and Psychiatric Epidemiology*, 43 (6): 483–489.

World Health Organization (WHO). 2007. 'What is Mental Health?'. Retrieved from http://www.who.int/features/qa/62/en/, 9 March 2014.

Yeh, C. J. 2003. 'Age, Acculturation, Cultural Adjustment, and Mental Health Symptoms of Chinese, Korean, and Japanese Immigrant Youths', *Cultural Diversity and Ethnic Minority Psychology*, 9 (1): 34.

Zahid, M. A., A. Fido, R. Alowaish, M. A. M. Mohsen and M. A. Razik. 2003. 'Psychiatric Morbidity among Housemaids in Kuwait III: Vulnerability Factors', *International Journal of Social Psychiatry*, 49 (2): 87–96.

Web Resources

International Labour Organization—Publications on Domestic Work, http://www. ilo.org/travail/Whatsnew/WCMS_173363/lang--en/index.htmhttp://www.ilo. org/travail/Whatsnew/WCMS_173363/lang--en/index.htm
International Organization of Migration—About Migration, http://www.iom.int/ cms/en/sites/iom/home.htmlhttp://www.iom.int/cms/en/sites/iom/home.html
Mind Health Connect—Service Directory, http://www.mindhealthconnect.org.au/ directoryhttp://www.mindhealthconnect.org.au/directory
National Domestic Workers Movement—http://ndwm.org/http://ndwm.org/
World Health Organization—Mental Health Publications, http://www.who.int/ mental_health/resources/publications/en/index.htmlhttp://www.who.int/ mental_health/resources/publications/en/index.html

7

Mental Health Issues of Home-based Elderly and Geriatric Social Work Intervention

Sheeba Joseph

Introduction

'The ageing process is of course a biological reality which has its own dynamic, largely beyond human control. However, it is also subject to the constructions by which each society makes sense of old age. In the developed world, chronological time plays a paramount role. The age of 60 or 65, roughly equivalent to retirement ages in most developed countries is said to be the beginning of old age. In many parts of the developing world, chrono-logical time has little or no importance in the meaning of old age. Other socially constructed meanings of age are more significant such as the roles assigned to older people; in some cases, it is the loss of roles accompanying physical decline, which is significant in defining old age. Thus, in contrast to the chronological milestones which mark life's stages in the developed world, old age in many developing countries is seen to begin at the point when active contribution is no longer possible (Gorman 2000). Certain physical signs mark an individual as old: toothlessness, balding or grey hair, hunched back, lameness, deafness. Increasing debility is the clearest signal that one is becoming old. People can be considered old because of certain changes in their activities or social roles. For example, people may be con-sidered old when they become grandparents, or when they begin to do less or different work during retirement. This chapter discusses the psychological problems faced by the home-based elderly. An attempt is made to examine the well-being and to make a profile of the health problems and the leisure time activities of elderly at home.

Natural Changes

Like every other period in the lifespan, old age is characterised by certain physical and psychological changes. Decline comes partly from physical and partly from psychological factors. The physical cause of decline is a change in the body cells not due to a specific disease but due to the aging process. But the elderly are more prone to diseases, syndromes and sickness than any other age group. The main changes are characterised by hair loss, wrinkles and liver spots on the skin, agility and slower reaction time. There is a consistent decline in the ability to see at low levels of illumination and a turn down in colour sensitivity. The ability to hear will decrease and marked changes in taste due to the atrophy of the taste buds in the tongue and inner surface of the cheeks. There is often a common physical decline, and people become less active.

There will be general reduction in the speed with which the individual reaches a conclusion in both inductive and deductive reasoning. The elderly tend to have poor recent memories but better remote memories. Generally, there is a decline in the sexual potency during the sixties, which continues as age advances.

Over the past few years, the world's population has continued on its remarkable transition path from a state of high birth and death rates to one characterised by low birth and death rates. At the heart of that transition is the increased number and proportion of the elderly. Ageing is an inevitable phenomenon in all biological species. It is a relentless process in life, leading to its extinction. While the developed regions of the world have already experienced their economic, social and medical consequences, the developing countries are currently facing a similar phenomenon. The improved standard of living and the advanced medical care have lengthened the average human lifespan.

Rao (1996) has suggested that ageing is not biological alone, but that psychological and sociological factors too are responsible for major changes in roles, status, health, looks and persona independents. Certain recent developments have given rise to some stress and strains that have increased the problems of the aged. These are

- Technological developments have caused tremendous changes in lifestyles and values. This greatly reduces dependence on age.
- High cost as well as lack of availability of rental accommodation in cities work as constraints in keeping the aged together.

- Migration of the younger generation leaving behind the aged tends to increase the problems of isolation and loneliness for the old staying behind.
- With the increasing employment of women in offices and factories and rise in career aspirations, there is reduced attention towards the older members, hence resulting in the establishment of nuclear families.

Old age is a part of the lifecycle about which there are numerous myths. This is characterised by a lack of social autonomy, unloved and neglected by both the family members and friends. They pose a threat to the living standards of younger age groups by being a burden to them. In other words, the elderly consume without producing. Ageing is a universal process. However, concern about the ageing of population is a relatively new phenomenon, which has come up very recently because of the significantly large increase in the number of the aged. In a way, the ageing of the society reflects triumph of civilisation over illness, poverty and misery.

Indian society is slowly getting transformed to be an industrialised modern urban society. These changes are responsible for causing many changes within the family structure. The joint family system is being replaced by the small nuclear family system. All these changes are the problem of the aged that are not entirely due to aging but to a large extent to the psychological environment—diminishing support systems and their inability to adapt to changes because of fear of changes. At this critical juncture of life, family has an important role to play.

The elderly wish to lead a happy and satisfying life with their family. However, not all elderly are found to succeed in adapting and adjusting to life's later circumstances. For some, life becomes almost intolerable due to the changing attitude of the younger members of the family, consequent to unsatisfactory financial and health status, low adjustment on the part of the elderly, thus resulting in discord between the elderly and the young and the young may stay away from parents or relocate them into an institution, slamming the hopes and aspirations of the elderly in vain.

The global scenario of aging is increasing faster than ever before. The number of elderly people is growing around the world chiefly because more children are reaching adulthood. In most parts of the world, women live, on an average, longer than men. In the United States, in the late 1990s, life expectancy at birth was 80 years for women and 73 years for men. In Western countries, the current lifespan is 80 years. Even in developing countries such as India, the average lifespan has increased from 32 years in

1951 to 65 years in 2005 and is estimated to cross 76 years by 2031. It is expected that by 2025 nearly 71 per cent of the world's elderly population will be living in the developing countries. As per the 2001 Census, 7.7 million people in India were of 60 years and is expected to reach 8.2 million by 2011. In India, lifespan for both sexes has increased. Now, India has the second largest elderly population in the world.

Ageing in India

India is the second largest country in the world, with 72 million elderly persons above 60 years of age as of 2001 as compared to China's 127 million. According to the projection, the elderly in the age group 60 and above is expected to increase from 72 million in 2001 to 171 million in 2031 and further to 301 million in 2051. Population above 70 years is projected to increase from 27 million in 2001 to 132 million in 2051. The elderly persons of 80 years and above are likely to improve their numbers from 5.4 million in 2021 to 32 million in 2051. A United Nations (UN) study report (2003) points out that by 2050 the ratio of youngsters and elderly will be equal. The percentage of elderly in the world population will increase rapidly from 9.5 per cent in 1995 to 20.7 per cent in 2050 and 30.5 per cent in 2150. According to the demographic estimation, the annual growth rate of the aggregate elderly population is 2 per cent in the developing countries.

The earlier social institutions and practices that we had, such as joint family, village, panchayat and caste system had to ensure a minimum security and protection to all, including the aged. The disintegration of the joint family system and impact of economic changes has brought into sharp focus the problems which the elderly now face in the country. A large number of adult members leave their homes in search of jobs. They may find jobs in some distant places and may not be able to look after their parents.

Common Problems of Old Age

Old age is a time when people need support and help from others. They may need human support on which they can rely; they feel happy and courageous when their loved ones are near them. When they feel this is lost, they may have emotional insecurity.

SOCIAL PROBLEMS

The disintegrating joint family system, rapid industrialisation and urbanisation and changing social values have together caused serious problems for the aged. They are treated like an unavoidable burden if they cease to remain productive members.

Employment is very important to the old persons not only for self support and independence but also for a healthy living and self-respect. Many of the problems confronting the aged may be attributed to a considerable degree of anxiety over loss of income, followed by loss of status which was previously enjoyed when engaged in such occupation. Majority of elderly people have financial problems. Many people who belong to the lower middle class group have economic problems. They do not have enough savings to take care of their needs so they depend mostly on their children. After retirement, their income generally decreases by 50 per cent or more. Older persons without adequate income cannot enjoy life and become a burden for their family. Such conditions prevent them from leading a satisfying life in the later years.

The quote from Sankarachari,'Your family is attached to you as long as you earn, with frail body and no income, no one in the house will ever care for you.'

The former joint family system is breaking down fast and at present, the elderly are left to the mercy of their own resources. The Hindu joint family system provided social security to the aged and took proper care of them. But now the situation has undergone a big change. The institution of 'joint family' has started disintegrating rapidly due to recent changes in social values, social structure and economy resulting from industrialisation and urbanisation and consequent morbidity. Poverty, unemployment, underemployment and inflation have rendered the family members unable to discharge their duties towards the aged.

Suitable housing conditions are important—housing of appropriate size, which offers safety, comfort and opportunity of choice between privacy and contact with the community.

SOCIAL ISOLATION

Social isolation and loneliness are also major aspects of old age. The concept of isolation implies a relative lack of participation in social relationships. Social relationship enables one to have social contact, interaction and communication. The isolation refers to two stages: Firstly, social isolation of the individual from his/her primary group, family and work. Secondly, one is isolated from the larger community.

Loneliness is an undesirable feelings of lack or loss of companionship. Many isolated people do not feel loneliness and some integrated people do feel lonely. Isolation may be the result of depression; loneliness and being alone are not the same.

The sociological aspects of individual ageing are concerned with changes in the circumstances or situations of the individual as a member of the family, community and society. Ageing is a time of physical and social loss, loss of children, spouse, friends, jobs and property and physical appearances. It is not a disease or a degenerative force, but an inherent part of life. The term old age usually implies some notion of decline and deterioration in health, vitality, social usefulness and independence.

Physical Illness

Physical illness is the most obvious problem among old persons. Many have one or more chronic health conditions, the most common of which are high blood pressure, heart diseases, arthritis and rheumatism. Older people take longer to recover from illness. Older people are less often afflicted with acute health problems such as cold or infectious diseases, than are younger persons. Severe chronic health problems can contribute to an aged person becoming socially isolated and in turn result in loneliness and depression.

Nutrition is a major problem among the elderly. Many live alone and there is a tendency for such persons not to consume a well-balanced meal because they believe that preparing meals for one person is too much trouble. Low income is another reason that malnutrition is common among older individuals. Some research indicates that many consider housing to be a major problem during later years of life. Suitable housing condition is important for anyone regardless of age.

A study conducted by Darshan and Ritu (2010) found the disease pattern of ear, nose and throat (ENT) and head–neck region in the geriatric population. A total of 3,303 patients were examined. Most of the patients suffered from ENT diseases. Malignancy of larynx was the most common cancer found in the study population. The number of geriatric patients examined in the outpatient department (OPD) was small as the elderly people had ardent belief in home remedies, traditional medicine and spiritual cures. So, by reforming policies and making innovative planning, we should try to change the quality of life of the elderly and add life to years, thus increasing longevity by reducing morbidity.

OCCUPATIONAL PROBLEMS

Occupational problems of ageing are generally accepted that the lack of employment security of older workers constitutes a significant social problem. The ever-increasing complexity of technological innovations has produced a labour market in which many older workers find themselves on the margins without any secure attachment to a job or even actually displaced and unable to find employment.

FINANCIAL PROBLEMS

Ageing to a certain extent is socioculturally determined. Elderly migrants are particularly lonely and isolated, especially when there are language barriers. Whether ageing can be termed successful depends on the interaction between the individual and his/her environment. Several recent studies emphasise the threats to self-identity and adaptive behaviour, which can arise from unsuitable, intrusive, demanding or limiting environments. Most of the elderly do have a living child, but the ability and willingness of that child to take care for an aged parent is decreasing. Family separations are likely to result in an aged individual living alone.

It is the women who usually take care of the elderly person in the family. However, in the present world they are finding it necessary to work outside the home both to augment the income and also to find personnel satisfaction. Women have been traditional caregivers for elderly parents and their removal from home during the time when elderly parents need increasing amounts of assistance with activities of daily living suggests that either the elderly will be less welcome in the home or will be a source of increased stress within the family. Once the elderly commanded great respect due to the traditional norms and values of Indian society.

PSYCHOLOGICAL PROBLEMS

The psychological changes that occur with age are, firstly, a steady decline in the speed with regard to physical activity. Secondly, there is an obvious loss in the realm of memory. 'Peripheral memories' are more important because these are involved in many aspects of mental activity. These peripheral memories when replaced by other pre-occupations or when intruded upon by much older memories result in making a person disoriented to time and place. Thirdly, psychological change is a gradual loss in the area of learning. The acquisition of a new skill is very slow and poor. Fourthly, there is a loss of confidence in their own ability and judgement. There is also a tendency among the old people to blame others when things go wrong. Another escape resorted to by the aged is withdrawal from social contacts. It may not only result in physical loss of contact but also brooding over the past or in one's own thoughts resulting in mental withdrawal. Older people also become more easily and quickly tired than younger people. Loud noises and bright lights cause fatigue.

Anantharaman (1981) found that loss of income, more free time, loss of friendship and work environment may be resources for negative self-conception in old age. Another psychological problem of older persons is the feeling of uselessness. Psychological and environmental factors leading to the emotional living of the aged are a sense of being unwanted, a sense of uselessness, a feeling of boredom due to the absence of a goal in life, the speed of modern living with changes in environment placing great stress and strain on the aged and finally the complexity of demands and natural thoughts of approaching death. A man's masculinity and feeling of importance is strongly associated with work and job performance. When this is taken away, his source of identity is removed. Retired men feel more useless than their wives.

Lena et al. (2009) showed in their study that a major proportion of the elderly were out of workforce, partially or totally dependent on others, and suffering from health problems with a sense of neglect by their family members. There is a growing need for intervention to ensure the health of this vulnerable group and to create a policy to meet the care and needs of the disabled elderly.

A psychologically devastating problem for older persons is that of isolation and loneliness. As people grow older in our society, there is a tendency to become more isolated with fewer contacts with peers and companions with whom he/she has shared the past. Forced retirement at the age of 60 and chronic health problems remove older persons from the mainstream of life. Some decline in the extended family system, many elderly do not live with their children as they often did in the past; their children become autonomous. This makes older parents concerned about being a burden on their children and hence this contributes further to their isolation.

Gupta (2005) explained that a survey was recently conducted by Age Care India, a national voluntary organisation, claiming that most of the aged are neglected and leading a woeful life. In urban areas, they have been isolated while this process has also started in the rural areas. The trend is mainly due to the growing cost of living, and the younger generation wanting to live an independent life. In many cases, the aged parents are forced to do odd jobs despite their poor health and are ill-treated on one pretext or the other by their children.

The increased isolation of many older persons leads to increased feeling of loneliness, which is one of the most painful problems during the later years. Research indicates that as many as 50 per cent of older women and 25 per cent of older men are abnormally anxious and worried. The older persons are likely to be irritable, quarrelsome and contrary. Fears and worries, disappointment and feelings of persecution are far more common than the pleasant emotional states.

Apathy is a psychological change where the old person takes no interest in himself/herself/friends/surroundings and leads almost an isolated life. This may come after an illness or gradually because there is nobody to care for him/her or to give affection and nobody is interested in his/her welfare. Hoarding is a common characteristic of old people. They have an inclination to gather things and to never throw them away. Aggressiveness and discontentment is another characteristic of old age behaviour. A sense of reduced power and position within the social environment could be the reason behind this.

Old people are generally quarrelsome because of their inability to accept disabilities and hence become irritable. Grumbling is usually a result of low morale and is common among old people.

Senile psychosis directly corresponds to the softening of the brain due to actual deterioration of the brain tissues and lack of adequate supply of blood to the brain. A mild case may show deterioration and being unaware of the month and the year; more severe would be not knowing where he/she is living, and not being able to recognise people.

PHYSICAL ABILITY

An old person does not have the physical ability of a young person. Walking can be an effort. Crossing a road can be impossible without assistance. It is common to hear of old people being knocked down by vehicles on the roads. They just cannot handle the traffic anymore.

LIVING ALONE

In the old days, most people did not go very far from their birthplace and thus families usually stayed together. The family unit was strong and practical. Today the family unit is breaking apart as young men and women travel widely in search of better jobs. So, the chances are that the old people are left alone and neglected. Sometimes they are not wanted by their children at all. The luckier ones may have a child or two staying with them. The less fortunate ones may have to pine their lives away in an old folks' home or in their now-empty house that once was filled with the sound of children's laughter. This neglect is a real problem in our society and what the old dread the most—being unwanted and uncared for in times of need.

INDIFFERENCE AND NEGLECT

There are other problems too which the old people face, but none can be as bad as the indifference and neglect of the young. The young have no time for the old even though the old have virtually no time left.

H. R. Sharma (2005) noted that even in villages, the situation is deteriorating. The status of the elders as advisors and spokespersons of the village and as guides of a family is no longer in evidence; on the other hand, the elderly people find it difficult to adjust with their own sons and daughters because of the generation gap and their varying perceptions. The result is that the seniors have to yield to the wishes of the juniors in the interest of peace in the family. If not, the life of the elderly becomes tormented and they develops a feeling of unwantedness. Thus, the aged suffer from numerous familial, social, economic, psychological and emotional problems.

Objectives of the Study

Against this backdrop, the study proposes to understand the adjustment problems shared by aged people living in their homes. By approaching and investigating the families, this study aims at the following:

- Examining the psychological problems faced by the elderly in a home-based context.
- Understanding the degree of well-being of the home-based elderly.
- Making a profile of common health problems faced by the elderly at home.
- Making a profile of leisure activities of the elderly in a home-based context.

Hypotheses

- Higher the family support, lower would be the psychological (stress, anxiety and depression) problems.
- There is a significant degree of negative co-relation between well-being and psychological status of the elderly.

Research Methods

Sample

The study included elderly participants residing at home. The elderly persons of both the sexes living at home were identified using the purposive random technique. Thus, a total number of 50 participants constituted the sample. The sample was selected from all socio-economic backgrounds in and around Bhopal district of Madhya Pradesh.

Tools and Techniques

The study was based on the quantitative survey and the qualitative interview methods. Appropriate tools were selected and constructed for data collection. It included measuring the psychological problems, the degree of family support as perceived by the old people in the family and health problems that included both the psychological and the physiological health indicators of the elderly people to examine their current health issues. The study also put an effort to find leisure time activities for the home-based elderly.

Patient Generated Index (PGI): A Well-being Scale (developed by Verma and Verma, 1988) was used to examine the subjective well-being of elderly. It has 20 items giving a single score. The score ranges from 1 to 20 and the scoring is done by adding the total items.

Leisure activities record: This record gives a list of 24 leisure time activities that were compiled by Willigen and Chadha (1990). The activities were classified under four major categories: cultural, physical, social and solitary activities.

Common ailments of old age checklist: This is a self-constructed list of ailments associated with old age. The respondents tick mark against those applicable to them.

Results and Discussion

The study focused on a four-fold objective and examined the physical and psychological problems of the home-based elderly. It was very evident that the elderly were facing multiple problems—physical, psychological and adjustment problems with the younger generation and social problems.

In Table 7.1, it is explicit from the findings that the well-being of the elderly in the age group of 60 to 65 years (M = 8.75) experiences better well-being than the other groups. When the measure of anxiety was analysed, there were no significant variations among the age groups from 66 to 70,

Table 7.1
Measure of Well-being, Anxiety and Depression due to Age

Age of the respondents		Well-being of the respondents	Measure of anxiety	Level of depression
60–65	Mean	8.7500	40.5000	22.0000
	N	16	16	16
	SD	3.25576	4.66190	4.95311
66–70	Mean	10.1429	36.7143	20.8571
	N	14	14	14
	SD	5.17177	3.95024	4.73704
71–75	Mean	8.0000	38.1875	23.5000
	N	16	16	16
	SD	3.96653	3.70978	4.04969
76–80	Mean	7.5000	38.7500	22.5000
	N	4	4	4
	SD	1.91485	2.21736	3.31662
Total	Mean	8.8000	38.5600	22.2000
	N	50	50	50
	SD	4.03050	4.19017	4.49943

N = number; SD = standard deviation.

71 to 75 and 76 to 80. However, it was interesting to know that the elderly in the age groups 60 and 65 years had a high level of anxiety (M = 40.5) when compared to their counterparts.

The research found significant correlation between many variables. A significant positive correlation was found among the variables such as anxiety, depression and social problems. The study evinced that well-being and anxiety, well-being and depression, physiological and psychological health and well-being has significant negative correlation as mentioned in Table 7.2.

Leisure time activities are a source of coping with physical and emotional stress and a source of successful ageing. As life expectancy increases, the involvement in leisure time activities also increases. The present research analysed the involvement of the elderly in leisure time activities. The activities were grouped into solitary and physical activities, social and cultural activities. Leisure time activities that are solitary in nature are reading newspaper, listening to radio, viewing TV, attending movies and reading religious books. Involving in household activities, personal hobbies, and morning and evening walks are other ways of spending time. The elderly show greater interest in various social activities such as visiting friends, looking after their grandchildren, visiting relatives and so on. The age group highly involved in leisure time activities is from 76 to 80 years (M = 16.0000). The respondents in the age group 66 to 70 years showed less interest in leisure activities (M = 14.0714).

The common health problems shared by the elderly are impairment of vision and hearing, blood pressure, bowel irregularities, backache, arthritis, chest pain, short-term memory problems, diabetes, heart diseases, cough, giddiness, weakness, prostates, cancer and insomnia. The mean score was found to be very high for vision impairment, blood pressure and backache than for other problems. In this context, many of the elderly people are not physically fit. They need proper and timely check-up and follow-ups. It is the family members' responsibility to make sure timely access to health care facilities for the older people are catered to.

Moreover, we can find hundreds of reasons that directly affect the elderly. However, in the research context, it was observed that atmosphere, food, medical care, lack of support from family members and social problems contribute to stressful situations for the elderly at home. They also feel the absence of peer group from where they can get comfort and enjoyment. To a great extent, interaction with the social support network will help them overcome their stress and loneliness. The social interactions and activities help people build a bond with each other to perform as an active well-being.

Table 7.2
Correlational Analysis

		Measure of anxiety	Level of depression	Well-being of the respondents	Social problems faced by the respondents	Family support of the respondents	Psychological and physical health
Measure of anxiety	Pearson Correlation	1	.609(**)	-.469(**)	.523(**)	.618(**)	-.436(**)
	Sig. (2-tailed)	.	.000	.001	.000	.000	.002
	N	50	50	50	50	50	50
Level of depression	Pearson Correlation	.609(**)	1	-.506(**)	.347(*)	.607(**)	-.747(**)
	Sig. (2-tailed)	.000	.	.000	.014	.000	.000
	N	50	50	50	50	50	50
Well-being of the respondents	Pearson Correlation	-.469(**)	-.506(**)	1	-.563(**)	-.479(**)	.678(**)
	Sig. (2-tailed)	.001	.000	.	.000	.000	.000
	N	50	50	50	50	50	50
Social problems faced by the respondents	Pearson Correlation	.523(**)	.347(*)	-.563(**)	1	.588(**)	-.528(**)
	Sig. (2-tailed)	.000	.014	.000	.	.000	.000
	N	50	50	50	50	50	50
Family support of the respondents	Pearson Correlation	.618(**)	.607(**)	-.479(**)	.588(**)	1	-.526(**)
	Sig. (2-tailed)	.000	.000	.000	.000	.	.000
	N	50	50	50	50	50	50
Psychological and physical health	Pearson Correlation	-.436(**)	-.747(**)	.678(**)	-.528(**)	-.526(**)	1
	Sig. (2-tailed)	.002	.000	.000	.000	.000	.
	N	50	50	50	50	50	50

* Correlation is significant at the 0.05 level (2 tailed).
** Correlation is significant at the 0.01 level (2 tailed).

The social and peer group interactions influenced in overcoming the depressive nature of the subjects through engaging in different activities that transform depression in the hidden areas of their memory. Generally speaking, most of the older people in India do not live alone. They attach themselves to their kin and kith in some way or the other. Thus, they find themselves in a web of socio-familial matrix. Therefore, the extent to which these socio-familial interactions are perceived to be meaningful and satisfying is to the extent to which they contribute, in turn, to general satisfaction. If the relationships with peers, children and others are satisfying, it would contribute to general satisfaction in their life. Though India is getting industrialised, modernised and urbanised at a fast rate, familial bond is yet to be disrupted to a significant extend. Old age is usually marked by a feeling of loneliness and unwantedness. During this phase, family serves as the basic support provider which in turn enhances the well-being of elderly. The elderly, like any other, is a social being, who lives in the social context. If he/she gets a positive stroke from his/her social support network, it is a satisfying experience.

Some of the aged were depressed because of their family members, especially the new generation. The elderly claimed that the young generation did not give proper attention and care to them. In their own house, they felt like strangers. In the present scenario, both the husband and the wife are engaged in their jobs and they are not able to spend quality time with their children. So how are they able to give time to the elderly parents at home? But it is the duty of the family members to give enough time to the elderly at home.

The physiological, psychological as well as the socio-economic changes with age may be a cause of greater severity of mental health problems in their later period of life. An elderly faces numerous fears and insecurities that may not be a characteristic of earlier life periods, like that produced during the old age. There is a widespread belief that emotional problems, particularly depression in old age, are infrequent in our country as compared to the West. The joint family system or other cultural practices that provide satisfaction and security to the elderly account for this. However, this notion does not hold true. Ramachandran et al. (1982) reported that the notion that psychiatric disorders in the aged in our country are infrequent appears to be a myth. The study found that about 33 per cent of the subjects above the age of 60 in the community were found to exhibit manifestations of mental illness.

A good percentage of the participants in the study were not aware of the support programmes from the Government. Appropriate guidance in this regard helps in making such social support programmes more effective.

Non-governmental organisations (NGOs) and some government agencies could provide necessary inputs to the elderly. Counselling or psychological treatment needs to be planned for people with withdrawal tendencies and depression.

Here is the necessity for introducing a geriatric social worker who can conduct the psychosocial assessment of an elderly and facilitate the elderly for optimal functioning in their life. Geriatric social work is a division of social work concerned with the welfare of the elderly. Geriatric social workers help the elderly deal with the problems that are psychological (alienation, hopelessness, loneliness), social, adjustment problems, economical and health-related. They encourage clients to participate in group activities. No doubt, professionals in this field are badly needed these days, as the population is getting older. The goal of geriatric social workers is to try and improve the quality of life of senior citizens and help alleviate the negative aspects of ageing. Geriatric social workers can find jobs in a variety of settings including retirement communities, nursing homes, hospitals, state and government agencies and hospices. They have a wide range of duties and usually specialise in one of the three areas. One of these areas is assessing the needs of senior citizens. These social workers work at family-service agencies or day-care centres, many of which have outreach programs.

Geriatric social workers are trained to recognise normal and abnormal ageing patterns. They help to decide which senior citizen needs home health aides, special transportation or similar services. It is very important to underline that with the help of these services, some elderly people may be able to live in their own homes when otherwise they would need a nursing home's care. Some of the geriatric workers are skilled in leading these activities or in arranging for others to lead. There are some geriatric social workers that are able to plan and organise services for the elderly; their function is to estimate the future needs and to plan how these needs can be best met. The goal of geriatric social workers is to help their clients apply for appropriate services. They also help sort out problems in the delivery of these services. They help the senior citizens live a healthier and more productive life. Geriatric social workers help seniors understand and effectively utilise the various social services and programs that are available to them. They also offer direct assistance, such as providing family support services and facilitating the co-ordination of medical care. Many geriatric social workers also offer counselling services, which often deal with end-of-life issues and other concerns common to senior citizens. Geriatric social work can help lower many of the risks associated with ageing.

Conclusion

Majority of the elders mentioned that sharing their problems with each other helps them to face difficulties. In that context, the researcher could conclude that people living at home are happy. However, sometimes they feel loneliness at home even when their family members are with them, and sometimes they face adjustment problems with the younger generation at home as well as in the society. They feel that the children too would become old one day and then they will understand that parents only want some time from the children. In the study, the researcher also found that if family support is high, the elderly people have less physical and psychological problems and when they get ill, they recover soon if they get proper care from their family members. Old people need some quality time, care and support from their family members. The present study seeks the intervention of geriatric social work in mitigating the problems of the elderly.

References

Anantharaman, R. N. 1981. 'Physical Health and Adjustment in Old Age', *Journal of Psychological Researches*, 25 (1): 46–50.

Beland, F. et al. 2006. 'A System of Integrated Care for Older Persons with Disabilities in Canada: Results from a Randomized Controlled Trial', *Journal of Gerontology: Series A: Biological Science and Medical Sciences*, 61 (4): 367–373.

Darshan and Ritu. 2010.' A Study of ENT and Head Neck Diseases in Geriatric Population at Tertiary Care Hospital', *Indian Journal of Gerontology*, 24 (4): 421–433.

Gorman, M. 2000. 'The Growing Problem of Violence against Older Persons in Africa', *Southern African Journal of Gerontology*, 9 (2):33-36.

Gupta et al. 2005. 'Concurrent Alcohol and Tobacco Use Among a Middle-aged and Elderly Population in Mumbai', *National Medical Journal of India*, 18 (2): 88–91.

Lena et al. 2009. 'Health and Social Problems of the Elderly: A Cross-sectional Study in Udupi Taluk, Karnataka', *Indian Journal of Community Medicine*, 34 (2): 131–134.

Ramachandran. V., M. ShardaMenon and S. Arunagiri. 1982.'Socio-cultural Factors in the Late Onset of Depression', *Indian Journal of Psychiatry*, 24 (3): 268–273.

Rao and Mandavilli. 1996. Accumulation of DNA Damage in Aging Neurons Occurs Through a Mechanism Other Than Apoptosis. J Neurochem 67 (4): 1559–1565.

Willigen, Van, J. and N. K. Chadha. 1990. 'Techniques for Collecting Social Network Data for Studies of Social Aging', Indian Journal of Social Work, 51 (4): 615–621.

Verma, S. K. and A. Verma. 1988. *Manual for PGI Well-being Measure*. Lucknow: Ankur Psychological Agency.

Web Resources

http://www.ehow.com/about_4678546_geriatric-social-work.html#ixzz1AH5XpBi6. (accessed 16 March, 2014)

United Nation Population Division. 2003. "World Population Prospects: The 2002 Revision". Available at http://www.un.org/popin/data.html. (accessed 11 April, 2014)

8

Ageing, Religiosity and Mental Health: Some Reflections

Braj Bhushan

Ageing

Although ageing is a natural process that everyone has to undergo, it assumes importance due to its strong association with 'physical incapacity, biological deterioration and disabilities, and psychological failures' (Bhattacharya 2005: 3). Demographic data show global increase in the population of senior citizens around the world. A close look at the government policies and existing infrastructure for social care and welfare indicates that most of us are not ready for the challenges that this growing gray population pose before us. This chapter will focus on the mental health issues pertaining to ageing and the role religion/spirituality have been found to play.

Scientific literature classifies age into five different subtypes: biological, chronological, psychological, functional and social age. Of them, psychological and social age are of our interest right now because the former refers to the adaptive capacity of the individual in the light of situational changes and life experiences, whereas the latter refers to the roles and social habits with respect to other members of the community.

The ageing process is associated with psychological problems, such as memory loss, feeling of insecurity, loneliness and uselessness as well as mental health problems of relatively grave nature, such as depression, phobia and fear of ageing. The increase of chronological age has imperative association with mental health problems, and this has attracted the attention of psychologists, sociologists and social workers. The World Health Organization (WHO) has defined mental health as 'a state of well-being in which the individual realizes his or her own abilities, can cope with the normal stresses of life, can work productively and fruitfully, and is able to make a contribution to his or her community' (WHO 2001: 1).

Anxiety and depression are the most common mental health problems reported among this age group. Although the present definition of mental health is more positively worded, practitioners and researchers have consistently focused on mental illnesses. Keyes (2005: 539) defines mental health as a 'complete state in which individuals are free of psychopathology and flourishing....with high levels of emotional, psychological, and social well-being'. In fact, 'mental health and mental illness are not opposite ends of a single continuum; rather, they constitute distinct but correlated axes that suggest that mental health should be viewed as a complete state' (Keyes 2005: 546).

India has the second largest geriatric population of the world, and it is expected to further grow in the decades to come (Rajan 2006). Figure 8.1 illustrates the projected growth of the geriatric population in the forthcoming censuses.

Taking into account that mental health and mental illness are distinct but correlated axes, it is important that the world's second largest populace be systematically studied. Gautam's (2011) study examined differences among three age groups (50–60 years, 60–70 years, and >70 years) for ten psychiatric indicators of mental health, namely anxiety, cognitive–competence, depression, psychoticism, fear of ageing, obsession–compulsion, paranoia, somatisation and mania in the Indian population. Her study indicated higher mania score in those between 50 and 60 years. An interesting finding of this study was that religiosity significantly affected all indicators of mental health except substance abuse, showing the positive effect of religiosity on mental

Figure 8.1
Projected Growth of the Geriatric Population in India

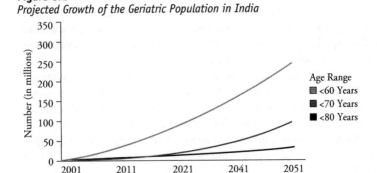

health. Several studies have highlighted the significant role of spirituality in the lives of people.

Technical literature makes distinction between religiosity and spirituality, although these terms are interchangeably used by common people. Belief in a kind of worship refers to religiosity. It includes certain practices and obligations. As described by Allport and Ross (1967), one can have intrinsic or extrinsic religious orientation. Intrinsic orientation is self-transcendental and the individual lives in the religion. On the other hand, extrinsic orientation is self-oriented and the individual uses religion in one's life. Contrary to this, spirituality refers to personal experiences lacking such obligations and practices usually associated with religiosity and 'connotes the self existential search for ultimate meaning through an individualized understanding of the sacred' (Wink and Dillon 2002: 79). Researchers do differentiate between practice-oriented and seeking-oriented spirituality (Wuthnow 1998). Hadzic (2011) has emphasised the acknowledgment of differences between different religions and the need to define spirituality in the context of a specific faith.

It is important to note that religiosity or spirituality is being referred to as a belief in a supreme power that does not require adherence to any particular religion. This has been referred to as transcendence. According to Piedmont (1999: 988), spiritual transcendence is 'the capacity of individuals to stand outside of their immediate sense of time and place to view life from a larger, more objective perspective'.

Recent research on the ageing population has focused upon attitudes and beliefs about mental health (Conner et al. 2010), life satisfaction (Berg et al. 2009), ageing-induced worry (Nuevo et al. 2009), personality traits and perceived social support among the depressed (Cukrowicz et al. 2008), health and changes in late-life drinking patterns (Moos et al. 2005), life strain and psychological distress (Boey and Chiu 2005), social support (Blazer 2005), family as care provider (Phillips and Chan 2002), and ageing and dependency (Yeon 2000). Interestingly, recent studies on mental health and ageing have also focused on attachment to God and recovery from psychosis (Prout, Cecero and Dragatsi 2012), religiosity and trajectories of depressive symptoms (Sun et al. 2012), experience of prayer during stressful life events (Miller, Gall and Corbeil 2011), and attitudes and beliefs about mental health (Conner et al. 2010).

Studies show significant increase in spirituality with respect to ageing. It augments from late middle age (mid 50s–60s) to old age (late 60s–mid 70s). Spirituality reflected in the late 60s is correlated to cognitive commitment. It is associated to meaning making and deriving purpose in life. Both of these positively relate to general psychological well-being (Debats 2000).

In an interesting qualitative study, Miller, Gall and Corbeil (2011) attempted extracting common themes based on the subjective experience of prayer and found three key themes: contextual information regarding the nature of significant life events, spiritual architecture of prayer, and spiritual relationship with the sacred.

According to the Census of India, the four major religions practised in India are Hinduism, Islam, Christianity and Sikhism. Buddhism, Jainism, Zoroastrianism and Judaism have a modest presence. Figure 8.2 shows the spread of distribution of different religions in India since 1961.

Bhushan and colleagues studied the majority (Hindus) and minority (Buddhist) religious groups in India in a series of studies, and the findings endorse the significance of religiosity/spirituality. Studying the minority religious group, Hussain and Bhushan (2011) attempted to extract culturally derived coping resources used by the Tibetan Buddhists living in India and found that Buddhist philosophy and community bonding were vital sources of strength for them. Further, the elements of community bonding and support included identity and belongingness, source of strength and platform for sharing. It is important to note that their religion seems to endow them with various protective schemas that help in attribution and meaning making. It also fosters a common sharing ground. In yet another study on these Tibetan Buddhists Hussain and Bhushan (2012) attempted to understand how they derive the meaning of their lives, by analysing semi-structured interview using interpretative phenomenological analysis.

Figure 8.2
Percentage Distribution of Different Religions in the Indian Population

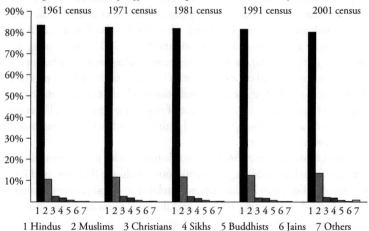

1 Hindus   2 Muslims   3 Christians   4 Sikhs   5 Buddhists   6 Jains   7 Others

Change in outlook, personal strength and meaningful relationships were the major themes emerging out of the narratives. Family and community were the components adding to meaningful relationship. In a quantitative study of a large number of elderly samples between the age of 50 and 90 years, Gautam and Bhushan (unpublished study) examined religious beliefs and practices, and their buffering impact on mental health. Results indicated that religiosity significantly affected mental health. Besides that preventive, reflective, strategic and emotional support seeking, instrumental support seeking and avoidance coping strategies mediated the relationship between religiosity and psychiatric indicators of mental health. Coping strategies are an important aspect of behaviour as it shows how a person responds to stressful life events. Older people try different strategies to cope with the stressors due to multiple and mixed nature of life experiences that they have had. Negative life events are likely to augment certain symptoms whereas positive reframing, planning and acceptance are part of behavioural alternatives that affect mental health, and this could have contributed to the finding.

Defining 'spirituality/religiosity [as] a stable characteristic' Folkman and Lazarus (1980) have also endorsed it as an important resource for coping. They have proposed 'spirituality as a dimension of successful ageing' linking it to better health outcomes (Folkman and Lazarus 1980: 49). Ellison and Levin (1998) found that religious practices and involvement were favourable for health inasmuch as they also helped cope with adversities. This finding has been corroborated by Koenig, McCullough and Larson (2001). It also positively affects mental health of older people (Levin and Chatters 1998).

It is argued that religious inclination is instrumental in developing behavioural, social, psychological and physiological mechanisms (Fetzer Institute and National Institute on Aging Working Group 1999). For instance, drug and alcohol abuse is less likely in highly religious people. Thus, the behavioural mechanism is moderated by religiosity. Religious groups have been observed to encourage supportive communities, thus integrating the social units. They lay down certain beliefs that are pertinent to mental health and coping strategies. This facilitates psychological mechanisms. Religious practices are also known for eliciting 'relaxation response', thus influencing the physiological reactions. It is evident that the psychosocial mechanisms get influenced by religiosity/spirituality. This has significance for social and community level workers.

Studies on religiosity and several psychiatric disorders confirm the positive role played by such commitments and practices. For instance, comparison between religious and non-religious groups confirm lower anxiety rate in people with religious commitment (Koenig et al. 1993; Thorson and

Powell 1990). Religiosity has been found to predict low depression and positive attitude towards life (Koenig 1995; O'Conner and Vallerand 1990). Irrespective of age, sex, race, social support and functional disability, the rate of depression in religiously active people has been less compared to those who are religiously inactive (cited in Koenig 1995). Sun et al. (2012) found that older adults with depressive symptoms frequently attending religious services reported fewer depressive symptoms. Those with high intrinsic religiosity at baseline showed sharp decline in the depressive symptoms over the four-year period. On the other hand, those with low intrinsic religiosity had short-term decline followed by increase in the depressive symptoms. Based on their findings, Sun et al. (2012) have strongly advocated the need for culturally appropriate patient care system. Their work also has implications for social workers so that the health and social support system can be further strengthened.

Prout, Cecero and Dragatsi (2012) examined the moderating role of attachment to God in the relationship between object representations of parents and psychotic disorders in schizophrenia or schizoaffective patients. The findings suggested association between recovery and benevolent representations of the parents. On the other hand, recovery was negatively associated with punitive representations of the parents. What was interesting was that the association between benevolent representations of father and recovery from psychotic disorders was strengthened by attachment to God. This attachment also acted as a buffer in mild-to-moderate punitive parental representations.

Religious involvement fosters group activities, and such groups are likely to offer occasions for sharing one's difficulties and adversities, thereby assisting in coping against life stress. Such group efforts might help building collective meaning of life. These meanings might be instrumental in deducing self-described cosmic connectedness which in turn could help maintain sense of meaning and purpose in the later years of life. All this becomes extremely important at the age which inevitably invites loss of relationship and productivity. Such combinations can seriously affect one's mental health. Studies suggest that despite such experiences, people with religious belief and practices find a sense of personal meaning to move ahead in their lives (Zinnbauer et al. 1997).

The main facets of religious orientation are forgiveness, acceptance and sublimation of locus of control. Besides these, evolution of social support system and religious coping are also noteworthy. Overall, the studies in the area of psychology suggest that religious involvement in old age plays a vital role in psychological well-being and the application of these findings are looked after. Leavey, Dura-Vila and King (2012) have examined the interface between religion and mental health care. They have argued the need for psychiatry and faith groups to explore the nature and boundaries of their relationship. Recently there has been advocacy for proactive ageing, suggesting successful ageing by invoking accumulated resources (Kahana, Kelley-Moore and Kahana 2012).

Implications for Social Work Practitioners

There has been advocacy for active ageing. According to the WHO (2002), 'active ageing is the process of optimizing opportunities for health, participation and security in order to enhance quality of life as people age'. This is a challenge that cannot remain restricted to the boundaries of any given discipline. The studies cited clearly indicate the cross-disciplinary implication of the findings. As a matter of fact, several disciplines have shown concern as to how people can be made to understand 'their suffering through their spiritual beliefs' (Puchalski and Romer 2000: 129). Self-understanding and imagination are important for healing (Stanard, Sandhu and Painter 2000), and social workers and mental health counsellors can play a vital role in facilitating it. Spirituality does seem 'to go hand in hand' with mental health counselling (Powers 2005: 217). At the international front, several counselling organisations, such as the American Counseling Association (ACA) and the Association for Spiritual, Ethical, and Religious Values in Counseling (ASERVIC) have been actively pursuing implications of spirituality in helping clients derive meaning out of their life experiences.

The economic divide further reshapes the challenge. The frail mental health services in the developing nations need to be strengthened. The spectrum of mental health service should not only restrict itself to diagnosis and treatment; rather, it should embrace promotion, prevention and support system. Certain types of discriminations based on gender and caste are known to us. With the increase in affordability and development of healthcare facility, the average age in countries like India has also gone up. The gradually increasing capable geriatric mass is getting aware of age discrimination also. Typically reported by those above 55 years, it has been found to negatively affect mental health. Irrespective of the economic divide, the stigma associated with mental health problems is a major challenge that the stakeholders have to take into account. The role of social work practitioners becomes very vital. They can really act as the agents of such social transformation. As the geriatric population is expected to rise in the decades to come, ensuring the participation of the gray population in meaningful activities remains an intricate task.

Conclusion

Several studies show increase in spirituality as a function of ageing. These changes in orientation play significant role in helping a person derive meaning in life. It not only becomes important for coping with adversities of life but also augments acceptance and forgiveness. Such research findings can be very vital for the management of age-related issues as well as mental health counselling.

References

Allport, G. W. and J. M. Ross. 1967. 'Personal Religious Orientation and Prejudice', *Journal of Personality and Social Psychology,* 5 (4): 432–443.

Berg, A. I., L. Hoffman, L. B. Hassing, G. E. McClearn and B. Johansson. 2009. 'What Matters, and What Matters Most, for Change in Life Satisfaction in the Oldest-old? A Study Over 6 years among Individuals 80+', *Aging & Mental Health,* 13 (2): 191–201.

Bhattacharya, P. 2005. 'Implications of an Aging Population in India: Challenges and Opportunities', paper presented at *The Living to 100 and Beyond,* Orlando, Florida, January 12–14.

Blazer, D. G. 2005. 'Depression in Late Life: Review and Commentary', *American Journal of Psychiatry,* 162 (4): 705–710.

Boey, K. W. and H. F. K. Chiu. 2005. 'Life Strain and Psychological Distress of Older Women and Older Men in Hong Kong', *Aging and Mental Health,* 9 (6): 555–562.

Conner, K. O., B. Lee, V. Mayers, D. Robinson, C. F. Reynolds, S. Albert and C. Brown. 2010. 'Attitudes and Beliefs about Mental Health among African American Older Adults Suffering from Depression', *Journal of Aging Studies,* 24 (4): 266–277.

Cukrowicz, K., A. Franzese, S. Thorp, J. Cheavens, and T. Lynch. 2008. 'Personality Traits and Perceived Social Support among Depressed Older Adults', *Aging and Mental Health,* 12 (5): 662–669.

Debats, D. L. 2000. 'An Inquiry into Existential Meaning: Theoretical, Clinical, and Phenomenal Perspectives', in G. T. Reker and K. Chamberlain (eds), *Exploring*

Existential Meaning: Optimizing Human Development across the Life Span, pp. 93–106. Thousand Oaks, CA: Sage Publications.

Ellison, C. G. and J. S. Levin. 1998. 'The Religion-health Connection: Evidence, Theory, and Future Directions', *Health Education and Behavior*, 25 (6): 700–720.

Fetzer Institute and National Institute on Aging Working Group. 1999. *Multidimensional Measurement of Religiousness/spirituality for Use in Health Research: A Report of the Fetzer Institute/National Institute on Aging Working Group*. Kalamazoo, MI: John E. Fetzer Institute.

Folkman, S. and R. S. Lazarus. 1980. 'An Analysis of Coping in a Middle-aged Community Sample', *Journal of Health and Social Behaviour*, 21 (September): 219–239.

Gautam, R. 2011. 'Geriatric Mental Health and Quality of Life: The Role of Life Events, Resilience, and Religiosity', Unpublished doctoral thesis, Indian Institute of Technology, Kanpur, India.

Gautam, R. and B. Bhushan. (n.d.). 'Religiosity and Geriatric Mental Health: Exploring the Mediating Role of Coping Strategies', Unpublished paper.

Hadzic, M. 2011. 'Spirituality and Mental Health: Current Research and Future Directions', *Journal of Spirituality in Mental Health*, 13 (4): 223–235.

Hussain, D. and B. Bhushan. 2011. 'Cultural Factors Promoting Coping among Tibetan Refugees: A Qualitative Investigation', *Mental Health, Religion & Culture*, 14 (6): 575–587.

———. 2012. 'Posttraumatic Growth Experiences among Tibetan Refugees: A Qualitative Investigation', *Qualitative Research in Psychology*, 10 (2): 204–216.

Kahana, E., J. Kelley-Moore, and B. Kahana. 2012. 'Proactive Aging: A Longitudinal Study of Stress, Resources, Agency, and Well-being in Late Life', *Aging & Mental Health*, 16 (4): 438–451.

Keyes, C. L. M. 2005. 'Mental Illness and/or Mental Health? Investigating Axioms of the Complete State Model of Health', *Journal of Consulting and Clinical Psychology*, 73 (3): 539–548.

Koenig, H. G. 1995. 'Religion and Older Men in Prison', *International Journal of Geriatric Psychiatry*, 10 (3): 219–230.

Koenig, H. G., S. M. Ford, L. K. George, D. G. Blazer and K. G. Meador. 1993. 'Religion and Anxiety Disorder: An Examination and Comparison of Associations in Young, Middle-aged, and Elderly Adults', *Journal of Anxiety Disorders*, 7 (4): 321–342.

Koenig, H. G., M. E. McCullough and D. B. Larson. 2001. *Handbook of Religion and Health*. New York: Oxford University Press.

Leavey, G., G. Dura-Vila and M. King. 2012. 'Finding Common Ground: The Boundaries and Interconnections between Faith-based Organisations and Mental Health Services', *Mental Health, Religion & Culture*, 15 (4): 349–362.

Levin, J. S. and L. M. Chatters. 1998. 'Religion, Health, and Psychological Well-being in Older Adults', *Journal of Aging and Health*, 10 (4): 504–531.

Miller, L. M., T. L. Gall and L. Corbeil. 2011. 'The Experience of Prayer With a Sacred Object Within the Context of Significant Life Stress', *Journal of Spirituality in Mental Health*, 13 (4): 247–271.

Moos, R. H., P. L. Brennan, K. K. Schutte and B. S. Moos. 2005. 'Older adults' Health and Changes in Late-life Drinking Patterns', *Aging and Mental Health*, 9 (1): 49–59.

Nuevo, R., J. L. Wetherell, I. Montorio, M. Ruiz, and I. Cabrera. 2009. 'Knowledge about Aging and Worry in Older Adults: Testing the Mediating Role of Intolerance of Uncertainty', *Aging and Mental Health*, 13 (1): 135–141.

O'Conner, B. P. and R. J. Vallerand. 1990. 'Religious Motivation in the Elderly: A French-Canadian Replication and an Extension', *Journal of Social Psychology*, 130 (1): 53–59.

Phillips, D. R. and A. C. M. Chan. 2002. 'National Policies on Aging and Long-term Care in the Asia-Pacific: Issues and Challenges', in D. R. Phillips and A. C. M. Chan (eds), *Aging and Long-term Care: National Policies in the Asia–Pacific*, pp. 1–22. Singapore: Institute of South East Asian Studies and Ottawa: International Development Research Centre.

Piedmont, R. L. 1999. 'Does Spirituality Represent the Sixth Factor of Personality? Spiritual Transcendence and the Five-Factor Model', *Journal of Personality*, 67 (6): 985–1013.

Powers, R. 2005. 'Counseling and Spirituality: A Historical Review', *Counseling and Values*, 49 (3): 217–225.

Prout, T. A., J. Cecero, and D. Dragatsi. 2012. 'Parental Object Representations, Attachment to God, and Recovery among Individuals with Psychosis', *Mental Health, Religion & Culture*, 15 (5): 449–466.

Puchalski, C. and A. L. Romer. 2000. 'Taking a Spiritual History Allows Clinicians to Understand Patients More Fully', *Journal of Palliative Medicine*, 3 (1): 129–137.

Rajan, S. I. 2006. 'Population Ageing and Health in India'. Mumbai: Centre for Enquiry into Health and Allied Themes. Retrieved from http://www.cehat.org/humanrights/rajan.pdf, 8 March 2014.

Stanard, R. P., D. S. Sandhu and L. C. Painter. 2000. 'Assessment of Spirituality in Counseling', *Journal of Counseling & Development*, 78 (2): 204–210.

Sun, F., N. S. Park, L. L. Roff, D. L. Klemmack, M. Parker, H. G. Koenig, P. Sawyer and R. M. Allman. 2012. 'Predicting the Trajectories of Depressive Symptoms among Southern Community-dwelling Older Adults: The Role of Religiosity', *Aging & Mental Health*, 16 (2): 189–198.

Thorson, J. A. and F. C. Powell. 1990. 'Meanings of Death and Intrinsic Religiosity', *Journal of Clinical Psychology*, 46 (4): 379–391.

Wink, P. and M. Dillon. 2002. 'Spiritual Development across the Adult Life Course: Findings from a Longitudinal Study', *Journal of Adult Development*, 9 (1): 79–94.

World Health Organization (WHO). 2001. *Strengthening Mental Health Promotion*. Fact Sheet No. 220. Geneva: WHO.

World Health Organization (WHO). 2002. *Active Ageing: A Policy Framework.* Report No: WHO/NMH/NPH/02.8. Geneva: WHO. Retrieved from http://whqlibdoc.who.int/hq/2002/WHO_NMH_NPH_02.8.pdf, 8 March 2014.

Wuthnow, R. 1998. *After Heaven: Spirituality in America Since the 1950s.* Berkeley, CA: University of California Press.

Yeon, K. C. 2000. 'Elder Care in Korea: The Future is Now', *Aging International,* 20 (1): 25–37.

Zinnbauer, B. J., K. I. Pargament, B. Cole, M. S. Rye, E. M. Butter, T. G. Belavich, K. M. Hipp, A. B. Scott and J. L. Kadar. 1997. 'Religion and Spirituality: Unfuzzying the Fuzzy', *Journal for the Scientific Study of Religion,* 36 (4): 549–564.

9

Mental Health and Well-being among Older Persons: Gerontological Social Work Perspectives

Ilango Ponnuswami and P. Udhaya Kumar

Introduction

The ageing of the world's population is a global phenomenon with extensive economic and social consequences. The ratio of the elderly population (60 years and older) is now 1 in 10. By 2050, those in the age group of 80 plus will represent 27 per cent of the older population (Tan 1999). Ageing of a population is a matter of great concern for the health sector. The elderly, on the whole, are less healthy than the non-elderly. Among the elderly, increasing age is associated with higher morbidity and higher use of health services (number of visits to doctors and hospitalisations; Sidik 2004). Some mental illnesses are particularly common in old age; others differ in clinical features and/or present particular problems in management. Social difficulties, multiple physical problems and sensory deficits are also common. Appropriate detection and management requires specialist knowledge and skills as well as multidisciplinary collaboration. Appropriate interventions for the major mental illnesses of old age can often either treat the elderly effectively or at least substantially improve the quality of life of patients and their families. The rise in the number of old people with mental health problems has necessitated the development of the specialty of psychiatry of the elderly. The emergence of the specialty of psychiatry of the elderly has helped to raise the status of this vulnerable group and has also fostered research that offers hope for better treatment and outcomes and provides an opportunity for training students in all health and social care–related disciplines (WHO 1996).

Mental Health and Healthy Ageing

Good mental health and emotional well-being is as important in old age as it is at any time of life. Many people fear growing old, and assume that old age is depressing and distressing, characterised by loss and disability, offering little to look forward to. But the reality is that older people are as capable as the younger people of enjoying life, taking on challenges, coping with difficulties, engaging in satisfying activities, supporting each other with warmth and good humour and making a real contribution to their families and communities, using their wealth of knowledge and experience (Nicholls 2006). The population of old people is increasing rapidly throughout the developed and developing countries. This reflects upon the improving health and social conditions and is a cause for celebration. Most older people remain in good mental as well as physical health and continue to contribute to their families and to society (WHO 1996). A number of reports in recent years have emphasised the need to focus on successful ageing and living well in later life. The World Health Organisation's (WHO) vision statement on active ageing states: 'Active ageing is the process of optimizing opportunities for health, participation and security in order to enhance quality of life as people age' (WHO 2002b).

Prevalence of Mental Illness among the Older Persons

Approximately 20 per cent of the older adults have a mental illness today, yet only half of these adults who acknowledge such problems receive treatment and only a fraction of them receive specialised mental health services (Dupree et al. 2005; U.S. Department of Health and Human Services 1999). There is a lack of treatment provided to older adults across all types of service settings (Kaskie and Estes 2001). It was estimated that, by 2030, 15 million adults aged 65 and older will be living with a major mental illness (Bartels et al. 2003). Mental disorders among older adults may substantially impair physical functioning and result in unnecessary hospitalisation or nursing home placement and increased rates of mortality. At the same time, individuals with physical health problems are more vulnerable to mental illness (Speer and Schneider 2003; U.S. Department of Health and Human Services 1999). Common psychiatric problems that prevail among elders are as follows:

Depression

Depression is the most common mental health problem of later life, affecting 10 to 20 per cent of older people (NIMHE 2005) and up to 40 per cent of older people residing in homes, yet in older people, depression is often underdiagnosed and undertreated. Older people in residential and nursing homes are two to three times more likely to experience depression than older people in the community (Godfrey and Denby 2004). Older people tend not to complain of being depressed, they are more likely to refer to physical symptoms, and some symptoms of physical illness are similar to those of depression. Physical illness is also a common trigger for depression in older people. Depression causes great mental distress and affects a person's ability to function day to day. When untreated, depression shortens life, exacerbates disability from medical illnesses, increases health-care cost and is the leading cause of suicide among older people. When treated, quality of life improves (NIMHE 2005). Suicide is a significant risk for older people who are depressed.

Suicide in Elderly

Suicide is an important issue, but is often misunderstood and underidentified among older persons. 'Suicidal thinking' and 'suicidal behaviour' refer to thoughts and actions that reflect the intent to do harm to oneself. These usually occur in the context of very severe depression, anxiety or other mental health problems. The highest suicide rates of any age group are among persons aged 65 years and older. A recent study showed that adults aged 65 and older make up 13 per cent of the population, but accounted for 19 per cent of all suicide deaths. Men are especially at high risk, and completed 84 per cent of the suicides among this age group (Wyman et al. 2010). Elderly people have a higher risk of completed suicide than any other age group worldwide (WHO 2002b). Despite this, suicide in elderly people receives relatively little attention, with public health measures, medical research and media attention focusing on younger age groups (Unchapher and Arean 2000). According to psychological autopsy studies of suicides in elderly people, 71 per cent to 95 per cent of the people had a major psychiatric disorder at the time of death (Conwell et al. 2002). Depressive illnesses are by far the most common and important diagnoses. Non-clinical cohort study of suicide in older adults suggests that the strongest predictor of suicide was severity of depression symptom (Ross et al. 1990). A recently published retrospective case-control study found that alcohol use disorders predicted suicide in older people (Waern 2003).

Anxiety

Sometimes feeling nervous, worried or jumpy is a part of normal life. However, when the nervousness feeling or anxious behaviour affects daily functioning and causes distress for a person, seeking professional evaluation is important. There are a number of different types of problems that are conceptually grouped together under the 'anxiety disorders.' These include obsessive-compulsive disorder (e.g., preoccupation with cleaning, checking locks or a fear of getting rid of things), post-traumatic stress disorder, panic disorder and specific phobias (such as a fear of heights or fear of dogs), as well as generalised anxiety disorder, characterised by excessive worry. There can be overlap among these disorders, as well as overlap among anxiety and depressive disorders (Wyman et al. 2010). Studies suggest that among the elderly, anxiety disorders are more common than depressive disorders, with prevalence rates of generalised anxiety disorder ranging from about 4 to 12 per cent. As with depression, research suggests that the rate of subclinical anxiety symptoms are much higher than more severe, 'diagnosable' disorder. The prevalence of subclinical anxiety is estimated at 17 per cent to 21 per cent (Himmelfarb and Murrell 1984). The high rate of co-morbidity between late-onset generalised anxiety disorder and depression in old age suggests that antidepressant medication should be the treatment of choice (Flint 1997).

Dementia

Dementia is an 'umbrella' term used to describe a collection of symptoms associated with physical changes in the brain that results in the gradual loss of mental functions such as memory and the ability to use words or to carry out previously familiar tasks. The cause of Alzheimer's is not yet known. The disease is usually characterised by a gradual deterioration over several years (Nicholls 2006). Chronic organic mental disorders, nowadays called dementias, are the main reason for the necessity of geriatric care units. Dementia is defined as a syndrome of acquired impairment of memory and other cognitive functions secondary to structural brain damage (Moroney et al. 1997).

Other Mental Illnesses

There are other mental health problems that exist in older adults, such as thought disorders (e.g., schizophrenia), bipolar affective disorder or 'manic-depression' (which is quite different from the other depressive disorders as discussed above, in terms of root causes, treatment and course over time), and maladaptive personality traits. In addition, the at-risk use of alcohol, street drugs or prescription medications among the elderly is an issue that has received increasing attention in the clinical and research arenas (Wyman et al. 2010).

Treatment for Mentally Ill Older Persons

There is clear evidence that older adults have high need for mental health services related to mental disorders such as depression, anxiety, substance abuse and cognitive impairment. Epidemiologic Catchment Area (ECA) data estimate a female and male prevalence for older persons living in the United States of all mental disorders as 13.6 per cent and 10.5 percent respectively (Wykle and Musil 1993). The treatment for mental illness among elderly includes restoration of health, improving the quality of life, minimising disability and preserving autonomy. Treatment must be adaptive to an individual patient's needs and to available resources. Its delivery usually requires cooperation between the multidisciplinary professionals involved as well as involvement of informal supporters. Early detection and intervention may improve prognosis, and education is required to counteract the therapeutic pessimism of both the professionals and the elder patients. Older people with mental illnesses may take longer to respond to treatment than their younger counterparts. Functional psychiatric illnesses in later life have a high rate of relapse; close follow-up and continued treatment may reduce this (WHO 1996).

Psychotherapy with older adults is very similar to psychotherapy with younger or middle-aged adults. However, most experts believe that some training and experience with elders, leading to 'geriatric cultural competence', is ideal for clinicians to be most effective in their work with the elderly (Wyman et al. 2006). Experienced geriatric providers agree that some adaptations may be needed to make the treatment maximally effective. These adaptations include taking time to socialise older adults to the process of psychotherapy, adjusting the pace of psychotherapy to account for age-related changes in information processing and allowing flexibility in the delivery of psychotherapy to overcome medical and physical barriers to care (Wyman et al. 2006).

Older people are particularly vulnerable to side effects of psychotropic drugs. Consideration must also be given to age-related changes in drug handling. Interactions between psychotropic drugs and older patients' co-morbid physical illnesses (and their treatment) are also common. Coexistent physical problems in older people with mental illness must be treated; this may facilitate treatment of mental illness. All psychotherapeutic techniques (e.g., supportive, psychodynamic and cognitive/behavioural) may be used with older people. Adaptations may be necessary to take into account any sensory or cognitive deficits (WHO 1996).

Barriers to Mental Health Services for Older Adults

Attitudes towards mental health services by older adults have been suspected as major barriers to seeking treatment. Reasons why older adults have been thought to reject mental health care include lack of education regarding mental health and generational negative attitudes or stigma surrounding mental illness. Birren and Renner (1979) suggested that older adults hold the attitude that seeking mental health services is a sign of personal weakness. Lebowitz and Niederehe (1992) propose that stigma of mental illness is especially strong in the current cohort of older adults who tend to associate mental disorders with personal failure or spiritual deficiency. Lack of knowledge of the range of mental health problems addressed by professionals and limited breadth of conceptions of the causes of mental disorders have also been hypothesised as barriers, particularly among the oldest cohorts (Currin et al. 1998). Lundervold and Young (1992) developed an instrument to assess older adults' attitudes and knowledge towards mental health services, and studied 50 older persons. They interpreted their findings as suggesting that older adults generally have negative attitudes and knowledge deficits regarding psychological services, but provided no comparison to younger individuals or normative data on their measure.

Research also suggests that current attitudes towards mental health services among the elderly may become increasingly positive. Currin et al. (1998) used a cohort design to assess this issue and found what may be a positive cohort shift in attitudes towards mental health services. Using two independent samples of older adults separated by a 14-year time interval, the researchers found that lack of knowledge regarding ageing and mental health, perceived barriers to the availability of services and older adults' negative expectations about effectiveness of treatment decreased among later-born cohorts of older persons. Analyses indicated that the more recent cohort of older adults held more positive attitudes towards mental health services than the earlier cohort. Zarit and Zarit (1998) reported that in their experience, older people viewed psychotherapy positively and were increasingly turning to mental health professionals for help with their problems. They suggested that older adults did not feel the stigma associated with seeing a mental health professional that prevailed in the past and that this trend was likely to increase with future generations.

Spirituality and Its Effects on Mental Health of Older Persons

Spirituality plays a significant role in the lives of elders' thoughts and behaviour. Spirituality develops throughout the human lifespan, from childhood to old age, and contributes uniquely to the achievement of a satisfactory life (Miller and Thoresen 2003). Spirituality has a strong impact on cognitive phenomena, affect and emotion, and personality that is being shaped and developed within a specific environment (Hill et al. 2000). Spirituality is highly related to developing a relationship with God, finding meaning and purpose in life and promoting personal growth (Julian 1992). Spirituality can be developed either through extrinsic motivation or intrinsic motivation (Donahue 1985). Individuals with extrinsic motivation make use of spirituality as a means by which they find security, sociability, self-justification or fulfil their primary needs. Conversely, people with an intrinsic motivation tend to internalise spirituality as a response to their inner spiritual needs. Some results suggest that intrinsically oriented people have healthier personalities, but extrinsic ones show higher levels of anxiety and depression (Smith, et.al; Shreve-Neiger and Edelstein, 2004). The relationship between spirituality and health has been reported in over a thousand studies and published in many medical and psychological papers (Koenig et.al 2001). In the nursing field, spiritual care has been taken into consideration since ancient times (Narayanasamy 1999). Spirituality is understood as something that motivates, enables, empowers and provides hope (Coyle 2002).

Spirituality appears to be preventative of mental disorders (Cohen and Koeing 2004). Many studies showed that spirituality has a positive correlation with life's satisfaction, happiness and higher morale. Additionally, a positive relationship with optimism and hope has been evidenced in 12 out of 14 studies with a sense of meaning and purpose in life (15 out of 16 studies), with social support (19 out of 20 studies) and with having higher marital satisfaction (35 out of 38 studies; Almeida et al. 2006). Spiritual people deal better with symptoms such as pain or fatigue (Brady et.al 1999). Also, as spiritual attitudes determine the way people approach, view and understand death, spiritual well-being brings hope to those for whom death is imminent (McClain et.al 2003). The spiritual concerns of older people are important to consider because they may act as potential resources for well-being in later life, helping to shape a meaningful and fulfilling existence. Spiritual resources may also assist an older person to successfully adjust to some of the changes associated with growing older (Baltes and Smith 2003).

Social Work Interventions for Geriatric Mental Health

Gerontological social work is concerned with maintaining and enhancing the quality of life of older adults and their families. It provides a holistic view of the patient/family. Gerontological social work is particularly concerned with ameliorating those physical, psychosocial, familial, cultural, ethnic and racial, organisational and societal factors that serve as barriers to physical and emotional well-being in later life. Interventions that enhance older adults' coping and problem-solving capabilities are perhaps the most basic and crucial aspects of gerontological social work. Gerontological social workers give special attention to the psychosocial meanings of change and loss, as well as to the underlying biological, psychological, cognitive and social factors experienced by the older adults and family (Dobrof 1998). Social workers who work across the health and behavioural health care continuum and in diverse settings such as adult protective service agencies, employee assistance programs, veterans' service programs and senior centres are well positioned and trained to support and advocate for older adults and their caregivers (NASW 2009). Gerontological social workers also play a vital role in promoting wellness, prevention, early intervention and outreaching services in health, behavioural health and social service programs for all older adults and their caregivers (IOM 2008).

Conclusion

Mental health issues in later life can have devastating effects on older people and those close to them. Older adults fear growing older and assume that old age is depressing and distressing, characterised by loss and disability, offering little to look forward to. But the reality is that older people are as capable as younger people of enjoying life, taking on challenges, coping with difficulties, engaging in satisfying activities, supporting each other with warmth and good humour and making a real contribution to their families and communities by using their wealth of knowledge and experience (Nicholls 2006). Attitudes towards mental health services held by older adults have also been suspected as major barriers to seeking treatment. Reasons why older adults have been thought to reject mental health care include lack of education regarding mental health and generational negative attitudes or stigma surrounding mental illness. Research also suggests that current attitudes towards mental health services among the elderly may be becoming increasingly positive. There is clear evidence that older adults have high needs for mental health services related to mental disorders such as depression, anxiety, substance abuse and cognitive impairment. Early detection and intervention may improve prognosis, and education is required to counteract the therapeutic pessimism of both professionals and elder patients. Most mental disorders are treatable once detected. Untreated mental disorders strongly impair life quality of patients and caregivers, cost money, promote further disability and burden for the public health system. Mental health is of tremendous importance for functional independence and quality of life among older adults. Since it is impossible not to have any somatic diseases in old age, it is essential to develop strategies to cope with these impairments, which in turn strongly depend on mental, that is on both emotional and cognitive health. It is important to emphasise that effective mental health care requires a team approach and spiritual care in both prevention and treatment of mental illness in old age.

References

Baltes, P. and J. Smith. 2003. 'New frontiers in the future of aging: from successful aging of the young-old to the dilemmas of the fourth age', *Gerontology: Behavioural Science Section/Review*, 49 (2): 123–135.

Bartels, S. J., A. Dums, T. Oxman, L. Schneider, P. Arean, and G. Alexopoulos. 2003. 'Evidence-Based Practices in Geriatric Mental Health Care: An Overview of Systematic Reviews and Meta-Analyses', *Psychiatric Clinics of North America*, 26 (4): 971–990.

Birren, J. E. and V. J. Renner. 1979. *Notes on the History Ning in Mental Health and Aging*. Washington, D.C.: National Institute of Mental Health, Center for Studies of the Mental Health of the Aging.

Brady, M., A. Peterman, G. Fitchett, M. Mo and D. Cella. 1999. 'A Case for Including Spirituality in Quality of Life Measurement in Oncology', *Psycho-Oncology*, 8 (5): 417–428.

Cohen, A. B. and H. G. Koenig. 2004. 'Religion and Mental Health', in C. Spielberger (ed.), *Encyclopedia of Applied Psychology*, 3: 255-258. Oxford, UK: Elsevier Academic Press.

Conwell, Y., P. R. Duberstein and E. D. Caine. 2002. 'Risk Factors for Suicide in Later Life', *Biological Psychiatry*, 52 (3): 193–204.

Coyle, J. 2002. 'Spirituality and Health: Towards a Framework for Exploring the Relationship between Spirituality and Health', *Journal of Advanced Nursing*, 37 (6): 589–597.

Currin, J. B., B. J. S. L. Hayslip and R. A. Kooken. 1998. 'Cohort Differences in Attitudes toward Mental Health Services among Older Persons', *Psychotherapy*, 34 (4): 506–518.

Dobrof, R. 1998. 'Journal Gerontological Social Work', *Journal of Gerontological Social Work*, 30 (3/4).

Donahue, M. J. 1985. 'Intrinsic and Extrinsic Religiousness: Review and Meta-analysis', *Journal of Personality and Social Psychology*, 48 (2): 400–419.

Dupree, L. W., M. Watson and M. G. Schneider. 2005. 'Preference for Mental Health Care: A Comparison of Older African Americans and Older Caucasians', *Journal of Applied Gerontology*, 24 (3), 196–210.

Flint, A. J. 1997. 'Epidemiology and Comorbidity of Anxiety Disorders in Later Life: Implications for Treatment', *Journal of Clinical Neuroscience*, 4 (1): 31–36.

Godfrey, M. and T. Denby. 2004. *Depression and Older People: Towards Securing Well-Being in Later Life*. Bristol: Policy Press.

Hill, P. C., K. I. Pargament, R. W. Hood, Jr., M. E. Muccullough, J. P. Swyers, D. B. Larson and B. J. Zinnbauer. 2000. 'Conceptualizing Religion and Spirituality: Points of Commonality, Points of Departure', *Journal for the Theory of Social Behaviour*, 30 (1): 51–77.

Himmelfarb, S. and S. Murrell. 1984. The Prevalence and Correlates of Anxiety Symptoms in Older Adults', *Journal of Psychology: Interdisciplinary and Applied*, 116 (2): 159–167.

Institute of Medicine (IOM). 2008. *Retooling for an Aging America: Building the Health Care Workforce.* Washington, DC: National Academies Press.

Julian, R. 1992. 'The Practice of Psychotherapy and Spiritual Direction', *Journal of Religion and Health*, 31 (4): 309–315.

Kaskie, B. and C. L. Estes. 2001. 'Mental Health Services Policy for the Aging', *Journal of Gerontological Social Work*, 36 (3/4): 99–114.

Koenig, H. G., M. McCullough, and D. B. Larson. 2001. *Handbook of Religion and Health: A Century of Research Reviewed.* New York, NY: Oxford University Press.

Lebowitz, B. D. and G. Niederehe. 1992. 'Concepts and Issues in Mental Health and Aging', In J. E. Birren, R. B. Sloane and G. D. Cohen (eds), *Handbook of Mental Health and Aging* (2nd ed.). Los Angeles: Borun Center for Gerontological Research.

Lundervold, D. A. and L. G. Young. 1992. 'Older Adults' Attitudes and Knowledge Regarding the Use of Mental Health Services', *Journal of Clinical and Experimental Gerontology*, 14 (1): 45–55.

McClain, C. S., B. Rosenfeld and W. Breitbart. 2003. 'Effect of Spiritual Well-Being on End-of-Life Despair in Terminally-Ill Cancer Patients', *The Lancet*, 361 (9369): 1603–1607.

Miller, W. R. and C. E. Thoresen. 2003. 'Spirituality, Religion, and Health. An Emerging Research Field', *American Psychologist*, 58 (1): 24–35.

Moreira-Almeida, A., F. L. Neto., H. G. Koeing. 2006. 'Religiouseness and Mental Health: A Review', *Revista Brasileira de Psiquiatria*, 28 (3): 242-250.

Moroney, J. T., E. Bagiella, D. W. Desmond, V. C. Hachinski, P. K. Molsa, L. Gustafson, A. Brun and P. Fischer. 1997. 'Meta-analysis of the Hachinski Ischiaemic Score in Pathologically Verified Dementias', *Neurology*, 49 (4): 1096–1105.

National Association of Social Workers (NASW). 2009. *Aging and Wellness. Social work speaks: National Association of Social Workers Policy Statements, 2009–2012* (8th ed., pp. 14–21). Washington, DC: NASW Press.

National Institute for Mental Health in England (NIMHE). 2005. *Facts for Champions* (p. 11). London: Department of Health.

Narayanasamy, A. 1999. 'Learning Spiritual Dimensions of Care from a Historical Perspective', *Nurse Education Today*, 19 (5): 386–395.

Nicholls, A. 2006. *Assessing the Mental Health Needs of Older People.* UK: Adults' Services, SCIE Guide.

Ross, R. K., L. Bernstein, L. Trent, B. E. Henderson and A. Paganini-Hill. 1990. 'A Prospective Study of Risk Factors for Traumatic Death in the Retirement Community', *Preventive Medicine*, 19 (1): 323–324.

Shreve-Neiger, A. K. and B. A. Edelstein. 2004. Religion and Anxiety: A Critical Review of the Literature. *Clinical Psychology Review*, 24 (4): 379–397.

Smith, T. B., M. E. McCullough and J. Poll. 2003. 'Religiousness and Depression: Evidence for a Main Effect and the Moderating Influence of Stressful Life Events', *Psychological Bulletin*, 129 (4): 614–636.

Speer, D. C., and M. G. Schneider. 2003. 'Mental Health Needs of Older Adults and Primary Care: Opportunity for Interdisciplinary Geriatric Team Practice', *Clinical Psychology: Science and Practice*, 10 (1): 85–101.

Tan, S. K. 1999.Mental Health and Ageing. Speech by the Minister of Community Development and Consumer Affairs at 'The Proclamation of the World Health Mental Day with the Theme Mental Health and Ageing', Malaysia.

U.S. Department of Health and Human Services. 1999. *Mental Health: A Report of the Surgeon General.* Rockville, MD: U.S. Department of Health and Human Services, Substance Abuse and Mental Health Services Administration, Center for Mental Health Services, National Institutes of Health, National Institute of Mental Health.

Unchapher, H. and P. A. Arean. 2000. 'Physicians are Less Willing to Treat Suicidal Ideation in Older Patients', *Journal of the American Geriatrics Society*, 48 (2): 188–192.

Waern, M. 2003. 'Alcohol Dependence and Alcohol Misuse in Elderly Suicides', *Alcohol Alcohol*, 38 (1): 249–254.

World Health Organization (WHO). 1996. *Psychiatry of the Elderly—A Consensus Statement.* Geneva: Author.

———. 2002a. *Suicide Prevention (SUPRE).* www.who.int/mental_health/prevention/suicide (accessed on 1 Aug 2004).

———. 2002b. *Strengthening Active and Healthy Ageing.* Geneva: World Health Organization.

Wykle, M. L. and C. M. Musil. 1993. 'Mental Health of Older Persons: Social and Cultural Factors', in M. A. Smyer (ed.), *Mental Health and Aging: Progress and Prospects* (pp. 3–17). New York: Springer Publishing Company.

Wyman, M. F., A. Gum and P. A. Areán. 2006. 'Psychotherapy with Older Adults', in M. E. Agronin and G. J. Maletta (eds), *Principles and Practice of Geriatric Psychiatry* (pp. 177–198). Philadelphia: Lippincott, Williams & Wilkins.

———. 2010. 'Psychotherapy with Older Adults', in M. E. Agronin and G. J. Maletta (eds), *Principles and Practice of Geriatric Psychiatry* (pp. 177–198). Philadelphia: Lippincott, Williams & Wilkins.

Zarit, S. H. and J. M. Zarit. 1998. *Mental Disorders in Older Adults.* New York: The Guilford Press.

10

Social Work Interventions for Comprehensive Psychosocial Care in Substance Use Disorders

Lakshmi Sankaran and Pratima Murthy

Introduction

Substance dependence is best understood in a bio–psycho–social framework, with counselling and rehabilitation forming critical components. The components comprise psychosocial interventions ranging from motivating an individual into treatment, facilitating lifestyle changes, strengthening coping skills, vocational training, reducing risk behaviour and prevention and management of relapses. Some of the specific strategies used in rehabilitation are individual counselling, motivational enhancement, brief interventions, cognitive behavioural interventions and skills training. The intensity, frequency and duration of psychosocial interventions vary on the type of treatment setting, that is, hospital, residential and community-based treatment. The interventions could be for individuals, family members or significant support persons (UNODC 2005).

Unfortunately, such treatment interventions, particularly in developing countries, are largely limited to specialised tertiary care addiction treatment centres and for those with late stage problems. Given the limited resources in developing countries such as India, it is a challenge to optimally use mental health human resources. There is a need to train social workers to offer effective rehabilitation and care for persons with substance use disorders (SUDs) keeping in mind the cultural milieu. In this chapter, we provide an overview of these approaches and discuss the role of social workers in the comprehensive management of SUDs.

Globally, the misuse of substances is associated with adverse consequences not only for the users, but also their families and communities. Different kinds of substances, including tobacco, alcohol and other drugs such as opioids, cannabis, stimulants, hallucinogens, inhalants are used for their intoxicating or mind-altering effects. SUDs include a range of problems including intoxication, harmful use, dependence (addiction), withdrawal and psychiatric problems associated with their use. A significant number of users who develop SUDs are found to contribute significantly to global illness, disability and death (WHO 2010). The UNODC (2011) notes that there continues to be an enormous unmet need for drug abuse prevention, treatment, care and support, particularly in developing countries and in their survey in 2011, it was noted that 15 to 39 million people between the ages of 15 and 64 used illicit substances at a level defined as 'problem use'.

The shortage of mental health professionals is well documented. The Atlas project of the WHO reports that all countries in southeast Asian region and nearly all countries in Africa have less than one psychiatrist for a population of one lakh (Patel and Thara 2003). To meet the mental health needs in India, there are about 3,500 psychiatrists, 1,000 psychiatric social workers, 1,000 clinical psychologists and 900 psychiatric nurses in India (Murthy 2000). Evidence shows that trained social workers are increasingly encountering problematic alcohol and other drug use among their service users and have identified areas of training needs and report lack of confidence when approaching substance use–related issues (Galvani and Forrester, 2008).

Given the limited resources in developing countries, it is a challenge to optimally use mental health human resources (in the form of trained mental health professionals) to offer effective rehabilitation and support for persons with SUDs. Unfortunately, in India, treatment interventions for SUDs are largely limited to specialised tertiary care in addiction treatment centres and only for those with late stage problems (Murthy and Nikettha 2007).

Many social workers (often specialised in medical and psychiatric social work) who are a part of the treatment team may not have had specific or formal training including exposure to SUDs and psychosocial interventions. A social worker has been defined as a 'change agent, a helper who is specifically trained and employed for the purpose of planned change and is expected to be skilled to work with individuals, families and the community and help in problem solving and coping capacities' (Barker 2003, cited in Zastrow 2010). In addition, the International Federation of Social Work (IFSW 2013) defines the profession of social work as one that 'promotes problem solving in human relationships and the empowerment and liberation of people to enhance well-being, utilising theories of human behaviour and social systems'. In such a case, for trained social workers, the principles of social work can serve as a guide in delivering psychosocial interventions for persons with SUDs including their families.

This chapter addresses a social worker's role in engaging a person with SUD and significant others in effectively dealing with the problem. Specific areas discussed include motivation enhancement, brief interventions, promotion of skills (communication, problem solving, assertiveness, drink refusal, stress and coping, relaxation), and relapse management, occupational help, working with couples and families, follow-up and after care.

Given below are social work principles. The psychosocial interventions used in addiction treatment centres are as follows.

Social Work Principles and SUD

According to the IFSW (2013), social work is based on 'respect for the inherent worth and dignity of all people, upholding and defending each person's physical, psychological, emotional and spiritual integrity and well-being'. Besides reiterating an individual's right to self-determination, and to participate as stated by IFSW, this chapter also recognises aspects such as the importance of treating and empowering each person as a whole that includes family and promoting their strengths. DuBois and Miley (1992) have outlined the social work's profession as being guided by a distinct set of values and ethics. These values are transformed into accepted practice principles for the purpose of intervention with clients and the nine social work principles have relevance in the Indian context in addiction treatment. They include the following:

Acceptance: This refers to genuine concern by a social worker in a professional relationship. It includes receptive listening, intentional responses that acknowledge the other person's viewpoint and mutual respect. Often, clients with SUDs may feel isolated and rejected by their local community and acceptance by the social worker is an important value. In a country like India where alcohol use is generally viewed with disapproval, this principle is important.

Affirming individuality: This means to 'begin where the client is' or to recognise the uniqueness with personalised understanding, freedom from bias, labelling, prejudices, stereotyping and recognising cultural diversity. Usually clients with SUDs are often criminalised or labelled as a 'drunkard' or 'junkie' and this may be their only identity where society is concerned.

Purposeful expression of feelings: Providing the client with opportunities to express, uncover and vent feelings is another aspect. Clients with SUD may have never had the chance to talk about their lives and difficult experiences and social workers during counselling can create this opportunity.

Non-judgemental: A non-blaming attitude and behaviour towards the client as being either good or bad or unworthy is important. In the context of SUD, clients may have many past experiences commonly viewed as being deviant and they may not fit into societal norms.

Objectivity: The avoidance of including personal feelings in a social worker's observations and understanding is important. For instance, a social worker may not approve of alcohol use in personal life and this value needs to be kept apart and to themselves.

Controlled emotional involvement: Sensitivity to client's feelings, an understanding based on knowledge of human behaviour, and responses guided by knowledge and purpose are the three components that play a role when working with a client.

Self-determination: The rights and needs of clients, their freedom in making their own choices and decisions are recognised and encouraged during the working relationship by a social worker. Here, innate capacity for self-determination by the client having SUD is encouraged.

Access to resources: Ensuring an individual's access to necessary resources, services and opportunities to improve social conditions and promotion of social justice through advocacy and legislative changes is the responsibility of a social worker. In the Indian context, the oppressed and disadvantaged persons with SUD and their families benefit from such actions.

Confidentiality: This refers to the right to a client's privacy about their identity, information shared during individual and group work and their expressed consent before psychosocial interventions begin. The stigma associated with use of alcohol in Indian society viewing itself as a 'dry culture' can call for secrecy about substance use information including treatment.

The above principles serve as a springboard for a social worker working in addiction treatment centres through their constant interplay with psychosocial care to facilitate change and growth in an individual's long-term goals at the same time restoring strength and dignity. Clinical social work has a primary focus on the mental, emotional and behavioural well-being of individuals, couples and families including a holistic approach to psychotherapy and the client's relationship to his/her environment specialised in treatment of psychiatric and substance disorders (NASW 2005). Where group processes are concerned, the role of the social worker as facilitator requires high level of training that resonates with basic social work principles. There can be treatment groups, psycho-educational groups and support groups for clients and their families and in addiction treatment centres they help to change unhealthy behaviour, learn new social skills, learn to trust and gain insight into personal problems, experience mutual support and achieve stated goals.

Psychosocial Interventions

Psychosocial interventions have been described to include a combination of psychological and behavioural strategies, which are used alone or in combination with pharmacotherapy and the level of intensity, frequency and duration of these interventions may vary depending upon the settings (ranging from outpatient, partial hospitalisation or residential-based treatment). According to Yadav and Dhawan (2007), treatment interventions for SUD (presented below) are commonly viewed from the lens of a bio–psycho–social condition requiring a multipronged approach of management.

Psychosocial Models in Addiction Treatment

In a paper titled 'Planning Psychosocial Interventions', Yadav and Dhawan (2007) report that the most often used bio–psycho–social model for addictive behaviours articulated by Donovan (1986) comprise the following components:

- Biomedical modalities focus on detoxification regimens, anti-craving medication, substitution treatment and other pharmacological approaches
- Psychological treatment modalities range from addiction counselling to psychodynamic and cognitive behavioural treatment modalities, insight-oriented therapy, behaviour therapy and motivational interventions.

- Sociocultural treatment modalities include therapeutic communities, vocational rehabilitation and culturally specific interventions.

The hitherto described components that comprise of psychosocial interventions could be used for individuals (or clients), family members or significant members and other support persons (UNODC 2005). Murthy and Nikettha (2007) state that psychosocial interventions in SUDs can be easily delivered with some training for mental health professionals placed in addiction treatment centres. The interventions may vary depending on the treatment setting and goals of treatment.

Yadav and Dhawan (2005) state that some of the important psychosocial interventions in treatment of SUDs are brief intervention, motivation improvement, relapse prevention (assertiveness, stress management, relaxation and refusal skills), network therapy (strengthening peer and social support by mobilising families and friends), community reinforcement approach (vocational counselling, social skills training, problem solving skills, creating self-help groups via communities in natural settings) and multi-systemic therapy (includes family, community and peer group). The mental health professionals including social workers use individual counselling, cognitive behavioural strategies and skills training for the various interventions. They add that effective management of SUD is to combine psychosocial care with pharmacological interventions (being complimentary to each other)—they caution that factors such as patient's characteristics (education, support systems, motivation)and therapist's skills (empathy and therapeutic alliance) could challenge effective delivery of services. DiNitto and McNeece's (2007) paper on addictions and social work practice state that with the growing number of evidence-based approaches for treatment of addictive behaviours, social workers need to discern and select ones that may be the most useful in their local context and practice.

An overview of some of the aforesaid interventions and the role of the mental health professionals including a social worker is presented in this chapter. The term mental health professional includes a social worker and has been used interchangeably throughout.

INDIVIDUAL COUNSELLING

Burnard (1995) defines counselling as a means by which 'one person helps another through purposeful conversation' and lists the essential elements of counselling skills to include empathy and warmth towards the client, genuineness (being interested), unconditional positive regard and concreteness (sticking to what is being said than implied). A sense of humour (a light approach that can often rescue situations), a sense of the tragic (recognising that humans have limitations) and self-awareness (of the counsellor's own limitations and strengths) has been included.

Competence in counselling, a component of psychosocial care, is essential for social work practice, and by using problem-solving approaches, counselling theories and practice bring about positive changes when working with individuals, families and communities (Zastrow 2010). Bringing about a change through counselling is a challenging component found in interventions such as motivation enhancement therapy, brief interventions, cognitive behaviour therapy and skills training, that is, drink refusal, assertiveness, to name a few (UNODC 2008).

Counselling services for the client are an indispensable part of treatment intervention regardless of the type of treatment setting. The counselling process serves to establish a rapport and create trust from the first interview session until the follow-up phase between the client and the mental health professional including a social worker at the treatment centre. The professionals' interpersonal skills, warmth and supportive style help clients during addiction treatment. The purpose of counselling is to be a good listener and to organise each case methodically and at the same time build a trusting relationship. Keeping progress notes and anticipating difficulties help to deal with difficult situations; careful planning is a part of good counselling practice. For the clients, the aim of counselling is to empower them to live their daily lives more effectively. The mutual process is to reduce the client's fear and distrust while encouraging the client to continue attending treatment and follow-up by providing a non-threatening environment.

According to Egan (2002), all helping frameworks for clients consist of four fundamental questions:

1. What is going on?

    – Facilitates the clients to tell their stories
    – Assists in breaking through blind spots that prevent clients from seeing their problem situations and unexplored opportunities
    – Enlists clients to choose the right problems and/or opportunities to work on

2. What solutions make sense for me?

    – Help clients to choose realistic goals that are the real solutions to key problems

- Helps clients find incentives to help them commit to change

3. What do I have to do to get what I need or want?

- Helps clients develop different ways to choose the best strategy to make a plan

4. How do I get results?

- Helps clients convert goal setting into solutions, results, outcomes or accomplishments. This is an ongoing process and part of the implementation phase

These four questions provide the steps, goals and actions towards better management of problems. The stages overlap and interact with one another.

For a social worker, the basic principles of social work such as confidentiality, objectivity, purposeful expression of feelings and controlled emotions come into play during counselling. In a report by the Bureau of Labour Statistics (2011), the work description for mental health and substance abuse social workers includes counselling of clients in individual or group sessions to assist them in dealing with substance abuse, mental or physical illness, poverty, unemployment or physical abuse including counselling family members to assist them to understand, deal with or support the client or patient with SUD including mental health problems.

MOTIVATIONAL ENHANCEMENT

One of the most challenging tasks in addiction treatment is to get people to change. A collaborative client–social worker relationship provides a partnership of support rather than persuasion or coercion. The main aim of motivational interviewing is to shift the client towards motivation for change emphasising that the process is voluntary and the decision to do so rests with the client. Jones' (2007) paper on 'Motivational Interviewing with Substance Abusers' reports that the client-centred approach which is the hallmark of social work is reflected in motivational interviewing resonant with social work values of a client's right to self-determination and not a top-down, authoritarian approach. Wahab (2005) similarly reports that motivational interviewing in addiction settings concerned with behaviour change was consistent with core social work values and ethics.

There are five stages or cycles observed during motivation beginning with pre-contemplation and terminating in the maintenance phase. A social worker's response in each stage is highlighted.

Stage 1. Pre-contemplation: Here, the client does not consider change and continues abusing the substance.

> Some common statements by clients are as follows:
> *'I drink alcohol to get a good night of sleep'; or 'Why should I stop smoking ganja, (marijuana) as it is only a herb'; or 'I use heroin to forget my problems'.*

Social worker's response: Allow the client to ventilate (on feelings, impact on others); provide information (about the client and the problem).

Stage 2. Contemplation: The problem related to alcohol/ drug use is acknowledged and the client weighs the pros and cons.

> Some common statements by clients are as follows:
> *'I guess I need to quit, but it may be difficult'; or 'I need to give up heroin but can I do it without pain?'*

Social worker's response: Facilitate discussion on the costs or benefits of quitting and a realistic evaluation based on feelings and cognition about alcohol/drugs.

Stage 3. Determination/Preparation: The client makes a decision to quit the drug/alcohol.

> Some common statements by clients are as follows:
> *'I want to stop drinking'; or 'I would like to start the treatment'.*

Social worker's response: Build on the confidence of the person's ability to change and commit to specific goals.

Stage 4. Action: The client takes concrete steps towards specific goals.
Social worker's response: Help the person make a plan and work towards the goal.

Stage 5. Maintenance: The client stays committed to the alcohol/drug free behaviour through a change in lifestyle.
Social worker's response: The person is encouraged by inclusion of support systems (relatives, significant others) around him/her in the treatment plan.

The readiness to change depends on the stage that the client is in, that is, while some motivated clients move smoothly from one stage to another (e.g., less difficult for a client in the stage of determination), there are others who may face difficulties (e.g., clients in an early, pre-contemplation stage).

Motivational interviews can be carried out as a separate session, though they are often used at first contact between the client and the treatment professional. It is usually integrated with other therapeutic interventions at different points of time. Repetition of motivational elements during each session increases the client's engagement and reinforces commitment towards maintaining recovery. Research on substance dependence reveals that such brief and timely interventions are more effective in contrast to long-term, intensive therapies. Also, a therapist's effects and characteristics are found to influence a client's dropout and considered as a common index of motivation. The four principles of motivational interviewing given below serve as a guide during the counselling sessions (see Box 10.1).

Box 10.1
Four Principles of Motivational Interviewing

1. Express empathy:

    – An accepting attitude facilitates change
    – Skilful reflective listening
    – Recognise ambivalence as normal

2. Develop discrepancy:

    – Encourage client to present arguments for change
    – Perceived discrepancy between present behaviour (of continuous substance abuse) and personal goals and values motivates change

3. Roll with resistance:

    – Avoid arguing for change (counterproductive)
    – Recognise resistance as a signal to respond differently
    – Encourage client to find new perspectives, resources, solutions (do not impose)

4. Support self-efficacy

    – Supporting client's belief to implement and succeed with specific tasks motivates change

Source: Miller and Rollnick (2002).

Brief Intervention

Brief interventions are now recognised as an important part of the overall approach to persons with risky patterns of substance use (Murthy and Nikketha 2007). Clients may have alcohol/drug pattern of consumption that is defined as at risk for future health problems and may not have problems or dependence-related issues. The aim of brief interventions is to reduce the prevalence of substance abuse and decrease consumption by early detection and intervention before it further progresses to dependence.

Benefits of Brief Intervention

- A cost effective and time efficient mode of intervention
- Provides the person with a realistic picture of substance use
- Corrects misconceptions regarding substance use
- Gives feedback regarding potential/actual harm/risk
- Encourages client's participation, motivation to change behaviour

Even though there are benefits as seen above, brief interventions should not be viewed as complete solutions as they are inadequate to handle complex psychosocial issues and severe dependence. Rather, it is usually a preventive method of primary care for individuals at risk in the community.

Steps in Brief Intervention

- Identification (clients are screened through instruments, question-naires to obtain medical and substance use history): Screening helps to understand the related risks to clients that can prompt them to consider changing their substance use behaviour. For a client, it helps the social worker to plan appropriate intervention. Some of the questionnaires for assessment and screening are the CAGE (screening test with four questions for alcohol-related problems) and the AUDIT (Alcohol Use Disorders Identification Test) questionnaires for alcohol, the ASSIST (Alcohol, Smoking and Substance Involvement Screening Test) for all drugs abuse and the Fagerstrom's Test for Nicotine Dependence (FTND).
- The next step is to assess the client's motivation to change (refer to section on motivation enhancement therapy). Based on the client's need and goals, the strategy is personalised; FRAMES (freedom, responsibility, advice, menu, empathy and self-efficacy) is used and offered in a non-judgemental manner.

About FRAMES: 'FRAMES' provides an outline on the important components of a brief intervention. The acronym stands for (NIAAA 1999)

- *Feedback* to clients about the risks associated with continued alcohol/drug use based on assessment
- *Responsibility* of an individual (based on choices) to cut down substance use is emphasised
- *Advice* on the importance of changing current pattern of substance use
- *Menu* of alternative change options, choices, setting of limits, learning to recognise high-risk antecedents and developing skills to deal and cope with everyday problems associated with alcohol/drug use
- *Empathy* including a warm, reflective and understanding style that is effective in the client's motivation and change compared to an aggressive, confrontational style
- *Self-efficacy* by encouraging optimism in the client to help in achieving the set goals including motivation enhancing techniques to develop, implement and commit to plans

Note on Brief Interventions:

- Typically of five to thirty minutes in duration
- Use of motivational interviewing and counselling techniques
- Used in settings such as general/emergency hospitals settings, community counselling centres, workplace settings, general practitioner settings
- With prior training, any health care professional can deliver brief interventions
- When a brief intervention is not successful in reducing alcohol/drug use, offer a more intensive treatment including referral to a specialist centre

COGNITIVE BEHAVIOURAL INTERVENTIONS

Psychosocial interventions that are cognitive oriented include thinking and behaving strategies that are useful to make lifestyle changes for risky drinkers including those with substance dependence. The interventions are based on behavioural learning principles and on the idea that re-learning and modifying behaviour is influenced by how people view themselves and others. The approach covers a range of strategies and techniques, which includes skills training and cognitive restructuring including behavioural couples' therapy. McHugh et al. (2010) reports that cognitive behavioural therapy (CBT) for SUDs has demonstrated efficacy as a monotherapy and when combined as part of treatment strategies.

SKILLS TRAINING

There is consistent evidence that skills training are a useful part of treatment intervention for clients aiming at reducing the use of drinking or towards total abstinence. The training is specially recommended for clients with a high risk of relapse as it compensates for skills deficits that have led to alcohol/drug use as a coping strategy. It is also beneficial for clients lacking relevant skills (observed during assessment and counselling sessions) such as assertiveness, problem solving abilities and communication (Murthy and Nikketha 2007).

In skills training, emphasis should be on

– Assessing client's need for learning specific skills
– Client's commitment to learning skills
– Breaking down behaviour using a step-by-step format during training
– Encouraging practice, refining and reinforcing skills at various stages
– Using both individual and group sessions for effective skills training
– Avoiding training clients in skills in which they are already adept

A brief note on some of the important skills and its main components is given below.

Communication Skills: Role play and modelling are useful in communication skills training for clients who feel uncomfortable and embarrassed in social gatherings. The aim is to teach clients skills related to active listening, starting and engaging in conversation, understanding social cues and to feel comfortable with silences including the expression of feelings and opinions. Good communication strengthens relationships and well-being especially in families coping with alcohol/drug-related problems. Effective communication is both what said (verbal), as well as non-verbal (using our body, facial expressions, gestures, tone of voice and our eyes).

Problem-solving Skills: The goal of problem solving is to assist clients to tackle life with a general set of skills that may threaten their commitment to change. There may be many situations in life where clients are faced with the inability to solve problems. Many problems may be related to issues arising out of use of alcohol/drugs; for example, facing life after addiction treatment can be stressful—it may mean clearing old debts and bills, finding a job or staying away from drinking friends.

The steps in problem solving are as follows:

1. Identify the specific problem
2. Brainstorm the different solutions
3. Select the best option
4. Make a plan to implement the option
5. Evaluate the outcome; if not satisfied, restart from 1.

Assertiveness and Substance Refusal Skills: Assertiveness training is equally effective for goals of moderation or abstinence. Problematic situations are role played and repeatedly practiced at the treatment centre. The gradual change in the client's thinking increases self-confidence and ability to be assertive. Clients having problems related to alcohol and drugs may often have difficulties in expressing feelings in a clear manner; for example learning to say a firm 'No' to situations that are at high risk for relapses including those that create feelings of discomfort. This can result in creating negative mood states such as anger, frustration, sadness and anxiety adding to interpersonal problems both at home and outside. Thus, the vicious cycle of both relapses and/or the risky use of substances recur.

> The client learns that being assertive means that he/she has
>
> - The right to express personal opinions and feelings
> - The right to request others to change behaviour that affects the person
> - The right to reject or accept requests without hurting others

> Types of assertive responses
>
> - Non-verbal: Maintain eye contact, speak in clear voice, keep an erect body posture, let your face talk, use gestures
> - Verbal: Talk with feelings, express your opinions when others disagree, accept responsibility

Refusal Skills: Clients often lack confidence in being assertive to say 'No' when pressurised by their peer group and others to drink alcohol or use drugs.

Statements that put pressure to use are as follows:

'Just one beer will not hurt you after treatment'
'Come join us at the bar to celebrate my job promotion'
'Have a drag of ganja (marijuana), it's only a herb'

Drink or drug refusal skills training teaches the person to develop and practice methods of effective responses. The repetitive use of assertive and refusal skills need to be encouraged in the client during counselling sessions extending to follow-up and aftercare stages to help maintain treatment goals (see Box 10.2).

Box 10.2
Refusal Skills

When refusing or saying 'No', emphasise on

- Coming up with alternative activities instead of using alcohol/drugs
  'Let us have fresh juice instead of beer';
  'I was just leaving, as I get up early to go jogging'

- Assertive, appropriate responses in dealing with social pressure
- Using strong body language, confident tone of voice and respond fast
  'No thanks, I have stopped using heroin';
  'I am on medication, I cannot drink'
  'I have a busy day at college tomorrow'

- Guilt-free feelings about saying 'No'
- Mastering skills through role play using groups (more effective than individual sessions)
- Incorporating relaxation and stress management to reduce daily tension

Relaxation Training Skills and Stress Management

Clients with alcohol- and drug-related problems may report that they get overwhelmed due to stress from various sources and display signs of tension. Deep muscle relaxation, relaxed imagery, yoga, tai chi, chanting and meditation are some techniques proven to help individuals relax by reducing anxiety. The client can be counselled to recognise the signs in advance and use relaxation techniques to reduce tension and prevent a relapse (Murthy and Nikettha 2007).

Anger Management

Users of substances are found to experience anger more frequently than non-users, are less in control of their angry feelings and alcohol is found to interfere with self-regulation skills. In an Indian study, it was found that alcohol use enhanced the expression of anger, aggressiveness and was perceived as a negative emotion (Sharma et al. 2012). Psycho-education for anger control was recommended as a part of treatment intervention.

CO-OCCURRING PROBLEMS

Besides the use of substances by individuals and families, the social worker needs to recognise co-occurring disorders such as anxiety, depression including severe mental health problems such as psychoses as well as risky temperaments (such as impulsivity, boredom, sensation seeking) as they can complicate the recovery processes. It is reported that more than 50 per cent of persons with substance use are known to suffer from mental illness while 70 per cent of those with mental illness use substances regularly (Kulhalli, cited in Murthy and Nikettha 2007). Timely referrals to the psychiatrist are important to treat problems related to mental health, assist with withdrawal symptoms and minimise the risk of relapse.

SPIRITUAL AND FAITH-BASED INTERVENTIONS

Spirituality plays a role in maintaining treatment gains and recovering individuals show more evidence of spirituality in comparison to those who relapse (Miller 2003). The 12 steps of Alcoholics Anonymous (AA) are explicitly spiritual and refer to surrendering oneself to a 'higher power'. Similarly, prayer, meditation and retreats are included as part of recovery.

LIFESTYLE CHANGES

These include simple measures such as healthy diets, exercise, structured daily routines, safe recreations and alternative methods to cope with stress, anger and loneliness. It also includes proactive measures to deal with high-risk situations that may cause relapses (avoiding being with friends who use drugs, avoiding smoking to prevent an alcohol relapse).

COGNITIVE RESTRUCTURING

Cognitive restructuring has shown to help persons identify and change irrational self-statements about their self-worth, counterproductive beliefs and views related to use of substances that contribute to relapse. The goal is to help the clients recognise when their erroneous thinking is likely to lead to the use of alcohol/drugs and the breaking away from such thoughts is by challenging and interrupting.

> Some points to remember:
>
> – Cognitive restructuring is effective when combined with skills training in other areas
> – The process is collaborative (between counsellor and client)
> – Recommended for those with no cognitive deficits
> – Useful for clients with additional problems such as anxiety and depression

COUPLES THERAPY

The overall goal of couples therapy is to improve relationship and communication including the commitment to change the behaviour associated with alcohol/drug use. Couples therapy includes skills therapy for partners and cognitive restructuring, improving a partner's coping with substance-related situations as well as improving the overall relationship functioning (Epstein and McCrady 1998).

Aim of Couples Therapy

– To improve interactions to support change in alcohol/drug using behaviour
– To address relationship problems by resolving conflicts without the use of substances
– To strengthen the coping, communication and problem-solving skills of the partner; help to deal with risky drinking,
– To encourage activities that do not involve alcohol/drug use
– Couples therapy can be offered and continued at follow-up
– Used for couples with moderate to low problems; couples living together
– The therapy should emphasise that alcohol/drug use is the problem

Such dyadic intervention among couples has been shown to have better treatment outcome compared to individual interventions (Nattala et al. 2010).

Relapse Prevention

Relapse is one of the most important problems in SUDs and should not be considered as an exception. The decision to change the pattern of substance abuse is a challenge to the person and difficulties during treatment are to be viewed as a natural part of the process. Given that there is a substantial relapse rate of return to problem drinking within the first year after treatment, relapse prevention is not an intervention in itself, but should be a part of the comprehensive treatment plan to reduce the risk of both problem and recurrent use of substances. Inclusion of skills training, cognitive restructuring and lifestyle balancing as part of treatment intervention addresses the immediate issues preceding relapse at the same time help with long-term precipitating factors.

Common Factors Associated with Relapse

Lapse refers to the initial episode of use of the substance following a period of abstinence.
Relapse refers to the failure to maintain a state, free from substances over time.

Many factors, also referred to as 'triggers', seen during different phases of treatment intervention contribute to a relapse. They are as given below:

− Coping skills inadequate
− Mood states: Negative emotions such as anger, sadness, frustration, boredom, guilt; including excessive happiness, excitement (positive mood)
− Poor social network, lack of social support, peer pressure, poor family support including unemployment
− Physiological factors: Craving (post-treatment), long-lasting withdrawal symptoms, that is, recurrent sleep disturbance after cessation of substances, chronic physical pain
− Beliefs: Client's view of substance dependence as a loss of control disease, low self-efficacy; for example:

   'I have relapsed after not using drugs for three months; what will my family think of me?'
   'I am worthless because I cannot stop drinking'

− Cognitive and behavioural factors: Over-confidence, false sense of perception to cope with high-risk situations including impulsivity; for example:

   'I can be with my friends when they smoke ganja as I have been away from drugs for a year'

'Let my colleagues drink; I have control and will drink only lime juice'

- Psychiatric conditions: Mood (depression) and anxiety disorders (panic attacks, generalized), drug induced psychosis, somatoform disorders, insomnia

The social worker should be alert to the above factors experienced by the client and take appropriate steps to address them. This would apply to a variety of clients in different treatment settings (outpatient, residential and community-based interventions).

High-risk Situations and Craving

The goal of relapse prevention strategies is to reduce the severity of relapse, help clients to reduce risky use or abstain from use of alcohol/drugs and improve psychosocial well-being. Relapse prevention is best after the acute withdrawal symptoms have subsided and is recommended for clients with moderate to severe alcohol-/drug-related problems.

The most important component in relapse prevention is to identify high-risk situations; for example, frequenting bars, meeting friends who use alcohol/drugs, weekends, payday, isolated living, family conflicts, work-related stress, tiredness and poor sleep. The assessment of co-morbid disorders, cognitive impairment including social and coping skills is included.

The next step is to address craving. Once the triggers that precede relapse are identified, the client is taught specific ways to handle craving. The client is reminded that feelings of craving to use the substance is episodic and range from high intensity to a gradual disappearing phase, that is, like a wave in the ocean. Hence, it is time bound and requires coping skills; for example, postponing the use of substance (by calling a support person, friend), recalling negative consequences, practicing the 4 D's and HALT including staying away from triggers or high-risk situations (Murthy and Nikketha 2007).

4 D's: Delay, Drink water, Distract, Deep breathing
HALT: Hunger, Anger, Loneliness and Tiredness

Strategies for relapse prevention should be reiterated during counselling as part of follow-up and aftercare sessions. They are as follows:

- Learning from triggers preceding lapse or relapse onto making specific plans to reduce future problems
- Strengthening coping responses (behavioural methods) with pervasive stressors through physical activities, use of relaxation techniques
- Strengthening coping responses (cognitive methods) with thoughts of negative consequences associated with the use of substances; delaying use of alcohol/drugs including distraction
- Handling negative mood states: Creating awareness of self-defeating thoughts, its adverse consequences; challenge, ignore thoughts; learn to accept self and have realistic expectations; for example,

> 'Each time I felt guilty about the past, I relapsed and went back to drinking; what is the point of thinking of the past?'

- Encouraging changes in client's lifestyle through recreational activities, hobbies to substitute activities related to use of alcohol/drugs
- Continuously use motivational interviewing and cognitive behavioural strategies to address issues concerning relapse (including lapse)
- Role playing, modelling of new behaviours to deal with high risk-situations; give direct feedback (during group and individual sessions)
- Plans for follow-up sessions, continuous contact and review treatment goals
- Psycho-education on relapse prevention for clients, family, support persons
- Referral to specialists for other issues threatening future relapse

Adjunct Pharmacotherapy

Pharmacological therapies are part of treatment and an adjunct to relapse prevention for clients with alcohol-/drug-related problems. Medication to decrease craving or replace the harmful substance is usually started within one week of detoxification and prescribed for three to six months; in some cases up to a year. Medication is also prescribed for co-existing psychiatric disorders. Clients often find it difficult to comply with medication. However, those who are compliant with both psychosocial treatments including medication are likely to have a smoother recovery.

Occupational Rehabilitation

It is well known that substance use or abuse leads to deterioration on occupational functioning and productivity at the workplace. The unemployed client faces greater problems after recovery, where the likelihood of relapse is high. Conditions that need attention when planning occupational rehabilitation:

- Night shifts, rotating shifts, over-time (especially faced by information technology and business outsourced employees working across different time zones); seasonal work, labour intensive jobs, pressure at work
- Monotonous work routine, boredom
- Use of substances as a part of work culture, business parties, availability of alcohol/drugs near workplace
- Availability of disposable income; pay day (high chance of risky use of alcohol/ drugs)

Thus, plans for relapse treatment should be tailored to the needs of each client.

Workplace Interventions

Substance use problems can be effectively identified and addressed through workplace interventions, where early identification, prompt intervention and supervised follow-up can result in better outcome. Systematic worksite interventions for alcohol-related problems have been shown to produce significant long-term improvements in both alcohol consumption and work efficiency (Murthy and Sankaran 2009).

Working with Families

Families living with a person with alcohol-/drug-related problems are affected by overall family dysfunction and view the problem as a shameful secret. Family members can have high hopes, experience great relief and joy over the person's abstinence from alcohol/drugs after treatment intervention. Treatment intervention should be directed to include families (and children) to enhance their own individual well–being and at the same time equip them to manage future problems that may be experienced by the person recovering from SUD.

Problems faced by family members: As the alcohol/drug problem escalates and intensifies over time, the family tries to deal with each new crisis resulting in their lives becoming as dysfunctional as the addicted family member. The family members, especially the spouses of the client, are exposed to high levels of violence. Many clients are usually found to be under the influence of alcohol prior to the assault. Children witnessing these scenes may be left with emotional scars. Some parents may be prone to neglecting their children and this could result in emotional distancing.

Problems commonly face by children having a parent with substance use disorder:

- Lack of positive role models
- Witnessing fights, violence at home
- Dropping out of school; forced to work due to financial crisis
- Poor contacts with relatives, others
- Risk of early use due to home environment (imitating parent's drinking through modelling; parent asking child to light a cigarette or get drinks)
- Emotional and behavioural problems

The more serious the alcohol/drug problem in the person, the less the spouse is able to perform the various roles and responsibilities competently. Many spouses/partners may have psychological problems such as depression, anxiety, low esteem including disturbed sleep and appetite. Stress may frequently culminate in suicidal ideation (Murthy 2008). The spouse may be vulnerable to drinking or drug problems, misuse of medication (e.g., tranquilizers, sedatives, and antidepressants) used as a coping mechanism or misguided exercise to control her spouse's drinking. Hence, the family as a unit, attempts to maintain equilibrium or balance in their lives at any cost (referred as *homeostasis*). The role of the social worker is to prepare the family for this long and continuous process of recovery.

Some common issues faced by families during the client's recovery phase are given below:

- Family members taking total responsibility for a state free from substance use and not considering recovery as the client's responsibility
- Treating client with caution or like a 'brittle doll' fearing that saying anything could cause conflict making the person use alcohol/drugs again

- Lack of trust, fear or suspiciousness undermining genuine efforts made by recovering person, for example, reddening of eyes mistaken for a relapse
- Excluding client from taking up old roles at home and outside, for example, paying bills, school fees, shopping
- Family's reluctance in not letting old feelings go; making negative remarks or unwillingness to acknowledge client's recovery or progress
- Poor social contact to avoid embarrassment at public occasions caused by alcohol-/drug-related problems by client
- Continuing problems such as poor family or couple interactions, unsettled debts, difficulty with job, sexual problems

Intervention for families: The social work code of ethics directs social work professionals working in the area of addiction to include strengths and resiliencies and the involvement of family members in the intervention process (NIAAA 2005). The social worker should provide the families including children a chance to make meaning out of a difficult situation or adversity encouraging an *optimistic approach*—in this case, the addiction treatment itself may be a traumatic experience. Helping the family view and approach crises is important for well-functioning families, helps to improve coping styles and contributes to resilience among family members (Sankaran et al 2008). It is important to involve the family from the beginning of treatment to plan recovery at a more realistic level.

The aim of family counselling is as follows:

- To create safe, accepting and supportive environment for family members to discuss problems, needs, feelings due to the alcohol-/drug-related problems
- To help family members 'recover' and improve their well-being (independent from the addict's recovery); offer medical/psychiatric help.
- To empower families to tackle future issues and support to the client through psycho education on alcohol/drugs, consequences
- To provide information on relapse prevention, that is, help family members identify high-risk situations, management of relapses, follow-up
- To equip families (including children) to restore healthy family functioning and individual well-being by improving family interactions, skills related to parenting, communication, assertiveness, stress, coping and anger management

- To strengthen supports (material and emotional) including meeting new non–alcohol-/drug-using friends
- To revitalise rituals and routines through structured plans of daily routines engaging the family as a unit, for example, eating a meal together, watching television, recreational activities; celebrating family traditions, visiting relatives, celebrating birthdays; celebrating festivals/ holidays. Such rituals and routines are considered to play a protective role in delaying early onset of alcohol/drug use by reinforcing a sense of family identity for the children (Muralidharan and Sankaran 2007).

> *Family rituals and activities*: Families that maintain their important rituals (despite severe parental drinking) are found to have a strong collective sense of identity (this identity is separate from the identity of that of an 'alcoholic family'). Pre-existing rituals are actively protected by the family members and the parent's intoxicated behaviour is rejected by confrontation and clear expression of disapproval. The idea is that the rituals may often be continued by the children when they turn into adults. These communicate important messages to the children that there is a possibility of taking effective control of the present and future life events.

- To provide families with directory of services such as addiction treatment centres (both private and government services at district/state levels), tobacco cessation clinics, addresses of AA, Al-Anon and Al Ateen meetings, vocational guidance/training centres, legal aid, micro-credit groups for women, voluntary organisations/clubs

Follow-up and Aftercare

Complete recovery includes a change in use/abuse of substances, working through the problems in thinking, behaviour, lifestyle issues, interpersonal relationships and day-to-day functioning. Treatment at the primary phase is to stabilise the client; the major part of recovery starts later. For example, the client may be alcohol/drug free but can be irritable and disengage from the environment. The social worker greatly influences the recovery process by being supportive, non-judgemental and sensitive to the difficulties during the client's recovery phase. Recent technology such as mobile telephones, text messages, internet contact offer opportunities for follow-up and support even when face-to-face contact is not practical or feasible (Murthy and Subodh 2010).

What helps in recovery?

- A structured treatment program and daily routine to strengthen commitment to remain free from alcohol/drugs
- Physical well-being to improve health, that is, regular mealtimes, cessation in use of tobacco, coffee or tea, junk food; regular sleep; exercise routines; maintaining personal hygiene; addressing medical problems like gastritis, neuritis, respiratory problems, pain and so on.
- A productive work routine for a sense of fulfilment and financial stability
- Regular follow-up contact is very important to identify and prevent relapses. In our experience, relapses are extremely common between three to six months following treatment (Prasad et al. 2000) and follow-up support is very important to prevent relapse (Murthy et al. 2009).
- Having fun without drugs, engaging in leisure and recreational activities, different from past
- A value-based lifestyle and shift from negative thinking, impulsiveness; respecting other's needs, feelings; accepting responsibility
- Increasing social support, engaging with family members, strengthening ties with parents, sibling, spouse and children; forming new relationships with alcohol-/drug free persons; contact with self-help groups (see box).

Self-help groups or peer-led groups are a part of treatment intervention during the recovery stages. The client usually identifies with the peer groups who are seen as strong motivators and primary agents of change. The membership is voluntary and the groups are open. Confidentiality and anonymity is maintained. Examples of self-help groups are Alcoholic Anonymous (AA), Narcotics Anonymous (NA) and Al Ateen (groups for teenagers).

Conclusion

The influences of SUDs on individuals' well-being and mental health have been presented in this chapter. Empowering and supporting them to effectively deal with substance use problems and restore or strengthen overall wellness, functioning with respect to family, work and society are important goals in psychosocial care and treatment of SUD. Integration of social work principles in the wide array of psychosocial interventions helps to focus on building individual skills, enhancing motivation, improving support for recovery and addressing relapse in SUDs.

References

Bureau of Labour Statistics. 2011. Summary Report for 21–1023.00. Mental Health and Substance Abuse Social Workers. Wage data and 2010–2020 Employment Projection. ('Projected growth' represents the estimated change in total employment over the projections period [2010–2020].)

Burnard, P. 1995. *Counselling Skills Training: A Sourcebook of Activities*. New Delhi: Viva Books Private Ltd.

DiNitto, Diana M. and C. Aaron McNeece. 2007. Addictions and Social Work Practice (Chapter 8). Retrieved from www.lyceumbooks.com/... lWorkIssuesOpps_Chapter_08.pdf (access date 1 May 2014)

Donovan, J. M. 1986. 'An Etiologic Model of Alcoholism', *American Journal of Psychiatry*, 143 (1):1–11. (Cited in Murthy, P. and Nikketha Bala Shanthi, S. 2007. *Psychosocial Interventions for Persons with Substance Abuse: Theory and Practice*. Bangalore: NIMHANS. Available at: www.cawnet.org/...sychosocial+a ssessment+forms+for... http://www.whoindia.org/LinkFiles/Mental_Health_&_ substance_Abuse_psychosocial_Interventions_for_persons_with_substance_ abuse.pdf) http://www.imarksweb.net/book/substance+abuse

DuBois, B. and K. K. Miley. 1992. *Social Work: An Empowering Profession* (pp. 135–141). Boston: Allyn and Bacon.

Egan, G. 2002. *The Skilled Helper: A Problem-Management and Opportunity-Development Approach to Helping* (7th ed.). Pacific Grove, CA: Brooks/Cole.

Epstein, E. E. and B. S. McCrady. 1998. 'Behavioral Couples Treatment of Alcohol and Drug Use Disorders: Current Status and Innovations'. *Clinical Psychology Review*, 18: 689–711.

Galvani, S. and D. Forrester. 2008. *What Works in Training Social Workers about Drug and Alcohol Use? A Survey of Student Learning and Readiness to Practice* (Final Report for the Home Office). Available online in PDF at: www.beds.ac.uk

International Federation of Social Workers (IFSW). 2013. Definition of Social Work. Available at: ifsw.org/policies/definition-of-social-work/ (accessed on 18 March, 2013)

Jones, L. K. 2007, May/June. 'Motivational Interviewing with Substance Abusers—The Power of Ambivalence'. *Social Work Today*, 7 (3): 34.

Kulhalli, V. (2007). Psychosocial Interventions—Opportunities and Challenges. (Cited in Murthy, P. and S. Nikketha Bala Shanthi. 2007. *Psychosocial*

Interventions for Persons with Substance Abuse: Theory and Practice. Bangalore: NIMHANS. Available at: http://www.whoindia.org/LinkFiles/Mental_ Health_&_substance_Abuse_psychosocial_Interventions_for_persons_with_ substance_abuse.pdf)

McHugh, R. K., B. A. Hearon and M. W. Otto. 2011.'Cognitive-Behavioral Therapy for Substance Use Disorders', *Psychiatric Clinics of North America*, 33 (3): 511–525. doi: 10.1016/j.psc.2010.04.012

Miller, W. R. 2003. 'Spirituality as an Antidote for Addiction', *Spirituality and Health.*

Miller, W. R. and S. Rollnick. 2002. *Motivational Interviewing: Preparing People for Change* (2nd ed.). New York: The Guilford Press.

Muralidhar, D. and L. Sankaran. 2007. 'Strengths Based Approach in Social Work Practice with Families Having Alcohol Problems', *Handbook of Psychiatric Social Work*. NIMHANS: Bangalore.

Murthy, P. 2008. *Women and Drug Use in India—Substance, Women and High Risk Assessment Study.* United Nations Office on Drugs and Crime. Available at: http://www.unodc.org/documents/southasia//reports/UNODC_Book_ Women_and_Drug_Use_in_India_2008.pdf (accessed 18 March, 2014)

Murthy, P. and B. N. Subodh. 2010, March. 'Current Developments in Behavioural Interventions in Tobacco Cessation' *Current Opinion*, 23 (2): 151–156.

Murthy, P. and L. Sankaran. 2009. Workplace Well-Being. Integrating Psychosocial Issues with Health. Bangalore: National Institute of Mental Health and Neuro Sciences and the Printers Bangalore Pvt. Ltd.

Murthy, P., P. K. Chand, M. G. Harish, K. Thennarasu, S. Prathima, Karappuchamy and N. Janakiramiah. 2009. Outcome of Alcohol Dependence: The Role of Continued Care, *Indian Journal of Community Medicine*, 34 (2): 148–151.

Murthy, P. and S. Nikketha Bala Shanthi. 2007. *Psychosocial Interventions for Persons with Substance Abuse: Theory and Practice.* Bangalore: NIMHANS. Available at: http://www.whoindia.org/LinkFiles/Mental_Health_&_substance_Abuse_ psychosocial_Interventions_for_persons_with_substance_abuse.pdf

Murthy, R. S. 2000. *Development of Mental Health Care in India 1947–1995.* New Delhi: Voluntary Health Association of India.

National Institute on Alcohol Abuse and Alcoholism (NIAAA). 1999. Brief Intervention for Alcohol Problems, April 1999, No: 43

———. 2005. Social Work Education for the Prevention and Treatment of Alcohol Use Disorders. Available at: http://pubs.niaaa.nih.gov/publications/Social/ Module 10HEthnicity & Culture/ Module10H.html accessed on 21 May 2007.

National Association of Social Workers (NASW). 2005. *Standards for Social Work Practice in Health Care Settings.* Washington, DC: Author.

Nattala, P., K. S. Leung, Dr Nagarajaiah, M.P., and P. Murthy. 2010. 'Family Member Involvement in Relapse Prevention Improves Alcohol Dependence Outcomes: A Prospective Study at an Addiction Treatment Facility in India', *Journal of Studies on Alcohol and Drugs,* 71 (4): 581–587.

Patel, V. and R. Thara. 2003. *Meeting Mental Health Needs of Developing Countries—NGO Innovations in India.* New Delhi: Sage Publication.

Prasad, S., P. Murthy, D. K. Subbukrishna and P. S. Gopinath. 2000. 'Treatment Setting and Followup in Alcohol Dependence' *Indian Journal of Psychiatry,* 42 (4): 387–392.

Sankaran, L., D. Muralidhar and V. Benegal. 2008. 'Strengthening Resilience within Families in Addiction Treatment', *The Indian Journal of Social Work,* 69 (1).

Sharma, M. K., L. N. Suman, P. Murthy and P. Marimuthu. 2012. 'Relationship of Trait Anger with Quality of Life and Anger Control among Alcohol Users', *Open Journal of Psychiatry,* 2 (4): 249–252. Available at: http://www.SciRP.org/journal/ojpsych (accessed 18 March 2014)

UNODC. 2005. World Drug Report 2005. Retrieved from www.unodc.org/...c/en/data-and-analysis/WDR-2005.html. Accessed 1 May 2014.

UNODC. 2011. World Drug Report 2011. New York: United Nations.

Wahab, S. 2005. 'Motivational Interviewing and Social Work Practice', *Journal of Social Work,* 5 (1): 45–60.

WHO. 2010. *Management of Substance Abuse.* Geneva; Author. Available at: http://www.who.int/substance_abuse/facts/index.html (accessed on 22 October, 2014)

Yadav, S. and S. Dhawan. 2007. Planning Psychosocial Intervention. Helping Persons with Substance Abuse Series. Psychosocial Interventions for Persons with Substance Abuse: Theory and Practice. Bangalore: NIMHANS, Deaddiction Centre.

Zastrow, C. 2010. The Practice of Social Work—A Comprehensive Work Text (9th ed.). BROOKS/COLE Cengage Learning: California (USA).

Web Resources

What works in training social workers about drug and alcohol use?
www.beds.ac.uk

International Federation of Social Workers
ifsw.org/policies/definition-of-social-work/

Spirituality as an antidote for addiction. Spirituality and Health, New York, NY.

Psychosocial Interventions for Persons with Substance Abuse: Theory and Practice. NIMHANS, Bangalore
http://search.mywikilocal.com/index.php?query=Substance%20Abuse%20Evaluation%20Template

Women and drug use in India—Substance, women and high risk assessment study. United Nations Office on Drugs and Crime
http://www.unodc.org/documents/southasia//reports/UNODC_Book_Women_and_Drug_Use_in_India_2008.pdf

United Nations Office on Drugs and Crime. Thematic pamphlets (Assessing a person, Recovery, Individual counselling, Family and drug addiction, Family counselling, Aftercare services, Crisis intervention, Relapse management, Prevention in the community)
http://www.unodc.org/india/thematic_pamphlets.html retrieved from www.nimhans.kar.nic.in/cam/html/resources.html
Management of substance abuse
http://www.who.int/substance_abuse/facts/index.html
Spirituality and Substance abuse treatment
www.ncbi.nlm.nih.gov/pmc/articles/PMC2943841/
Addictions and Social Work Practice- Diana M. DiNitto and C. Aaron McNeece
VIDENCE-BASED ADDICTIONS PRACTICE
lyceumbooks.com/pdf/SocialWorkIssuesOpps_Chapter_08.pdf

11

The Dead End: Reflections on Suicide in Developing Economies of South-East Asia

Sonny Jose, Reeja P. S. and Faheema Mustafa

Introduction

This chapter, thematic in nature, attempts to sensitise the reader to the phenomena of suicide as a major mental health menace. The Dead End, demystifies the phenomena, exposing the vicious cycle that hastens suicide, revisiting various theoretical frameworks and qualifying suicide as a normal impulsive response to a perceptually abnormal situation. This chapter describes suicide in India, as a developing economy, much a representation of developing economies in South-East Asia, overwhelmed by the proliferation of suicide, and more specifically, delves in-depth on the southern state of Kerala, which despite favourable sociopolitical indices is fast emerging as the suicide capital of the world. Based on evidence culled from secondary data, this chapter attempts an incisive analysis of the context, understanding and grounding it on research evidence, examining various strategies adopted over the years, and to finally present plausible social work interventions at micro-, mezzo- and macro-levels.

Case Study 1

Bindu is a 39-year-old divorcee and a mother of two teenage girls. She has had a successful, well-paying career as an executive secretary of a multinational company (MNC) for the past several years. Even though she has worked for the same, thriving company for over six years, she's found herself worrying constantly about losing her job and being unable to provide for her children. Despite the best of efforts, she hasn't been able to shake the negative thoughts. When alone in office, she often paces and ends up feeling restless, fatigued and tense. She's had embarrassing moments in and during meetings where she has lost track of what she was trying to say. When she goes to bed at night, it's as if her brain won't shut off as she finds herself mentally rehearsing all worse-case scenarios regarding losing her job, including ending up homeless. Although afraid of ending life, she occasionally contemplates on how to.

Case Study 2

Haseena is a graduate who reported to a gynaecologist with continuous bleeding. Her woes began with the love of her life, Salman, turning paranoiac. Haseena met Salman five years ago and fell madly in love with him. Salman immigrated to the Gulf for work and has been away for over three years. Although they speak every day, of late Salman is becoming extremely possessive about Haseena. He asks her almost all the time where she has been, whom she talks to and every little detail of the conversations. He cannot stand her interacting with other males. Although Haseena is innocent and pleads with Salman all the time, he is not convinced. His behaviour has become so intense over the past one year. He even calls-up her friends to enquire about her whereabouts, almost hourly. Haseena has been having recurrent bleeds almost every fortnight lasting for over 10 days at a stretch. Of late, she has lost her appetite and sleep and is contemplating of ending her life. Although mortally afraid, she dared to cut her wrists on two occasions. Hailing from an agrarian background, she has known of Furedan as an effective pesticide known for its fatality.

Portrayed as 'homicide turned 180°', suicide is described as an act of self-harm undertaken with the intention of ending one's own life. Emile Durkheim, a sociologist, defines suicide as a term to apply to any type of death 'resulting directly or indirectly from a positive or negative act of the victim, which he knows will produce this result' (Durkheim 1897/1951). Suicide is perceived as the culmination of an impulsive act, a normal reaction to an abnormal situation. Although research and popular conceptualisations on suicide posited that suicides are the result of impulsive, 'on-a-whim' decisions, recent research demonstrates that most suicides are not attempted impulsively, and in fact involve a plan (Smith et al. 2008). Whatever be the case, it implies the end of the tunnel—the dead end!

Suicide is a worldwide phenomenon and perceived differently. It is generally undertaken across cultures in the West as an escape, an act out of desperation, often emerging out of psyche-ache caused by alienation (Shneidman 1993). In the Orient, suicide in general is perceived as an act of honour; an example is the *Kamikazi* Bombers, essentially aircrafts transformed into pilot-guided explosive missiles during World War II. The Oriental cultures abound with other examples; women of conquered and defeated provinces in war stabbed themselves to death to avoid being raped and dishonoured. Sati, the Rajput custom of the widowed jumping into the funeral pyre of her deceased beloved, extols the virtue of suicide. Others explain it in terms of an act of penance for one's own failure in any major undertaking one; in Japan, valiant warriors once defeated, cut themselves with the sword rather than be killed by the enemies. Spies as well as suicide bombers of the modern age are heard of carrying cyanide capsules to be consumed on being captured.

In India, suicide is referred to as *khud-khushi* the Urdu word, which implies killing oneself. In Kerala the Malayalam equivalent for suicide is *athma-hatya*, which literally translates into 'annihilating the soul', bringing in existential and moral overtones. Thus, in this post-modern era it would be worth to consider various explanations as to how suicide is perceived. This chapter discusses the statistics on suicide, ventures into plausible explanations to the phenomena that increasingly confounds human sensibility.

Murder by Numbers: The Theory

The most profound discourse on the melancholic tale of suicide was initiated by Emile Durkheim. Steven Luke, who translated Durkheim's inimitable magnum opus 'Le Suicide' (1897/1951) writes that "development of industry and the almost infinite extension of the market, from top to bottom of the scale" had aroused greed that was 'unable to find ultimate foothold'. In modern towns driven by commerce and enterprise, men lost 'closeness' (warmth) as 'the cold winds of egoism froze their hearts and weakened their spirits'. As a consequence, 'the bond attaching man to life slackens because the bond which attaches him to society is itself slack'. Emile Durkheim postulated that suicide happened too little or too much of either integration or regulation. He went on to classify suicide on the basis of different types of relationship between the actor and his/her society (Pope 1981). **Egoistic suicide** happens when a person is not adequately integrated into the immediate society. Thus, he/she is socially isolated because he/she has 'no place' in the society. Such 'over-individuation' forces the person to destroy himself/herself. **Altruistic suicide** is suicide committed for the benefit of others and it occurs when there is close intimacy and attachment with individuals or among a group of individuals. It occurs when individuals and the groups are too close and intimate. Altruistic suicide results from the over-integration of an individual into the society; for example, suicide bombers. **Anomic suicide** is an outcome of social anarchy (anomie) or breakdown of social equilibrium. It takes place in a situation that crops up suddenly; for example, bankruptcy or after winning a lottery. The last type of suicide, **fatalistic suicide,** is the tangential opposite to anomic suicide. This type of suicide is due to over-regulation in society. Under overregulation, the individual feels too stifled, unable to experience his/her own individuality. This is best illustrated by a victim of torture or when a slave commits suicide. It has been noted in the realm of mental health, that it is the perceived erosion or absence of social support (integration) and approval (regulation) that precipitates the majority of the suicides (see Figure 11.1).

Baumeister (1990) conceptualised suicide as a means of escape from aversive self-awareness. He proposed that when individuals experience aversive self-awareness, they attempt to alleviate these feelings by achieving a state of 'cognitive deconstruction', which is characterised by a constricted, present focused time perspective and cognitive rigidity.

Van Orden et al. (2006) showed that a measure of perceived burden-someness—the view that one's existence burdens family, friends and/or

Figure 11.1
Typology of Suicide Based on the Dimensions—'Regulation' and 'Integration'*

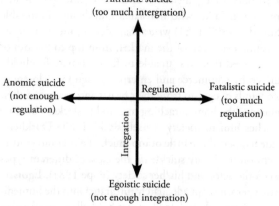

* Described by Emile Durkheim.

society—was a robust predictor of suicide attempt status and of current suicidal ideation, even controlling the powerful suicide-related covariates such as hopelessness.

The World

Worldwide, suicide rate or 'global mortality' is 16 per 100,000 (WHO 2011). Suicide is considered as one of the most fatal, considering that it claims a large numbers of people. In the United States alone, more than 34,000 people kill themselves each year.

With urbanisation happening at a rapid pace, suicide is now considered a leading cause of death by the WHO. In fact, in the United States, it is the 11th leading cause of death among Americans. However, suicide deaths are only a part of the problem. It is a culmination of a host of factors including stress, alienation and depression, that is considered a bane of modern day living. In fact, more startling is the fact that many people attempt suicide (termed as *suicide attempted*) than actually dying (*suicide completed*). In India, families with a history of suicide (suicide survivors) and suicide attempters are alienated simply because this act is regarded primarily as unethical and as something unnatural.

India

Suicide has been escalating at an alarming rate in India between 1995 and 2010. The social changes that followed the drastic geo-politics had a profound influence on people during these years. This may be generally attributed to the economic crisis (inflation) as well as the chaos due to the post-Gulf (Kuwait) war in India following the structural adjustment programs (SAPs) with the World Bank, ending up in the rolling introduction of the New Economic Policy (NEP), that forced the national government to reverse social expenditure in sectors namely agriculture, education and social welfare. Subsidies were cut thus mounting stress on the farmers as well as the middle class. The suicide rates peaked during 1999. Subsequently, 2000 onwards there has been a gradual regression in suicide rates. The growing public awareness regarding the warning signs and the role played by non-governmental organisations (NGOs) and the access to counselling services can be attributed to why the suicide rates have stabilised at 10.5 per 1,00,000 (NCRB 2010; see Table 11.1).

Going into details, interestingly, Uttar Pradesh and Bihar, which have much higher populations and far lower levels of literacy, report fewer suicides. In 2002, Uttar Pradesh and Bihar accounted for 4.8 per cent and 1.7 per cent, respectively, of the total number of suicides in the country. The south of India comprising the states of Andhra Pradesh, Karnataka, Tamil Nadu and Kerala famed as the information technology hub is taking the worst hit. Even as early as 2004, *The Lancet* reported that around 50,000 people in the four states of Kerala, Karnataka, Tamil Nadu and Andhra Pradesh and the union territory of Pondicherry kill themselves every year. This statistic becomes even more alarming if one were to consider that the total number of suicide cases recorded in the whole of India in 2002 was only 1,54,000.

Table 11.1
Variation in Suicide Rates in India between 1995 and 2010

(Sl)	Year	Total no. of Suicides in India	Estimated Mid-year Population (in lakhs)	Rate of Suicide
1	1995	89,178	9,160.0	9.7
2	1996	88,241	9,319.0	9.5
3	1997	95,829	9,552.0	10.0
4	1998	1,04,713	9,709.0	10.8
5	1999	1,10,587	9,866.0	11.2
6	2000	1,08,593	10,021.0	10.8
7	2001	1,08,506	10,270.0	10.6
8	2002	1,10,417	10,506.0	10.5
9	2003	1,10,851	10,682.0	10.4
10	2004	1,13,697	10,856.0	10.6
11	2005	1,13,914	11,028.0	10.3
12	2006	1,18,112	11,198.0	10.5
13	2007	1,22,637	11,365.5	10.8
14	2008	1,25,017	11531.3	10.8
15	2009	1,27,151	11694.4	10.9
16	2010	1,34,599	11857.6	11.4

Source: NCRB 2010.

The suicide rate spiralled to 11.6 per cent between 2005 and 2009. Some startling facts were cited by the *Times of India* (*TOI 2007*). The total number of suicides at a staggering 1,27,151, meant that 15 suicides took place every hour. Specifically, every day an average of 223 men and 125 women (89 housewives) committed suicide. While social and economic issues have precipitated men to commit suicide, it was more emotional and personal reasons that prompted women to commit suicide. Reeja (2011) postulates that failure in fulfilling the primary adult male role (economic success) is more visibly obvious than failure in the primary female role (success in relationships), thus increasing the propensity of men to kill themselves. As per the National Crime Records Bureau (NCRB) data, the issues that drove men over the edge were disrepute in the society, failure in examinations and unemployment. On the other hand, women committed suicide when they found out about their spouses' illicit relationships, cancellation of the wedding or when they were unable to bear a child or face divorce (Shastri 2012). One in every three victims of suicide fell in the age group between 15 and 28 years. Those below the 29 year age bracket killed themselves due to unemployment, examination failure, poverty and dowry disputes. The number of suicides due to unemployment increased by 18.8 per cent, and those due to professional or career failures went up by 15.1 per cent.

The metros topped in terms of the highest numbers; Bangalore registered 2,167, Chennai followed with 1,412 suicides, Delhi with 1,215 and Mumbai with 1,051 suicides. Thus, one may conclude that the metros in the south had a higher propensity for suicide. *The Lancet* authoritatively states that the suicide rates among young men and women in southern India are the highest in the world. A study by the Christian Medical College, Vellore, on teenagers in Tamil Nadu in 2002, especially in the Vellore region, found that the average suicide rate for women is as high as 148 per 1,00,000, and 58 per 1,00,000 for men. To put it most simplistically, out of every three cases of suicide reported every 15 minutes in India, one is committed by a youth in the age group of 15 to 29. In the union territory of Pondicherry alone, every month at least 15 youths between the ages of 15 and 25 commit suicide. In 2002, there were 10,982 suicides in Tamil Nadu, 11,300 in Kerala, 10,934 in Karnataka and 9,433 in Andhra Pradesh. Another group that is most affected are farmers. In 2003, the largest number of farmers— around 175—committed suicide in Andhra Pradesh. This is attributed to the indebtedness on account of continuous crop failure due to climate change.

The contours of desperation that culminate into suicide has two India— the urban and the rural. Dr Hansal Bhachech, a city-based psychiatrist, understands the upward swing in suicides as a by-product of urbanisation

(*Sinha* 2012). The issues of women living in urban and rural areas are different. While in urban areas we see more frustration among housewives due to restrictions by family, in rural areas, it is more to do with limited opportunities. With the crumbling family system and migration of rural population to urban centres, women get caught in the whirlwind of change. They see their role as a thankless job in the family set-up and hardly see a way out. There are innumerable instances when new environment preys on the innocence of rural women, eventually luring them into being trafficked.

As discussed by Guha (2004), the level of alienation experienced in the late 19th century France, is the same that pervades the 21st century India. It should come as no surprise that Bangalore, India's Silicon City, with as many as 2,000 cases registered every year, accounting for 17 per cent of all the suicides in the country, is also India's Suicide City. Here, so far there have been no significant biases as far as gender is concerned. However, it discriminates significantly with regard to age—majority of suicides are undertaken by those between twenty and thirty years of age—and also professionals. Many of these are software professionals. The age group between 20 and 30 is the time when stress peaks, especially with work, marriage and parenting, all coinciding. Software professionals are subject to stress due to deadlines, high pressure at work and competition, transient relationships. Bhachech, a noted psychiatrist, vouches that 'in personal relationships too, tolerance levels have reduced (substantially)' (*TOI* 2007).

Behind these very individual tragedies are some very social processes. Within a generation, this sleepy cantonment town has been transformed into a bustling metropolis. No city in India, and possibly even the world, has changed quite so much so soon. The most striking manifestation of this is in the city's skyline; with the lovely white bungalows built in British style of architecture that once were Bangalore's signature, it has given way to large apartment complexes and even larger shopping malls.

Fuelling this transformation of the built environment are changes in economy and society. A rapid rise in incomes has led to a still more rapid rise in desires. The young in Bangalore want a great deal more success than their parents; and they want it more quickly. These ambitions are stoked by the press, which gives disproportionate coverage to men and women who are young and yet famous and rich—or rather, famous because they are rich. At least in Bangalore, the media has time for only three kinds of heroes: beauty queens, cricketers and software titans. The gross mismatch between aspirations (ideals) and actual achievement amounts to stress affecting their mental health and well-being.

Dramatically, one in every five suicides was said to be committed by a housewife (NCRB 2010). The NCRB statistic for 2011 shows 24,596 housewives accounted for 51.5 per cent of the female victims. Out of these, 43.6 per cent were in the age group of 15 to 29. These figures are alarming because in India most women are homemakers. This may suggest how marriage and other stressors that subsequently arise are significant factors precipitating suicide (*TOI 2007*). Initially, we perceived it to be connected to dowry-related deaths or harassment by in-laws. Deeper probing indicates of a paradigm shift in the reasons why homemakers are taking their lives. It is the apparent 'lack of individual identity' that is one of the main reasons driving suicides in urban, literate India where, increasingly, parents do not differentiate between daughters and sons (Sinha 2012). Increasingly, women aspire to be more than just someone's wife or daughter-in-law. When unable to self-actualize, they suicide to escape aversive self-awareness (Baumeister 1990). He proposed suicide as an escape from self and is analysed in terms of motivations to escape from aversive self-awareness. It is also seen as an ultimate step in the effort to escape from self and the world. However National Crime Records Bureau (NCRB 2011) statistics of India claim that while social and economic causes have led most of the males to commit suicide, its emotional and personal causes have mainly forced women to end their lives.

Dr Nagpal J. of the Institute of Mental Health and Life Skills Promotion, New Delhi, postulates that a negative self-image is a very crucial issue with young women today, especially if they are not employed. In India, many of the professional, career-oriented men marry expecting their equally-qualified bride to become a 'homemaker'. Given the over glorification by the society of a working woman, it was only natural that a qualified woman, who is not employed despite being qualified, feels incomplete. In other words, brilliant girls are not allowed to work or even pursue a vocation as the family does not need their money. Given this, it is only inevitable that existential questions start bothering such homemakers, who need to keep themselves engaged for personal satisfaction. This leads to depression, which in turn becomes the flagging point for an eventual suicide.

Kerala: The Suicide Capital?

Kerala, the country's first fully literate state, with education and social indices at par with those of the West, has the highest number of suicides. The gravity of the situation is visible in the fact that approximately 32 people commit suicide in Kerala every day (NCRB 2008). Table 11.2 displays some relevant statistics churned out by the NCRB followed by some discussion:

The rate of suicide in Kerala is consistently high and is almost three times India's national average (Figures 11.2 and 11.3). Any day, it is estimated that about 26 persons take their lives, of them 18 are men and eight are women. The overall male–female suicide fatality ratio is 73:27, with the male suicide rate rising since 1996. In the eight years between 1995 and 2003, suicide incidences rose by 17.8 per cent; suicide rate rose by 9.6 per cent, with the peak happening in 1999. Subsequently, there has been a gradual decrease with the Kerala State Mental Health Authority (KSMHA) launching a campaign for suicide prevention under the leadership of late Dr Suraraj Mani, the then Secretary of the KSMHA. There was an initiative to establish hot lines for suicide prevention manned by voluntary counsellors. Two NGOs, Thrani-FIRM and Maithri were actively involved in popularising such interventions then unheard of.

As much as 80 per cent of suicidal deaths in Kerala take place among the age group of 15 to 59 years. As many as 91 suicidal deaths in 2007 were

Table 11.2

Gender-wise Incidence and Rate of Suicides in Kerala between 1995 and 2007

Year	Estimated Mid-year Population (in 1,00,000s)			Suicide Incidence			Suicide Rate (per 1,00,000 of population)		
	Male	Female	Total	Male	Female	Total	Male	Female	Total
1995	147.79	154.54	302.33	5615	2397	8012	37.99	15.51	26.50
1996	148.97	156.09	305.06	5414	2672	8086	36.34	17.12	26.51
1997	150.15	157.66	307.82	6215	2746	8961	41.39	17.42	29.11
1998	151.35	159.25	310.60	6503	2803	9306	42.97	17.60	29.96
1999	152.55	160.85	313.41	6853	2925	9778	44.92	18.18	31.20
2000	153.77	162.47	316.24	6609	2695	9304	42.98	16.59	29.42
2001	154.99	164.11	319.10	6787	2785	9572	43.79	16.97	30.00
2002	156.23	165.76	321.99	7165	2645	9810	45.86	15.96	30.47
2003	157.47	167.43	324.90	6935	2503	9438	44.04	14.95	29.05
2004	158.73	169.11	327.84	6598	2455	9053	41.57	14.52	27.61
2005	159.99	170.80	330.81	6830	2414	9244	42.69	14.13	27.94
2006	161.27	172.50	333.81	6583	2443	9026	40.82	14.16	27.04
2007	162.55	174.21	336.84	6588	2374	8962	40.53	13.63	26.61

Note: Population figures are calculated from the Census of India data for years 1991 and 2001, assuming equal per year growth rates.

Figure 11.2
Suicide Rate in Kerala—Trend during 1995 to 2007

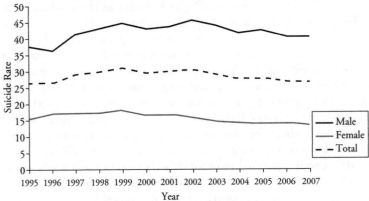

Figure 11.3
Age Distribution and Gender Differences of Those Who Died due to Suicide in Kerala (Year: 2007)

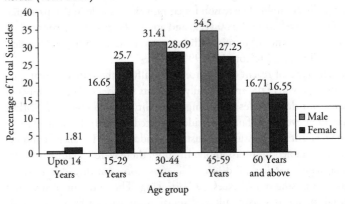

accounted by children below 14 years of age, among children below 14 years of age; incidence among girls exceeds that among boys. Sanjay Chugh, a psychiatrist and founder chairman of the International Institute of Mental Health, explains that girls attempt suicide more often, but more boys end up dying as their attempts are successful. He goes on to add that adolescent girls seek support from family and friends to deal with emotional stress during examination. But as boys are less expressive, they tend to suppress their feelings of inadequacy and fear of poor performance. This often drives them to suicide to end their frustration.

Young women of the age group 15 to 29 years are more prone to suicide, with the male–female ratio for that age group being 39:61 against the overall ratio of 74:26. The present trend of high tele-density and the resultant use of mobile phones and the internet has also contributed significantly to the rise in the number of crimes—cyber as well as crimes against women. There has been a steep increase in cyber crimes involving the girl child. The excessive use of the mobile and the chats often find the girl child falling prey to false love and ending up being cheated and dragged into human trafficking. Once into it, there is no coming back, especially in a conservative society that stigmatises and eventually discriminates against her. Being alienated, she has no other option but to commit suicide. Such an eventuality could have been contained to a great extent if the child had better resilience. Mental health could have been augmented, provided the social support systems—the family as well as the immediate society—realised the need to help the child recoup and regain self-esteem, and thereby ensure mental health.

The next modal population is the aged, among whom suicide proneness is acute. The middle aged marked by the age group of 45 to 59 years too are suicide prone. With this age group, the male–female ratio attempts to balance almost equally at 56:44. The reason for committing suicide in this particular age category as well as in the 60 years and above age group is accounted on grounds of occurrence of terminal illness or severe and debilitating physical illnesses (Leikin and McCormick 1991).

Another trend of recent emergence, especially in the state of Kerala, are family suicides, where the entire family attempts suicide. In large number of such cases, murder-suicides is a strong possibility. A study by the KSMHA says that 39 of every 100 family suicides reported across India, take place in God's own country. The study has just been endorsed by Kerala's Economic Review 2010, tabled in the assembly. In 2009, there were 13 family suicides in Kerala, which totalled 38 deaths. The most common thread is a case of indebtedness arising out of excessive borrowing. The resultant relative and sudden fall of status—economic and social—can act as a factor that adds impetus to suicide.

Modus Operandi

The modus operandi for suicide was predominantly hanging by noose made of rope, dhoti or saree (the traditional 8 meter wrap around). This was followed by consuming poison usually rodent poison or agricultural poison (such as Furedan) that is freely dispensed at general stores. This was the most popular modus operandi adopted in the case of family suicides. Those engaged in agriculture consumed insecticides. Given the accessibility of the rope and poison, lethality is generally regarded high (Figure 11.4).

It is interesting to probe into the patterns of district wise. Suicide is maximum in Wynad, Kollam and Idukki districts. Among these Wynad and Idukki are dominantly agrarian in nature, and the farmer suicides happening in these districts have gained national attention putting the respective state governments into the defensive. The farmer suicides occurring here are by and large considered altruistic, as the father and mother who plunge into indebtedness due to repeated crop failure, scheme to annihilate the entire family so that none of them have to face the brunt of the debt incurred. Suicide rate is high in Thiruvananthapuram, Palakkad and Thrissur districts, while the suicide rates remain steady in Kannur, Eranakulam, Kasaragode, Kottayam, Alleppey and Kozhikkode districts. The latter group consists of districts that have the largest migrant population (Table 11.3).

The most notable in terms of rate of increase in suicide is Thiruvanantha-puram district, where suicide has spiralled from 17.2 per 1,00,000 population in 1995 to 34.6 per 1,00,000 population in 2008. Thiruvananthapuram, known as the 'pensioners' paradise' and population consisting of individuals having migrated from mostly central and north Kerala, is by nature heter-ogeneous and less gregarious. For these reasons, the social capital may be considered low, perhaps best described as referred to by as Durkhiem as state

Figure 11.4
Means Adopted by Those Who Died by Suicide in Kerala (Year: 2007)

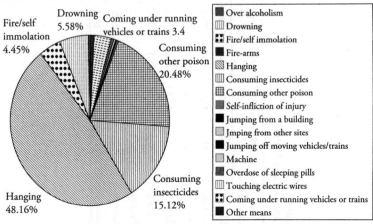

Table 11. 3
Regional Classification

District \ Year	1995	1996	1997	1998	1999	2000	2001	2002	2003	2004	2005	2006	2007	2008
Idukki	48.6	41.1	43.3	43	43	41.5	49.2	49.7	51	42.4	40.3	38.6	39.5	34.6
Kollam	32	33.5	32.1	31.2	33.4	33.2	33.9	43.6	43.1	41	42.4	41.3	42	36.4
Wynad	44.4	39.1	38.6	39.4	51.7	48.4	39.8	40.6	45	36.5	38	40.1	36.5	38.2
Trivandrum	17.2	33.2	40.6	41.3	39.8	41.4	41.4	38.5	32.7	35.5	37	37.8	37	34.6
Thrissur	37.5	33.1	35.1	35.3	37.1	34	34.3	34.5	33.7	31	31.6	30.3	27.7	27.1
Palakkad	32.3	32.7	33.4	33.2	34.1	34.4	33.1	32.9	33.1	33	35.8	34.5	32	29.2
Kozhikode	22	21.4	24.5	24.6	24.8	23.7	25.5	24.3	22.7	21.4	22.3	22	22	19.7
Malappuram	12	10.1	14.6	14.2	13.5	14.7	11.7	11.8	12.9	12.8	12	11.3	10.6	10.6

of anomie. As opposed to this, suicide rate is consistently low in Malappuram district, which is by nature homogeneous, as it is largely a laidback rural community, predominated by Islam. The Islamic population being gregarious by nature, Malappuram may be considered to be blessed by such factors that add up to its social capital, which works in a protective manner.

Socio-economic Considerations

A significant social variable that moderated suicide is the marital status. Being married increased the possibility of suicide (Figure 11.5). This needs to be read together with several other considerations—the gender and the age. It is found that being a woman in the age group of 19 to 29 and married increased the propensity to suicide. In context of Kerala, marriage usually is perceived as the girl moving away from the security of her family into her spouse's home. This is usually followed by stressors especially in terms of adjustment to a new family culture and the in-laws that might be generally against the girl's marital expectations. The expectations include child bearing. The Kerala society being generally patriarchal, the preference of gender of the first born being male can cause stress for the new parents. The stress is higher especially if the girl is a working mother.

Looking at occupation-wise distribution of completed suicides, one realises that the fact that a woman is a housewife increases the propensity towards committing suicide. Most of the girls in Kerala are well educated

Figure 11.5
Social Status of Those Who Died by Suicide in Kerala (Year: 2007)

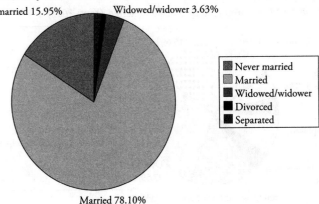

Never married 15.95%   Widowed/widower 3.63%

■ Never married
▨ Married
■ Widowed/widower
■ Divorced
■ Separated

Married 78.10%

and the absence of an opportunity to engage oneself in accordance with their expectations can affect their self-esteem. The same can be equally if not more damaging for men. High aspirations, the low employment rates and poor entrepreneurship skills are the reasons why men who are usually unemployed attempt suicide. Almost equally likely is the fact that the person is an agriculturist. Agriculture in Kerala is increasingly becoming an untenable proposition. The skyrocketing land prices, the high cost of labour and a rollback on subsidies, unpredictable rainfall patterns have played chaos with agriculture. This connection between social change as stressor affecting mental health is discussed is discussed subsequently (see Figure 11.6).

The suicide rate in Kerala escalated to about 32 per 1,00,000 persons in 2002, at that point in time, thrice the rate of the whole of India. This points to the dismal state of mental health in South India, especially Kerala. Mental health experts attribute this to 'acute stress factors', that include (Thomas 2011):

- Family conflicts, family dysfunction and domestic violence
- Academic failures, examination failure
- Unfulfilled romantic ideals, love affair failures
- Consumerism fuelled by credit lenders and hire–purchase schemes
- The widening gap between people's aspirations and actual capabilities
- Disintegration of traditional social support mechanisms—joint families and emergence of nuclear families
- Alcohol abuse
- Financial instability, bankruptcy
- Growing population of the aged

Figure 11.6
Professions of Those Who Died by Suicide in Kerala (Year: 2007)

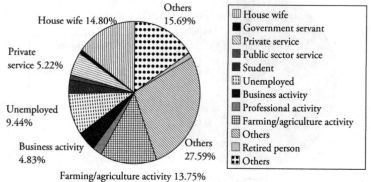

- Failure of crops, huge debt, escalating costs of cultivation and shrinking yield

The Final Analysis

In the final analysis, one may conclude that the case of Kerala is a case of lope-sided development. In spite of it's impressive standards of living statistics—life expectancy, literacy, health care indices that poised Kerala as an ideal model for socio-economic development—Kerala demonstrates an equally startling trend in mental health, for the wrong reasons. In mental health, Kerala boasts of the highest trends in terms of suicide (Halliburton 1998), the magnitude being almost triple the national average, a rate 50 per cent more than the second highest state. Laymen may attribute this to urbanisation loosening the grip of tradition, break up of extended family and spirituality, abetted by the influence of media. However, we have no evidence to establish these contentions.

A more tenable argument is the lack of match between educational status (literacy) and the adequate number of jobs. This sounds more logical considering the fact that higher literacy and education has spiralled the expectations and aspirations of the average *Malayalee*, which does not essentially commensurate with the rate of employment (Halliburton 1998). Halliburton further goes on to record that a secular ideology, loosely translating into a general apathy towards religiosity, does not aid the individual to philosophise on the meaning of suffering and self. This precipitates a sense of meaninglessness in the purpose of living. In other words, contrary to the belief that development in its present form has helped generate opportunities for self-realisation as well as well-being—material, personal and social—it would be more logical to conclude that the present mode of development has created more setbacks.

The remarkable social change that has happened especially with the Gulf boom, the decade following the Gulf War, and the technology explosion leading to the proliferation of internet and high tele-density need to be read alongside. Social change abetted by opening of borders, resulting in migration and technological explosion has induced psycho-pathology. Very early studies—Fortes and Mayer (1969), who did a longitudinal study on social change happening in Tallensi; Eguchi (1991), who studied how the proliferation of electricity, communication and transportation impact on mental health; Carstairs and Kapur (1976: 176), who studied the impact of family disorganisation on mental health—have substantiated this direct relation between social change and psycho-pathology. The social change is quite evident in the state of Kerala in its high rate of migration, consumerism, stress-inducing educational system, spiralling aspirations, disorganisation of the joint and even extended family systems into nuclear families, growth of multimedia communications and its abuse and so on. All of these in a sense create anarchy, resulting in a kind of alienation. Family disorganisation is a very significant variable. NCRB statistics seem to indicate that two of the four most common cited explanations for suicide were 'quarrel with spouse' or 'quarrels with in-laws'. Along with this, the trend towards nuclear families which are essentially filocentric is an alarming issue. Being filocentric, such families live 'for' and around their children, thereby generating future citizens, who are by-and-large intolerant, impulsive and expect immediate satiation of their individual needs with scant disregard for any other logic—as to whether it is really a need rather than a want, or it is being tenable. Any denial of these wants translates into behaviour that is incommensurate with the situation. Their decisions are momentous and they generally resort to very drastic actions. The learning from this wisdom is to understand the importance of perceiving and proacting on the development in a manner it unfolds. Life-skill education needs to be imparted at both individual and group level in order to assist the individual to negotiate his/ her way in the society during adolescence when biophysical and psychosocial challenges are most evident. At the macro-level, governments need to consider not just sustainable development, but also at the next level, inclusive development, one that would not only sustain, but also provide happiness and well-being to its citizens, in short mental health.

Intervention

From the social work point of view, intervention may be undertaken at three levels—micro, mezzo and macro. The following are some of the approaches that may be undertaken in the Kerala context.

At the Micro-level

One of the major impediment that a *Malayalee* experiences when it comes to problem solving is the tendency to over-rationalise. *Malayalees* tend to rationalise personal problems to the extent that they deny the psyche-ache, the real hurt that is simmering within. Step 1, first and foremost, is to help the individual to realise when he/she has a problem. This is the easiest way to understand any preoccupation and the resultant ambivalence that clouds his/her understanding. Step 2 is to teach the individual to *ask* for help. Step 3 is getting the person to realise the need to trust and identifying somebody whom he/she can trust. Step 4 is to help the individual to understand the need to express his/her feelings with someone he/she can trust and do the same.

Being a helper by default, individuals need to be taught to administer psychological first aid. The key to suicide prevention is to *ask!* A myth as in any culture, the most frequently asked question (FAQ) about suicide intervention is that whether asking someone about his/her intentions for suicide would not induce the thought of suicide into the person? This apprehension is out of place considering the potential benefits of being able to make a correct assessment and getting the person to spill the beans, much before the individual resorts to the fatal act! Thus, one should leave no stone unturned in making an assessment of suicidal ideation and inclination. The following are five questions that may be put to the subject in an ascending order (Mani and Jose 2000):

1. Have you felt you are *lonely*?
2. Have you felt that there is *no one to love you*?
3. Have you thought there is *no point in living*?
4. Have you ever *intentionally* tried to *hurt* yourself?
5. Have you ever *thought of killing* yourself?

With each question in the lower order being answered in the affirmative, one may progress down to this protocol, and finally end up asking 'how?', in the process, making a good assessment of the lethality of the individual subject in question. This may also help in isolating and eliminating the materials, whereby defusing the possibilities to a great extent.

At the Mezzo-level

One of the basic assumptions regarding suicide attempts is the perception that there is an absence of social support or a sense of belongingness. Given this, it pays to encourage individuals to communicate with fellow beings especially when they are in a state of emotional distress and confusion. 'When you are in distress talk to a friend; when your friend is in distress listen to them' could be a good policy to follow. The absence of communication creates ambivalence that is often a precursor to suicide attempt.

There are excellent models in Kerala, yet to hit the limelight. The *tharakoottam* movement initiated by Pankajakshan Mash, in late 1980s, is one such example. Each *tharakoottam* is a neighbourhood group consisting of five to 10 households, within a 'stone's throw' distance, that convenes meetings on a weekly basis. Activities in these congregations include sharing of news, personal achievements and sorrows, pitching in as a good samaritan by wilfully sharing of money, resources and food in an exigency. As a practice, the neighbours pitch in for a household that hosts a visitor, to ensure that the neighbour gets quality time with the visitor.

Similarly steps may be taken to strengthen interpersonal communication by ways of informal gatherings at the workplace. This may in turn facilitate closer ties between colleagues. The same may be applied at home, encouraging the upkeep of ties with the extended family such as cousins, in-laws and relatives, and making them realise the importance of intervening when close relatives or family members are in distress.

Instituting peer counsellors in schools or at the workplace may be a good strategy. The social worker identifies those who have the aptitude, and are better positioned to identify and befriend those in distress; train them to identify those in distress, undertake psychological first aid, and eventually refer them to professional social workers or even interface them with the health care system.

At the Macro-level

Just like financial capital, social capital can only be developed provided there is proper planned investment in developing relationships. There needs to be a public policy to ensure mental health and encourage and nurture the building of social capital. This may be possible by means of instituting clubs and recreation groups.

We also need to educate public about the warning signs of suicide. The public needs to be educated that encountering crisis is something common and normal, and that it is a temporary phase to be tided over rather than stigmatised. This awareness can be supported by establishing befriending and counselling services especially targeting high-risk groups—adolescents, young adults especially women, middle aged and the aged. To prevent harassment and distressing of the already 'distressed', the social worker may liaison between the police, the fire service, the 1089 ambulance service and the judiciary. A good preventive strategy may be undertaken by 'catching them young' and administering capacity building and skill development training, especially in life skill training for children at the school level. At the preadolescent and adolescent levels, vocational guidance and counselling may be organised to assist pupils in aptitude testing, ensuring realistic choice as well as goodness of fit in the vocations they aspire for. At the young adolescent level, one may promote job-oriented education and encourage entrepreneurship, especially given the high unemployment rates in Kerala. It is also imperative to prepare young adults for a marital life by the family life-cycle approach, by way of pre-marital guidance and counselling during the initial years, later convening encounter groups post-marriage, at later points of the family life cycle—adjusting to partner; birth of the first, second and third child; getting the children to school; eventually at a point of child leaving school; preparing for the marriage of the children and separation; death of the spouse; preparing for one's own death. Equally important are promotion of family life education and family budgeting. For those in employment, the social worker may provide career planning and counselling service at critical junctures—at the point of induction, at the point of marriage, midlife especially when career-doldrums occur, and at the point of retirement.

It would be advisable to design a dedicated suicide intervention policy with specific protocols such as (U.K. National Commission on Suicide 2001):

- Constitution of 24-hour crisis teams
- Assertive outreach and hospital follow-up
- Policies on non-compliant and dually diagnosed patients
- Multidisciplinary post-suicide review of suicides to find out risk factors that will be of use in the treatment of other at risk clients
- Specialised training
- Aggressive treatment of patients with mental illness and co-morbid substance abuse

Conclusion

Suicide is a major menace to both worlds—developing and the developed. This thematic chapter explains the context in which suicide occurs, as well as exposes it as a natural phenomenon that could befall anyone, anytime. Suicide was found to be associated with social structures, psychological and social relationships, which are in a state of flux given the fast changing geopolitical occurrences. The chapter also recommends specific strategies and policies at the micro-, mezzo- and macro-levels, to enhance personal competence as well as augment social capital, towards preventing and alleviating this grave menace to mental health, especially in cash-strapped developing economies.

References

Ananthakrishnan, G. 2011, 13 February. 'In Kerala, Suicide Runs in the Entire Family', *Times of India*.

Baumeister, R. F. 1990. 'Suicide as Escape from Self', *Psychology Review*, 97 (1): 90–113.

Carstairs, G. M. and Kapur R. L. 1976. *The Great Universe of Kota: Stress, Change, and Mental Disorder in an Indian Village*. California: University of California Press.

Durkheim, E. 1951 (1897). *Suicide: A Study in Sociology* (J. A. Spaulding and G. Simpson, trans.). London: Routledge.

Eguchi, Shigeyuki . 1991. 'Between Folk Concepts of Illness and Psychiatric Diagnosis: Kitsune- Tsuki (Fox Possession) in a Mountain Village in Western Japan', *Culture, Medicine and Psychiatry*, 15 (4): 421-451.

Government of India. 2006. 'Accidental Deaths and Suicides in India 2006'. New Delhi: NCRB.

———. 2008. 'Accidental Deaths and Suicides in India 2008'. New Delhi: NCRB.

———. 2010. 'Accidental Deaths and Suicides in India 2010'. New Delhi: NCRB.

Halliburton, M. 1998. 'Suicide: A Paradox of Development in Kerala', *Economic and Political Weekly*, 33 (36/37).

Leikin, S. and R. A. McCormick. 1991. 'Terminal Illness and Suicide', *Ethics Behaviour*, 1 (1): 63–68.

Mani, S. and S. Jose. 2000. *Telephone Counsellor's Training Manual*, Trivandrum: Thrani-FIRM.

Meyer, F. 1969. *Kinship and the Social Order*. Chicago: Aldine.

Pope, W. and N. Danigelis. 1981. 'Sociology's One Law', *Social Forces*, 60 (2): 496–514.

Reeja, P. S. 2011. *Causes and Consequences of Suicide: A Case study of Kerala* (Unpublished Thesis), University of Kerala, Thiruvananthapuram, India.

Roy-Byrne, P. 2012. 'Broad Mental Health Service Changes Can Prevent Suicide', *Journal Watch Psychiatry*. Doi:http://dx.doi.org/10.1056/JP201203050000001.

Shastri, P. 2012, 1 July. 'Distressed Men On Suicide Spree', *Times of India*. Available at: lite.epaper.timesofindia.com/mobile.aspx

Shneidman, E. S. 1993. 'Suicide as Psychache'. *Journal of Nerve and Mental Disorders*, 181: (3): 145–147.

Sinha, K. 2012. 'Suicide May Soon be Leading Cause of Death in India, Reveals Study'. *Times of India*, p.4

Smith, A. R., T. K. Witte, N. E. Teale, S. L. Kings, T. W. Bender and T. E. Joiner 2008. 'Revisiting Impulsivity in Suicide: Implications for Civil Liability of Third Parties'. *Behavioural Science Law*, 26 (6): 779–797.

The Times of India. 2007. Over 5,200 Suicides in One Year. Retrieved from http://timesofindia.indiatimes.com

Thomas, J. 2011, 11 February. 'Housewives committing suicide'. *Times of India*.

Van Orden, K. A., M. E. Lynam, D. Hollar and T. E. Joiner, Jr. (2006). 'Perceived Burdensomeness as an Indicator of Suicidal Symptoms'. *Cognitive Therapy and Research*, 30: (4): 457–467.

Web Resources

Web-based Injury Statistics Query and Reporting System (WISQARS) for Disease Control and Prevention URL: http://www.cdc.gov/injury/wisqars/index.html

National Crime Records Bureau URL:http://www.ncrb.nic.in

PART 2

Challenges and Way Forward

Challenges and Ways Forward

S. Kalyanasundaram

A broken leg can be remembered and located: "It hurt right below my knee, it throbbed, I felt sick at my stomach." But mental pain is remembered the way dreams are remembered—in fragments, unbidden realizations, like looking into a well and seeing the dim reflection of your face in that instant before the water shatters.

Tracy Thompson (Pulitzer Prize finalist, 1988)
in *The Beast: A Reckoning with Depression*

Mental illnesses are misunderstood; they are obscured by myths, misconceptions and stigma. There exists a broad range of illnesses in the neuropsychiatric spectrum, each with varying set of symptoms and experiential consequences. Instances abound in literature as well as professional and laypersons' day-to-day experiences of this 'invisible' malady, where ill persons and their families shy away from seeking help.

Mental illnesses are not uncommon; they are just under recognized. The World Health Organization (WHO) estimates that neuropsychiatric disorders contribute to 13 per cent of the global burden of disease (WHO 2011). Though the extent of the burden varies from country to country, neuropsychiatric disorders account for a substantial amount of the disease burden in every country of the world.

Over the last two decades, however, it is gratifying to note that mental health is gradually gaining priority in the global health agenda. Increasing attention has been brought to the detrimental impacts of neuropsychiatric disorders on individuals, families and communities (WHO 2011).

There are several key areas in the global mental health scenario as well as those in developing countries such as in the Indian context that require attention.

Investment in Mental Health

Mental and neurological disorders are accompanied by significant emotional and financial burden on individuals, their families and society as a whole. The estimated cost of mental health problems in developed countries is between 3 per cent and 4 per cent of gross national product (GNP). There is an enormous gap between the need for treatment of mental disorders and the resources available. In developing countries, the figures are startling with the treatment gap being close to 90 per cent (WHO 2003).

Investing in mental health today can generate enormous returns in terms of reducing disability and preventing premature death and it is best done in the realm of financial and human resources. Mental health service delivery in low-resource settings such as India requires integrating mental health with the existing rubric of primary health care. It requires a paradigm shift in how services are offered—service delivery must involve the local communities for it to be acceptable, successful and sustainable. Nagaraja and Murthy (2008) quoting the *Lancet* series on Global Mental Health (2007) emphasise that mental health investment in primary health care is important.

Community Mental Health

The need for community mental health care has been proposed by several authors (Tansella and Thornicroft 1999; Ustun and Sartorius 1995). Some of the relevant concerns are:

- Mental disorders seen in primary care settings are a major public health problem and these create a substantial burden to society.
- Most primary care professionals are aware of psychological disorders, but the transition from clinician recognition to the actual treatment is very low.
- Mental health treatment should be an integral part of primary care.
- Primary care doctors will need to be trained to recognise and treat major mental disorders.

Increasingly, there has been a debate between those who favour providing mental health treatment and care in hospitals, and those who prefer providing it in community settings. The psychiatric consumer community has been at the forefront in the devolution of care from deinstitutionalisation and to provide services through community care. There is good evidence to show that these community mental health services are clinically effective (Leff et al. 1994; Marks et al. 1994) and more cost-effective (Knapp et al. 1997).

Evidence-Based Practices

Effective mental health interventions must include practices that are known to or likely to contribute in a positive way to recovery. Evidence-based practices (EBPs) refer to clinical practices for which scientific evidence of improvement in consumer outcomes has been consistent (Dixon et al. 2001). EBP requires demonstrable impact in a practice setting—there is the issue of efficacy versus effectiveness (the effect of the intervention in a research setting vs. in a practice setting). It is imperative that mental health practitioners be skilled at reading and interpreting research.

In the Indian scenario, a major challenge in the mental health care scenario is the serious lacuna of practice that is backed by rigorous scientific evidence. For instance, one of the observations with regard to the National Mental Health Programme (NMHP) implementation has been that changes in functioning have not kept pace with EBPs even after nearly three decades of 'implementation'. This is largely due to the fact that adequate numbers of trained mental health professionals are still not in place, due to both delays in recruitment and financial remuneration and service conditions not being attractive enough (Rao, in Nagaraj and Murthy 2008).

Nagaraja and Murthy (2008) quote Isaac et al. (2007) who notes that in developing countries, there is a great mismatch in the areas of mental health research, practice, policy and services in comparison to developed countries. However, the authors are optimistic that, of late, with increase in collaboration in research, availability of treatment including low-priced psychotropics and a growing emphasis on the need for mental health policy in some low-income countries, the bleak scenario is likely to change.

Emerging Knowledge Base for Indian Mental Health Scenario

In the Indian scenario, the expanding knowledge base fuelled by research that is shaping practice and mental health service delivery has been a heartening trend. Murthy (2004), outlining the priority areas for mental health research, suggests a greater focus on course, outcomes, indicators and specific vulnerable groups among others as topics for generation of new knowledge.

The contribution of the Indian Council of Medical Research (ICMR) is noteworthy in this context. The ICMR is the apex body for the formulation, coordination and promotion of biomedical research in India (ICMR 2011). Mental health is one of the emerging research priorities, and attention to mental health research has been intensified progressively (Murthy 2007). Apart from clinical studies, ICMR has also developed intervention modules in community care for the elderly, substance use, and indicators of community well-being, to name a few (Shah et al. 2005).

Research Practice

Research in mental health cannot be an end in itself. Research makes its mark on society only when it is translated into practice in service delivery. In the Indian context again, practice based on research is sporadic and not given due accord. Agarwal (2012) notes that some of the maladies affecting psychiatric research are lack of research cadre, absence of long-term financial support and poor documentation of clinical work.

There are innumerable indigenous models of service delivery but there is a dearth of published material. Psychiatric rehabilitation in the Indian scenario is one such area. In a review article, Chandrashekar et al. (2010) note that there are innovative initiatives across the country pertaining to various aspects of rehabilitation such as assessment of rehabilitation needs and different rehabilitative approaches. They also point out that there are meagre publications in this area of work in India, and stress the need for mental health professionals to publish the models they follow across the country.

However, a heartening development as mentioned earlier is the pioneering role of the ICMR which has given a big push to mental health research since the 1980s. This research has not only brought to light the importance of understanding mental disorders such as schizophrenia in the cultural context, but has also shown the feasibility of developing models involving schools, primary health care and general practitioners, as well as working with families. This new knowledge has continuously supported the development of mental health programmes (Murthy 2011).

Mental Health Promotion

An increasingly popular thrust in mental health services has been the shift from curative to preventive services. Mental health promotion involves adopting an approach based on a positive view of mental health rather than emphasizing mental illness and deficits.

The scope and outcome of mental health promotion activities is potentially wide. Mental health is a community responsibility, not just an individual concern. The social and economic costs of poor mental health are high and the evidence suggests that they will continue to grow without community and government action.

Mental health promotion works at three levels: strengthening individuals, strengthening communities and reducing structural barriers to mental health (Mentality 2003). This framework is useful for conceptualising the entry points for promotion within a mental health policy. Structural barriers to mental health can be reduced through initiatives to reduce discrimination and inequalities and to promote access to education, meaningful employment, housing, health services and support to those who are vulnerable.

The Ottawa Charter of Health Promotion (WHO 1986) provides a foundation for health promotion strategies and can be considered a guide for the promotion of mental health. It draws attention to individual, social and environmental factors that influence health. Its main strategies are building healthy public policies, creating supportive environments, strengthening community action, developing personal skills and reorienting health services.

The understanding of local factors relevant to a community, the empowerment of that community to solve its own problems and the subsequent improvement in the determinants of mental health demonstrate why the community development approach is a key strategy for mental health promotion.

In rural India, for instance, poverty, inequality, gender discrimination and domestic violence are major contributors to mental illness. Related factors that have been linked to mental ill health in the literature are also found, including low self-esteem, learned helplessness, less security, higher levels of adverse life events, social isolation and distress (Cullen and Whiteford 2001; Mumford et al. 1997; WHO 1990). In addition, unemployment, financial and economic deprivation, low social status, low levels of education and female gender have also been implicated.

Hermann et al. (2004) recommend that the promotion of mental health can be achieved by effective public health and social interventions. These include

- early childhood interventions,
- economic and social empowerment of women,
- social support to old age populations,
- programmes targeted at vulnerable groups such as minorities, indigenous people, migrants and people affected by conflicts and disasters,
- mental health promotion activities in schools,
- mental health interventions at work,
- housing policies,
- violence prevention programmes, and
- community development programmes.

Intersectoral collaboration and sustainability of programmes are the keys to effective programmes for mental health promotion. Involvement of all stakeholders, ownership by the community and continued availability of resources facilitate sustainability of mental health promotion programmes. Again, as in other fields, more scientific research and systematic evaluation of programmes are needed to increase the evidence base as well as to determine the applicability of this evidence base in widely varying cultures and resource settings.

International action is necessary for generating and disseminating further evidence, for assisting low- and middle-income countries in implementing effective programmes (and not implementing those that are ineffective) and for fostering international collaboration.

What Are Some of the Suggestions/ the Way Forward

Reducing the Treatment Gap

There is a need to increase services and efforts to reduce the treatment gap (Thirunavukarasu 2011). To overcome barriers to closing the gap between resources and the need for treatment of mental disorders, and to reduce the number of years lived with disability and deaths associated with such disorders, the WHO has created the Mental Health Global Action Programme (mhGAP; WHO 2003)

Generation of Human Resources

It is important to have a well-trained, competent and professional set of persons who can implement services effectively as well as efficiently. In developing countries, there is a widely acknowledged paucity of mental health professionals (WHO 2011). In the Indian scenario, successful ongoing efforts in the direction of generating manpower have been training of primary health care doctors and general physicians, primary health care workers and specialist training (Nagaraja and Murthy 2008).

Role of the Non-governmental Sector

The non-governmental sector is increasingly a major player in the mental health scenario in developing countries, especially in India. It is crucial to tap and mobilise resources in this sector and increase government support to the non-governmental sector. The growing role of non-governmental organisations (NGOs) that provide services for suicide prevention, disaster care and school health programmes, in which non-specialists and volunteers play an important role, has tremendous importance for India as NGOs can bridge the gap of human resources. One viable model of intersector collaboration is the public–private partnership (Murthy 2011).

Strengthening Community Mental Health Initiatives

Existing community mental health services must be diversified, planned and coordinated to address the multiple needs of people with mental disorders and to enable them to live a full community life.

Several proven models of community-based service provision need to be utilised judiciously depending on the sociocultural and resource context.

It would be preferable if context-specific models are encouraged and empirically tested rather than merely adopting Western models.

One must not lose focus of the need for strengthening residential services in the community. These arrangements vary from country to country, depending on the particular context of social and health care provision.

Crisis intervention services need to be provided in association with primary care providers, who are usually the first 'port of call' in a crisis. This requires good referral and linkage systems with primary care services, as well as with mental health services in general hospitals.

Research in community mental health services must be encouraged, especially in the area of service delivery; for example, by investigating the effectiveness of different models of service delivery. Community mental health services have first-hand knowledge of delivering community-based services, and this can usefully feed into the framing of research priorities and questions.

Linkages of community mental health services with other service/welfare sectors are essential. People with mental disorders have multiple needs related to health, welfare, employment, housing, criminal justice and education. For these reasons, community mental health services need to work collaboratively with other sectors and establish clear referral pathways, mutual supervision and training.

Emphasis on Dignity

Restoring dignity is an essential and basic ingredient in the culture of healing, offering hope and consequently, recovery-oriented services. Unfortunately, the lived experience of mental illness, constantly battling stigma and discrimination at various levels often strips the person of his/her self-worth and identity. Non-acknowledging of suffering from others, be it family, employer, peer or even treating professionals, is in itself a dignity-depriving experience (Kalyanasundaram and Sekhar 2011). Mental health services, irrespective of the setting, must be offered in a humane and sensitive manner while being professional in approach. The thrust in mental health training must be not only towards creating a cadre of knowledgeable and competent professionals, but also those that are caring and approachable.

Whither Deinstitutionalisation?

There are several unsettling questions pertaining to the issue of deinstitutionalisation that are staring us in the face and need answers: Has deinstitutionalization served its intended purpose? Can we do away with institutional care completely; especially, in the Indian context where traditional family support systems are disintegrating and there is complete absence of state welfare/social security measures for the psychiatrically disabled? Are there not some of those who are chronically ill, who will need to be taken care of by the state? The need of the hour is to have some well run facilities staffed by properly trained mental health professionals, who will not only run such institutions efficiently but also ethically, keeping in mind the welfare of the those who suffer from such devastating conditions.

Need for a Multidisciplinary Approach

The needs of persons with mental illness are varied and can be effectively addressed only by a multidisciplinary approach. There is a need for greater collaboration among various professionals involved in delivering mental health care services. A mix of persons with different professional expertise helps integrate the medical and psychosocial models of intervention. Use of a multidisciplinary team is more effective for optimum and efficient patient care (Pollock 1986; Liberman et al. 2001)

Role of Training

One of the areas that require close attention is training in mental health. Annual manpower generated per a 100,000 population in the South-East Asian region (WHO 2011) was 0.02 psychiatry graduates, 2.96 nurses, 0.01 psychologists, 0.06 social workers and 0.02 occupational therapists. The scenario in India (WHO 2005) was 0.2 psychiatrists, 0.05 psychiatric nurses, 0.03 psychologists and 0.03 social workers, per 100,000 population. At any given point in time, it is fairly evident that there are not enough trained professionals to cater to the needs of those with mental illnesses (Sinha and

Kaur 2011), more so in psychosocial rehabilitation (Gangadhar 2008). This obviously imposes a great deal of burden on the available professionals. One of the recommendations could be to open up many more centres to provide training for mental health workers at all levels and disciplines. Although there are not many centres that offer such training exclusively in this area, it should be possible to provide short-term training for those working in the area of psychiatric rehabilitation to equip them with the required knowledge and skill set. It is also important to get people with the right aptitude who will be able to work in this difficult area where results are not immediate. Training must inculcate core values such as compassion and caring guided by ethics, to make an impact in this challenging area of managing those with severe dysfunctioning.

In this section, special attention has been paid to explore the main challenges that human service professionals in the mental health field have to face. Dr Francis and Dr Mark David Chong will discuss the social justice and human rights issues in mental health social work practice with the support of some case studies. Further, Dr Harris will share her ideas about ethical considerations in mental health research and practice and this will lead the reader through to establish a research practice framework for his/her practice. Community engagement and community partnership has been identified as key factors in mental health promotion and treatment. Dr Chitra, a psychiatrist, through her chapter explains the need for establishing community partnerships and discusses the role of NGO's in mental health care in India with the help of case illustrations. Taking the discussion further Dr MacMohan will take the reader through a discussion on the emerging knowledge base in mental health field and implications for social work practice. In the last chapter, drawing on from field experiences and direct practice with clients, Prof. Ilango and Dr Francis will address some of the challenges faced by the social work profession and will outline some strategies for ways forward.

In conclusion, we still have 'miles to go' towards providing the kind of support and help that individuals with chronic mental illness deserve. It can only be achieved if all the people concerned work in tandem to help them fulfil their dreams and aspirations. Society will have to play its role in embracing them back into its folds, without any reservations, so that they can feel less stigmatised and be part of the larger community like any other member. After all, they too only have an illness like anyone else who may suffer from any other chronic medical disease.

References

Agarwal, A. K. 2012. *Status of psychiatric research*. Available from: http://neuroscienceacademy.org.in/pub/Set%2012.pdf. (accessed on 5 May 2014)

Chandrashekar, H., N. R. Prashanth, P. Kasthuri and S. Madhusudhan. 2010. 'Psychiatric Rehabilitation', *Indian Journal of Psychiatry*, 52 (supplementary 1), 278–280.

Cullen, M. and H. Whiteford. 2001. *The Interrelations of Social Capital with Health and Mental Health: Discussion Paper*. Canberra: Mental Health and Special Programs Branch, Commonwealth Dept. of Health and Aged Care. Available from http://www.health.gov.au/internet/publications/publishing.nsf/Content/mental-pubs-i-intsoc-toc-mental-pubs-i-intsoc-3. (accessed on 3 May 2014)

Dixon, L., W. R. McFarlanem, H. Lefley, A. Lucksted, M. Cohen, I. Falloon, K. Mueser, D. Miklowitz, P. Solomon and D. Sondheimer. 2001. 'Evidence-Based Practices for Services to Families of People with Psychiatric Disabilities', *Psychiatric Services*, 52 (7): 903–910.

Gangadhar, B. N. 2008. 'Human Resource Development in Mental Health Care', in D. Nagaraja and P. Murthy (eds), *Mental Health Care and Human Rights* (pp. 281–290). New Delhi: National Human Rights Commission.

Herrman, H., S. Saxena and R. Moodie. 2004. *Promoting Mental Health: Concepts, Emerging Evidence, Practice* (A Report from the World Health Organization, Department of Mental Health and Substance Abuse in collaboration with the Victorian Health Promotion Foundation and the University of Melbourne). Geneva: World Health Organization.

Indian Council of Medical Research. 2011. *Evaluation of District Mental Health Programme: Final Report Submitted to Ministry of Health and Family Welfare*. New Delhi: Indian Council of Medical Research. Available from: http://mhpolicy.files.wordpress.com/2011/05/evaluation-of-dmhp-icmr-report-for-the-ministry-of-hfw.pdf. (accessed on 3 May 2014)

Kalyanasundaram, S. and N. Sekhar. 2012. 'Creating Supportive Communities in Mental Health: The RFS (I) Experience in Bangalore, India'. in P. Venkat, C. Lesley, F. Abraham, and B. Stefan. (eds), *Papers in Strengths Based Practice* (pp. 176–190). New Delhi: Allied Publishers. Available from http://www.academia.edu/2324023/Papers_in_Strengths_Based_Practice. (accessed on 3 May 2014)

Knapp, M., D. Chisholm, J. Astin, P. Lelliott and B. Audini. 1997. 'The Cost Consequences of Changing the Hospital-Community Balance: The Mental Health Residential Care Study', *Psychological Medicine*, 27 (3): 681–692.

Leff, J., G. Thornicroft, N. Coxhead and C. Crawford. 1994. 'The TAPS Project 22: A Five-Year Follow-Up of Long-Stay Psychiatric Patients Discharged to the Community', *British Journal of Psychiatry*, 165 (suppl 25): 13–17.

Liberman, R. P., D. M. Hilty, R. E. Drake and H. Tsang. 2001. 'Requirements for Multidisciplinary Teamwork in Psychiatric Rehabilitation', *Psychiatric Services*, 52 (10): 1331–1342.

Marks, I. M., J. Connolly, M. Muijen, B. Audini, G. McNamee and R. E. Lawrence. 1994. 'Home-Based Versus Hospital-Based Care for People with Serious Mental Illness', *British Journal of Psychiatry*, 165 (2): 179–194.

Mentality. 2003. *Making It Effective: A Guide to Evidence Based Mental Health Promotion*. Radical mentalities—briefing paper 1. London: Mentality. Available from http://www.centreformentalhealth.org.uk/pdfs/makingiteffective.pdf. (accessed on 3 May 2014)

Mumford, D. B., K. Saeed and I. Ahmad. 1997. 'Stress and Psychiatric Disorder in Rural Punjab: A Community Survey', *British Journal of Psychiatry*, 170 (5): 473–478.

Murthy, R. S. 2004. 'Mental Health in the New Millennium: Research Strategies for India (Editorial)', *Indian Journal of Medical Research*, 120 (2): 63–66. Retrieved from http://medind.nic.in/iby/t04/i8/ibyt04i8p63.pdf. (accessed on 3 May, 2014)

———. 2007. 'Mental Health Programme in the 11th Five Year Plan (Editorial)', *Indian Journal of Medical Research*, 125 (6): 707–711. Available from http://icmr.nic.in/ijmr/2007/june/editorial.pdf. (accessed on 3 May 2014)

———. 2011. 'Mental Health Initiatives in India (1947–2010)', *National Medical Journal of India*, 24 (2), 98–107. Available from http://www.nmji.in/archives/volume-24/issue-2/medical-society-ii.pdf. (accessed on 3 May 2014)

Nagaraja, D. and P. Murthy. 2008. 'Future Directions for Mental Health Care in India', in D. Nagaraja and P. Murthy (eds), *Mental Health Care and Human Rights* (pp. 281–290). New Delhi: National Human Rights Commission.

Pollock, L. 1986. 'The multidisciplinary team', in C. Hume and I. Pullen (eds), *Rehabilitation in Psychiatry–An Introductory Handbook*. Edinburgh: Churchill Livingstone.

Rao, K. 2008. 'Quality Assurance in Mental Health: A Blueprint for Change, in D. Nagaraja and P. Murthy (eds), *Mental Health Care and Human Rights* (pp. 85–99). New Delhi: National Human Rights Commission.

Shah, B., R. Parhee, N. Kumar, T. Khanna and R. Singh. 2005. 'Mental Health Research in India' (Technical Monograph on ICMR Mental Health Studies). New Delhi: Division of Noncommunicable Diseases, Indian Council of Medical Research. Available from www.icmr.nic.in/publ/Mental%20Helth%20.pdf. (accessed on 3 May 2014)

Sinha, S. K. and J. Kaur. 2011. 'National Mental Health Programme: Manpower Development Scheme of Eleventh Five-Year Plan', *Indian Journal of Psychiatry*, 53 (3): 261–265.

Tansella, M. and G. Thornicroft. 1999. '*Common Mental Disorders in Primary care*. London: Routledge.

Thirunavukarasu, M. 2011. 'Closing the Treatment Gap', *Indian Journal of Psychiatry*, 53 (3): 199–201.

Ustun, T. B. and N. Sartorius. 1995. *Mental Illness in General Health Care: An International Study*. Chichester: Wiley.

World Health Organization (WHO). 1986. Ottawa Charter for Health Promotion. Geneva: World Health Organization. Available from www.who.int/healthpromotion/conferences/previous/ottawa/. (accessed on 3 May, 2014)

————. 1990. *The Introduction of a Mental Health Component into Primary Health Care*. Geneva: World Health Organization. Available from http://www.who.int/mental_health/media/en/40.pdf. (accessed on 3 May 2014)

————. 2003. *Investing in Mental Health*. Geneva: World Health Organization. Available from http://www.who.int/mental_health/media/investing_mnh.pdf. (accessed on 3 May 2014)

————. 2005. *Mental Health Atlas: 2005*. Geneva: World Health Organization. Available from www.who.int/mental_health/evidence/mhatlas05. (accessed on 3 May 2014)

————. 2011. *Mental Health Atlas–2011*. Geneva: World Health Organization. Available from http://whqlibdoc.who.int/publications/2011/9799241564359_eng.pdf. (accessed on 3 May 2014)

12

Social Justice and Human Rights Issues in Mental Health Practice

Mark David Chong and Abraham P. Francis

Introduction[1]

Time and time again we see so many people with mental health issues struggling to negotiate their normal day-to-day activities. Often, even the simplest of tasks can prove to be a daunting endeavour for such mentally ill patients who suffer from 'a clinically diagnosable disorder that significantly interferes with … [their] cognitive, emotional or social abilities' (Australian Health Ministers 2003: 5). To make matters worse, mentally disordered

---

[1] I would like to convey my appreciation once more to Dr Abraham Francis for providing me with the opportunity to co-author this chapter with him. His guidance and wisdom as an 'academic-practitioner' in social work has made this a wonderful learning experience for me (a criminologist and lawyer), and I hope that, God willing, this will be the first of many more exciting collaborative endeavours to come. I am also deeply indebted to my wife, Sharon, who had to endure many nights alone because I was working on this chapter. Furthermore, I would like to express my thanks to Ms. Margaret Henni, my research assistant, for proofreading the manuscript. We are likewise humbled by the guidance provided to us by the referees and the editorial board. That said, any mistakes contained herein, are mine and Dr Francis' alone. As always, we hope that this chapter will be a blessing to our readers, and in particular, our students. Be inspired—YOU CAN MAKE A DIFFERENCE! Last but certainly not the least, we thank our heavenly Father for providing us with the perseverance, inspiration and insight to complete this worthwhile endeavour. We could not have done this without you, Lord—*Ad majorem Dei gloriam.*

people are frequently stigmatised by their own communities—their mental condition seen as a mark of innate inferiority (consider by way of illustration, the role eugenics played in this regard) or of retribution (see e.g., how some religions characterised mental illness as punishment for a sinful life). Others even viewed mental illness as a particularly fortuitous invitation to abuse or marginalise their vulnerable victims. While this may seem unthinkable to most, the unfortunate reality is that it happens all too often. On top of having to cope with the more direct effects of being psychologically and/or emotionally impaired, mentally ill people around the world face a range of other challenges. Many live in 'socially unjust' environments where they are either institutionally blocked from receiving much needed health care and/ or social services, or more tragically, find themselves unnecessarily institutionalised or even abused in residential mental health facilities. Furthermore, opportunities for employment, educational/training facilities, housing, transport and leisure activities are likewise limited for people suffering from mental disorders (Drew et al. 2011: 1666). Such acts of social exclusion, discrimination and abuse are not only morally reprehensible but are arguably also egregious breaches of their human rights, especially since these victims represent a particularly vulnerable section of our society, and hence deserve protection. The *Preamble to the United Nations Declaration of Human Rights* (1946) specifically acknowledged that the foundation of freedom, justice and peace in the world was premised on recognising our inherent dignity as being members of the human family, as well as the inseparable inalienable rights afforded equally to all of us by virtue of our common human condition. As Ife (2008: 1) pointed out:

[H]uman rights represent one of the most powerful ideas in contemporary discourse. In a world of economic globalisation where individualism, greed and becoming rich are seen as the most important things in life…the idea of human rights provides an alternative moral reference point for those who seek to reaffirm the values of humanity.

This chapter will therefore attempt to elaborate upon these key issues by (a) outlining the nature and scope of the relevant human rights regimes; (b) uncovering the extent to which such human rights abuses have occurred; (c) the role social workers may play in protecting the human rights of mentally ill clients; and finally (d) canvassing possible solutions that social workers may implement so as to prevent future violations, or at least remedy some of their more deleterious effects.

Understanding the Nature and Scope of Human Rights Regimes

In a recent study that interviewed 51 mentally ill people from across 18 low-to middle-income countries in Asia, South America, Africa, the Middle East and Eastern Europe, Drew et al. (2011) observed that despite expressing a diverse range of definitions concerning what human rights meant to them personally, certain common themes were nevertheless identified (p. 1666). For instance, these rights were thought of as being prerogatives integral to being human, and hence entitled them to inalienable access to basic necessities such as food, health care, education and employment; as well as higher social needs, for example, freedoms of expression and from being discriminated against (Drew et al. 2011: 1666). These human rights were seen to be indispensable tools that could be used to 'live a decent life in society' or to lead a 'harmonious and happy' existence in their respective communities (Drew et al. 2011: 1666).

Echoing this underlying sentiment, Dudley et al. (2012) noted:

> [R]ights in general, or 'human rights' as a sub-class, may be regarded as special normative entities and strong entitlements but also sets of social practices… which apply to everyone, by virtue of their dignity as humans. While rights have moral, political, and legal functions, they are pre-legal, pre-political, and peremptory in nature. Rights are primarily concerned with human capacities to flourish and develop without arbitrary impediment; they signify the incalculable worth of and potential of all humanity. (p. 3)

Dudley et al. reinforced this point by highlighting that 'human rights especially apply to disadvantaged and marginalised groups for whom realising rights is imperative to achieving full potential' (2012: 3). Regrettably, a large number of mentally ill people fall within this sorry predicament, and for them, achieving their full potential in communities where they are usually stigmatised as 'the other', is a bleak prospect indeed (Thesen 2001; Lauber and Rossler 2007). And yet, can we really contend that the wants and needs of these 'others' are somehow so fundamentally different from 'ours'? Or that their hopes and dreams are so distinct and perverse, that it justifies denying them a sense of fulfilment? On the contrary, it is arguable that their expectations of life are far from unique. In fact, they are remarkably similar to 'ours'. Just like 'us'—the so-called 'mentally competent'—these 'others' merely want to have an adequate standard of living; to be healthy, both physically and mentally; to exercise legal capacity and personal freedom; to be safe from harm, torture, 'cruel, inhuman and degrading' treatment/punishment; to be free from exploitation, violence or abuse; and to enjoy their civil, cultural, economic, political and social rights (Drew et al. 2011: 1665).

To accomplish such ends, these legitimate expectations were enshrined in the *United Nations Universal Declaration of Human Rights* (1948), and thereafter entrenched in a number of international treaties, including for example, the

- *Convention on the Elimination of all Forms of Racial Discrimination (1966)*
- *International Covenant on Economic, Social and Cultural Rights (1966)*
- *International Covenant on Civil and Political Rights (1966)*
- *Convention on the Elimination of All Forms of Discrimination against Women (1979)*
- *Convention against Torture and other Cruel, Inhuman or Degrading Treatment or Punishment (1984) and its Optional Protocol (2002)*
- *Convention on the Rights of the Child (1989)*
- *Convention on the Rights of Persons with Disabilities (2006)*

For a more comprehensive list of these instruments, please refer to Chapter IV (Human Rights Section) of the United Nations Treaty Collection at the following website:

<http://treaties.un.org/Pages/Treaties.aspx?id=4&subid=A&lang=en>.

With the exception of the *2002 Optional Protocol to the Convention against Torture and other Cruel, Inhuman and Degrading Treatment or Punishment*, Australia has signed and ratified all of the other treaties (United Nations Treaty Collection, n.d.). As for India, this nation has likewise ratified the above instruments apart from the 1984 *Convention against Torture* (United Nations Treaty Collection, n.d.). Similar to that of Australia, Indonesia has also ratified/acceded to all of the above treaties with the exception of the *2002 Optional Protocol* (United Nations Treaty Collection, n.d.). The United States however has only signed and ratified the following treaties (United Nations Treaty Collection, n.d.):

- *Convention on the Elimination of all Forms of Racial Discrimination (1966)*
- *International Covenant on Civil and Political Rights (1966)*

- *Convention against Torture and Other Cruel, Inhuman or Degrading Treatment or Punishment (1984)*

As for the rest, with the exception of the *2002 Optional Protocol,* which it has taken no action, the United States has only signed the following international agreements:

- *International Covenant on Economic, Social and Cultural Rights (1966)*
- *Convention on the Elimination of All Forms of Discrimination against Women (1979)*
- *Convention on the Rights of the Child (1989)*
- *Convention on the Rights of Persons with Disabilities (2006)*

It should be noted that once ratified (and not merely signed), a country (subject to any reservations made) will be bound by all the terms of the said treaty.

While all of these instruments sought to protect our fundamental rights as human beings, there were no conventions that specifically addressed the needs of mentally ill people until 2006. The only comparable instrument was the non-binding *United Nations Principles for the Protection of Persons with Mental Illness and the Improvement of Mental Health Care* (1991) that attempted to establish minimum threshold levels of human rights standards and compliance within mental health systems across the world (Dudley et al. 2012: 28). This was later augmented by a number of guidelines, principles and a resource book that was produced by the World Health Organisation (WHO) to assist nations in implementing the said *1991 Principles* (Dudley et al. 2012: 28). Nevertheless, it was not until 2006 that the United Nations enacted a treaty that was solely designed to protect the human rights of the disabled, including those who were mentally ill. The 2006 *Convention on the Rights of Persons with Disabilities* thus stands out from among the previously listed human rights treaties as being primarily concerned with safeguarding the interests of people who have 'long-term ..., mental, [or] intellectual ... impairments which in interaction with various barriers may hinder their full and effective participation in society on an equal basis with others' (Article 1). This instrument was deliberately intended to

promote, protect and ensure the full and equal enjoyment of all human rights and fundamental freedoms by all persons with disabilities, and to promote respect for their inherent dignity. (Article 1)

Thus, mentally ill people residing in signatory states would be guaranteed the following rights to

- *Life* (Article 10);
  - o   Every human being, regardless of his/her mental capacity, has an inherent right to life, and signatory states must ensure that persons with disabilities are able to enjoy this right to the same extent as persons not suffering from such disabilities.
- *Equal recognition before the law* (Article 12);
  - o   Every person, including those suffering from a disability, is regarded equal before the law. Consequently, signatory states must ensure that this right is not violated but rather enjoyed by persons of disability in all aspects of life (for example, the right to control their finances; own or inherit private property; have access to loans/mortgage etc.), and to be given support to facilitate the exercise of this right.
- *Access to justice* (Article 13);
  - o   Signatory states must ensure that persons of disability have access to the civil and criminal justice systems in their countries, and to that end should encourage appropriate disability awareness training and so on, for its administrative and enforcement officers.
- *Life and liberty of the person* (Article 14);
  - o   Signatory states must ensure that persons of disability are entitled to enjoy their liberty and security of person to the same extent as others who are not disabled.
- *Freedom from torture or cruel, inhuman or degrading treatment or punishment* (Article 15);
  - o   This would also include the freedom from being subject to medical or scientific experimentation without the person's consent.
- *Mental and physical integrity* (Article 17);
  - o   Every person with disabilities has a right to respect for his/her physical and mental integrity on an equal basis with others.
- *Liberty of movement and nationality* (Article 18);
  - o   Persons with disabilities must be allowed freedom of movement, to choose their residence and to their nationality, just as others who do not suffer from any disability. Similar rights, if appropriate, are also extended to children who suffer from disabilities as well.

- *Living independently and being included in the community* (Article 19);
  - o   Persons with disabilities have equal right to live, be included and participate fully in the community, and to that extent the signatory state must take effective and appropriate measures so as to facilitate the enjoyment of such a right.
- *Personal mobility* (Article 20);
  - o   Signatory states should take effective measures to facilitate the personal mobility of persons with disabilities, as this will allow them to maintain their independence.
- *Freedom of expression and opinion, and access to information* (Article 21);
  - o   This would also include the freedom to seek, receive and impart ideas on an equal basis with others and through all forms of communication of their choice.
- *Respect for privacy* (Article 22);
  - o   Signatory states must ensure that persons of disability are not subjected to arbitrary or unlawful interference with their privacy, family, home or correspondence or to any unlawful attacks on their honour and reputation.
- *Respect for home and family* (Article 23);
  - o   Signatory states must eliminate discrimination against persons with disabilities in all matters pertaining to marriage, family, parenthood, relationships, guardianship, wardship, trusteeship and adoption. Similar protection, if appropriate, is also extended to children who suffer from disabilities as well.
- *Education* (Article 24);
  - o   Signatory states must ensure that persons of disability are afforded an inclusive educational system at all levels (for example, primary, secondary, tertiary and vocational etc.), and that it also includes lifelong learning opportunities.
- *Habilitation and rehabilitation* (Article 26);
  - o   Signatory states must organise, strengthen and extend comprehensive habilitation and rehabilitation services and programmes in areas of health, employment, education and social services to enable persons with disabilities to attain and maintain maximum independence and participation in all aspects of life, as well as full physical, mental, social and vocational ability.
- *Work and employment* (Article 27);
  - o   Signatory states must safeguard and promote this right, which also includes that opportunity to gain a living by work freely chosen

as well as being employed in an open, inclusive and accessible environment for persons with disabilities.

- *Adequate standard of living and social protection* (Article 28);
  - o This would include adequate food, clothing, housing, living conditions, clean water, disability-related services, gender equality, poverty reduction programmes, public housing as well as retirement benefits and so on, for persons with disabilities and for their families.
- *Participate in political and public life* (Article 29);
  - o Signatory states must guarantee that persons with disabilities will still be able to exercise their political rights and to fully participate in public life.
- *Participate in cultural life, recreation, leisure and sport* (Article 30)
  - o This would include being able to enjoy access to cultural materials, television programmes, films, theatre and so on.

Perhaps one of this treaty's most significant provisions relates to a mentally ill person's *right to health* under Article 25. This provision stipulates that 'persons with disabilities have the right to enjoyment of highest attainable standard of health without discrimination on the basis of disability'. This entails ensuring that such health services are, among other criteria, accessible, affordable, gender sensitive, disability appropriate, comprehensive and of comparable quality to that offered to non-disabled patients (please note that this provision is an adapted version of the earlier Article 12(1) of the *International Covenant on Economic, Social and Cultural Rights* 1966; see also McSherry 2008: 774–775).

Human Rights Abuses Perpetrated against Mentally Ill People

Although not enumerative in nature, the ensuing analysis will attempt to offer the reader a cross-sectional glimpse of the type of marginalisation, exploitation and mistreatment that mentally ill people are often subjected to. This would include, for example, social exclusion, discrimination and marginalisation; limited or restricted employment opportunities; physical and sexual assaults; lack of accessibility to mental health and/or medical services; being unnecessarily institutionalised; inadequate opportunities to live independently within their communities; not being allowed to marry or to have a family and economic exploitation (Drew et al. 2011: 1666). For deeper insight into the monitoring of such human rights abuses, please refer to the work done by the Committee on the Rights of Persons with Disabilities at the following website:

<http://www.ohchr.org/EN/HRBodies/CRPD/Pages/CRPDIndex.aspx>

This is an independent body established by the United Nations Office of the High Commissioner for Human Rights for the purpose of monitoring the implementation of the 2006 *Convention on the Rights of Persons with Disabilities*. Another useful resource is the Institutional Treatment, Human Rights and Care Assessment (ITHACA) Project, an initiative funded by the European Commission that is designed to 'document the range of experiences of people with mental illness across Europe' (ITHACA, n.d.). Its purpose-driven toolkit may be used to independently monitor and measure human rights abuse in mental health and social care facilities. It is also premised on the principles and values articulated in the *United Nations Convention on the Rights of Persons with Disabilities* (ITHACA, n.d.).

The illustrations outlined below will draw upon some of the more egregious experiences suffered by mentally ill people in India, Australia, the United States and Indonesia.

Indian Case Studies

Case Study No. 1: Akhtar and Jagawat (1993: 115) noted that out of the 2,785 patients who were admitted to the psychiatric outpatient department (OPD) of the Central Institute of Psychiatry, 70 of these patients were physically restrained. While the proportion of patients so encumbered was relatively small (around 2.5 per cent), the authors noted a worrying trend that

> [p]atients who belonged to a lower socio-economic group and from a rural background had a significantly higher usage of restraint; also, patients [who suffered from] a shorter duration of illness or an abrupt onset with a diagnosis of MDP [Manic Depressive Psychoses]-Mania [ICD-9] were more frequently brought tied to the OPD. (Akhtar and Jagawat 1993: 115)

Furthermore, although most of these patients were perceived to be assaultive and threatening, others were restrained because of the fear that they would jump out of a train or bus, were unwilling to go to the OPD or were tied up in anticipation that they would become violent in the future (Akhtar and Jagawat 1993: 116–117). Akhtar and Jagawat however argued that while:

> [a]cts of violence (30%) and suicidal threats (10%) may be said to be [the] only plausible reason of restraint[,] ... [a]nticipating violence, wandering tendencies, ease of transporting the mentally ill to a mental hospital, unwillingness for treatment and a past history of unpredictable behaviour cannot be adequate justification for restraining a psychiatric patient. (1993: 117)

Case Study No. 2: Having interviewed 146 female psychiatric in-patients, Chandra et al. (2003: 207–208) discovered that 30 per cent of them had been coerced into having sexual activity primarily by their husbands, intimate partners or people who held positions of authority within the community (e.g., an employer, village chief, etc.), with 14 per cent of them reporting that some form of violence or threat of violence had been involved. Unfortunately, most of these sexual assaults were not recorded in these patients' medical records.

Case Study No. 3: Loganathan and Murthy (2011) recently conducted a study that deeply delved into the lives of 118 men and 82 women who were suffering from schizophrenia in India. The authors sought to uncover the personal experiences of these patients, and in particular, the nature and extent to which they had been socially stigmatised by their communities. As a result of suffering from schizophrenia, many male respondents often found themselves facing considerable cultural barriers to marriage, and even when they were successful in securing a spouse, these marriages were usually filled with conflict, ridicule and shame, particularly from their in-laws. Consequently, many respondents preferred not to disclose their disease to anyone (Loganathan and Murthy 2011: 572–573). The female respondents however tended to experience:

> Coercion to not have children, be forced to have an abortion because of beliefs that her child would be born with mental illness; or suffer forced separation from her children, and divorce. Another recurrent theme in this domain involves having to endure abuse from a mother-in-law. (Loganathan and Murthy 2011: 573)

Finally, this study discovered that many of the respondents were unable to secure and/or retain employment easily, particularly those in the government sector. Furthermore, most were bullied or ridiculed at work. As a coping measure, some chose to conceal their mental illness from their employers and colleagues (Loganathan and Murthy 2011: 574–575).

Australian Case Studies

Case Study No. 4: The Australian legislative senate commissioned a wide-ranging study in 2005, with the aim of examining the measures taken by the government to address and meet the needs of those requiring mental health services within the country. After receiving over 800 submissions, hosting extensive public hearings and visiting many mental health facilities across Australia, the Senate Select Committee on Mental Health, in its first report, acknowledged:

> [M]ental illness raises many human rights issues. People with mental illness experience discrimination within society, and even within the health care system; mental illness can cause significant social disadvantages that under-resourced services may fail to adequately address; during episodes of acute illness, a person with mental illness may be unable to assert his/her rights at the very time when those rights may be the most vulnerable to being breached; people experiencing acute mental illness may be treated against their will, or confined against their will, which can be a serious threat to their rights. (Senate Select Committee 2006: 27)

The Select Committee noted that many consumers were denied access to mental health services because of lack of resources provided to mental health facilities by the government (Senate Select Committee 2006: 30). Perhaps even more tragically, when some of these consumers eventually accessed these facilities, they were abused by the mental health system because of 'hostile environments, mental health staff ignoring or dismissing ... [their] personal feelings, physical abuse and forced treatment' (Senate Select Committee 2006: 30).

In this latter regard, 'forced treatment' included involuntary admission, and the Senate Select Committee observed that such practices were common in many facilities, and perhaps a 'norm in acute inpatient settings' (Senate Select Committee 2006: 37). In certain circumstances, some in-patients were even threatened with involuntary admission protocols if they wanted to leave the hospital without the attending physician's permission (Senate Select Committee 2006: 37). It is arguable that such coerced or potentially coerced admission and/or treatment provided to the patient (particularly if he/she has not perpetrated an offence that deserves incarceration) would be in breach of his/her human rights unless the hospital had complied with the relevant mental health laws that specifically allowed for such extreme measures to be taken. For example, if the mentally ill patient's health or safety was at risk or if he/she represented a threat to the community, then they may be involuntarily institutionalised (i.e., 'scheduled' or 'sectioned') even though they had not committed a serious crime (Senate Select Committee 2006: 37). And yet, although ostensibly sanctioned by the relevant law, Smith (2012) nevertheless showed just how 'unjust' such legal rules can be, highlighting in particular that mandatory detention and treatment in New South Wales during the 1980s did not require, among other safeguards, corroborating evidence to prove that the person was suffering from a mental illness, legal representation for the patient at committal hearings or the need for the patient's family or carers to be consulted beforehand.

Likewise other areas of great concern for the Select Committee included the extent to which a mentally ill patient's right to privacy should be sacrificed in favour of providing his/her carers' with information about his/her diagnosis, treatment and prognosis. This was a particularly thorny issue because there were instances when protecting that privacy led to the patient being abandoned, and in some cases, the patient successfully committing suicide. Thus, even though 'the right to privacy, should be respected ... this should not become an excuse for failure to engage with the families of those with mental illness, inadequate discharge planning or failure to implement appropriate community care' (Senate Select Committee 2006: 40).

Case Study No. 5: In a 2010 nation-wide study conducted by the Australian government's Department of Health and Aging, around 1.5 million people between the ages of 18 and 64 years were surveyed to obtain 'updated information on the lives of people with psychotic illness who received public specialised mental health services' (Morgan et al. 2011: 1). Unfortunately, 37.9 per cent of those who were suffering from such mental disorders reported that they had experienced some form of stigma or discrimination because of their psychotic condition (Morgan et al. 2011: 63). In this regard, more female respondents (46.9 per cent) appeared to have been discriminated against than the male respondents (31.8 per cent; Morgan et al. 2011: 63).

Furthermore, 22.7 per cent of the respondents complained that the fear of being stigmatised or of being discriminated against had prevented them from *even* attempting to do the things that they would like to do, while 20.3 per cent who had actually suffered from such discrimination expressed their regret that their bad experiences had stopped them from continuing with certain types of activities (Morgan et al. 2011: 63). Not surprising, 38.8 per cent of those mentally ill respondents who were employed, refused to disclose their psychological conditions to their employers (Morgan et al., 2011: 63).

As for being criminally victimised, the respondents who were suffering from psychosis were much more likely to have been assaulted, robbed and/or had their residences broken into, than the general population (Morgan et al. 2011: 63). For example, 24.8 per cent had reported that they had been a victim of an assault as opposed to 4.8 per cent of the general population who had been similarly victimised (Morgan et al. 2011: 63).

An American Case Study

Case Study No. 6: Solitary confinement (e.g., *supermax* facilities) in American prisons is increasingly being used to punish or control mentally ill prisoners (Metzner and Fellner 2010: 104). When such a punishment is administered to mentally *healthy* prisoners, many of them go on to suffer from 'anxiety, depression, anger, cognitive disturbances, perceptual distortions, obsessive thoughts, paranoia, and psychosis' (Metzner and Fellner 2010: 104). Those who are already suffering from serious mental illness become even more mentally unbalanced as '[t]he stress [of solitary confinement], lack of meaningful social contact, and unstructured days can exacerbate symptoms of illness or provoke recurrence' (Metzner and Fellner 2010: 105). Consequently, many of those who survive this traumatic experience require crisis care and/or psychiatric hospitalisation. For those less fortunate, the morgue ends up as the most likely destination given that a significant number end up committing suicide (Metzner and Fellner 2010: 105).

Indonesian Case Studies

Case Study No. 7: In Jakarta, on the island of Java, was the scene of a horrific media report involving the deaths of hundreds of chronic mentally ill patients from 2007 to 2009 (Minas 2009: 1). They were housed in congested shelters, and they died from malnutrition and diarrhoea. Even some of those who had been transferred from these shelters to a mental hospital died during this period. Minas noted that this was not the first time one of these shelters had been caught out for human rights abuses against their mentally ill patients (2009: 1). The 2009 inquiry by the Head of the Jakarta Health Agency discovered that these shelters were dismally overcrowded, unconscionably understaffed and woefully underfunded (Minas 2009: 2).

As a result, these institutions had become unhygienic environments, and their patients uncared for and malnourished (Minas 2009: 2). *Case Study No. 8*: The province of Aceh on the island of Sumatra commonly used physical restraints and confinement as a way of containing the problem that mentally ill people posed to their communities (Puteh et al. 2011: 1). Known as '*pasung*', these measures were considered to be necessary given 'the problem of looking after a severely mentally ill family member, concerns about risk to the mentally ill member or to others, and inaccessible, unaffordable, ineffective psychiatric treatment services' (Puteh et al. 2011: 1). The infliction of *pasung* was by no means gentle, and often entailed the:

> securing [of] ankles in wooden stocks, chaining and tying by rope to immovable objects (e.g., a building or a tree), locking in a confined space such as a cage or a box, and often a combination of confinement and restraint. (Puteh et al. 2011: 1–2)

Puteh et al. lamented that even though:

> such practices constitute a severe form of abuse of the human rights of persons with mental illness they have attracted little sustained attention from policy-makers, human rights activists and professional groups. (Puteh et al. 2011: 2)

As the above examples indicate, the range of violations against the human rights of mentally ill people can be quite varied, both in terms of their nature as well as of their consequence. While some breaches may be relatively less serious than others, it is also equally apparent that mentally ill people are extremely vulnerable to abuse from so many different quarters of society, and hence are deserving of greater protection. Social workers, among other professions, may be able to play an important role in this regard.

Protecting the Human Rights of Mentally Ill Clients

This chapter suggests that given its 'caring' and 'social justice' ethos, social workers are ideally positioned to assist in alleviating the suffering of mentally ill people. According to the Australian Association of Social Workers (AASW), 'the purpose of practice is to promote recovery, restore individual, family, and community well-being, to enhance development of each individual's power and control over their lives, and to advance principles of social justice' (2008: 8). More particularly, the AASW explained that 'the domain of social work in mental health is that of the social context and social consequences of mental illness' (2008: 8). Social workers are thus actively involved 'with issues of stigma and discrimination, of political freedoms and civil rights, of promoting access to necessary treatment and support services, and of promoting consumer and carer rights to participation and choice in mental health services' (AASW 2008: 8–9). They are, unabashedly, ardent defenders of the mentally ill (Lundy 2011: 41)—a role which is entirely consistent with the philosophical approach taken by the *Convention on the Rights of Persons with Disabilities 2006*. This treaty has been described as a 'seismic shift in the treatment of people with disabilities' (Dudley et al. 2012: 32) because it radically repudiates our traditional assumption that the mentally ill are welfare cases in need of paternalistic benevolence rather than being autonomous agents who are entitled to *demand* their government's medical treatments and social services simply because they are human beings and citizens of their respective countries. However, as Bland et al. (2009: 4) clarified, if the above mentioned aims of social work practice are to be realised, social workers must argue for a broader agenda in mental health. That is, an agenda that looks beyond the dominance of 'narrow, clinical concepts of illness and treatment', to interventions more inclusive of a variety of practice methods, such as individual counselling, community work, group work, social action, social planning and social policy (Bland et al. 2009: 4). With such a foundation (both aspirational and practical), social workers are constitutionally imbued with the ability to craft creative and morally inspirational solutions—qualities that are necessary given how insurmountable the problem of curtailing human rights abuses will be.

Possible Solutions

As highlighted in the previous section, social workers are clearly able to play a pivotal part in either reducing these human rights contraventions or in diminishing the misery and distress suffered by their mentally ill clients as a result of being marginalised, exploited and/or mistreated simply because of their psychosocial disorders. Some of these measures include the following:

- Initiating public awareness and anti-stigma campaigns through various vehicles of the mass media (television, radio, newspapers etc.) to demystify and debunk the erroneous beliefs surrounding mental illness (e.g., the myth that *all* mentally ill people are violent and erratic in their behaviour);

- Augmenting the professional and educational training that governments provide to their health care practitioners so that they will be better equipped to serve the mentally ill;
- Increasing governmental funding allocated to health care services specifically for the mentally ill;
- Improving the quality of mental health services, particularly those that are provided within the community;
- Empowering and encouraging greater involvement of the mentally ill in their treatment and rehabilitation within their communities;
- Putting in place effective and humane laws and public policies that are designed to defend the mentally ill from abuses as well as to endorse greater respect for their human rights;
- Promoting and supporting greater opportunities for the mentally ill to form organisations that will advocate their interests better;
- Ensuring that human rights compliance and abuses are regularly and efficiently monitored and assessed and
- Making certain that these mental health initiatives and programmes are an integral part of the government's overall health and development policies (Drew et al. 2011: 1668–1672).

Notwithstanding the width and depth of these initiatives, it is still arguable that many of them can be successfully implemented through direct social work practice. Such an approach would not only encompass the provision of face-to-face clinical services (e.g., micro-level intervention through individual casework or counselling), but also the establishment of macro-level collaborative relationships with other key institutional, organisational and professional actors, as well as the practice of advocacy (Hepworth et al. 2013: 15, 26). In fact, one of the underlying principles of direct practice especially exemplifies just how suitable social workers are in addressing the human rights abuses afflicting the mentally ill. As a philosophical tenet of social work direct practice, Hepworth et al. (2013: 29) suggested that:

> [b]ecause social work clients are often subject to poverty, racism, sexism, heterosexism, discrimination, and lack of resources, social workers negotiate systems and advocate for change to ensure that their clients obtain access to their rights, resources and treatment with dignity. They also attempt to modify or develop resource systems to make them more responsive to client needs.

While micro-level intervention (e.g., clinical social work) may ameliorate some of the personal costs suffered by their mentally ill clients as a result of these human rights abuses, it will only be through macro-level intervention that deeper social reform can take place. At this domain, social workers become 'professional change agents who can assist community action systems composed of individuals, groups, or organizations in dealing with social problems' (Hepworth et al. 2013: 15). In this role, social workers will strive towards reducing the occurrence of human rights abuses at a systemic level by developing and mobilising adequate and appropriate resources; effectively employing advocacy and social action initiatives; organising the community; improving organisational environments and effecting, where necessary, organisational change (Hepworth et al. 2013: 441).

Conclusion

As the above analysis shows, people who suffer from mental illness are significantly disadvantaged on so many different levels. Their lives are constantly undermined not only by the direct consequences of being mentally ill but also by the marginalisation, discrimination and abuse that they face as a result of their psychological and/or emotional impairment. Demonised as the 'other', mentally ill people are viewed with suspicion and derision, and are often victimised because of their inherent vulnerabilities. The challenges that they face are not only at an inter-personal level but, more tragically, are embedded within the social system itself—culture, science, politics, religion, economics—all of which converge and result in either creating environments that are conducive for human rights abuses, or are breaches of human rights in themselves.

Many social workers however are equipped to address some of these issues at both micro and macro levels of intervention. In this regard, clinical social work practice can potentially ease the personal suffering associated with such abuses. Macro-level initiatives, on the other hand, require social workers to operate outside of their clinical comfort zones, and to engage more vigorously at an institutional level to implement systemic restructuring, particularly those measures that seek bottom-up community engagement and transformative responses. Although advocacy is a key feature in such endeavours, it should be noted however:

> Practicing human rights is much broader than advocacy. Advocacy is important and has played a vital role in the promotion and protection of human

rights, but to understand human rights work only as advocacy is unnecessarily limiting. By using some of the ideas of community development practice, which is broader and holistic, we can significantly extend the practice of human rights from below. (Ife 2009: 201)

Consequently, addressing these human rights abuses will require root and branch reform that will go beyond immediate clinical treatment, and to that extent social workers must develop, in addition to their clinical skills, a whole host of other core competencies to prepare themselves for broader macro-level direct practice work. This will entail, as Bland et al. (2009: 12) pointed out, '[s]ocial workers, nurses, psychologists, occupational therapists, and psychiatrists ... [sharing] a body of knowledge, skills and values' by learning from one another through the medium of multi-disciplinary teams—an initiative previously envisaged by the Australian National Mental Health Strategy 2003–2008 (Australian Health Ministers 2003). This is the path that social workers must take if they are to remain true to their calling—one that leads them to creating a more socially just world.

Summary

We often see so many mentally ill people struggling to negotiate their normal day-to-day activities because they suffer from 'a clinically diagnosable disorder that significantly interferes with ... [their] cognitive, emotional or social abilities'. To make matters worse, case studies from India, Australia, the United States and Indonesia highlight the fact that mentally disordered people are also frequently stigmatised by their own communities. Such acts of social exclusion, discrimination and abuse are not only morally reprehensible but are arguably egregious breaches of their human rights as well—rights that are protected by a range of international treaties and conventions. Given their 'caring' and 'social justice' ethos, as well as the wide array of interventional tools that they have at their disposal, social workers are in a strong position to play an important role in either protecting their mentally ill clients from human rights violations and/or assisting in the healing process as a result of such abuse. Such intervention may encompass both micro and macro level initiatives, with the former involving, for example, individual casework and counselling, while the latter engages in advocacy and the establishment of collaborative relationships with other key institutional, organisational and professional actors.

References

Akhtar, S., and T. Jagawat. 1993. 'Restrained Psychiatric Outpatients: Necessity, Justification or Violation of Human Rights?', *Indian Journal of Psychiatry*, 35 (2): 115–118.

Australian Association of Social Workers (AASW). 2008. *Practice Standards for Mental Health Social Workers*. Canberra, ACT: Author.

Australian Health Ministers. (2003). *National Mental Health Plan 2003–2008*. Canberra, ACT: Australian Government.

Bland, R., N. Renouf and A. Tullgren. 2009. *Social Work Practice in Mental Health*. Crows Nest, NSW: Allen & Unwin.

Chandra, P. S., S. Deepthivarma, P. Michael, B. C. Kate and M. P. Shalinianant. 2003. 'A Cry from the Darkness: Women with Severe Mental Illness in India Reveal Their Experiences with Sexual Coercion', *Psychiatry Prax*, 66 (4): 323–334.

Drew, N., M. Funk, S. Tang, J. Lamichhane, E. Chávez, S. Katontoka, S. Pathare, O. Lewis, L. Gostin, and B. Saraceno. 2011. 'Human Rights Violations of People with Mental and Psychosocial Disabilities: An Unresolved Global Crisis', *Lancet*, 378 (9830): 1664–1675.

Dudley, M., D. Silove and F. Gale. 2012. 'Mental Health, Human Rights, and Their Relationship: An Introduction', in M. Dudley, D. Silove and F. Gale (eds.), *Mental Health and Human Rights: Vision, Praxis, and Courage* (pp. 1–49). Oxford, Oxfordshire: Oxford University Press.

Hepworth, D. H., R. H. Rooney, G. D. Rooney, K. Strom-Gottfried and J. A. Larsen. 2013. *Direct Social Work Practice: Theory and Skills* (9th ed.). Pacific Grove, CA: Brooks/Cole.

Ife, J. 2008. *Human Rights and Social Work: Towards Rights Based Practice*. Port Melbourne, VIC: Cambridge University Press.

———. 2009. *Human Rights from Below: Achieving Rights through Community Development*. Port Melbourne, VIC: Cambridge University Press.

Institutional Treatment, Human Rights and Care Assessment Project (ITHACA). n.d. The Problem Available at: http://www.ithacastudy.eu/theproblem.html (accessed 19 March 2014).

Lauber, C. and W. Rossler. 2007. 'Stigma towards People with Mental Illness in Developing Countries in Asia', *International Review of Psychiatry*, 19 (2): 157–178.

Loganathan, S. and S. R. Murthy. 2011. 'Living with Schizophrenia in India: Gender Perspectives', *Transcultural Psychiatry*, 48 (5): 569–584.

Lundy, C. 2011. *Social Work, Social Justice and Human Rights: A Structural Approach to Practice* (2nd ed.). Toronto, Ontario: Toronto University Press.

McSherry, B. 2008. 'Mental Health and Human Rights: The Role of the Law in Developing a Right to Enjoy the Highest Attainable Standard of Mental Health in Australia', *Journal of Law and Medicine*, 15 (5): 773–781.

Metzner, J. L., and J. Fellner. 2010. 'Solitary Confinement and Mental Illness in U.S. Prisons: A Challenge for Medical Ethics', *The Journal of the American Academy of Psychiatry and the Law*, 38 (1): 104–108.

Minas, H. 2009. 'Mental Health and Human Rights: Never Waste a Serious Crisis', *International Journal of Mental Health Systems*, 3 (12): 1–3.

Morgan, V. A., A. Waterreus, A. Jablensky, A. Mackinnon, J. J. McGrath, V. Carr, R. Bush, D. Castle, M. Cohen, C. Harvey, C. Galletly, H. J. Stain, A. Neil, P. McGorry, B. Hocking, S. Shah and S. Saw. 2011. *People Living with Psychotic Illness 2010: Report on the Second Australian National Survey*. Canberra, ACT: Commonwealth of Australia.

Puteh, I., M. Marthoenis and H. Minas. 2011. 'Aceh Free Pasung: Releasing the Mentally Ill from Physical Restraint', *International Journal of Mental Health Systems*, 5 (10): 1–5.

Senate Select Committee on Mental Health. 2006. *A National Approach to Mental Health: From Crisis to Community*. Canberra, ACT: Senate Committee on Mental Health.

Smith, M. 2012. 'Detained, Diagnosed, and Discharged: Human Rights and the Lived Experience of Mental Illness in New South Wales, Australia', in M. Dudley, D. Silove and F. Gale (eds.), *Mental Health and Human Rights: Vision, Praxis, and Courage* (pp.376–382). Oxford, Oxfordshire: University Press.

Thesen, J. 2001. 'Being a Psychiatric Patient in the Community: Reclassified as the Stigmatized "Other"', *Scandinavian Journal of Public Health,* 29 (4): 248–255.

United Nations Treaty Collection. n.d. Chapter IV: Human Rights. Available at: http://treaties.un.org/pages/treaties.aspx?id=4&subid=A&lang=en (accessed 19 March 2014).

Web Resources

Australian Association of Social Workers http://www.aasw.asn.au/ (accessed on 19 March 2014).

Australian Department of Health and Aging (Mental Health Section) http://www.health.gov.au/mentalhealth (accessed 19 March 2014).

Australian Human Rights Commission http://www.hreoc.gov.au/ (accessed 19 March 2014).

Australian Institute of Health and Welfare (Mental Health Section) http://www.aihw.gov.au/mental-health/ (accessed 19 March 2014).

ITHACA (Institutional Treatment, Human Rights and Care Assessment) Project http://www.ithacastudy.eu/index.html (accessed 19 March 2014).

Mental Health Council of Australia http://www.mhca.org.au/ (accessed 19 March 2014).

United Nations Committee on the Rights of Persons with Disabilities http://www.ohchr.org/EN/HRBodies/CRPD/Pages/CRPDIndex.aspx (accessed 19 March 2014).

United Nations Treaty Collection http://treaties.un.org/Pages/Treaties.aspx?id=4&subid=A&lang=en (accessed 19 March 2014).

13

Ethical Considerations in Mental Health Research for Evidence-Based Practice[1]

Nonie Harris

Introduction

The purpose of this chapter is to explore ethical research practice in the field of mental health and in doing so, to contribute to the overall development of the research capacity of mental health practitioners and researchers (Gould 2010). Social work practice is changing; research is now an integral part of practice. The need for practitioners to be able to engage in research is becoming more important for clients, organisations and communities. We should assume that research and practice are not mutually exclusive and that as practitioners, committed to social justice and human rights, we are also social researchers who embrace these same commitments. This chapter explores the link between socially just practice, research and ethics and highlights the political nature of not only knowledge creation but also the relationship between a researcher and the researched. The chapter concludes that our commitment to our clients and their communities is strengthened not only by an evidence base but also by ethical research practice that embodies and manifests the principles of human rights and social justice.

---

[1] This paper was presented in part as a keynote presentation at the International Conference on Child and Adolescent Mental Health, 18th and 19th January, 2013, Tamil Nadu, India.

The Importance of Social Research and Evidence-Based Practice

Social work practice is changing; research is now an integral part of practice. The need for practitioners to be able to engage in research is becoming more important for both clients and organisations. Rubin and Babbie (2005: 5) point out that

> even if you never consider yourself a researcher, you are likely to encounter numerous situations in your career when you'll use your research expertise and perhaps wish you had more of it. For example, you may supervise a clinical program whose continued funding requires you to conduct a scientific evaluation of its effects on clients ... You may be involved in community organizing or planning and want to conduct a scientific survey to assess a community's greatest needs ... You may be engaged in social reform efforts and need scientific data to expose the harmful effects of current welfare policies and thus persuade legislators to enact more humanitarian welfare legislation.

The Australian Association of Social Workers (AASW) states: 'Research is key to the continued development of the theory and knowledge base of social work practice' (2008: 6). This professional practice standard emphasises the importance of the creation of an evidence base to inform our practice, that as social work practitioners we continue to monitor and evaluate what we do in a structured way, and that through these processes we are accountable for the quality and effectiveness of our practice. Practitioners also need to undertake research to determine the needs of clients, to test new ideas and to confirm practice wisdom. Research underlies the accomplishment of all of these expectations.

Maschi and Youdin maintain that 'research has always been a systematic agent of change and an organizing frame used to develop individual- and community-level interventions and to monitor the desired outcomes' and that as practitioners we need to 'reclaim research for practice and action' (2012: xviii). Social research is, therefore, a systematic task that involves gathering and analysing information for the purposes of taking action and affecting positive social change. Data collection and analysis can occur within qualitative and/or quantitative methodological frameworks, using a variety of data gathering methods as appropriate to the topic. (Later in this chapter, I will briefly explore the particular relevance of a qualitative methodology.) Additionally, sound research practice rests on assumptions about the nature of scientific inquiry and the scientific method that 'seeks truth through observed evidence—not through authority, tradition or ideology ... [and] that the observations, that accumulated that evidence, should have been systematic and comprehensive' (Rubin and Babbie 2005: 19).

According to Brian Sheldon (2001), the history of evidence-based practice in social work began in the 1930s in the United States, and since that time social workers and practitioners have conducted research and used the generated evidence to evaluate and inform their practice. Bland et al. define evidence-based practice as 'the conscientious, explicit and judicious application of best research evidence to a range of clinical domains: diagnostic tests and interventions of a therapeutic nature' (2009: 41). Sheldon (2001) and Bland et al. (2009) identified the kinds of research and research-related activities that were relevant to acquiring best evidence—for example, clinical trials, conducting comparative and longitudinal studies, drawing together separate but similarly relevant studies, using qualitative in-depth interviews, case studies, focusing on the causes of social problems and accessing relevant research from other disciplines.

Practice guided by research is fundamental to the accountability and justification of our practice decisions. Accountability is valid motivation but as Leanard Gibbs says the motivation for our evidenced-based practice comes, 'First from the heart, from your dedication to do no harm, from your determination to make better judgments and decisions, wherever possible, in collaboration with your clients. Your second source of motivation may come from your practical nature' (2003: 8).

Although, research as an evidence base for social work practice is an accepted principle of the profession, the reality is that most practice decisions are made without a strong evidence base (Fook 2003; Harvey et al. 2013). Indeed a recent review of social work research literature by Harvey et al. (2013) identified a low level of published research relevant to everyday practice decisions. Fook (2003) also notes that there is variation in what is understood to be practice-relevant research. At the conservative end of the continuum, valuable research is seen as positivist, evaluative and instrumental, while others take a broader view encompassing 'any research activities which aim to improve practice' (Fook 2003: 50). Further, Fook specifically defined practice research as 'research which is directly about practice, or which concentrates on applying results of other research directly to practice' (2003: 51). Fook continues her discussion by expanding her focus beyond narrow definitions of practice research to ethical practice and evidence-based practice, thus framing our understanding of practice-relevant research in a more complex way.

Evidence-based practice research that aligns with positivist notions of the researcher as expert can also raise ethical questions for practitioners who value service user knowledge and are sensitive to 'power differences, cultural contexts and the impact of social disadvantage in assessing social situations' (Harvey et al. 2013: 2). Chan and Ng (2004) draw links, relevant to this chapter's focus on research ethics, between research practice and an awareness of intolerance for injustice. They ask that we embrace the 'virtues of mutual respect and tolerance of diversity, rational thought and commitment to a defensible moral code' (Chan and Ng 2004: 313). This claim supports the connection between evidence-based practice, a commitment to social justice and ethical research practice.

Particularly, as practitioners in the in the mental health field, we are committed to socially just practice that aims to make a positive difference to the lives of our clients and their communities. Further, we have the belief that 'human rights are important, and that they are particularly important for the human service professions in general, and for social workers in particular... human rights can provide social workers with a moral basis for their practice' (Ife 2009: 1). We assume, as previously stated, that research and practice are not mutually exclusive and that therefore as practitioners, committed to social justice and human rights, we are also social researchers who embrace these same commitments. Such commitments assume a connection to ethical research practice.

Social Research Ethics

The Australian National Health and Medical Research Council (NH&MRC 1999: 1) clarifies the role of ethics in social research:

> Ethics and ethical principles extend to all spheres of human activity. They apply to our dealings with each other, with animals and the environment. They should govern our interactions not only in conducting research but also in commerce, employment and politics. Ethics serve to identify good, desirable or acceptable conduct and provide reasons for those conclusions ... The primary purpose of a statement of ethical principles and associated guidelines for research involving humans is the protection of the welfare and the rights of participants in research.

Codes of ethical research practice with human participants were originally established in the Nuremburg Code, adopted during the Nuremburg

Military Tribunal held after World War II (Neuman 2011). These codes were enshrined in the *Universal Declaration of Human Rights* in 1948, and form the basis of current ethical practice in social research. Central to the codes of ethical research practice is the notion of informed consent. That is at no time should research participants feel coerced into participating in the research: 'It is not enough to get permission from people; they need to know what they are being asked to participate in so they can make an informed decision' (Neuman 2003: 124).

Research today, as in the past, involves ethical dilemmas. Glesne and Peshkin (1992) refer to the complexity of ethical considerations in research noting that a brief acknowledgment of ethical standards at the commencement of a project is not enough. All interaction throughout the research project should be viewed in the context of ethical behaviour. Ethical considerations are positioned within the context of power relations, most commonly between the researcher and the respondent. There are a number of strategies the researcher can use to promote an ethical research process: acknowledgement of the impact of power and difference; reflexivity; attention to research practices and the adoption of protocols for ensuring ethical standards are adhered to (Hesse-Biber and Yaiser 2004). Of course, some theorists (Roberts 1981; Oakley, 1999) have wondered if ethical research is even possible since all research is embedded in oppressive material realities. Nevertheless, the researcher, acknowledging the complex contexts within which research is undertaken, should prioritise ethical research practice. Ramazanoglu and Holland (2002) specifically suggest: 'You will need to work out your ethical position in relation to the researched, your accountability for the research, how you should present yourself (and) what the researched are to be asked to consent to' (p. 157).

Further, I argue, as ethical social researchers we should be concerned with issues of power and, specifically, how patterns of domination and subordination are reproduced in the relationship between the researcher and respondent. Positivists accept the implicit authority of the researcher, failing to acknowledge the potentially exploitative nature of the research relationship (Oakley 1981; Stanley and Wise 1983). The taken-for-granted superiority of the 'objective' scientific mind concerned early critical theorists such as Horkheimer, who challenged the apolitical, ahistorical positioning of the scientist claiming that the scientist and the person should not be separated (Stanley and Wise 1983; Horkheimer 1989). Implicit in this separation is a failure to recognise that the scientist is embedded in oppressive social structures and is implicated in supporting and reproducing oppression.

Dismantling these power relationships is a primary task for social researchers. The unchallenged researcher and researched relationship is like a 'colonial power relationship—the oppressor defines the problem, the nature of the research, (and who is researched) ... Research is inherently value laden and reflects the power structures within which the research exists' (Hesse-Biber and Yaiser 2004: 107).

Thus far I have acknowledged the link between socially just practice, research and ethics, and highlighted the political nature of not only knowledge creation but also the relationship between researcher and researched. I have noted that ethical research should occur within a framework that is sensitive to politics and power. I have also provided a brief history of research ethics and noted particularly the importance of informed consent. I argue that all these considerations are vital to our exploration of ethical research within the area of mental health practice.

Justifying Research in the Mental Health Field

Mental health research is important. A review of mental health literature reveals extensive reference to research in the field. The research varies and is large and small scale; primary and secondary; quantitative, qualitative or mixed method. Its relevance to the field is unquestionable. Srinivasa Murthy (2011) acknowledges the contribution of research to our understanding of mental disorders and notes: 'This new knowledge has continuously supported the development of mental health programs' (p. 104). Research not only describes the practice field, it also provides the evidence on which to base our practice and it is a mechanism for linking theory and practice. Such links 'stress the important relationship between research and practice effectiveness' (Trevithick 2012: 57).

Ethics, values and the need for effective practice justify research in the mental health field. Daisy Bogg (2010) begins her exploration of *Values and Ethics in Mental Health Practice* by drawing connections between personal and professional values and how we articulate our mental health practice, where we privilege 'principles of hope, self-efficacy, personal dignity, self determination and person centredness' (p. 11). Ethical research practice clearly links to these values, principles and standards; providing mental health practitioners with a strong imperative and justification for their practice-based research. Research is justified not only by commitment to the ethical principles that underlie sound research but also because mental health practitioners occupy 'a unique situation to influence the social service delivery system because of their rich experiences across an array of mental health client problems' (Boyd and Koor 2002: 300).

Ethical Social Research Practice

When we specifically consider undertaking research in the field of mental health—whether our research is with clients, practitioners, agencies or governments—our priority is to embed our research activity in ethical principles that acknowledge politics and power and principles that value of human rights and social justice. But what strategies can a researcher use to ensure that their research practice reflects these principles and values? A number of authors have provided guidance in this area and recommended that the basic tool in this process is reflexivity. Reflexivity refers to 'the tendency to reflect upon, examine critically, and explore analytically the nature of the research process' (Fonow and Cook 1991: 2). Hesse-Biber and Yaiser (2004) argue that reflexivity is a powerful tool for recognising the researcher's own social position and assumptions; and reflexivity is the first part in the process deconstructing the authority of the researcher. They recommend that researchers convey their own positionality to respondents and to the research audience. The researcher should also engage in processes that promote collaborative research. 'This includes building on the existing achievements of service user researchers in initiating and leading research collaborations' (Gould 2010: 180). The principles of collaboration and reflection should guide and inform all research in the mental health field.

I also argue that mental health researchers particularly value opportunities for clients to tell of their own experiences, to share clients' knowledge and to explore experiences relevant to client's lives. Capturing service user knowledge in a way that encourages the respondent to tell their story in a safe and respectful environment can, in many cases, be best achieved using a qualitative methodology. A qualitative methodology encourages deep engagement with the respondent and can allow the respondent to share information beyond the original research vision of the practitioner. A qualitative methodology uses data-gathering techniques such as in-depth interviewing and case studies to provide access to rich data on the lived experience of service users. These methods encourage us to respectfully and collaboratively engage with service users' understanding of the research purpose and benefit—privileging their voices.

Of course, research that articulates the values of respectful and collaborative engagement assumes that some of the research in the field will involve primary research with clients. It is imperative therefore that we consider the vulnerability of people who have a mental health condition and the implications of this vulnerability for research protocols. Informed consent is at the heart of our considerations. Informed consent assumes the following:

- The person making the decision must be able to understand the necessary information and be able to use that information to reach a decision.
- The person must know all the necessary facts, be offered all available choices and be aware of any risks associated with these choices.
- The person must reach a decision voluntarily and not because they have been coerced into it (O'Connor et al. 1998: 228).

It is important that we recognise that our clients' status—for example, as children and adolescents with a mental health condition, may diminish their capacity to give informed consent to participate in research projects. Their capacity to understand the nature and the intent of the research may also be diminished. As practitioners we must recognise that in relation to our clients, we are in a position of power—after all we may control the resources on which their well-being depends. In such circumstances, consent from clients to participate in our research may at best be uninformed and at worst given in a context of fear of significant negative consequences—amounting to a perception of coercion. As practitioners and social researchers, we must recognise the general principle that 'it is unethical to involve "incompetent" people (e.g., children, mentally disabled) in our study unless we have met two conditions: A legal guardian grants written permission, and we follow all ethical principles against harm to participants' (Neuman 2011: 151). Of course, we must refer to our country-specific ethical research guidelines. Although, generally, meeting these requirements would mean, for example, that we reflect on our position of power and the impact of that position on potential respondents, that we engage collaboratively with parents, guardians and clients in the formulation and design of the research project, and that the intent and requirements of involvement in the research are articulated in a way that is sensitive to the needs of our client group.

Given these considerations we can assume that socially just research practice means that

- As researchers, we accept responsibility for the ethics of our research.
- We avoid research that will cause harm to our participants.
- We recognise the vulnerability of our clients and the consequent impact on their capacity to give informed consent.
- Respondents are free to withdraw from the study at any time during the study, even if they have initially consented to participate.
- We ensure that the participation of the respondent and the information they provide is confidential and their anonymity is preserved.
- We approach our research in the spirit of collaboration and partnership.
- We clearly articulate the purpose and design of our study and disclose the nature of any sponsorship of the study.
- We give due consideration to the possible consequences and repercussions of our research and the publication of our results.
- The intention of our research is to improve the quality of life of our clients and their communities.

Conclusion

The purpose of this chapter is to explore ethical research practice in the field of mental health and in doing so, to contribute to the overall development of the research capacity of mental health practitioners and researchers (Gould 2010). At the beginning of this chapter, I focused on the political nature of knowledge, knowledge production (that is research) and the research act itself. This 'truth' about research sets the scene for conducting ethical research and, particularly, ethical research in the area of mental health. As social scientists and practitioners in the field of mental health, we are concerned with making respondents and their experiences visible, exploring and understanding the context in which we practice and, most importantly, promoting positive social change (Roberts 1981). Emeritus Professor Jim Ife argues: 'From a human rights perspective, social work research needs to address a human rights agenda... [and] research that aims to further the cause of human rights must itself respect human rights principles in its own methodologies' (2009: 179–181). This consistency between what we aim to achieve and how we go about achieving our goals is at the heart of ethical research practice. We also recognise, as social researchers and practitioners committed to a human rights perspective, that socially just research forms the basis of socially just practice. These connections lead us to one conclusion—that our commitment to our clients and their communities is strengthened not only by an evidence base but also by ethical research practice that embodies and manifests both the principles of human rights and social justice.

References

Australian Association of Social Workers. 2008. *AASW practice standards for social workers*. Canberra: Author.

Bland, R., N. Renouf and A. Tullgren. 2009. *Social Work Practice in Mental Health: An Introduction*. Crows Nest: Allen and Unwin.

Bogg, D. 2010. *Values and Ethics in Mental Health Practice*. Exeter: Learning Matters Ltd.

Boyd, S. and W. Korr. 2002. 'Social Workers as Program Evaluators and Researchers', in K. Bentley (ed.), *Social Work in Practice in Mental Health: Contemporary Roles, Tasks and Techniques* (pp. 297–321). Belmont: Brooks/Cole Cengage Learning.

Chan, C. and S. Ng. 2004. 'The Social Work Practitioner-Researcher-Educator: Encouraging Innovations and Empowerment in the 21st Century', *International Social Work*, 47 (3): 312–320.

Fonow, M. and J. Cook. 1991. 'Back to the Future: A Look at the Second Wave of Feminist Epistemology and Methodology', in M. Fonow and J. Cook (eds), *Beyond Methodology: Feminist Scholarship as Lived Research* (pp. 1–15). Bloomington: Indiana University Press.

Fook, J. 2003. 'Social Work Research in Australia', *Social Work Education: The International Journal*, 22 (1): 45–57.

Gibbs, L. 2003. *Evidenced-Based Practice for the Helping Professions: A Practical Guide*. Pacific Grove: Brooks/Cole-Thomson Learning.

Glesne, C. and A. Peshkin. 1992. *Becoming Qualitative Researchers: An Introduction*. New York: Longman.

Gould, N. 2010. *Mental Health Social Work in Context*. New York: Routledge.

Harvey, D., D. Plummer, A. Pighills and T. Pain. 2013. 'Practitioner Research Capacity: A Survey of Social Workers in Northern Queensland', *Australian Social Work*. Doi: 10.1080/0312407X.2012.754916

Hesse-Biber, S. N. and M. Yaiser. 2004. 'Difference Matters: Studying across Race, Class, Gender and Sexuality', in S. N. Hesse-Biber and M. Yaiser (eds), *Feminist Perspectives on Social Research* (pp. 101–120). Oxford: Oxford University Press.

Horkheimer, M. 1989. *Critical Theory: Selected Essays*. New York: Continuum.

Ife, J. 2009. *Human Rights and Social Work: Towards Rights-Based Practice* (Revised edition). Melbourne: Cambridge.

Maschi, T. and R. Youdin. 2012. *Social Worker as Researcher: Integrating Research with Advocacy.* Boston: Pearson.

National Health and Medical Research Council (NH&MRC). 1999. *National Statement on Ethical Conduct in Human Research.* Canberra: Australian Government.

Neuman, L. 2003. *Social Research Methods: Qualitative and Quantitative Approaches* (5th ed.). Boston: Allyn and Bacon.

———. 2011. *Social Research Methods: Qualitative and Quantitative Approaches* (7th ed. and International ed.). Sydney: Pearson.

Oakley, A. 1999. 'People's Ways of Knowing: Gender and Methodology', in S. Hood, B. Mayall and S. Oliver (eds), *Critical Issues in Social Research: Power and Prejudice* (pp. 154–170). Buckingham: Open University Press.

O'Connor, I., J, Wilson and D. Setterland. 1998. *Social Work and Welfare Practice* (2nd ed.). Melbourne: Longman.

Ramazanoglu, C. and J. Holland. 2002. *Feminist Methodology: Challenges and Choices.* London: Sage.

Roberts, H. (ed.). 1981. *Doing Feminist Research.* London: Routledge and Kegan Paul Ltd.

Rubin, A. and B. Babbie. 2005. *Research Methods for Social Work.* New York: Wadsworth.

Sheldon, B. 2001. 'The Validity of Evidence-Based Practice in Social Work: A Reply to Stephen Webb', *British Journal of Social Work,* 31 (5): 801–809.

Srinivasa Murthy, R. 2011. 'Mental Health Initiatives in India (1947–2010)', *The National Medical Journal of India,* 24 (2): 98–107.

Stanley, L., and S. Wise. 1983. '"Back to the Personal" or: Our Attempt to Construct "feminist research"', in G. Bowles and R. Duelli-Klein (eds), *Theories of Women's Studies* (pp. 192–209). London: Routledge and Kegan Paul.

Trevithick, P. 2012. *Social Work Skills and Knowledge: A Practice Handbook* (3rd ed.). New York: McGraw-Hill.

14

Community Mental Health and NGO Engagement: The Kerala Experience*

Chitra Venkateswaran, Sonny Jose and Abraham P. Francis

Introduction

Mental and neurological disorders affect nearly 13 per cent of the world population. In fact, one out of every four people around the globe experience a mental illness that warrants diagnosis and treatment. Mental disorders cause considerable burden on individuals, families and societies. Human, social and financial resources are needed to provide access to effective and humane treatment for people with mental disorders. Mental health and mental illness is a part of every country, culture, age group and socio-economic status.

In India, around 6 per cent of 1.21 billion population are reportedly affected by varying mental problems. The disparity between the number of mentally ill, treatment facilities and trained professionals result in a large 'treatment gap' in the community. Community mental health programmes are essential to address this gap, to reach out to a major percentage of people who live with little access to good care, especially those economically deprived. Establishment of autonomous organisations to provide accountable and evidence-based good-quality care and development of appropriately trained human resources has been suggested as one of the methods to improve

* The contributors of this chapter acknowledge and appreciate the efforts of the numerous NGOs and voluntary organisations around the country providing a yeoman service in the area of mental health care. We have only highlighted a few of them and have used a case to illustrate the point regarding the importance of the NGO sector. We wish to punctuate how collaborative practice models can be developed in a given local context and further discuss the role of social workers. This could be explored with the students in the class by bringing in appropriate local case studies.

mental health care. This chapter illustrates the case of Mehac Foundation, a non-governmental organisation (NGO), as an earnest initiative to integrate community and key persons into community mental health as an initiative to provide quality mental health care.

Mental and neurological disorders, account for 12.3 of the total disability adjusted life years (DALYs), contributing to 13 per cent of the global burden of disease, and almost half of the 10 leading risk factors that cause about one third of premature deaths (WHO 2011). An analysis of trends suggests that this burden will increase steeply to the extent of 15 per cent in the year 2020 (WHO 2011). Despite substantial evidence, mental health still remains one of the most neglected and a poorly researched area of public health, particularly in lower middle income countries (LMICs; Rochon et al. 2004; Sharan et al. 2007). The most common forms of psychiatric disorders seriously restricting meaningful participation in society and affecting quality of life include unipolar depression, alcoholism, schizophrenia, bipolar depression and dementia.

South Asia has its own share of problems. The fact that South Asia suffers from shortage of manpower, especially psychiatrists and hospital beds, for the increasing population in this region, is a major concern (Kallivayalil 2004). Zeroing in on India, 6 per cent of a staggering 1.21 billion population is reported to be afflicted by varying degrees of mental problems. All of this is in spite of India having a national mental health policy and specific program formulated as early as 1982. This is in sharp contrast to more than 40 per cent of countries that have no laws, rules or regulations for mental health (Mental Health Atlas 2011). This National Mental Health Policy operational through the National Mental Health Programme (NMHP) in 1982 laid an emphasis on 'building up mental health intervention programmes at the district level' (NMHP 1982). But 30 years later, much desires to be done to achieve this goal. The average allocation for mental health care stands at a mere 0.83 per cent of the public health budget, situating India alongside 30 other countries, whose mental health budget is less than 3 per cent. In addition, the existing infrastructure in education generates only about 320 psychiatrists, 50 clinical psychologists, 25 psychiatric social workers and 185 psychiatric nurses per year (Murthy 2011). This deficit leading to an average national deficit of psychiatrists of around 77 per cent, precipitates a gross disparity resulting in a large 'treatment gap' in the community. The apathy depicted above, in many ways, is a reflection of the stigma and discrimination against the mentally ill at the administrative level. It is not only economic deprivation or the lack of development, but rather the sociocultural climate in large parts of the country that treats mental health like a curse.

People living with mental illness suffer twice over—from the illness itself and also because they are shunned by their families and often exiled from their communities and isolated by society (WHO 2011). Stigma associated with mental illness is arguably the greatest obstacle to the path of recovery from mental illness in India. Patients with mental health problem are often perceived as 'accursed, punished for wrong doings in earlier births' and the same is endorsed by superstitions. It is only natural logic that communities segregate the afflicted and their families, further stigmatising and discriminating them both. Consequently, this already morbid picture becomes murkier. As an illustration, as many as half the people, who have schizophrenia, live in the community without treatment (Isaac et al. 2007; Saravanan et al. 2010; Thirthalli et al. 2010). Rural India scored high on stigma scores and 'deployed a punitive model towards the severely mentally ill' when compared to the urban group; urban Indians showed a strong link between stigma and 'not wishing to work' with a mentally ill individual (Jadhav et al. 2007). Most of the mentally ill do not have access to organised services, causing such patients to suffer from significant disability, burdening the family and caregivers emotionally and financially, and jeopardising them further. Hence, in a country like India and most of the South Asian countries, there is a compelling need to initiate and facilitate services reaching out to people in the rural parts. Here comes the relevance of community health.

Community Mental Health: Its Need and Relevance

Smukler and Thornicroft have defined community psychiatry as follows (cited in Thara et al. 2010):

> Community psychiatry comprises the principles and practices needed to provide mental health services to a local population by (i) establishing population-based needs for treatment and care; (ii) providing a service system linking a wide range of resources of adequate capacity, operating in accessible locations and (iii) delivering evidence based treatments to people with mental disorders.

Community psychiatry usually has the following key components (WHO-HEN 2010):

- Crisis intervention/emergency/acute services
- Treatment services (multidisciplinary out-patient teams)
- Case management

- Psychiatric rehabilitation (within the fields of housing, work, education and socialising)
- Day care

The 'principles' of community psychiatry include (Caplan and Caplan, cited in Thara et al. 2010) the following:

1. Responsibility to a population, usually a catchment area defined geographically
2. Treatment close to the patient's home
3. Multidisciplinary team approach
4. Continuity of care
5. Consumer participation
6. Comprehensive services

Community psychiatry has been shaped by the mental health services in the Western countries and connected with 'de-institutionalisation' movement in the West during the mid-1960s (Koyanagi 2007). De-institutionalisation evolved as a process of replacing long-stay psychiatric hospitals with less-isolated community mental health services, for those diagnosed with a mental disorder or developmental disability (Stroman 2003) to protect them from harmful effects of long-term institutionalisation in mental hospitals (Léouffre and Tempier 1998).

In developing countries such as India, where there are inadequate number of institutions for the mentally ill, most care takes place in the community and family. Hence, in contrast, community psychiatry in India and other developing countries refers to the establishment or development of new services and programmes in the community, rather than the process of de-institutionalisation. The primary emphasis here is to integrate mental health with primary care services through community based mental health care services.

Community mental health services are intended to support or treat people with mental illness in a domiciliary setting, instead of a psychiatric hospital (asylum). Community mental health refers to a system of care wherein the patient's community, and not a specific facility such as a hospital, is the primary provider of care for people with a mental illness. The goal of community mental health services often includes much more than simply providing out-patient psychiatric treatment (Bentley 1994); it involves the vast resources in the community including supported housing with full or partial supervision (including halfway houses), psychiatric wards of general hospitals (including partial hospitalization), local primary care medical services, day centres or clubhouses, community mental health centres and self-help groups for mental health. India and especially Kerala, given their persisting family and caste structures offer a lot of social support and social networks that would augment recovery.

Community Mental Health: A Global Picture

A balance of community- and hospital-based services is the most effective form of comprehensive mental health care. Community mental health considers vital community resources—NGOs; consumer and family associations; traditional, indigenous and alternative health care systems; community-based social and rehabilitative services, as well as informal resources like family, friends and other social networks.

Globally, two-third of the countries claim at least some community care facilities for mental health. Only about half the countries in Africa, eastern Mediterranean and Southeast Asia region provide community-based care (Saxena 2008), whereas continued efforts are underway to provide community-based mental health care in Sri Lanka, Pakistan and India (Farooq et al. 2001). Increasing number of NGOs across the world focus on various aspects of mental health ranging from awareness to clinical management, advocacy and legal issues. WHO-AIMS (2005) data suggests that only 46 per cent of low-income countries have user and family associations, in comparison to 88 per cent of LMICs and 100 per cent of upper middle income countries. Thus, people with mental health needs and their families tend to have fewer opportunities to participate in decision making about treatment; this is true in all countries, especially in low-income countries. It has been realised that in countries such as India, integration of mental health into the primary care services is the most appropriate way to extend mental health care to the population, given its vast network of primary health centres.

Rationale behind Community Mental Health in India

In India, NMHP mandates the implementation of national mental health services; given the severity of issues plaguing mental health, it has been evaluated as ineffective. The national policies that determine the functioning of the NMHP are faulted for the following reasons (Murthy 2011):

- A top-down approach programme, least sensitive to the cultural aspects of the country
- WHO policies seemingly driving the programmes rather than local needs, reducing efficacy
- The lack of involvement of community care and community leaders

Despite the negativity, one should not under-rate the creative interventions and substantial progress made in priorities areas—setting up of psychiatric beds in general hospitals, suicide prevention, care of elderly, substance use and disaster programmes, as well as the setting up of day care centres, half-way homes, long-stay homes and rehabilitation facilities.

Responses from the Government

In India, one of the main strengths of the national programme has been the integration of mental health care with general primary health care fostering a more effective community-based service. There are various attempts on this line. One such attempt is the public health initiative called the *District Mental Health Programme* (DMHP), operational in 127 districts in India (Report of District Mental Health Programme 2011). This service undertakes mobile clinics in the communities to identify persons with mental illnesses, provide care and rehabilitate locally, thereby reducing the load on hospitals. This also reduces stigma by promoting integration and improving public awareness. However, there have been significant problems due to deficits in implementation, operation, coordination, monitoring as well as manpower (Kumar 2005a; 2011).

The *National Rural Health Mission (NRHM)* (2004) is another effective government initiative to engineer change to public health delivery. It brought on agenda inclusiveness of the health needs for the disadvantaged, as well as the health equity to a perceptible extent. The NRHM, committed to health of vulnerable populations, brought flexibility to funds like the central and the state, focussed on primary health care, public–private partnerships, developed time-bound deliverables. Further, it regulated and accredited medical facilities, regulated education and training of human resources and maintained quality systems for medications. The NRHM scheme works at the primary care level with exclusively female field workers designated as ASHA (Accredited Social Health Activists), supervised by the health inspectors and public health nurses, with wide reach within the community. Although mental health is not a priority on the NRHM agenda, individual states have set their own priorities and stand to gain more support and advancement through this programme (Kumar 2005b).

The community-level decentralised services that focus on integration at the primary health care level should be aggressively pursued with an adequate number of staff specific to this programme, rather than loading the already exhausted staff in primary health centres. The community health workers, ASHA under the NRHM scheme, junior public health nurses, health inspectors and nurses play an important role in improving awareness, identifying persons and following up. Alongside this, public–private partnership as well as partnerships with NGOs working in the community must be enhanced to allow better access, acceptance and gain support from volunteers.

Community Mental Health Services by the Voluntary Sector

Presence of the voluntary sector may be regarded as the best indicator or a civil society. In India, the voluntary sector has been active in setting up facilities in the community, addressing several aspects of mental health by generating awareness, providing care and shelter, both for short and long periods, care for special/vulnerable groups such as the elderly, women, differently abled children and children with severe deficits. Suicide prevention and disaster care may be regarded as other important areas of engagement and intervention. Benefits of regular treatment include reducing disability and burden, especially the financial costs of the family (Thirthalli et al. 2010).

Establishment of autonomous organisations to provide accountable and evidence-based good-quality care and development of appropriately trained human resources has been suggested as one of the methods to improve mental health care (Reddy et al. 2011). Such organisations are accepted by the community, and thus well utilised. However, there have been very few attempts to evaluate and consolidate such experiences.

Approximately, 88 per cent of the countries have at least one NGO that is active in mental health. Common NGO activities include advocacy, mental health rehabilitation and direct service provision. However, in most low- and middle-income countries, the population coverage and the range of services provided by NGOs are not comprehensive.

In India, Schizophrenia Research Foundation (SCARF Chennai), Manas (West Bengal), Shristi (Madurai) and Sangath (Goa) focus on several areas including child development, adolescent health and mental health; Sneha (Chennai), Medico-Pastoral Association (Bangalore), Saarthak (Delhi) work in suicide prevention; Banyan (Chennai) provides shelter and care for women living with mental illness; Alzheimer and Related Disorders Society of India focuses on dementia, while T. T. Ranganathan Clinical Research Foundation (TTK Foundation) Chennai and Total Response to Alcohol and Drug Abuse (TRADA) Kerala, addresses alcohol use (Thara et al. 2010). Nav Bharat Jagriti Kendra (NBJK) Hazaribagh is one of the the few organisations working in partnership with 23 NGOs in 14 rural districts of Bihar and Jharkhand, eastern states of India. The growth of family/user NGOs such as Action for Mental Illness (ACMI) Bangalore, ASHA (Chennai) and inclusion of mental health by NGOs primarily into other areas of health are refreshing developments. Ashagram (Madhya Pradesh) with primary focus on physical disabilities has grown to include rehabilitation of people with severe mental disorders. Much of research evaluating models of interventions in the community are at the behest of such NGOs. Despite overlaps, the activities of NGOs can be mainly grouped into the following:

- Treatment, care and rehabilitation
- Community-based activities
- Prevention, advocacy and empowerment
- Research and training

Mental Health Care in Kerala

Kerala, located in south-western India with a population of 33 million (Census India 2011), projects favourable social indices, compared to the rest of the country, especially in literacy, social awareness, per capita GDP and economic productivity. The Human Development Index (HDI) of Kerala is the best in India. This is reflected in many health parameters (Mannarth 2009). Yet, one million persons are estimated to be currently in need of mental health services; almost half of them suffer from severe mental illness. Kerala accounts for 10.1 per cent of all suicides occurring in India, though the population accounts for only 3.4 per cent, with mental illnesses reported to be the reason behind 90 per cent of the suicides in the state (National Crime Records Bureau (NCRB) 2010) is a matter of great concern.

The Comptroller and Auditor General (CAG 2010: 5) report on the utilisation of health funds in the state, revealed the fact that the state failed to utilise most of the funds it received from the Union Government in March 2010. The CAG took exception that Kerala failed to conduct a survey to identify the mentally ill persons in spite the National Human Rights Commission (NHRC) recommending it (CAG 2010: 6). The report highlighted that the shortage of manpower in various categories in the three mental health centres (MHCs) ranged between 64 and 94 per cent. This shortfall was due to lack of qualified psychiatrists, clinical psychologists, psychiatric nurses and social workers (CAG 2010: 12). However, the State Mental Health Authority (SMHA) is upgrading the mental health care infrastructure and has initiated action in conducting the survey (CAG 2010: 6). This apathy has significant social implications and highlights the relevance of community mental health.

There are approximately 1,800 psychiatry beds in public sector and 143 private mental hospitals are available in Kerala. The District Mental Health Programme (DMHP) active in the eight districts—Thiruvananthapuram, Thrissur, Kozhikode, Kannur, Kasargode, Malappuram, Idukki and Wayanad—of Kerala has its own limitations especially with regard to resources. In Kozhikode, the Institute of Mental Health and Neurosciences works along with the DMHP, NRHM and the community-based palliative care network to provide care in five northern districts (Krishna Kumar 2010).

There are many NGOs offering regular and continuous medically supervised care. A special mention has to be made about the tremendous progress in the palliative care movement, which has grown to be a social and public health milestone. Beginning as an out-patient clinic with a home care program in Kozhikode as the Pain and Palliative Care Society (Bollini et al. 2004), the movement evolved into a successful community led programme (Paleri and Numpeli 2005) motivating the health authorities to draft a policy for palliative care at the state level. Its salience lies in its principles and the possibility of replicating the model to any health sector. The programme has now started including mental health as one of its components.

Implications for Social Work in Community Mental Health

The above-mentioned discussions highlight two things—one, the existence of a persistent, ever-widening gap between what is needed for mental health care and what is available in many societies including the affluent ones in the West and secondly, there immense prospects of graduating from the conventional institutionalised approach, to the community-based approach. This beckons social work to mobilise and bridge the gap between the demand and resources, as well as to generate community involvement.

Social workers claim better access to individuals suffering from mental disorders as their role demands spending time with clients and their social systems. Social workers realise that mental distress may be caused or compounded by poor living conditions and difficult personal circumstances. Social workers are therefore crucial in the road to recovery from mental illness precisely because their focus is personal, giving practical support and help to resolve problems of living that might otherwise appear insurmountable to someone who is also trying to deal with his/her mental distress. This type of support not only contributes to recovery from a period of illness, it can also help reduce the likelihood of a further episode recurring (Gilbert et al. 2010). This provides an exciting opportunity for high impact work.

Clinical social work is also in a position to shape the mental health care system through creative utilisation of research-informed assessment and intervention tools, and through development of innovative models of evidence-based practice. Social workers ideally act as trailblazers in bringing to the fore the contribution of social care to the wider determinants of mental health and well-being (Gilbert et al. 2010); Gilbert and his fellow authors firmly set social work as one of the most vital components in a truly whole-person and whole-systems approach to mental health.

Strengths-Based Social Work Perspective in the Context of Community Mental Health

The general approach to mental health being top-down and deficit-oriented as constructed with the medical model, has resulted in the isolation, labelling and stigmatisation of the mentally ill. Hence, mental health context aspires a deliberate shift from deficits to strengths-based focus in the mental health care delivery. In other words, a shift from the currently practiced deficit model, to the community-based model will open up a host of options to the client and his/her context, including the augmentation of non-financial and social capital resources.

The strengths-based social work practice perspective fits in well in the mental health setting. In this approach, social work can focus on two important dimensions of intervention when dealing with individuals within communities. Firstly, is the focus on clients as 'treasure troughs' of resources capable of experiencing and learning from adversities, discerning what's right and best for them, and eventually evolving a process of self-healing and transformation. This ascribes 'expertness' to the client. Secondly, individuals live in a diverse eco-system (person-in-environment) that provides for the client's 'frame of reference' and the context to the challenge; it highlights where 'created resources' may be located and incorporated in the journey towards recovery (Francis 2012). Moreover, social participation can enhance health, particularly if this takes place in the cultural context. Being connected to the community, feeling included in a shared culture, having access to both informal and formal services, mitigates risks and provides opportunities to feel safe and be healthy in a community. Studies have suggested that low levels of social participation can limit access to social support and networks, which can then have a negative effect on health (Chenoweth and Stehlik 2004; Seyfang 2003).

Specific Roles for Social Work in Mental Health

Mental health settings usually include services in three broad levels of health care application: prevention, treatment and rehabilitation. It is recognised that individual social workers may practice exclusively within one setting, or transcend the boundaries of all three, in attempting to respond to diverse needs—client, family and community.

Prevention: In this context, social work aims to reduce the incidence of disease or dysfunction by modifying stressful environments within the community and strengthening the ability of the individual to cope. Prevention involves the promotion and maintenance of good health through education, attention to adequate standards for basic needs and specific protection against known risks. In mental health settings, preventive activities include public and client education regarding emotional self-care and healthy relationships, building community knowledge and skills (community development), social action and advocacy for social justice. In the context of Mehac, this is achieved through active engagement of community volunteers, alongside clinicians, social workers and ASHA workers.

Treatment: Social workers work to reduce the prevalence (number of existing cases) of a disorder or dysfunction and includes early diagnosis, intervention and treatment. Treatment activities are focused on individuals experiencing acute psychiatric symptoms, emotional trauma, relationship problems, stress, distress or crisis and include assessment, risk management, individual, couple, family and group counselling, intervention or therapy and advocacy. Social work uses relationship as the basis of all interventions. Locating and mobilising with community support would make treatment more manageable.

Rehabilitation: Social work aims at retraining and rehabilitation and to ensure maximum use of remaining capacities by the individual. In mental health settings, rehabilitation activities focus on clients who are disabled by mental illness and may include individual, couple, family and group interventions to build knowledge and skills, provision of specialised residential, vocational and leisure resources and advocacy to ensure the development of needed services and to change community attitudes. The same can be achieved by way of income generating initiatives (IGPs). One particular model of community-based rehabilitation has been shown to be effective for schizophrenia in a state in northern India (Chatterjee et al. 2003).

Case Study: Mehac Foundation

The Mental Health Care and Research Foundation (Mehac Foundation) is a not-for-profit organisation registered as a charitable trust (Registration no: 1850, October 2008, New Delhi, India; registered under the Act of Registration of Deeds) with the objective of advancing public health initiatives in the sphere of mental health care in India through widespread community participation (Mehac 2012).

History and Context

The establishment of Mehac can be traced to its roots in the palliative care movement in north Kerala; these initiatives in palliative care, involving people, indicate the efficacy of the community model. Two of Mehac's promoters—Mr. P. K. Ashok Kumar, one of the trustees, and Dr Chitra Venkateswaran, the lead clinician—have actively contributed to this community-based movement. Although initially, people with cancer and other terminal illnesses were the prime beneficiaries, the movement subsequently grew to encompass people with many chronic diseases. To incorporate the principles of palliative care for mental health was regarded as both a challenge and an exciting opportunity. Mehac Foundation has adapted the principles of this public health initiative specific to mental health care. This movement has actually enabled the community to own health care programmes, take responsibilities in policies and don an active role in the expansion of the programme.

Several other factors highlighted in this chapter have motivated the incorporation of this organisation. The development and existence of the mental health care system as an organisational and clinical entity, not integrated with the general health care apparatus, leave most institutions bereft of community orientation or participation. A large section of the needy remains deprived of care, long-term care, as well as continuous availability of medications. The Mehac model involves empowering local communities to impart free mental health services to fellow human beings under the guidance and supervision of trained medical professionals. Mehac's focus is on initiating, facilitating and augmenting the mental health component of existing general and primary health care services, providing free and quality care through a network comprising of a variety of local institutions and individuals to function as mental health care coordinators.

Community Engagement in Service

The local partners who take the lead in the programmes include those involved in community services and social upliftment, as well as the delivery of medical care. Regular clinics are conducted by the Mehac team with consistent follow-up with the help of people living in the same area. These projects draw strength from people who volunteer in various capacities. The clinical volunteers take the lead role in identifying persons with mental illnesses and their families, monitoring the care of the patients and coordinating with their families. They play an active role in understanding the nature of the illnesses and the treatment offered. They have an important role in educating people about the mental illnesses, thus contributing to awareness, demystifying and handling stigma related to psychiatric problems. To ensure adherence to treatment is maintained, to raise an alert if side effects are present, to enable quick management of emergencies are also part of their responsibilities. The therapeutic interventions, advocacy and mobilisation of resources reflect engagement of the community in means of direct social work practice (Mustafa 2010).

The team in the field is multidisciplinary in nature and includes psychiatrists, social workers and junior psychologists along with people belonging to the local areas functioning as volunteers. The work ranges from assessments, clinical management with cost effective medications, behavioural interventions, psychotherapy and counselling by the team. The team coordinates interdisciplinary services to a specified client, group or population, with active support of volunteers who perhaps incorporate the case management strategy (Mustafa 2010). Psycho-education and training form another important component. The main method of making a presence in the community has been through providing home-care services for mentally ill people. Training and awareness sessions for the local partners and volunteers are also important components. This echoes of community development strategy borrowed from social work method.

Mehac projects make use of an information technology–oriented, internet-based record system, which facilitates instant access to clinical and patient data to key clinical personnel. This in turn ensures quick response from the clinical personnel in emergencies, ensuring project management and administrative as well as effective service delivery.

Projects

Pilot project: The first project was initiated in 2008 in the north of Kerala in two districts: Malappuram, one of the poorer districts that lags behind other districts in literacy and education standards, though it has contributed immensely to Kerala's cultural traditions; and Wayand, in the north-east of Kerala, is a hilly district, which has the largest tribal population in the state and a high incidence of mental illness issues and suicide.

The programme focused incorporating the mental health component into the already existing palliative care units with a strong voluntary network. Offering care for mentally ill under the same roof as other chronic diseases managed by same set of volunteers helps in handling stigma issues effectively.

The first two years witnessed Mehac providing supervised psychiatric care to around 700 people with various mental illnesses of varying degrees. These two years also proved the feasibility and effectiveness of such a model. This encouraged Mehac to expand its services. There was a need to grow to the southern part of Kerala and part of the initial team remained back to continue the initial project. Mehac Foundation shifted to start newer projects in southern Kerala. The initial projects still continue and have expanded in north Kerala under Mental Health Action Trust, Kozhikode. This has led to continuity of work in north Kerala and also the chance to start new ones.

Services in South Kerala and Its Growth

South Kerala has relatively less strong palliative care networks compared to the north. To identify partners interested to collaborate in such ventures was a challenge. Programmes were started in 2010 in Ernakulam and Alleppey, two districts in southern Kerala. These two districts lack a district mental health programme, and further, do not have any strong, active community-based networks. Till date four clinics run in Alleppey and two in Ernakulam, with two more to begin in the months to follow. Most of the clinics are operated on a weekly basis. Two clinics are conducted on a monthly basis, in distant places, such as in Attapadi, where the population is mainly tribal, and in Elappuly, both in Palakkad district.

Partnerships in the Community

Mehac collaborates with the local governing body, the Panchayat in three of the projects; Muhamma in Alleppey, Chottanikkara and Kanjoor in Ernakulam. Recently another Panchayat, South Mararikulam in Alleppey, have initiated a programme for children focusing on learning disorders, behavioural problems and life-skills education. The involvement of Panchayat as the main stakeholder is encouraging as it points to an objective measure of community involvement. This would lead to sustainability of the programme. Moreover, the need is also felt from the side of the local authorities rather than Mehac imposing a model of care. The Panchayat takes responsibility for issuing free medications to the people and the ASHA volunteers of the NRHM programme take an active role. In the Panchayat wards, which are a subdivision to allow convenience in governance, members also take an important role.

Mehac has also initiated collaboration with two long-stay homes that look after patients with chronic mental illnesses. Patient population included persons wandering on the streets as well as those abandoned by the family. The aim in such institutional care is to improve the quality of care, provide regular and supervised care, engage interventions by social workers, undertake rehabilitation and most importantly to encourage the family to take the members back to their homes. The continuity of care in the community is offered by outpatient review.

Lessons from This Experience

Feasibility of the model: The model of organised care is feasible and people benefit to a great extent. Integration of mental health care is possible with primary health care. This present model can be implemented in a cost effective manner.

Partnerships: Striking up collaborations and partnerships with other organisations and individuals, including governmental bodies are possible and effective. Sharing the goal and working together can be planned and implemented.

New practice models: Mehac has been able to engage in new programmes focusing on a range of issues which are essentially based on the needs of the community engaged with.

Role of people in community: Mehac has been able to improve awareness and generate favourable attitude among the people involved, regarding mental health. There has been an increase in the interest and in the referral of people needing help from the community. People take an active role in such socially-relevant health problems.

Challenges

The sustainability and scope of the programmes depend on the availability of funds and support, which is a key problem. Expansion of programme depends on more staff and manpower. Long-term employment and continued commitment from staff and volunteers are issues that need to be addressed. Collaboration with governmental bodies not only encounters resistance, but also does suffer because of the bureaucracy and 'red-tapism' leading to delays and poor implementation. There is an acute shortage of psychiatrists who are willing to take up community-based work, especially to work in an NGO. There is also the unattractiveness of having to work in a rural environment, which challenges the comfort of systems found in hospitals. Psychologists and social workers are very keen in getting involved in these projects. However, focus on monitoring and review is not pursued with the same intensity as project work in the field.

Mehac Experience and Implications for Social Work

Social work is an enabling profession grounded with knowledge, value base and specific skills administered to empower individuals, groups and communities to live life to its fullest. As a profession, social work subscribes to the person-in-environment (PIE) concept, and integrates treatment of individuals, groups and communities in three domains—micro-, messo- and macro. At the micro-level it focuses on assisting the individual locate resources within the person and in the immediate environment, and mobilise the family in ensuring support to the person. At the messo-level, the social institutions (school in the case of a child, organisations in the case of those employed) of relevance to the life stage are mobilised and negotiated into supporting the individual in their journey towards recovery. The macro-level intervention demands advocacy to influence policy formulation and legislations; ideally we are also required to bring about desirable social changes and dispel stigma.

The Mehac experience in community mental health revealed to the actors the following challenges:

1. Rampant stigma and discrimination presenting an obstacle to treatment and recovery

2. Inertia on the part of the community to get involved in community mental health initiative
3. Lack of awareness as well as infrastructure pertaining to rehabilitation and organised care

Awareness and Stigma

In India, stigma and limited awareness of mental illness still remain a major obstacle to provision of care to the mentally ill (Shrivasthava et al. 2012). The community perceives mental illness as a low priority, leading to poor investment in resources, economics and manpower in this area of health, although continuous efforts are showing promising changes. The Mehac experience has been very rewarding in handling stigma. The volunteers live in the same village and take active responsibility in providing care. They also help in improving awareness through their social interactions. Integrated services thus reduce discrimination to a large extent and change attitudes towards mental health problems.

Home-care services also play a significant role in giving the community a convincing message of the need for care. Given the alternative models of handling the mentally ill, isolating people with illness in tiny rooms or sheds or chaining them which are still prevalent, can slowly be changed. Integration services can also ensure closer medication review and thus reduce visible markers of illness and treatment of such side effects of antipsychotics. The community also takes an active part in the care of wandering or homeless people who are otherwise ignored.

Stigma, sadly does not only have an impact on the affected individual, but also scars the families across generations. This may have implications on marriage or social standing that is quite palpable when home care visits are carried out. Stigma is also attached to the institutions providing care, medications and even with the mental health workers. A global programme against stigma and discrimination has reduced or even removed stigma in a number of countries where it was implemented (Sartorius 2007). Local initiatives have been identified as having significant contribution. An integrated, community-based approach is one of the most effective methods to address these social factors that form a barrier to deliver good care. Thus, NGOs emulating models similar to Mehac can make leeway in the combat against stigma and discrimination.

Community Participation and Education

Models with community participation have shown remarkable progress in addressing the social and societal determinants of chronic illnesses. The Mehac initiative promotes income-generating activities for people with illnesses and families along with setting up of self–help groups of people with mental illness and their families. Along with participation, education of people involved in cases, especially the volunteers, health workers, nurses and families is an important focus to enable delivery of good care. These carers also learn about the feasibility of such programmes by actually participating. This adds to their confidence in dealing with families with mental illness. They not only transform into role models for their community as they start visiting people they had once stigmatised and avoided before, but also encourage the mentally ill as well as their families to approach for care or arrange for home care visits, ensuring better treatment compliance. The carers and the beneficiaries communicate more effectively, using shared cultural expressions and thus contribute to better treatment compliance as well as substantial reduction in stigma and in fighting discrimination.

Thus, the involvement of stakeholders in community mental health has been a learning experience. Participation arising out of awareness of the social responsibilities of individuals in terms of looking after the vulnerable sections of their own community (Sallnow et al. 2005) and collaborating with medical personnel was found to lead to better outcomes. In a country such as India, a person with an illness comes with a huge load of economic problems associated with social isolation and suffering. Hence, given the fact that mental illness comes with an extra burden of stigma and discrimination, the community definitely benefits from a participatory model. Such a demand for palliative care and support within the community, served the very purpose of existence and the objectives set by Mehac.

Transformation in Nature of Services Provided

Mehac has experienced quite an effective team where the volunteers in the community took up the role of coordinating care; the nurse and social workers played a role in stepped care in treatment by providing medications, psycho-education, supportive counselling/psychotherapy, facilitating changes if necessary, acting as the link person and also helping to prevent relapses. This is in tune with the principles of 'organised care' (Lazarus and Freeman 2009) where case management, stepped care and collaborative care forming three overlapping approaches are offered as alternatives for delivery of care. The social workers along with the nurses could garner support from the immediate family and the community members who were significant in changing the attitudes towards mental illness and stigma that once existed in the community. This allowed the psychiatrist more time and space to plan the treatment regime, focus more time on people not improving or difficult to manage and recommend additional methods of management. The team working together towards a single goal aims at collaborative care. There is increasing evidence of the effectiveness of 'collaborative care' (Gilbody et al. 2003), a multifaceted organisational intervention involving new staff and ways of working (Von Korff et al. 2001). This is especially relevant in low resource settings and when there is paucity of referral resources.

Case management essentially involves assigning responsibility for coordinating the care of a patient to a particular member of the health care team. This allows for systematic monitoring of adherence to treatment and indicators of progress or relapse and triggers follow-up in case of treatment default. Mehac executed the same effectively by assigning non-specialist, low-cost personnel such as health workers or community-based volunteers to undertake the same. Considering the need for consistent supervision and technical input at every stage, the social worker acted as a go between the clinician and others who follow-up while the patient is back in the community. There are times when the medication may not be locally available or may be even too expensive. Here the social worker negotiates with the specialist, discusses alternatives and mobilised resources—internal and external—so that treatment is complied with.

Stepped care is providing care in a triaged manner where low-intensity interventions can be delivered to a proportion of persons who would benefit from such interventions, but do not require more aggressive care (Katon et al. 1999). Most of these people can be taken care of at home. In a community-based setting, there may be many people with chronic psychotic illnesses who suffer from severe disabilities and who could benefit from low doses of antipsychotic medications as well as other forms of support including psycho-education, regular follow-up and interventions to improve social and occupational functioning. Those identified as needing more specific or intense treatment can move to the next step of care. In particular, people with severe symptoms such as aggression, violence, wandering tendencies, can be given more potent medications requiring psychiatric review or even referred for in-patient treatment. Alternately, those who are recovering consistently may be elevated to the next level—rehabilitation. In the Mehac experience, the social workers and other team members, as well as stakeholders were trained in identifying between patients by way of 'triage'.

Collaborative care demands collaboration between people working in the community, primary health care workers and mental health workers leading to better outcomes in symptom control, compliance and adherence to treatment. A tiered approach with case management at the primary level, stepped care and effective collaboration results in establishing a service of good quality (Gilbody and Bower 2005). The social worker's role is to assist the client achieve proper integration into the immediate community that the person is rehabilitated into. The social worker needs to negotiate with the stakeholders to provide better integration back into the society.

Rehabilitation

The focus of medical and social care is to reinstate the affected, as far as possible, to the previous level of functioning. This becomes all the more meaningful if the entire community becomes involved. Community-based rehabilitation depends on the engagement of the community in managing disability. It is naturally difficult for people to understand the enormous disability that mental illness can bring to an individual, whereas this is well understood for physical disabilities (Chandrashekhar et al. 2010). A positive social milieu is seen to improve compliance, facilitate recovery and also encourage locally feasible rehabilitation programmes. The role of the social workers in this context is to design programs and activities of socio-economic relevance that would provide a venue for interaction between the mentally ill being rehabilitated, as well as to ensure meaningful and productive employment. Income-generating programs suited to the needs and local ethos have to be designed.

Rehabilitation methods should be planned in collaboration with the participants from the community as they need to be individualised to each person, taking into consideration the severity of his/her disability, and in tune to his/her cultural and social milieu. Community-based rehabilitation also addresses other barriers to equitable access in health programmes such as poverty, being part of a disadvantaged group socially and female gender.

Conclusion

Community mental health has progressed to a great extent influencing mental health care and advocacy. In spite of the severe morbidity faced and challenges that the mental illnesses impose in a society, there have been positive steps to address the issue. NGOs have had a definite role in developing models and programmes that can be adapted and used by public health sector. The community-base approach to mental health would benefit immensely only if the deficit-based approach is forsaken for a more proactive, strengths-based social work practice perspective (SBP). In this perspective, the community is perceived as a resource, and its engagement and integration into the treatment process will improve recovery and ambulation into productive living. Partnerships possible and effective between local NGOs, public sector, the local self-government (LSG) institutions and private organisations foster ownership, which is a significant advance in the combat against stigma. Mehac Foundation has been able to develop programmes in the community and partner with people in the community to provide good quality care. The value and practice of social work in community mental health care has improved the quality of care. Though the present focus is on strengthening and consolidation existing programmes, there is a need for expansion and growth of Mehac that depends on partnerships, collaboration especially with public health sector.

In summary, mental health is an issue of global concern, given its prevalence and variance in manifestation. There have been various initiatives in the form of DMHP and lately, the NRHM involving ASHA workers. Yet, these well-intended initiatives have not served their purpose of existence totally, as it has not been organic and accountable for the absence of community participation. The present chapter showcases the experiences and learnings of Mehac Foundation in Kerala. It goes into highlighting pointers for specific areas of intervention in mental health, especially in dealing with stigma and discrimination, engaging the community, as well as in providing organised care and rehabilitation.

References

Bentley, K. 2005. 'Women, Mental Health and the Psychiatric Enterprise: A Review', *Health and Social Work, 30(1)*.

Bollini, P., C. Venkateswaran and K. Sureshkumar. 2004. 'Palliative Care in Kerala, India: A Model for Resource-Poor Settings', *Onkologie*, 27 (2): 138–142.

Chandrasekhar, H., C. Naveen Kumar, N. R. Prasanth and P. Kasthuri. 2010. 'Disabilities Research in India', *Indian Journal of Psychiatry*, 52 (1): 281–285. doi: 10.4103/0019-5545.69252

Chatterjee, S., V. Patel, A. Chatterjee and H. A. Weiss. 2003. 'Evaluation of a Community-Based Rehabilitation Model for Chronic Schizophrenia in Rural India', *British Journal of Psychiatry*, 182 (1): 57–62. doi:10.1192/bjp.182.1.57

Chenoweth, L. and D. Stehlik. 2004, January–March. 'Implications of Social Capital for the Inclusion of People with Disabilities and Families in Community Life', *International Journal of Inclusive Education*, 8 (1): 59–72.

Comptroller and Auditor General (CAG) Report. 2010. *Performance Audit.* Health and Family Welfare Department. Government of Kerala. Available at: http://mhpolicy.files.wordpress.com/2011/05/cag-report-on-audit-of-mh-sector-in-kerala-2010.pdf (accessed 19 March 2014).

Farooq, S. and F. A. Minhas. 2001. 'Community Psychiatry in Developing Countries—A Misnomer?' *Psychiatric Bulletin*, 25: 226–227. Doi:10.1192/pb.25.6.226

Francis, A. 2012. 'Journey towards Recovery in Mental health', in V. Pulla, L. Chenoweth, A. Francis and S. Bakaj (eds), *Papers in Strengths Based Practice* (pp. 19–33). New Delhi: Allied Publishers.

Gilbert, P. 2010. *Social Work and Mental Health: The Value of Everything.* Dorset, UK: Russell House Publishing Ltd.

Gilbody, S., Paula Whitty, Jeremy Grimshaw, Ruth Thomas. 2003. 'Educational and Organisational Interventions to Improve the Management of Depression in Primary Care: A Systematic Review', *The Journal of the American Medical Association*, 289 (23): 3145–3151.

Gilbody, S. and P. Bower. 2005. 'Managing Common Mental Health Disorders in Primary Care: Conceptual Models and Evidence Base', *British Medical Journal*, 330 (7495): 859–842.

Isaac, M., P. Chand and P. Murthy. 2007. 'Schizophrenia Outcome Measures in Wider International Community', *British Journal of Psychiatry*, 191 (50): 71–77. doi: 10.1192/bjp.191.50.s71

Jadhav, S., R. Littlewood, A. G. Ryder, A. Chakraborty, S. Jain and M. Barua. 2007. 'Stigmatization of Severe Mental Illness in India: Against the Simple Industrialization Hypothesis', *Indian Journal of Psychiatry*, 49 (3), July–September: 189–194.

Kallivayalil, R. A. 2004. 'Mental Health Issues in South Asia Region', *Indian Journal of Psychiatry*, 46 (4): 295–298.

Katon, Wayne, Michael Von Korff, Elizabeth Lin, Greg Simon, Ed Walker, Jurgen Unutzer, Terry Bush, Joan Russo and Evette Ludman. 1999. 'Stepped Collaborative Care for Primary Care Patients with Persistent Symptoms of Depression: A Randomized Trial', *Archives of General Psychiatry*, 56 (12): 1109–1115.

Koyanagi, C. 2007. *Learning From History: Deinstitutionalization of People with Mental Illness as Precursor to Long-term Care Reform* (Report on Kaiser Commission). Washington: Judge David L. Bazelon Center for Mental Health Law.

Kumar, A. 2005a. 'District Mental Health Programme in India: A Case Study', *Journal of Health and Development Health*, 1 (1): 25–35.

———. 2005b. 'National Rural Health Mission and Mental Health'. *Health Action*, 18 (11). Available at: http://ssrn.com/abstract=1409063 (accessed 19 March 2012).

———. 2011. 'Mental Health Services in Rural India: Challenges and Prospects', *Health*, 3 (12): 757–761. doi:10.4236/health.2011.312126

Krishna Kumar, P. 2010. 'Impact of Community Mental Health Programs of Institute of Mental Health and Neuro Sciences, Kozhikode (IMHANS)', *Kerala State Mental Health Authority Newsletter*, 1 (9): 1–4.

Lazarus, R. and M. Freeman. 2009. *Primary-Level Mental Health Care For Common Mental Disorder in Resource-Poor Settings: Models & Practice—A Literature Review.* Pretoria, South Africa: Sexual Violence Research Initiative, Medical Research Council.

Léouffre, P. and R. Tempier. 1998, May. 'Deinstitutionalization in Psychiatry: Revising Our Principles of Community Psychiatry or Failure of Deinstitutionalization!', *Canadian Journal of Psychiatry*, 43 (4): 403–410.

Mannarth, S. C. 2009. *Financing Mental Health Care in India.* Basic Needs Policy Study. Retrieved from http://www.basicneeds.org/download/PUB%20-%20Financing%20Mental%20Health%20Care%20in%20India%20-%20 BasicNeeds%20Policy%20Study%202009.pdf. Accessed on 28/03/2014.

MEHAC Foundation. n.d. Available at: www.mehacfoundation.org (accessed 19 March 2014).

Murthy, R. S. 2011. 'Mental Health Initiatives in India (1947–2010)', *The National Medical Journal of India*, 2 (2): 98–107.

Mustafa, F. 2010. *Mental Capital of Undergraduate Female Students* (unpublished dissertation), Mahatma Gandhi University, Kottayam, Kerala, India.

National Crime Records Bureau. 2010. *Accident Deaths and Suicides in India.* Ministry of Home affairs. Government of India. Available at: http://ncrb.nic. in/ADSI2010/ADSI2010-full-report.pdf. Accessed 28 May 2012.

Mission Document. 2004. National Rural Health Mission, 2005-2012. Ministry of Health and Family Welfare: Government of India.

Office of the Registrar General and Census Commissioner. Ministry of Home Affairs, Government of India. 2011. *Census India.* Available at: http://censusindia.gov. in/2011-prov-results/prov_data_products_kerala_.html (accessed 20 March 2014).

Paleri, A. and M. Numpeli. 2005. 'The Evolution of Palliative Care Programmes in North Kerala', *Indian Journal of Palliative Care*, 11 (1): 15–18.

Reddy, S. K., V. Patel, P. Jha, V. K. Palul, A. K. ShivKumar and L. Dandona. 2011. 'Towards Achievement of Universal Health Care in India by 2020: A Call to Action', *The Lancet*, 377 (9767):760–768.

Report of Evaluation of District Mental Health Programme. http://mhpolicy.files. wordpress.com/2011/05/nimhans-report-evaluation-of-dmhp.pdf (accessed 20 March 2014).

Rochon, P. A., Mashari, A., Cohen, A., Misra, A., Laxer, Streiner, D. L., Dergal, J. M., Clark, J. P., Gold, J., and Binns, M. A. 2004. 'Relation between Randomized Controlled Trials Published in Leading General Medical Journals and the Global Burden of Disease', *Canadian Medical Association Journal*, 170 (11): 1673–1677.

Sallnow, L. and C. Shabeer. 2005. 'The Role of Religious, Social and Political Groups in Palliative Care in Northern Kerala', *Indian Journal of Palliative Care*, 1 (1): 10–14.

Saravanavan, B., K. S. Jacob and J. Shanthi. 2010. 'Outcome of First-Episode Schizophrenia in India: Longitudinal Study of Effect of Insight and Psychopathology', *British Journal of Psychiatry*, 196 (6): 454–459. doi: 10.1192/bjp. bp.109.068577

Sartorius, N. 2007. 'Stigma and Mental Health', *The Lancet*, 370 (9590): 810–811. doi: 10.1016/S0140-6736(07)61245-8

Saxena, S. 2008. 'Mental Health: A Global Perspective from the World Health Organization, Making Mental Health a Global Priority', *World Mental Health Day*, 3–8.

Scott, A. and B. Guo. 2012. HEN Synthesis Report,'For Which Strategies of Suicide Prevention is There Evidence of Effectiveness?'. Copenhagen: WHO.

Seyfang, G. 2003. 'Growing Cohesive Communities One Favour at a Time: Social Exclusion, Active Citizenship and Time Banks', International Journal of Urban and Regional Research, 27(3): 699-706.

Sharan, P., I. Levav, S. Olifson, A. Francisco and S. Saxena (eds). 2007. *Research Capacity for Mental Health in Low- and Middle-Income Countries: Results of a Mapping Project*. World Health Organization and Global Forum for Health Research: Geneva.

Shrivasthava, A., M. Johnston and Yves Bureau. 2012. 'Stigma of Mental Illness-1: Clinical Reflections', Mens Sana Monographs, 10(1): 70-84.

Stroman, D. 2003. *The Disability Rights Movement: From Deinstitutionalization to Self-determination*. University Press of America: New York.

Thara, R., S. Rameshkumar and C. G. Mohan. 2010. 'Publications in Community Psychiatry', *Indian Journal of Psychiatry*, 52 (1): 274–S277. doi: 10.4103/0019-5545.69248

Thirthalli, J., B. K. Venkatesh and M. N. Naveen. 2010. 'Do Antipsychotics Limit Disability in Schizophrenia? A Naturalistic Comparative Study in the Community', *Indian Journal of Psychiatry*, 52 (1): 37–41.

Von Korff, Miachel, Wayne Katon, Terry Bush, Elizabeth H., B.Lin, Gregory E. Simon, Kathleen S., Evette Ludman, Edward W. and Jurgen Unutzer. 1998. 'Treatment Costs, Cost Offset, and Cost Eeffectiveness of Collaborative Management of Depression', *Psychosomatic Medicine*, 60 (2): 143–149.

World Health Organization (WHO). 2002. *The World Health Report 2002: Reducing Risks, Promoting Healthy Life.* Geneva: Author.

————. 2005. *World Health Organization Assessment Instrument for Mental Health Systems (WHO-AIMS 2.2).* Geneva: Author. Available at: http://www.who.int/mental_health/evidence/WHO-AIMS/en/

————. 2011. Mental Health Atlas. Geneva: Author. Retrieved from http://www.who.int/mediacentre/multimedia/podcasts/2011/mentalhealth_17102011/en (accessed 28 March 2014).

————. 2011a. *Mental Health Atlas.* Geneva: Author. Available at: http://www.who.int/mental_health/publications/mental_health_atlas_2011/en/index.html (accessed 20 March 2014).

————. 2011b. *Prevention and Promotion in Mental Health. Geneva 2011.* Available at: http://www.who.int/mental_health/media/en/545.pdf (accessed 20 March 2014).

15

Emerging Issues for Social Work Practice

Anthony McMahon

Déjà Vu

Recovery, well-being and social justice are not what people think of as emerging issues in mental health social work practice. Yet, the idea of mutual relationships, the best outcome for the client to function in his/her family and his/her society, a just, fair and supportive society in which to live are concepts as old as social work itself and still of importance today. Recovery, well-being and social justice are emerging issues for each generation of people with mental health concerns. The issues of those who suffer mental illness are about their own functioning, their relationships with loved ones and their community and their ability to gain some control over what may often be a fairly chaotic life. Workers who can ensure that the sufferers can have hope, meaning and purpose as they live their life are what they want.

Not all emerging issues are new. In many ways, any discussion of emerging issues for social work practice is going to go over old ground. The issues that have been discussed in the past are still prevalent. For example, 'Mental health problems account for a large proportion of the disease burden among young people in all societies' (UNICEF 2011: 27) and 'health systems have not yet adequately responded to the burden of mental disorders; as a consequence, the gap between the need for treatment and its provision is large all over the world' (WHO 2013: 5). The incidence of mental health issues and an inadequate response have been, are, and will continue to be emerging issues for social work practice. In that sense, old issues are also emerging issues.

Thus, it is tempting to set out a list of current issues and say that these are the issues for the future. Likely contenders might be issues such as evidence-based practice, community mental health, mental health promotion and education, research into mental health issues or clinical breakthroughs. All of these issues are very important and will be important in the future. Each one will require the focus and work of different groups of social workers working in mental health. But, if we are looking at social work as a profession, these issues are too narrow in themselves to give a sense of direction for mental health practice in social work.

A better starting point is that old focus of social work, the person in his/her environment (Germain and Gitterman 1980). This notion, seminal in social work theory (Hamilton 1951), is that the individual can only be understood properly within the contexts of his/her social, political, familial, physical, economic and spiritual environments or, as the practice standards of mental health social workers in Australia put it, 'Social work practice occurs at the interface between the individual and the environment: social work activity begins with the individual, and extends to the contexts of family, social networks, community, and the broader society' (AASW 2008: 8).

If we take this foundational understanding of social work as the basis for delineating emerging issues, then the very definition of mental health practice in social work itself sets out emerging issues for practice. 'The purpose of practice is to promote recovery, restore individual, family, and community well-being, to enhance development of each individual's power and control over their lives, and to advance principles of social justice' (AASW 2008: 8). Recovery practice, well-being and social justice, therefore, are significant future issues for social work practice in mental health. Each of these issues requires us to forsake a negative and deficit understanding of mental health practice, which would focus on stigma, an individual's lack of capacity and on mere amelioration of his/her mental illness.

The Recovery Perspective

The attitude, skills and behaviour of the worker who is working with those with mental health problems are crucial to gaining positive outcomes. If the worker is focused on pathology and deficits, that is what he/she will find in the clients. If the workers see clients as unworthy or incapable of active participation in their own emancipation, then the clients will not be able to be agents of their own change. Thus, while the worker's knowledge and skills are important, his/her values are paramount. The basis of all work with others has to be the realisation of everyone's innate human dignity. From this flows the attitudes that ensure that professional practice respects and strengthens the clients' dignity and supports the clients' journey with mental illness and their own personal, spiritual and emotional resources.

The recovery perspective has been around for some time and in that sense it is not an emerging issue. However, it sufficiently challenges many professional understandings of mental illness that it continually needs re-emphasising and re-implementing. In contrast to the focus on a client's symptoms and his/her alleviation, a recovery perspective focuses on people's better functioning in their own environments. In this, it is allied with Saleeby's (1992) strength perspective with its focus on what strengths a person brings to life situations.

The recovery perspective originated in consumer/ex-patient support groups where the idea of becoming a functioning member of society was paramount. Recovery 'is a way of living a satisfying, hopeful, and contributing life even with limitations caused by illness. Recovery involves the development of new meanings and purposes in one's life as one grows beyond the catastrophic effects of mental illness' (Anthony 1993: 527). In this perspective, recovery is not a linear journey and as such the needs, intensity and duration of support may vary at any time during the recovery journey. The emphasis is on a person's capacity, confidence and self-reliance rather than on his/her pathology. It is a way of working for the real world.

One dynamic element of the recovery perspective is hope. Hope is central to recovery and is fostered by assisting people to have control over their own lives. 'There is no single definition of the concept of recovery for people with mental health problems, but the guiding principle is hope—the belief that it is possible for someone to regain a meaningful life, despite serious mental illness' (Mental Health Foundation 2013). The idea of the possibility of change is central to social work practice; hope is the client's realisation of that same possibility.

Well-Being

Well-being is more than the absence of negative psychological conditions. The World Health Organisation (WHO) defines wellness as:

> Wellness is the optimal state of health of individuals and groups. There are two focal concerns: the realization of the fullest potential of an individual physically, psychologically, socially, spiritually and economically, and the fulfilment of one's role expectations in the family, community, place of worship, workplace and other settings. (Smith et al. 2006)

The WHO definition of wellness is a definition that applies to everyone; it does not separate humanity into the pathological and the non-pathological. In a similar way to the concept of recovery, the worker does not concentrate on the pathology of the client but on the total environment/situation of the person. Again, this is a way of working that is fundamental to social work practice.

Just as importantly, realising or reaching a position of well-being requires a holistic focus: 'realization of the fullest potential of an individual physically, psychologically, socially, spiritually and economically' (Smith et al. 2006). But it is not just about the individual, it is also about that individual's place 'in the family, community, place of worship, workplace and other settings'. Mental health practice thus becomes not just about the person but the person in their environment. All these definitions and concepts draw us away from a focus on individual pathology, which is often the focus of mental health practice, to a focus on a person's journey and place within his/her own social context.

Well-being can seem a nebulous concept but it does provide a more humane way of understanding mental illness and its consequences than as a mere health problem 'that significantly affects how a person feels, thinks, behaves, and interacts with other people' (Australian Government Department of Health and Ageing 2013). Significantly, both the definition of mental illness and the concept of well-being centre on the question of forming meaningful relationships (or not). Relationships are also a central tenet of the recovery model where an individual's ability to function in various environments is a marker of his/her ability to deal with mental illness. Relationships/connections are central to a person's understanding of his/her own well-being and happiness. Social work has always been about relationships and the concept of well-being needs to become the main focus of social work practice whether in the field of mental health field or any other.

The mental health social worker, in promoting well-being, must also look after himself/herself. There are workers who are subject to the same issues as their clients: agitation, excessive worry, persistent anxiety, hyperactivity, obsessive behaviour and even self-harm. In fact, and often because of the stressful work we do, the very things we suggest and try to instil in clients, such as self-awareness, reflection, mindfulness, emotional maturity and a certain balance in life, are the same things workers need as well. Social workers must have balance in their own lives and take steps for reflection, recreation and restoration. The WHO definition of mental health as 'a state of well-being in which every individual realizes his or her own potential, can cope with the normal stresses of life, can work productively and fruitfully, and is able to make a contribution to his/ her community' applies as much to mental health workers as to any other section of society.

Social Justice

Another old social work issue that continues to be constantly emerging is social justice. It might seem a long way from a person's mental illness to a socially just society, but it's not. The way in which a society is organised can increase mental health problems or help to alleviate them. Poverty, unemployment, lack of social cohesion and deprived neighbourhoods can exacerbate mental illness. Socio-economic inequality can worsen the prevalence of mental disorder and curtail access to treatment (Lorant et al. 2003). More equal societies tend to have better mental health; income inequality tends to cause more and greater social problems (Wilkinson and Pickett 2009).

Social justice is also about relationships. Social justice tries to ensure that people treat each other fairly and equally. The international definition of social work states: 'The social work profession facilitates social change and development, social cohesion, and the empowerment and liberation of people. Principles of social justice, human rights, collective responsibility and respect for diversities are central to social work' (International Federation of Social Workers 2013). Working for social justice so that society is fairer, more caring and more supportive of individuals, families and communities is work that enhances mental health. Working to eradicate or alleviate the causes of mental illness is just as important as helping individuals and families deal with the consequences of that mental illness. The real challenge is to foster everyone's well-being by creating a civil society based on social justice and a rigorous concern for the common good.

It is a temptation for social workers to accept economic and materialist explanations of society rather than challenge them. Most pernicious is the acceptance of inequality and poverty as normal and right (see Holman 1993, for a critique of this position). While individual social workers may work to get justice for individuals and families, there is a tendency in the profession to complain rather than organise. Yet the profession has often confronted injustice and oppression, and this has never been more pertinent than now when economic and social inequalities continue to create the conditions that exacerbate mental health issues.

Emerging Issues?

These three topics—recovery, well-being and social justice—are not what people think of as emerging issues in mental health social work practice. The words may be slightly different but they are really tried and true concepts in social work. The idea of mutual relationships, the best outcome for the client to function in his/her family and his/her society, a just, fair and supportive society in which to live are concepts as old as social work itself. In what way are they emerging issues?

As I said at the beginning, there could have been a list of important issues for practitioners of one sort or another. And that would have truthfully answered the question. But at a deeper, more basic level, especially in mental health, these three issues continue to be important. Because they are always at the fore for social work practitioners, in that sense, they are always emerging issues: 'The disorders are pervasive in their impact across multiple and major life domains—they are not so much medical disorders as disorders of life itself' (Bland and Tullgren 2011: 26). And like life itself, they are always there.

These three concepts will also be emerging issues for each generation of people with mental health concerns. Just because we might have a broad historical vision and can see changes over time does not mean that the people we work with see much more than their own particular concerns. Their issues are about their own functioning, their relationships with loved ones and their community and their ability to gain some control over what may often be a fairly chaotic life. Workers who can ensure enhanced 'development of each individual's power and control over their lives' (AASW 2008: 8) are what they want.

And that is the real emerging issue, how to ensure some measures of self-control over the social worker's own life for those who suffer poor mental health. And the social worker's job is to assist the sufferer to have hope, meaning and purpose as he/she lives his/her life.

References

AASW. 2008. *Practice Standards for Mental Health Social Workers.* Australian Association of Social Workers, Barton ACT. Available at: http://www.aasw.asn. au/document/item/17 (accessed 30 November 2012).

Anthony, W. A. 1993. 'Recovery from Mental Illness: The Guiding Vision of the Mental Health Service System in the 1990s'. Reprinted from *Psychosocial Rehabilitation Journal, 16* (4), 11–23. Available at: http://www.bu.edu/cpr/repository/articles/pdf/anthony1993.pdf (accessed 29 April 2013).

Australian Government Department of Health and Ageing (2013). *What is Mental Illness?* Available at: http://www.health.gov.au/internet/main/publishing.nsf/content/B7B7F4865637BF8ECA2572ED001C4CB4/$File/whatmen.pdf (accessed 29 April 2013).

Bland, R. and A. Tullgren. 2011. 'Mental Illness, Social Work and Social Justice', in P. Jones, D. Miles, A. Francis and S. P. Rajeev (eds), *Eco-social Justice: Issues, Challenges and Ways Forward* (pp. 25–44). Bangalore: Books for Change.

Germain, C. and A. Gitterman. 1980. *The Life Model of Social Work Practice.* New York: Columbia University Press.

Hamilton, G. 1951. *Theory and Practice of Social Casework.* New York: Columbia University Press.

Holman, B. 1993. *A New Deal for Social Welfare.* Oxford, UK: Lion.

International Federation of Social Workers (IFSW). 2013. *Global Definition of Social Work.* Available at: http://ifsw.org/get-involved/global-definition-of-social-work (accessed 29 April 2013).

Lorant, V., D. Deliege, W. Eaton, A. Robert, P. Philippot and M. Ansseau. 2003. 'Socioeconomic Inequalities in Depression: A Meta-Analysis', *American Journal of Epidemiology, 157* (2): 98–112.

Mental Health Foundation. 2013. *Recovery.* Available at: http://www.mentalhealth.org.uk/help-information/mental-health-a-z/R/recovery (accessed 29 April 2013).

Saleeby, D. 1992. *The Strengths Perspective in Social Work Practice.* White Plains, NY: Longman.

Smith, B., K. Tang and D. Nutbeam, D. 2006. WHO Health Promotion Glossary: New Terms. *Health Promotion International,* 21 (4): 340.

UNICEF. 2011. *The State of the World's Children.* Available at: http://www.unicef.org/sowc2011/pdfs/SOWC-2011-Main-Report-chapter-2_12082010.pdf (accessed 29 November 2012).

Wilkinson, R. G. and K. E. Pickett. 2009. *The Spirit Level: Why More Equal Societies Almost Always Do Better.* London: Allen Lane.

World Health Organization (WHO). 2013. *Draft Comprehensive Mental Health Action Plan 2013–2020.* Available at: http://apps.who.int/gb/ebwha/pdf_files/WHA66/A66_10-en.pdf (accessed 28 April 2013).

Web Resources

Australian Department of Health and Ageing: Principles of Recovery Oriented Mental Health Practice: http://www.health.gov.au/internet/main/publishing.nsf/content/DA71C0838BA6411BCA2577A0001AAC32/$File/servpri.pdf

Bill Jordan: *Social Work and Wellbeing*: http://russellhouse.co.uk/pdfs/
socialworkandwellbeing.pdf

Amartya Sen on Justice: How to do it better (book review): http://www.economist.
com/node/14164449

Amartya Sen on Justice and Injustice (Youtube): http://www.youtube.com/
watch?v=IRErRJY4zTM

16

Future Directions and Implications for Social Work Practice in Mental Health

Abraham P. Francis and Ilango Ponnuswami

Introduction

Social work practice in mental health is an important area of practice. Throughout this book, we have emphasized the various dimensions of social work practice in mental health. Whether one is employed as a social worker in hospital settings, community settings or involved with rehabilitation activities, one thing that should influence our practice is our code of ethics and adherence to the principles of social work values and principles. Social work has been defined by the International Federation of Social Workers (IFSW 2012) as a profession that 'promotes social change, problem solving in human relationships and the empowerment and liberation of people to enhance well-being. Utilizing theories of human behavior and social systems, social work intervenes at the points where people interact with their environments. Principles of human rights and social justice are fundamental to social work.' Social work, as a profession, has come a long way in India after 75 years of existence and growth. However, when we attempt a SWOT analysis of the profession as such, there are lot of things which need to be done to make the best use of the enormous opportunities that lie ahead in the future and to face the threats with which we may be confronted. While it is an undeniable fact that the profession, unlike many other professions of the contemporary period, has withstood all vagaries of forces operating in the socio-economic and political milieu in the country, it is also an equally undeniable fact that the profession has not kept pace with the rapidly changing conditions and requirements. However, it is not too late and still, there is ample scope for the profession to correct its course and evolve itself as a highly respected profession with due recognition in society.

Social Work in Mental Health Field

Since its inception in India, the profession has been actively involved in the field of mental health. The pioneer in social work education Tata Institute of Social Sciences (then known as Sir Dorabji Tata Institute of Social Sciences) in Mumbai had mental health projects such as a Child Guidance Centre even as early as the 1930s. Besides, psychiatric social work, together with medical social work (nomenclature changed recently as Clinical Social Work in most of the places) has been a very important specialisation in the schools of social work and even in schools where there are no specialisations, psychiatric social work has been taught as an important subject. All over the country, social workers are involved in various mental health initiatives, be it governmental or non-governmental. Premier mental health institutes such as NIMHANS, Bangalore; PGI, Chandigarh; and Central Institute of Psychiatry, Ranchi, have rigorous clinically oriented psychiatric social work training leading to an M.Phil degree. These institutions also have psychiatric social work departments whose members are actively involved as members of the psychiatric team in various settings such as adult psychiatry units, family psychiatry units, child guidance clinics, de-addiction centres, psychiatric rehabilitation departments, community psychiatry departments and even related units such as neurology and neurosurgery. Very recently, the Union Health Minister Ghulam Nabi Azad has stressed the need for increased mental health manpower that includes psychiatric social workers (only 300 in the whole country as of now) and has expressed concern over the gross inadequacy of mental health professionals (*Times of India* 2012).

Research-Informed Practice

Historically, social workers have not always emphasised the importance of research knowledge for practice decision making as much as other professions have. In 1979, a sociologist, Simpson, shared his perceptions of social work practitioners and their relationship with research. He noted that practitioners tend to shun abstract knowledge and to rely instead on (a) humanitarian impulse, (b) occupational folklore and (c) common sense. He also observed that most of the knowledge that is used for practice decision making is drawn from the work of researchers in other fields. He went on to describe social work literature as permeated with faddism and lacking an empirical base.

But recent years have seen a significant upsurge in the interest of evidence-based research (EBR) and evidence-based practice (EBP) in the field of social work in India, particularly in the field of mental health (Ponnuswami and Francis 2012). Social work practitioners, academics and researchers have started talking about the importance of EBR and EBP at various professional events all over the country and many have even started sharing the processes and outcomes of their EBR and EBP by way of conference presentations and even some publications. The Council on Social Work Education (CSWE), the organisation responsible for the accreditation of Bachelors of Social Work (BSW) and Masters of Social Work (MSW) programs, recognises the importance of research content in social work curricula. The Educational Policy and Accreditation Standards (EPAS; Council on Social Work Education 2008) specify that research content and skills must be taught in both undergraduate and graduate social work education programs. Standard 2.1.6 maintains that social workers:

- Use practice experience to inform research;
- Employ evidence-based interventions;
- Evaluate their own practice;
- Use research findings to improve practice, policy and social service delivery;
- Comprehend quantitative and qualitative research and
- Understand scientific and ethical approaches to building knowledge.

Quite unfortunately, due to the absence of a CSWE in India, there are still no regulatory mechanisms regarding this matter. However, almost all over the country, with some exceptions, schools of social work do have research methodology as an important component in the social work curricula and most of them also have a mandatory requirement for Masters students to undertake a research project and an ensuing dissertation and viva-voce.

Evidence-Based Practice (EBP)

Even though EBR is a much talked about subject, social workers have also started thinking about EBP. Theoretically, EBP consists of a five-step process (Strauss et al. 2005: 3–4):

> **Step 1.** Convert our need for information about the causes of the problem, and for possible interventions, into an answerable question.
> **Step 2.** Track down the best evidence with which to answer that question.
> **Step 3.** Critically appraise that evidence for its validity, impact, and applicability.
> **Step 4.** Integrate the critical appraisal with our clinical expertise and the client's unique values and circumstances.
> **Step 5.** Evaluate our effectiveness and efficiency in carrying out steps 1–4 and seek ways to improve our practice.

Still, there is much to be desired with regard to EBP in India since there are no proper institutional systems and mechanisms in place. Unlike Western countries and some countries in the northern hemisphere, there are no structured and systematised procedures that social workers are expected to follow in their regular practice in different settings. For example, there is enormous paper work and documentation that needs to be done by social workers as per the requirements of the General Social Care Council in the United Kingdom. In fact, there have been reports of increasing dissatisfaction or rather frustration among social workers regarding the quantum of paper work required at the cost of even neglect of the clients in contravention to the basic principles of the profession.

Mental Health Promotion

Mental health promotion involves actions to create living conditions and environments that support mental health and allow people to adopt and maintain healthy lifestyles. These include a range of actions to increase the chances of more people experiencing better mental health. A climate that respects and protects basic civil, political, socio-economic and cultural rights is fundamental to mental health promotion. Without the security and freedom provided by these rights, it is very difficult to maintain a high level of mental health. National mental health policies should not be solely concerned with mental disorders, but should also recognise and address the broader issues that promote mental health. This includes mainstreaming mental health promotion into policies and programmes in government and business sectors including education, labour, justice, transport, environment, housing and welfare, as well as the health sector.

Promoting mental health depends largely on inter-sectorial strategies. Specific ways to promote mental health include:

- Early childhood interventions (e.g., home visits for pregnant women, pre-school psychosocial activities, combined nutritional and psychosocial help for disadvantaged populations);
- Support to children (e.g., skill-building programmes, child and youth development programmes);
- Socio-economic empowerment of women (e.g., improving access to education and microcredit schemes);
- Social support for elderly populations (e.g., befriending initiatives, community and day centres for the aged);
- Programmes targeted at vulnerable groups, including minorities, indigenous people, migrants and people affected by conflicts and disasters (e.g., psychosocial interventions after disasters);
- Mental health promotional activities in schools (e.g., programmes supporting ecological changes in schools and child-friendly schools);
- Mental health interventions at work (e.g., stress prevention programmes);
- Housing policies (e.g., housing improvement);
- Violence prevention programmes (e.g., community policing initiatives) and
- Community development (CD) programmes (e.g., 'Communities That Care' initiatives, integrated rural development) (WHO 2012).

When we go through the list of various mental health promotion activities outlined above, it is too obvious that most of the activities suggested fall well within the ambit of the professional domain of social work. Premier mental health institutions in India such as NIMHANS have been doing almost all the activities mentioned in the World Health Organisation (WHO) list and it is also to be noted that most of these activities of mental health promotion are planned, organised, coordinated, implemented and evaluated by professional teams led by psychiatric social workers in India. However, it must be mentioned here that that there has been an emphasis on early intervention, promotion and prevention in mental health services in

Australia as well. According to the Commonwealth Department of Health and Aged Care (2000), there is a growing body of interest internationally in the promotion, prevention and early intervention for mental health. In this regard, '[m]ental health promotion is any action taken to maximise mental health and well-being among populations and individuals. Prevention refers to interventions that occur before the initial onset of a disorder to prevent the development of the disorder. Early intervention comprises interventions that are appropriate for and specifically target people displaying the early signs and symptoms of a mental health problem or mental disorder, and people developing or experiencing a first episode of mental disorder' (2000: 4).

Community Approaches to Mental Health

The Sheffield Health Authority uses the following definition of CD, specifically as it relates to health:

> **Community development in health** aims to enable the active involvement of people, especially those most oppressed and marginalised, in issues, decision-making and organisations which affect their health and lives in general. It can take place at the grass roots, in neighbourhoods or communities of interest and also at an organisational level in policy, planning and service delivery. It is based upon people identifying their own needs and how these can best be met. It involves enabling people to come together to share experience, knowledge and skill; to support their participation and encourage their involvement in influencing policy making and service development on issues which concern them. Integral to the CD approach is a commitment to equal opportunities and confronting inequality and discrimination. A CD approach to health emphasises the holistic nature of health, and a positive approach to health, well-being and its promotion. (Sheffield Support Team 1993, as cited in Smithies and Webster, 1998)

Even though the above definition does not mention the aspect of mental health specifically, it does recognise the holistic nature of health and well-being that certainly includes the dimension of mental health. In India, CD is a field that has always been a 'very much sought after' specialisation among social work students because of the fact that it is CD field, that too the unimaginably huge non-governmental organisation (NGO) sector, which, till today, employs a vast majority of social work graduates, even social workers with specialisations in other fields. Despite the fact that large number of professional social workers are employed in CD field, they have been concentrating mainly on the 'mainstream activities' such as economic and social empowerment. But now there is an increasing realisation of the importance of mental health and the government has keen interest in involving the NGO sector. We find social workers getting actively involved in mental health activities using CD/or community approaches.

Advocacy and Social Justice

Mental health advocacy can be performed by several different types of organisations. However, it is especially important that organisations of mental health service users emerge to have a voice in shaping policy and public opinion. Organisations of family members of people with mental disorders, professional organisations and NGOs working in the field of mental health can also play a vital role in mental health advocacy.

WHO provides technical assistance to governments to develop policies and programmes to promote mental health care and protect the rights of people with mental disorders (WHO 2005). However, governments are unlikely to be able to design and implement adequate mental health policies without the involvement of those who will be most directly affected by these policies. Furthermore, governments on their own often cannot adequately educate the public about mental disorders to create the social and cultural conditions necessary to eliminate stigma and discrimination against people with mental disorders. It is for these reasons that WHO is also working to promote the emergence of strong and independent mental health advocacy movements throughout the world. Advocacy efforts towards promoting and protecting the rights of people with mental disorders can educate the general public along with policy makers and help create the conditions necessary for positive reform. (This chapter draws heavily on the WHO publication, *Advocacy for Mental Health* [WHO 2003]).

Barring a few social workers here and there, by and large, social work professionals have not been actively engaging themselves in this important work of advocacy and human rights–based activities. This is not true just with reference to mental health but it is the same situation for other major social issues too. Thus, we feel that professional social workers should get involved and more desirably, spearhead such advocacy work.

Social Inclusion

Social exclusion is an avoidable reality in the daily lives of many people with mental health problems or intellectual disabilities. These people are among the most marginalised and stigmatised groups in our society. There is clear evidence that they may be excluded both because they have inadequate material resources and because they are unable to participate in economic or socially valuable activities. They may be isolated and excluded from social relations and the wider community, and excluded from basic civil and political processes. Importantly, they may also be excluded from basic health and social services. These social disadvantages are associated with both physical and mental health inequalities. Disadvantage in early life increases the likelihood of disadvantage in later life; disadvantage may also be transmitted across generations.

Recovery and Social Inclusion

The Recovery Model is considered to be the most effective model in the field of mental health all over the world. However, most of the literature describes recovery as 'individuals taking control of their lives' (Beers 1921/1981, Deegan 1996 and Leete 1989, cited in Topor et al. 2011). There is no single uniform definition on recovery as the individual journey itself is unique and personal. But one of the definitions that practitioners, researches and consumers most often refer to is the one offered by Anthony (1993), where he identifies recovery as

> a deeply personal, unique process of changing one's attitudes, values, feelings, goals, skills and/or roles. It is a way of living a satisfying, hopeful, and contributing life even with limitations caused by the illness. Recovery involves the development of new meaning and purpose in one's life as one grows beyond the catastrophic effects of mental illness. (p. 13)

Recovery, in the sense used here, does not necessarily mean 'clinical recovery'; rather, it is concerned with 'social recovery', the idea of building a life beyond illness, of recovering one's life, without necessarily achieving clinical recovery. The ideas of recovery are integral to the notion of socially inclusive practice and can be applied to the whole range of people, of any age, with mental health problems and those with intellectual disabilities. Hope, a sense of personal control and opportunity are key ideas relating to recovery. There is a creative synthesis between recovery and social inclusion: recovery requires and allows social inclusion both, and social inclusion helps to promote recovery. Both are the key concepts for modern consultants and psychiatric practice.

The focus on strengths and empowerment has gained considerable prominence over the last couple of decades. A strengths-based perspective in social work practice in mental health is an important area of practice. Some of the earlier chapters in this book have suggested that there has been a shift away from the focus on deficits and today the profession is actively involved in the field of building recovery, coping and resilience and building hope in the people and the communities. Thus, it is apt that more social workers should embrace the strengths-based practice as it clearly engages with a person's abilities, talents, possibilities, hopes and competencies. This is both a challenge and opportunity for the profession. Challenge because we have to revisit the way we have provided services from an expert point of view. Nevertheless, changing to accept the views of the clients and respecting their lived experience can be difficult for some. However, it offers opportunities for growth and development for the profession as it provides a new way to think, reflect and act to better support the clients in their way towards recovery. It is in this context the 'Ten essential shared capabilities', advocated by the UK Department of Health (Hope 2004: 3) becomes relevant for social work practice. Following is a list that describes these ten-shared capabilities.

1. Working in partnership
2. Respecting diversity
3. Practising ethically
4. Challenging inequality
5. Promoting recovery
6. Identifying people's needs and strengths
7. Providing service-user-centred care
8. Making a difference
9. Promoting safety and positive risk taking
10. Personal development and learning

Although there are debates around how these could be used in practice, these capabilities reflect many of the social work values and principles and hence this could be adapted to our professional practice with minimal difficulty.

Social Inclusion and Policy

Many aspects of social exclusion will require attention to structural changes in society and broader policy initiatives. Psychiatrists have a role to play in highlighting the associations between these policy and institutional factors and mental health problems. Reducing the social exclusion of people with mental health problems and those with intellectual disabilities should be an explicit policy directive. The psychiatric profession can act as a constant advocate for the promotion of social inclusion in all policies that affect people with mental health problems or intellectual disabilities.

Socially Inclusive Practice and Mental Health Services

A socially inclusive approach includes recovery-oriented practice, an emphasis on social outcomes and participation, and attention to the rights of people with mental ill health, as well as to citizenship, equality and justice and stigma and discrimination. Mental health professionals and social services must work in a socially inclusive and recovery-oriented manner. This can have benefits for service users, professionals and carers, in addition to producing wider economic and social benefits.

Developing Indigenous Approaches to Work With

Social workers in India, for far too long, have been relying heavily on Western models and approaches in their work with the mentally ill. There is a real need for social workers to develop, standardise and document the efficacy of local models/approaches grounded in Indian or Eastern philosophies. The vast repertoire of Indian or Eastern expertise and methods can be effectively used by social workers in the field of mental health in India.

Emphasis on Group Work Practice

Except for well-established and premier mental health institutes in the country, social workers have not been using group work methods in working with persons with mental health issues. There is too much preoccupation with individual client centred kind of interventions rather than group work interventions. However, McDermott (2003) noted that social workers should 'address the needs of people with particular problems who could benefit from educational material delivered in a focused way and then move on to explore that in the context of their lives and the ongoing stressors they encounter' (p. 121).

Documenting Experiences and Sharing

One of the major drawbacks is the lack of proper and systematic documentation and sharing of professional experiences and insights of social workers working in the field of mental health. Social workers do enormous amount of work but seldom bother to systematically document the processes and outcomes of their therapeutic interventions. While academics and social work students or research scholars present papers at conferences, the majority of social workers who do exemplary work fail to document their experience and share their insights with others.

Developing a Culture of Scientific Writing and Publication

Unlike the West where professionals concentrate equally on practice and scientific writing, somehow, in India, a vast majority of social work practitioners lack the ambition to engage in scientific writing and publication. The main reason for this is the absence of proper incentives and rewards for scientific writing and publication for the practitioners. Social work academics and research scholars do write and publish now and then because they receive some kind of incentives and rewards professionally.

Policy Development

Social workers should start exploring opportunities for influencing policy making for mental health. One of the ways they could do this is by doing 'policy studies' and probably the other way would be to get actively involved in advocacy for mental health.

Networking

Social workers in the mental health field all over the nation have to network among themselves to share practice knowledge, learning from one another and for documenting their contributions, which might influence policymakers to give due recognition to the role of professional social workers in the field of mental health. Networking has to be done locally, regionally and even nationally.

Continuing Education and Capacity Building of Professionals

One of the most serious lacunae in the field of social work in India is the complete absence of organised continuing education and skill upgradation. However, in Western countries, there is a heavy emphasis placed on continuing education and supervision. As Bland et al. (2009) notes:

> The word 'supervision' has a specific meaning in social work that goes beyond the concept of accountability in administrative and line management terms. The quality of social work supervision is central to the development and maintenance of high standards of practice. This applies to social workers at all levels and across the full range of practice roles. The primary purpose of supervision is to support and ensure competent independent practice. (p. 240)

The very concept of continuing education is very important in social work practice. Social work professionals continue to hold on to the knowledge, skills, methods and techniques that need to be strengthened through supervision and continuing education. Especially in the field of mental health, the social worker is a member of a multidisciplinary team where one is required to articulate the role and relevance of their practice. This can happen only if one is engaged in this process of continuing education and supervision. This is a challenge for the profession as documented by Bland et al. (2009). Although social workers have, by and large, always valued a supportive approach to supervision, this is not the case for all the mental health professions. Profession-specific supervision is not always available and, in many service settings, it is not sufficient (Bland et al. 2009: 240).

Working with Consumers and Caregivers

In Australia, social work is identified as one of the mental health disciples on a multidisciplinary workforce in the National Mental Health Strategy and the data suggest that, "a growing number of social workers are working with people with mental health conditions" (The National Mental Health Workforce Strategy 2011: 5). The purpose of social work is to support people's self-determination and to 'assist others to achieve more equitable relationships and greater power and control over their lives' (O'Connor et al. 2008: 53). The Australian Association of Social Workers (AASW) identifies social justice as a key value integral to ethical practice. Social justice considers issues of stigma, disadvantage, discrimination and marginality, and values the lived experience of mental illness and the importance of partnerships, mutuality, participation and choice (AASW 2010).

There is a growing movement throughout the United States (and the world) of people calling themselves consumers, survivors or ex-patients, who have been diagnosed with mental disorders and are working together to make change in the mental health system and in society. The consumer movement grew out of the idea that individuals who have experienced similar problems, life situations or crises can effectively provide support to one another. According to Sally Clay (http://www.sallyclay.net/), one of the leaders of this movement, the consumer/survivor communities began 25 years ago with the anti-psychiatry movement. In the 1980s, ex-mental patients began to organise drop-in centres, artistic endeavors and businesses. Now hundreds of such groups are flourishing throughout the country. Our conferences (many sponsored by NIMH) have been attended by thousands of people. More and more, consumers participate in the rest of the mental health system as members of policymaking boards and agencies.

The AASW (2008: 12) also identifies specific principles fundamental to social work practice in the area of mental health. These are:

- Emphasising personhood;
- Valuing the lived experience of individual consumers and family members and carers;
- Affirming the importance of partnerships and mutuality;
- Addressing powerlessness, marginality, stigma and disadvantage and
- Conveying empathy, compassion and hope.

Manpower Planning

Manpower planning may be viewed as foreseeing the human resources requirement of an organisation and the future supply of human resources and (a) making necessary adjustments between these two and organisational plans; and (b) foreseeing the possibility of developing the supply of manpower resources to match it with the requirements by introducing necessary changes in the functions of human resources management.

Positioning Social Work in Recovery Model

Recovery in general terms means the act or process of recovering/recuperating, especially from sickness, a shock or a setback. This term has been used in the mental health field also to reflect the process of recovering from mental illness. The idea that people can recover from mental illness has only come about in recent decades. There has been much discussion about recovery since the 1980s especially from the field written by consumers and thus the concept of recovery began to gain its legitimacy (Sullivan 1994). The concept of *recovery* offers social workers and other health professionals a new way of looking at their practice and it is in fact a challenge for the social work profession to reclaim the profession's traditional ways of strengths-based concepts in working with individuals and communities, thereby championing an alternative approach to practice (Francis 2012).

Conclusion

Social workers are employed in a variety of settings and hence they are required to demonstrate their skill base, theoretical knowledge and a positive attitude towards their work. This can be quite daunting and challenging. Thus, for enhancement of the quality of social work in mental health field, social workers need to develop their own tools for assessment of various psychosocial aspects and the efficacy of social work interventions. It could be done in a collaborative way, yet maintaining a profession-specific focus in the interventions. Besides, there is also a challenge to develop and standardise indigenous models of care in many practice settings. Social work training for mental health work should be modified in such a way so that all these aspects can be covered and discussed at length so as to make it more practice oriented rather than being purely 'academic'. As has been mentioned earlier in the book, this is an exciting and challenging time for the profession. There is a great need for professionally qualified mental health social workers. However, our training and education has not been able to bridge that gap against the demand. Social work profession has to come up with proper systems and procedures for supervision, standards of practice and peer-review mechanisms in professional practice. While we see that there are many issues in the field, we also anticipate a greater scope for social work practice in the field of mental health.

References

Anthony, W. 1993. 'Recovery from Mental Illness: The Guiding Vision of the Mental Health Services in the 1990's', *Psychosocial Rehabilitation Journal*, 16 (94): 11–23.

Australian Association of Social Workers (AASW). 2008. *AASW Practice Standards for Mental Health Social Workers*. Available at: http://www.aasw.asn.au/document/item/17 (accessed 19 March 2014).

———. 2010. *The AASW Code of Ethics*. Canberra: Author.

Bland, R., A. Tullgren and N. Renouf. 2009. *Social Work Practice in Mental Health: an introduction*. Allen and Unwin: NSW (Australia).

Commonwealth Department of Health and Aged Care. 2000. *Promotion, Prevention and Early Intervention for Mental Health—A Monograph*. Canberra: Mental

Health and Special Programs Branch, Commonwealth Department of Health and Aged Care.

Council on Social Work Education (CSWE). 2008. *Educational Policy and Accreditation Standards.* Available at: http://www.cswe.org/Accreditation/2008 EPASDescription.aspx (accessed 19 March 2014)

Francis, A. 2012. 'Journey towards Recovery' in V. Pulla, L. Chnoweth, A. Francis and S. Bakaj (eds.), *Papers in Strengths Based Practice.* Delhi: Allied Publishers.

Hope, R. 2004. *The Ten Essential Shared Capabilities: A Framework for the Whole of the Mental Health Workforce.* London: Department of Health/National institute of Mental Health, England. Available at: http://www.dh.gov.uk/prod_consum_ dh/groups/dh_digitalassets/@dh/@en/documents/digitalasset/dh_4087170.pdf

International Federation of Social Workers (IFSW). 2012. Definition of Social Work. Retrieved from http://ifsw.org/policies/definition-of-social-work

McDermott, F. 2002. *Inside Group Work: A Guide to Reflective Practice.* Crows Nest: Allen and Unwin.

Ponnuswami, I. and A. Francis. (eds.). 2012. *Professional Social Work: Research Perspectives.* New Delhi: Authors Press.

Straus S. E., W. S. Richardson, P. Glasziou and R. B. Haynes. 2005. *Evidence-Based Medicine: How to Practice and Teach EBP* (3rd ed.). New York: Churchill Livingston.

Sullivan, W. P. 1994. 'A Long and Winding Road: The Process of Recovery from Severe Mental Illness', *Innovations and Research in Clinical Services, Community Support and Rehabilitation*, 3 (3): 19–27.

The National Mental Health Workforce Strategy. 2011. Victorian Government Department of Health, Melbourne, Victoria. Retrieved from http://www.health. gov.au/internet/mhsc/publishing.nsf/content/7AB7430A612FAB6FCA257A5 D001B9942/$File/srat.pdf on 28 March 2014.

Times of India. 2012. 'Govt to Pick up Medical Tab for Poor'. Available at: http:// articles.timesofindia.indiatimes.com/2012-08-09/india/33117925_1_mental-disorders-psychiatric-nurses-anxiety (accessed 19 March 2014).

Topor, A., M. Borg, R. Mezzina, D. Sells, I. Marin and L. Davidson. 2006. 'Others: The Role of Family, Friends and Professionals in the Recovery Process', *American Journal of Psychiatric Rehabilitation*, 9 (1): 17–37.

World Health Organization (WHO). 2003. *Advocacy for Mental Health.* Available at: http://www.who.int/mental_health/policy/services/1_advocacy_WEB_07. pdf (accessed 19 March 2014).

———. 2005. *Mental Health Atlas.* Geneva: Author.

———. 2012. Mental Health Fact Sheet 2012. Retrieved from http://www.wpro. who.int/mediacentre/factsheets/fs_201203_mental_health/en/

Web Resources

http://heapro.oxfordjournals.org/content/21/1/70.full (accessed 19 March 2014)

www.lancs.ac.uk/users/phdu/download/manual.doc (accessed 19 March 2014)

http://www.bms.co.in/what-is-manpower-planning-discuss-the-process-and-importance-of-man-power-planning-in-an-organization/ (accessed 19 March 2014)

http://www.who.int/mediacentre/factsheets/fs220/en/ (accessed 19 March 2014)

http://www.who.int/mediacentre/factsheets/fs220/en/ (accessed 19 March 2014)

Appendix 1

Glossary

Note

Following are some of the key terms used in this text. The authors have provided some explanations about these terms. While all of them are not exact definitions, they offer some explanation in the context of their use in the text. Hence, they are to be understood in the context of the chapters and discussions.

Chapter 1

Abuse: Maltreatment that may cause potential damage in the normal growth and development of children.

Empowerment: Achieving social capability to engage with treatment and care services to gain appropriate strength for positive well-being and development. In a holistic context, empowerment facilitates connections between individual pain and sufferings and social and justice.

Resilience: Resilience allows to gain an insight and control regarding developmental needs and ability to manage challenges in life. For example, a resilient child will have age-appropriate understanding regarding his/her developmental needs, should be able to manage emotions in the face of complexities and challenges in social life and develop self-protection ability.

Social justice: According to Ife (2010: 148), 'Social justice refers to the concept of a society in which justice is achieved in every aspect of society, rather than merely through the administration of law. It is generally considered as a social world which affords individuals and groups fair treatment, equality and an impartial share of the benefits of membership of society'.

Chapters 2 and 3

Child mental health: A special field of mental health which gives a scope for mental health professionals to work on various issues that are known to have a significant bearing on the psychological, emotional and behavioural well-being of children.

Counsellors : Persons suitably qualified in subjects related to human behaviour and engaged in professional guidance of individuals who seek help for their personal and emotional concerns.

School mental health: It is a field speciality in mental health practice to address varied psychosocial problems that affect learning, development and adjustment in significant ways in school settings.

School social work: It is a field of activity in professional social work with a focus on psychosocial problems of students in school setting and intervening suitably at the individual, group, community and societal level.

Chapter 4

Adolescent: A person in the stage of adolescence, which is the developmental stage that occurs from puberty to maturity lasting from the age of 12 to 18 years.

Children's home: According to Juvenile Justice (Care and Protection of Children) Act, 2000 'Children's home means an institution established by the state government or by a voluntary organisation and certified by that government under Section 34 (1), that is, for the reception of a child in need of care and protection during the pendency of any inquiry and subsequently for their care, treatment, education, training, development and rehabilitation'.

Intervention: It is defined as an influencing force or act that occurs to modify a given state of affairs. In the context of behavioural health, an intervention may be any outside process that has the effect of modifying an individual's behaviour, cognition or emotional state.

Psychosocial well-being: It is a term frequently used to catch all aspects of children's psychological development and social adjustment. The five proposed main domains of psychosocial well-being are cognitive abilities and cultural competencies, personal security, social integration and social competence, personal identity and valuation, sense of personal agency and the emotional and somatic expressions of well-being.

Chapter 5

Gender: Gender is a social construct as opposed to just considering the biological attributes of being male or female. Gender suggests that being male or female in a society is influenced by cultural, historical and societal norms and expectations for women and men and not just determined by the sex of a person.

Macro-level social work: It refers to social work interventions undertaken at the societal level, aiming to influence policy, socio-political or legal systems or even social change; methods used include community development, policy formulation, advocacy or even social action.

Meso-level social work: It refers to social work interventions undertaken with families, groups and communities to help them function in a manner desirable and in tandem with their goals; the method used is social group work and community organisation.

Micro-level social work: It refers to social work interventions undertaken with individuals or families to change their particular circumstances; the method used is social case work.

Pathologising: Pathologising describes the idea that a person's distress, ill health or behaviour is labelled by finding a fault or defect in the individual. This label is then used as a lens to view the person and his/her situation rather than maintaining openness to the person's experience.

Violence: It can take many forms; the checklist in chapter 6 indicates some of the behaviours that constitute violence.

Chapter 6

Mental health: Mental health is defined as a state of well-being in which every individual realises his or her own potential, can cope with the normal stresses of life, can work productively and fruitfully, and is able to make a contribution to her or his community. The positive dimension of mental health is stressed in WHO's definition of health as contained in its constitution: 'Health is a state of complete physical, mental and social well-being and not merely the absence of disease or infirmity' (WHO 2013).

Migration: It is 'the process of social change whereby an individual moves from one cultural setting to another for the purposes of settling down either permanently or for a prolonged period' (Bhugra and Jones 2001: 216).

Stressors: Significant life events and chronic on-going difficulties related to migration and work are stressors in the context of this chapter discussion.

Chapter 8

Religiosity: This is an indicator of belief-induced worship practiced by an individual.

Spirituality: A range of personal experiences that is driven by a search for the sacred and seeking meaning of life.

Chapter 9

Ageing: Ageing as a concept in this book addresses both the individual subjective experience of growing older and the collective experience of growing numbers of older persons in the society.

Mental illness: It is a 'clinically diagnosable disorder that significantly interferes with an individual's cognitive, emotional or social abilities' and would include, for example, a whole range of short- or long-term anxiety, affective (or mood) and substance use disorders (Australian Health Ministers 2003).

Chapter 10

Brief interventions: To reduce prevalence of substance abuse, decrease consumption by early detection and intervention before progress to dependence.

Cognitive behavioural interventions: These include thinking and behaving strategies that are useful to make lifestyle changes for risky drinkers including those with substance dependence.

Individual counselling: A person helps another through purposeful conversation with empathy, warmth, genuineness, unconditional positive regard and concreteness.

Interventions for family: To help families including children approach crises situations, better coping styles, strengthen resilience and supports.

Mental health professionals: Psychiatrists, psychiatric social workers, psychologists and psychiatric nurses, occupation therapists or people who have been professionally trained to work in the sector.

Motivational enhancement: The collaborative client–social worker relationship that provides a partnership of support to get people to change.

Occupational rehabilitation: Requisite training for livelihood or an occupation after recovery.

Psychosocial models: Biomedical, psychological and sociocultural treatment modalities that are culture specific.

Psychosocial interventions: Psychological and behavioural strategies used alone or in combination with pharmacotherapy.

Relapse prevention: A part of the comprehensive treatment plan to reduce the risk of both problem and recurrent use of substances.

Skills training: A step-by-step format during training to encourage practice and reinforcement through individual/group sessions aimed at reducing drinking or total abstinence.

Social worker: A person formerly trained (in theory and practice) to be a change agent to work with individuals, families and communities.

Substances: Tobacco, alcohol and other drugs such as opioids, cannabis, stimulants, hallucinogens, and inhalants used for intoxicating or mind-altering effects.

Substance use disorders: A range of problems such as intoxication, harmful use, dependence (addiction), withdrawal and psychiatric problems associated with use.

Chapter 11

Developing economies: It refers to economies or nations with a low-living standard, undeveloped industrial base and low human development index (HDI) in relation to other countries.

Social capital: It is the collectivity of institutions, relationships and norms that shape the quality and quantity of a society's social interactions.

Social work intervention: It refers to systematic psychosocial interventions with individuals, groups and communities at various levels—micro, meso and macro—with mobilisation of resources—internal and external—towards achieving desirable ends.

Suicide: It refers to any act of deliberate self-harm intended at taking one's own life, which ends in death.

Chapter 12

Direct social work practice: It is an approach that would encompass not only the provision of face-to-face clinical services, but also the establishment of macrolevel collaborative relationships with other key institutional, organisational and professional actors, as well as the practice of advocacy.

Human rights: 'Human rights refer to the basic rights and freedoms to which all humans are entitled. They are socially sanctioned entitlements to the goods and services that are necessary to develop human potential and well-being' (Ife 2010: 148).

Chapter 13

Ethical research: This is concerned with the 'dilemmas and conflicts that arise over the proper way to conduct research. Ethics define what it is or is not legitimate to do, or what moral research involves' (Neuman 2003: 116).

Evidence-based practice: When practitioners use their own and others' research to evaluate and inform their practice.

Social research: This is a systematic task that involves gathering and analysing information for the purposes of taking action and affecting positive social change.

Chapter 14

DALYs: It is the sum of years of potential life lost due to premature mortality and the years of productive life lost due to disability.

Global burden of disease: This is a measure of disability-adjusted life years (DALYs) assigned to a certain disease/disorder, which is a sum of the years lived with disability and years of life lost due to this disease within the total population.

Non-governmental organisations (NGOs): NGOs are institutions recognised by governments as non-profit or welfare oriented, which play a key role as advocates, service providers, activists and researchers on a range of issues pertaining to human and social development.

Panchayat: Panchayat means a village council in India, of self-government constituted for the rural areas.

Chapters 15 and 16

Consumers: In the discussion, we have referred to the term as people who describe and self-identify as users of mental health services, and/or have been diagnosed with mental illness and have been active in mental health consumer/survivors/service user movement that is aiming to bring change. We also acknowledge that there are some other similar terms also used in practice such as 'patient', 'service user' 'client' and survivor etc.

Person in environment—PIE: The concept 'person in environment' is seen as a practice orienting perspective for social work practice and education. This perspective is based on the notion that an individual and his or her behavior cannot be understood adequately without consideration of the various aspects of that individual's environment (social, political, familial, temporal, spiritual, economic, and physical).

Recovery: Anthony (1993: 13) identifies recovery as a deeply personal, unique process of changing one's attitudes, values, feelings, goals, skills and/or roles. It is a way of living a satisfying, hopeful, and contributing life even with limitations caused by the illness. Recovery involves the development of new meaning and purpose in one's life as one grows beyond the catastrophic effects of mental illness.

References

Anthony, W. 1993. 'Recovery from Mental Illness: The Guiding Vision of the Mental Health Services in the 1990s', *Psychosocial Rehabilitation Journal*, 16 (4): 11–23

Australian Health Ministers. 2003. *National Mental Health Plan 2003-2008*. Retrieved from http://www.aph.gov.au/parliamentary_business/communities/senate/former_committees/mentalhealth/report/eo1

Bhugra, D. And Jones, P. 2001. 'Migration and Mental Illness', *Advances in Psychiatric Treatment*, 7(3): 216-222. Retrieved from http://apt.rcpsych.org/content/7/3/216.full.pdf+html?sid=994ce9f3-3b3e-4075-8dcb-0fc3cbd61195.

Ife, J. 2010. *Human Rights from Below: Achieving Rights through Community Development*. Cambridge University Press: Australia.

———. 2010. 'Human Rights and Social Justice', in *Ethics and Value Perspectives in Social Work*, (ed.) M. Gray and S. Webb. Basingstoke: Palgrave Macmillan.

Neuman, L. 2003. Social Research Methods: Qualitative and Quantitative Approaches (5th ed.). Boston: Allyn and Bacon.

WHO. 2013. Mental Health: A State of Well-being. Retrieved from http://www.who.int/features/factfiles/mentalhealth/en. Accessed on 28 March 2014.

Appendix 2

Reflective/Practice Questions

The authors of the respective chapters have provided a number of practice/reflective questions. They are presented here according to the chapter numbers. You are invited to look at these questions and engage in critical reflections that will enhance your thinking and practice skills. Some of the questions are based on case studies and they are presented here as well. All other questions related to the concepts and ideas expressed in the chapter.

Chapter 1

1. What is the purpose of therapeutic work with children and adolescent?
2. Why is psychosocial approach important?
3. What is the purpose of using different games in therapy?
4. How would you ensure that social justice is adhered in your therapeutic intervention?

Chapter 2

1. Psychiatric social work and school social work: Do they conflict or complement each other?
2. Can we envisage the future of school mental health where school social workers take a leadership role to shape the mental health policy as well as provide services for school children?
3. School social workers, school counsellors, student counsellors, school psychologists, clinical psychologists and psychiatrists: How can you help school administrators to identify these professionals, their roles and take appropriate help for the school mental health programme?

Chapter 3

1. What are some of the child and adolescent mental health issues in India?
2. Based on reading this chapter, what are some of the strategies that can be applied in practice?
3. What are some of the initiatives taken by the government and non-government agencies in addressing child and youth mental health issues?
4. Based on your field work or practice experience, can you identify some of mental health needs of young people in your city/town? As a social worker how will approach these? Discuss.

Chapter 4

1. Comment about the possibility of replicating the study/program in other regions. What difficulties are foreseen?
2. What are some of the issues and challenges you may face as a social worker in implementing the program?
3. If the social worker has to prepare the package for boys what modifications need to be made in the contents and methodology?
4. Why do you think these kinds of interventions are needed for this identified group?

Chapter 5

1. How could you respectfully and safely explore women's experience of violence?
2. What information would you need if you want to refer a woman who has experienced violence to a support group, another service or a mental health practitioner?
3. What can social workers do to end violence against women?

Chapter 6

1. What is the relationship between migration and mental health?
2. Why are women migrants from disadvantaged and marginalised sections of the society vulnerable to mental ill health?
3. What are the main vulnerability factors that could lead to the development of mental disorders?
4. How can social workers promote the mental well-being of migrant women?

Chapter 7

1. What are the psychological problems faced by the elderly?
2. What is geriatric social work and mention the role of geriatric social worker in dealing the problems of elderly?
3. What are the natural changes observed among old age people?

Chapter 8

1. How does one explain the mental health issue of nonreligious persons?
2. Does religiosity/spirituality provide directionality or add valence to one's effort to remain productive during the process of ageing?
3. Does the investment of belief in the supreme power shifts the locus of control, thus increasing the level of acceptance?
4. How does a social work practitioner engage in the field with a client on the issue of spirituality such that the ethical code of conduct is not violated?

Chapter 9

1. What are some of the mental health issues among the older populations?

2. What are some of common strategies that a social worker could use in working with older people living with a mental health condition?
3. Visit a home for the aged during this semester and discuss your observations with your classmates. Reflect on the ethical issues that could be confronted by a social work practitioner in his/her practice.
4. Discuss on the relationship between spirituality and health.

Chapter 10

1. What is the status of mental health resources in developing countries?
2. Discuss some of the social work principles and its relevance in addiction settings.
3. What is the model commonly used in addiction treatment? Describe the components of psychosocial intervention
4. What does the term FRAMES mean in brief intervention?
5. How do skills training help the client with SUD? Name some skills you think are important and why do you think so?
6. What is meant by high risk and relapse? How can the client be helped to manage a risky situation after treatment?
7. Why should the family and children be included in treatment? Discuss how family rituals help.
8. What are the factors that help in recovery? How do self-help groups play a role?
9. State some reasons why follow-up and after care is important in addiction treatment?

Chapter 11

1. What are the complex psychosocial factors interacting, which compel individuals to deliberate self-harm?
2. What are the better strategies that social workers may incorporate to prevent and handle deliberate self-harm?
3. What are major considerations to be kept in mind while handling issues of suicide in developing economies?

Chapter 12

1. Why should social workers extend their skill sets to not only include clinical expertise but also advocacy and community development practice if they want to service mentally ill clients?
2. What challenges would a social worker face when attempting to provide assistance and support to mentally ill clients who have had their human rights breached?
3. How would you encourage social work students to appreciate the need to adopt a holistic and multidisciplinary approach when addressing human rights abuses against the mentally ill?

Chapter 13

1. Why do you think research is important in mental health practice?
2. What do you think are some of the ethical considerations that you need to consider when you are conducting research with mental health consumers or clients?
3. Discuss some of the challenges that you may encounter when researching in the mental health field.

Chapter 14

1. Define community mental health as perceived in the West and the Orient.
2. Could you describe the role of NGOs in community mental health in developing countries? What are some of the models?
3. What are the typical challenges faced by the human service professionals in community mental health and in working in a multidisciplinary team?
4. Discuss the role of professional social workers in destigmatising and improving service in mental illness in the communities.

Chapter 15

1. Why does the author write about general issues rather than concentrate on discrete mental health practice issues? Is it a valid stance to do this? Argue for and against his focus.
2. What is the place of hope in mental health social work practice? How does a worker assist a person to have hope?
3. The concept of well-being is very subjective. Discuss how it can be a useful concept in social work practice. List a number of ways a social worker could ensure his/her own well-being.

Chapter 16

1. What is evidence-based practice?
2. What is mental health promotion and why is so important in developing countries?
3. Based on the chapter, discuss the implications of mental health social work practice in your country?
4. What do you understand by community mental health and discuss the role of a social worker?

About the Editor and Contributors

Editor

Abraham P. Francis is a senior lecturer at the James Cook University in Australia with international exposure and extensive experience in community development and mental health. He taught social work at the Delhi University in India and also worked as a senior mental health social worker with the Country Health South Australia, before moving to Townsville to join the James Cook University. He held a stint in Queensland health as Assistant Director of Social work. Dr Francis is associated with many voluntary organisations, associations, professional bodies and developmental projects, both in Australia and India. Dr Francis has established international partnerships and research collaborations with universities and non-government organisations in Asia. He is the convener of the international consortium on strengths-based social work practice in mental health and has been the founding honorary director of the DePaul International Centre for Wellbeing, India. Dr Francis is passionate about working and researching in strengths-based practice in mental health. His other research interests are in the field of communities, criminal justice, international social work and gerontological social work. He can be contacted at abraham.francis@jcu.edu.au

Contributors

Braj Bhushan, PhD, is Associate Professor of Psychology at the Indian Institute of Technology, Kanpur, India. Earlier he served at the Indian Institute of Technology, Guwahati, as a Senior Lecturer and at Kyushu University, Japan, as a visiting professor. He has two books, seven book chapters and 32 journal articles to his credit. He also serves on the editorial board of Internet Journal of Medical Research. Besides this, he has worked as an ad-hoc reviewer for several major journals in the area of psychology. His areas of specialisation include Cognitive Neuropsychology, Cognitive Factors in Design and Trauma Psychology.

Mark David Chong is currently the Director of Research Education as well as a Lecturer in Criminology and Criminal Justice Studies at the School of Arts and Social Sciences, JCU. He is also an external assessor (grant applications) for the Social Sciences and Humanities Research Council of Canada. Dr Chong graduated with a PhD in Law from the University of Sydney, where he received his Law School's Longworth Scholarship (2003), the Cooke, Cooke, Coghlan, Godfrey and Littlejohn Scholarship (2004), and the Longworth Scholarship for Academic Merit (2006). His current research interests include: Social Problems, Criminal Justice Social Work, Social Control and Law and Order Issues, Policing, Crime Prevention and Community Safety, Punishment and Sentencing, Municipal and International Criminal Law, Juvenile Justice and Psychology and Crime.

Archana Dassi is currently an Associate Professor in social work with Department of Social Work at Jamia Millia Islamia, New Delhi. She has extensive experience in working with adolescents and children. She has initiated and developed a number of personality development programmes and capacity development programs for adolescents in India. She has also worked as a psychiatric social worker in Child Guidance Centre in Delhi. Archana's doctoral research was on *Social Tolerance and Deviant Behaviour of Children in a Slum in Delhi*. She has published two books and many articles on themes related to children, adolescents and family in national and international journals. She regularly conducts training programmes on child rights, gender issues, disability and HIV/AIDS with different stakeholders at micro and mezzo levels.

Kalpana Goel is an academician and a researcher in the Social Work and Rural Practice Unit at the Centre for Regional Engagement, University of South Australia. She has extensive teaching and research experience in social work and community development. She has widely published in the area of migration, migrant settlement, unorganised sector, mental health and teaching and learning. She is a member of the Australian Association of Social Work, Refugee and Migration Research Network and the Centre for Rural Health and Community Development.

Nonie Harris is currently a Senior Lecturer in the Department of Social Work and Human Services at JCU where she teaches undergraduate research methods and in the honours' programme. Nonie's postgraduate research and publications have focused on feminist methodologies, feminist theory, mothering and child care policy in cross national contexts. Nonie has achieved scholarly recognition at both national and international levels through the publication of results from child care policy research funded by grants from the Don Chipp Foundation and the Ian Potter Foundation.

Sonny Jose is an Associate Professor in Social Work at the Loyola /College of Social Sciences, Thiruvananthapuram. An accomplished trainer as well as a trained psychotherapist and counsellor, he tapered his five year long clinical practice to take-up teaching in social work, which he has been doing for the past 13 years. He did his doctorate in social networks. His passion is in teaching psychology and counselling. He is also engaged in research in the areas of Suicide Prevention, Gerontology and Gender and officiates two major research projects with the Indian Council of Social Science Research (ICSSR) and the University Grants Commission (UGC).

Sheeba Joseph is presently working as Head, Department of Social Work, Bhopal School of Social Sciences. She is associated with SAKSHAM, GFATM R7 (Global Fund to Fight HIV/AIDS, Tuberculosis and Malaria) project as the Faculty-in-Charge which is a counselling component with an all India outreach. She is the Editor in Chief of *BSSS Journal of Social Work*, and member, editorial board of *Learning Community*. She has presented papers in national and international conferences and published articles in refereed journals. Her areas of interest are geriatrics, women and child welfare and social work intervention in the community settings.

S. Kalyanasundaram holds an MMBS from Madurai Medical College, Madras University. He later did his MD in Psychiatry from NIMHANS Bangalore in 1975. Then he joined the Faculty of NIMHANS and served for five years as an Assistant Professor. He was the former President of Indian Psychiatric Society (IPS), Karnataka Branch and South Zone, and the first chairperson of 'Rehabilitation Psychiatry', the Sub-Specialty Section of the Indian Psychiatric Society.

Dr Kalyanasundaram is also one of the founder members of the Richmond Fellowship Asia Pacific Forum and former president of this body. He was an associate editor of the *International Psychogeriatrics Journal*. Presently, he is the Honorary Chief Executive Officer of the Richmond Fellowship Society (India), Bangalore, and deeply involved with Richmond Fellowship Society (India) and Psychiatric Rehabilitation.

Sheeja Remani B. Karalam is a MA (Sociology), MSW and PhD in Social Work and has 17 years of teaching and research experience at university levels. Presently, she is an Associate Professor at Department of Social Work, Christ University, Bangalore. She has the credit of authoring and co-authoring five books in the fields of social work and has published 11 papers on various research aspects in social work. She has presented research papers in national and international seminars. She has extensively worked on the well-being of adolescent girls in communities and institutions in terms of research and intervention program at field level. She has completed Minor Research Project funded by the Government of Karnataka, India, and has also undertaken Major Research Project on evaluation of the Government of India Scheme "Ujjawala" in Karnataka State funded by Christ University, Bangalore.

Abul Khan is a clinical social worker–cum–psychosocial therapist with over 18 years practice experience with diverse cross-cultural client groups in India, UK and Australia in areas of substance misuse, community development, teaching, child protection and child and adolescent mental health. Khan has completed a postgraduate research from the United Kingdon on Substance Abuse Management and currently he is undertaking a PhD study on Child Protection Management through Family Empowerment at JCU, Townsville, while working as a Senior Child and Adolescent Mental Health Clinician for the Victoria Government. Khan is a member of Australian College of Social Work in clinical specialty division.

V. Sayee Kumar is a qualified clinical social worker from the discipline of psychiatric social work. He had his advanced clinical training from National Institute of Mental Health and Neuro Sciences—NIMHANS, Bangalore in India. He also has his academic credentials in Applied Psychology, Human Resources, Counselling and Guidance. With over two and half decades of experience, he is actively involved in areas of postgraduate teaching, training, research, counselling, case work and psychotherapy. His experience includes two assignments outside India. It was to lead Student Counselling Services in the very large CBSE Indian Schools at Bahrain and Muscat, each with more than of 5,000 students. He has designed and conducted numerous workshops on skill and capacity building for various categories of people in counselling and other mental health areas. Kumar offers consultancy in areas of Counselling and Psychotherapy with special interest in Cognitive Behavior Therapy and Child and Adolescent Guidance.

Anthony McMahon is the Director of Centacare Catholic Family Services Townsville, an agency that provides counselling and community services across North Queensland. He has worked as a community worker, social worker and social work academic. He is the author of a number of books and journal articles on social policy, social welfare history, and child protection and indigenous issues. He is an Adjunct Professor in the School of Arts and Social Sciences, JCU, Australia.

Pratima Murthy is a professor of Psychiatry at the National Institute of Mental Health and Neuro Sciences (NIMHANS), Bangalore, where she presently heads the Centre for Addiction Medicine. She has provided consultancies to several UN organizations, including the UNESCAP in assessing drug abuse in the Maldives. She has been involved in framing national guidelines for tobacco cessation and has been a gender consultant for the UN Technical Advisory Group on HIV and Injection Drug Users (IDUs) and to the United Nations Office on Drugs and Crime (UNODC). She is also on the advisory group on IDU prevention at National AIDS Control Organisation (NACO) and a co-director on the Fogarty-ICHORTA training grant in mental health.

Faheema Mustafa is a Research Associate attached to Loyola College of Social Sciences, Thiruvananthapuram, India. Graduating with First Rank in BA Sociology from Calicut University, she undertook MSW from MG University. Her promotive mental health enthusiasm found her working in the Community Health Department in MES Medical College Hospital in areas including de-addiction and tobacco cessation, geriatric counselling, health education, and child and adult counselling. She also initiated a Geriatric Clinic with the Muslim Educational Society Medical College Hospital (MESMCH).

Ilango Ponnuswami is currently Professor, Department of Social Work, Mangalore University, Mangalagangotri. He obtained his MA in Social Work from the Loyola College, MPhil in Psychiatric Social Work from the National Institute of Mental Health and Neuro Sciences (NIMHANS), and PhD Degree in Social Work by the Bharathidasan University in 1996. Dr Ilango has also edited six books on various aspects of social work practice and education in India. He is an Editorial Board Member of the *Journal of Transformative Education* (an International Journal) published by SAGE and has been serving as a reviewer for reputed international journals such as *International Social Work* and *Oxford Journal of Gerontology*.

Reeja P. S. is an Assistant Professor with Department of Sociology, BCM College, Kottayam. She is also a visiting faculty to the Institute of Distance Education, University of Kerala. Her keen interest in Suicidology found her pursuing her PhD on the topic Causes and Consequences of Suicide—A Case Study of Kerala.

Lakshmi Sankaran lives in Chennai in South India. She is a trained social worker with a PhD from NIMHANS, Bangalore (Department of Psychiatric Social Work). She works as a counsellor in a clinic and is part of a mental health team in a rural mental health centre in India. She was a faculty in a Course on Counseling Psychology and has worked in Mental Health Settings as a trainer. Sankaran has also worked as an Assistant Professor, Department of Psychology (Counseling), Christ University, Bangalore. Currently, she is a consultant (Academic and Research) with 'The Banyan', Rural Mental Health Project, Chennai.

Rosamund Thorpe is Professor Emeritus of Social Work at JCU and is a volunteer community social worker with the Family Inclusion Network, a service-user support and advocacy organisation in which families and supportive professionals work together to achieve greater social justice for children and families caught up in the child protection system. Thorpe's research and practice activities also include the fields of domestic and family violence, Aboriginal and Torres Strait Islander approaches to social welfare practice, community work, service user involvement in human services and counter-oppressive approaches to social work.

P. Udhaya Kumar is a full-time PhD Scholar at the Department of Social Work, Bharathidasan University. Earlier, he served as a Lecturer in Social Work at the Urumu Dhanalakshmi College, Tiruchirappalli. He has presented more than 20 papers in national and international conferences and has published articles/chapters in national peer-reviewed journals and edited books. His specific interests are in mental health, spirituality and old age.

Chitra Venkateswaran (MD Psychiatry) is the founder/clinical director of Mehac Foundation which is an NGO working towards improving the quality of life of mentally ill people in Kerala and India. She also holds the post of Associate Professor in Psychiatry in Department of Psychiatry and is faculty at the Department of Oncology and Palliative Care of Amrita Institute of Medical Sciences, Kochi. Venkateswaran was an UICC International

Research Fellow from 2006 to 2008. As part of this fellowship, she has been doing research on screening tools for psychological distress in palliative care in Leeds.

Ines Zuchowski is a social worker, currently employed as a Lecturer at JCU in the field of education. She graduated with a Bachelor of Social Work from JCU in the early 1990s. The main focus of her work has been preventing violence against women and children and addressing this through individual intervention, group work and community development strategies. Ines has been teaching at JCU since 2007. She is currently undertaking a PhD in social work and her topic is External Supervision in Social Work Placements.

Index